CAPODIMONTE
AND I VERGINI

DECUMANO MAGGIORE

SPACCANAPOLI

EDO AND
EL NUOVO

**CAPODIMONTE AND
I VERGINI**
Pages 90–101

DECUMANO MAGGIORE
Pages 74–89

SPACCANAPOLI
Pages 60–73

0 metres	500
0 yards	500

EYEWITNESS TRAVEL

NAPLES
& THE AMALFI COAST

EYEWITNESS TRAVEL

NAPLES
& THE AMALFI COAST

LONDON, NEW YORK,
MELBOURNE, MUNICH AND DELHI
www.dk.com

Produced by Fabio Ratti Editoria Libraria
e Multimediale Milano, Italy

PROJECT EDITOR Giovanni Francesio
EDITORS Barbara Cacciani, Giorgia Conversi, Elena
Marzorati, Michele Di Muro
DESIGNERS Paolo Gonzato, Carlotta Maderna, Stefania Testa
MAPS Paul Stafford

DK Publishing, Inc.
PROJECT EDITOR Fiona Wild
EDITORS Francesca Machiavelli, Naomi Peck, Rosalyn Thiro

CONTRIBUTORS Patrizia Antignani, Mariella Barone, Ciro
Cacciola, Angela Catello, Daniela Lepore, Emilia Marchi,
Kirsi Viglione, Beatrice Vitelli
ILLUSTRATORS Giorgia Boli, Paola Spampinato, Nadia Viganò

ENGLISH TRANSLATION Richard Pierce

Reproduced by Lineatre Service, Milano
Printed and bound in China by Toppan Printing Co.
(Shenzhen Ltd)

First American Edition, 2000
07 08 09 10 9 8 7 6 5 4 3 2

Published in the United States by DK Publishing, Inc.,
375 Hudson Street, New York 10014

Reprinted with revisions 2003, 2005, 2007

Copyright © 2000, 2007 Dorling Kindersley Limited, London
A Penguin Company

Published in Great Britain by Dorling Kindersley Limited.

A CATALOGING IN PUBLICATION RECORD IS
AVAILABLE FROM THE LIBRARY OF CONGRESS.

ISSN 1542-1554
ISBN 978-0-75662-502-3

FLOORS ARE REFERRED TO THROUGHOUT IN ACCORDANCE WITH
EUROPEAN USAGE; IE THE "FIRST FLOOR" IS THE FLOOR ABOVE GROUND LEVEL.

Front cover main image: Positano, the Amalfi Coast

◁ **Marina Grande, Sorrento**

CONTENTS

The Farnese Hercules

INTRODUCING NAPLES

The Spaccanapoli district

Panoramic view of the Forum at Pompeii, with Vesuvius in the background

Outdoor eating, Bay of Naples

Pizza Napoletana

The church and cloisters of Santa Chiara

HOW TO USE THIS GUIDE

This guide helps you to get the most out of your visit to Naples. It provides both expert recommendations and advice as well as useful practical information. The first chapter, *Introducing Naples*, sets the city in its rich and varied geographical and historical context. *Naples at a Glance* gives you a brief overview of the main sights in the city, as well as cultural background. *Naples Through the Year* describes events and festivals season by season. *Naples Area by Area* describes the main sightseeing areas in detail, with maps, illustrations and photographs. *Pompeii and the Amalfi Coast* covers this region's splendid archaeological sites and also features an itinerary for a coastal boat trip. Information on hotels, shops, restaurants and bars is covered in *Travellers' Needs*, while the *Survival Guide* contains practical advice – for example, how to use the local transport networks.

FINDING YOUR WAY AROUND THE SIGHTSEEING SECTION

The city has been divided into six colour-coded areas, each with its own chapter. A description of the history and features of each area is followed by a Street-by-Street map focusing on the main attractions. The sights are numbered for easy reference. The most important sights in each area are described in detail in two or more pages.

Each area has a colour-coded thumb tab.

Locator map

A locator map shows where you are in relation to the other areas in the city.

A suggested route includes the most interesting and attractive streets.

The area shaded pink is shown in greater detail on the Street-by-Street Map on the following pages.

1 Introduction to the Area
The sights are numbered and located on an area map which also shows public transport stops and car parks. The major sights are listed by category: churches and cathedrals, museums and galleries, streets and squares, marketplaces, historic buildings, parks and gardens.

2 Street-by-Street Map
This gives a bird's-eye view of the heart of the sightseeing area. The numbers refer to the fuller descriptions provided on the following pages.

The list of star sights indicates places no visitor should miss.

NAPLES AREA MAP

The coloured areas on this map *(see inside front cover)* correspond to the seven main sightseeing areas. Each area is covered in full either in the *Naples Area by Area (see pp44–129)* section or in the *Pompeii and the Amalfi Coast (see pp130–173)* chapter. The map showing the centre of Naples *(pp14–15)* also locates all of the major sights and monuments in the city.

Numbers refer to each sight's position on the area map and its place in the chapter.

Practical Information provides all the information you need to visit the sights, including map references to the *Street Finder (see pp228–43)*.

The Visitors' Checklist provides all the practical information needed to plan your visit.

3 Detailed Information on Each Sight

All the most important sights in Naples are described individually. They are listed in order, following the numbering on the area map, which appears at the beginning of each chapter. The key to the symbols used is shown on the back flap for easy reference.

Stars indicate the features you should not miss.

The timeline lists the most important events in the history of the building.

4 Naples' Top Sights

Historic buildings are dissected to reveal their interiors. Museums and galleries have colour-coded floorplans to help you locate the major works exhibited.

M. Vesuvio.

Veduta di Castel del Ovo.

La Lanterna
Toro di S.t Vincenzo.

1. Isola de Ischia.	17. Castel nuovo.	23. d' Arsenale Oreficina.	30. Presidio de Pizo falco.	32. Vescovato.
2. Isola de Procia.	18. Castel S.t Elmo.	24. Lanterna.	31. Scola di Bombardieri.	33. Gesu Nuovo.
3. Palazzo del Vice Re.	19. Castel del Ovo.	25. Torre di S.t Vincenzo.		34. S. Chiara.
	20. Torrione del Carm.	26. Molo.		35. S.t Dominico.
	21. Fort. novamente	27. Dogana Grando.		36. la Spir. Sant.
	fatto.	28. Dogana della farina.		37. la Carmine.
	22. d' Arsenal delle Callere.	29. Forni del Biscotti.		38. la Nunziata.

GOLFO

INTRODUCING NAPLES

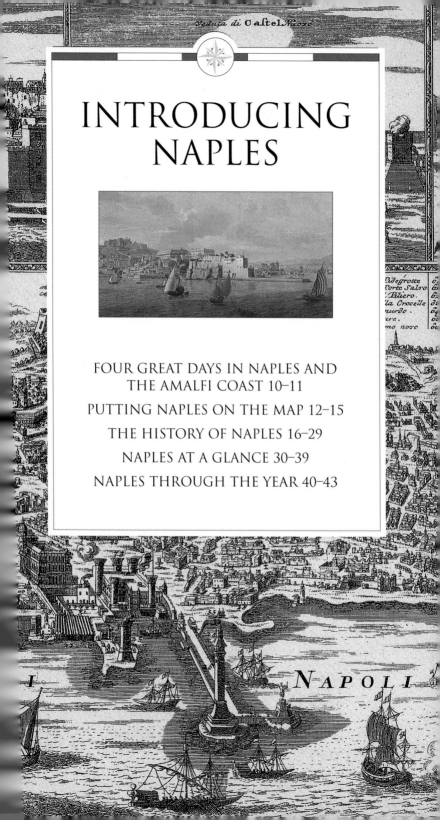

NAPOLI

FOUR GREAT DAYS IN NAPLES AND THE AMALFI COAST

Majolica plate made in Vietri

Visitors to Naples and the Amalfi Coast could be overwhelmed by the amount of things there are to see and do. Castles, palaces and museums, miles of breathtaking coastline, as well as plenty of culinary delights make Italy's third largest city and its surrounding area a treasure trove for travellers. These four itineraries offer a bit of everything, from a walk among ruins to a day exploring churches and shops, and from a drive along the spectacular coast to activities for children. All sights are cross-referenced to more information within the guide so that you can tailor the day to suit your needs. Price guidelines include the cost of public transport, food and admission charges.

The Duomo altar, Naples

CHURCHES AND SHOPPING

- **The magnificent Duomo**
- **Spaccanapoli shopping**
- **Lunch at a pizzeria**
- **Cloisters of Santa Chiara**

TWO ADULTS allow at least €50

Morning

Start on Via Duomo at Naples' most sumptuous Gothic cathedral, the **Duomo** *(see pp82–3)* – if it is May or September, you may be lucky enough to witness the liquefaction of San Gennaro's blood. From the Duomo enter the **Pio Monte della Misericordia** *(see p81)*. Its walls house one of Cara-vaggio's most celebrated masterpieces, *The Seven Acts of Mercy*. Afterwards, step into the heart of Naples' historic centre for a bit of retail therapy. Known as **Spaccanapoli** *(see pp62–3)*,

this narrow, vibrant street cuts the original Roman dimensions of the city in half and is crammed with churches, historic *palazzi*, shops and cafés. Seek out the artisan workshops on Via San Gregorio Armeno selling intriguing terracotta objects, from nativity scenes *(presepe)* and statuettes of **Pulcinella** *(see p39)* to good luck charms. Stop for lunch at one of the neighbourhood pizzerias for a classic pizza Margherita, topped with tomato, mozzarella and basil.

Afternoon

Continue along Spaccanapoli to the church of **San Domenico Maggiore** *(see p68)*. Its artworks, including Pietro Cavallini's frescoes in the Brancaccio chapel, are not to be missed. Pause for an espresso and *babà* (rum baba) at **Scaturchio** *(see p203)* before heading to Piazza del Gesù with its gaudy spire, the **Guglia dell' Immacolata** *(see p65)*. In the same piazza the church of **Gesù Nuovo** *(see p64)* stands

out for its diamond-pointed stone façade. Across from here is the church of **Santa Chiara** *(see pp66–7)* with its beautiful cloisters and the Museo dell'Opera di Santa Chiara, which houses parts of the church's original interior. Head for **Piazza Bellini** *(see p78)* for a look at the excavated ancient Greek walls and round off the day with a relaxing apéritif.

A FAMILY DAY

- **The port of Mergellina**
- **Visit the oldest aquarium in Europe**
- **Ancient Castel dell'Ovo**
- **Palazzo Reale**

FAMILY OF 4 allow at least €100

Morning

Start the day by exploring the charming port of **Mergellina** *(see p119)* with its wonderful views and stop at **Chalet Ciro** *(see p202)* for some of Naples' best ice cream. Head along the **Lungomare** *(see p116)* to the

Boats in harbour at the port of Mergellina

Villa Comunale *(see p117)*. Built on the order of the Bourbon sovereigns in the 1700s, it is the only public park near the historic centre so it is perenially popular with kids, and an ideal spot for a run about. Afterwards visit the oldest aquarium in Europe, with its array of local fish, attached to the **Stazione Zoologica** *(see p117)*. Continue along the Lungomare, taking in the sun and sea, boats and bathers, until the imposing Castel dell'Ovo comes into view. Stop for lunch at any one of the many restaurants in the Borgo Marinaro.

Afternoon
Explore the **Castel dell'Ovo** *(see p116)* – children love running around its ramparts – then head to Piazza del Plebiscito, to visit the **Palazzo Reale** *(see pp50–1)* and afterwards to enjoy the jugglers and busking musicians in the square. End the day with a hot chocolate from **Caffè Gambrinus** *(see p52)*.

The excavation area, Herculaneum

VIEWS OF THE AMALFI COAST

- **Majolica tiles at Vietri**
- **Lunch in Ravello**
- **Amalfi's striking cathedral**
- **Charming Positano**

TWO ADULTS allow at least €80

Morning
Begin the day's spectacular drive in **Vietri** *(see p161)* one of Italy's largest producers of ceramic tiles, particularly the colourfully painted majolica tile. Then take the coastal road inland towards **Ravello** *(see p160)*. Verdant and tranquil, it is arguably the best known stop on the Amalfi coast tour for spellbinding views of the sea. Must-see sights here include the splendid Duomo, the church of Santa Maria a Gradillo, and the villas Rufolo and Cimbrone. Break for lunch

at **Da Salvatore** *(see p200)*, which is also justly renowned for its stunning panoramas.

Afternoon
From Ravello, head back to the coastal road. Take a moment to stop at **Amalfi** *(see p159)* to admire the magnificent Duomo di Sant' Andrea, situated just steps away from the town's only car park. Its impressive 11th-century bronze doors were brought here from Constantinople.

From Amalfi the coastal road cuts through precipitous cliffs to **Positano** *(see p158)*. Often considered to be the jewel of the Amalfi coast, it is a picture postcard of pastel houses set steep into a hillside with fishing boats dotted in the sea below. Spend an hour or so wandering the picturesque narrow alleys or browsing the many boutiques and craft shops. Then round the day off with a relaxing beachside glass of *prosecco* (sparkling wine) at sunset.

Breathtaking view of the coast from Amalfi

RUINS AND CRATERS

- **Portici villas**
- **The ruins at Herculaneum**
- **Mercato di Resina**
- **Awesome Mount Vesuvius**

TWO ADULTS allow at least €70

Morning
Take the Circumvesuviana train to **Portici** *(see p140)*. The town and surrounding area are famous for their abundance of 18th-century aristocratic villas, including the royal palace. Back on the Circumvesuviana continue to the Ercolano Scavi stop and the ruins of **Herculaneum** *(see pp144–5)*. Destroyed by Vesuvius in AD 79 *(see pp18–19)*, it is a good alternative to **Pompeii** *(see pp146–9)* as its smaller scale makes a two-hour tour possible. Remaining in the town of Ercolano next visit the colourful **Mercato di Resina** *(see p208)* – an enormous flea market known for its antique costumes. For a picnic lunch, head to the town centre and grab a sandwich from **Viva Lo Re** *(see p198)* then take the provincial road up to the **Vesuvius Observatory** *(see p142)*.

Afternoon
Continue on foot for the three-hour round hike to the crater of **Vesuvius** *(see pp142–3)*. Afterwards take the Circumvesuviana to **Torre del Greco** *(see p141)* and end the day shopping for the famous coral jewellery produced and sold here.

Putting Naples on the Map

Naples is the third largest city in Italy
after Milan and Rome, and the largest
city in Southern Italy. The population
of the city proper *(see pp14–15)* is
1,250,000, rising to almost three
million when the suburbs are taken
into account. The city faces the great
sweep of the splendid Bay of Naples,
extends into the fertile Campania plain,
and occupies high ground and hollows
formed by ancient volcanic craters.

Satellite image of the Bay of Naples and Mount Vesuvius

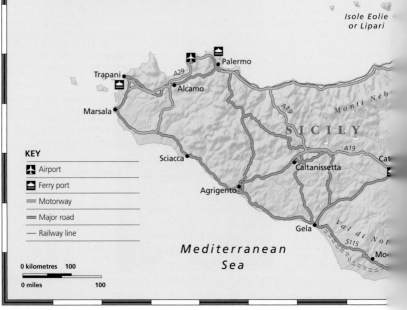

Tyrrhenian Sea

Isole Eolie or Lipari

KEY

✈ Airport

⛴ Ferry port

═ Motorway

═ Major road

— Railway line

0 kilometres   100

0 miles   100

Mediterranean Sea

Foggia
Barletta
Cerignola
Molfetta
Le Murge
Bari
Melfi
Altamura
Fasano
PUGLIA
Potenza
Matera
Brindisi
BASILICATA
Taranto
Penisola Salentina
Lecce
Galatina

Maratea

Sibari

Ionian Sea

Rossano

Cosenza

CALABRIA
Crotone
Lamezia Terme
Catanzaro
Vibo Valentia

Aerial view of Naples

Reggio di Calabria

ormina

ta

usa

EUROPE

NORWAY   FINLAND
SWEDEN   ESTONIA
RUSSIAN FED
LATVIA
DENMARK   LITHUANIA
REP OF IRELAND   GREAT BRITAIN   NETHERLANDS   POLAND   BELARUS
BELGIUM   GERMANY   CZECH REPUBLIC   SLOVAKIA   UKRAINE
FRANCE   SWITZ   AUSTRIA   HUNGARY
CROATIA   ROMANIA
ITALY   SERBIA   BULGARIA
Rome   MONTENEGRO
ALBANIA
SPAIN   Naples   GREECE
PORTUGAL
ALGERIA   TUNISIA

Central Naples

The old town is divided into six distinct areas. From the 16th century on, the administrative and commercial centre of Naples developed around Toledo and Castel Nuovo. The old city centre is described in the chapters on Spaccanapoli and Decumano Maggiore. The Vergini district, immediately north of the Foria gorge, leads to the park of Capodimonte with its Royal Palace. The Certosa di San Martino and Castel Sant'Elmo dominate the Vomero hill. In the Chiaia area, a few steps from the most elegant shops in Naples, places such as Castel dell'Ovo and Mergellina are surrounded by greenery and the sea. To the west are the lovely inlets and villas of Posillipo.

The Certosa di San Martino, on the Vomero

The Cappella Caracciolo di Vico in San Giovanni a Carbonara

Castel Nuovo, known locally as Maschio Angioino

The tiled cloister of Santa Chiara

The fountain of *Christ and the Samaritan* in the cloister of the convent of San Gregorio Armeno

Castel dell'Ovo, seen from the bay

KEY

▧	Major sight
M	Metro station
⛴	Ferry port
🚡	Funicular
P	Car park
ℹ	Tourist information
✚	Hospital with casualty unit
⚑	Police station
✝	Church
✡	Synagogue
⊠	Post office

0 metres 500
0 yards 500

CAPODIMONTE AND I VERGINI

Reggia di Capodimonte

PIAZZA S. EFRAMO VECCHIO

ORTO BOTANICO

PIAZZA CARLO III

PIAZZA SANSEVERO

VIA FORIA

CORSO GARIBALDI

L.GO MIRACOLI

PIAZZA MIRACOLI

S. Giovanni a Carbonara

P.ZA TEATRO S. FERDINANDO

P.ZA VOLTURNO

P.ZA PAGANO

P.TTA S. CARLO ALL'ARENA

P.TTA DEI LEPRI

P.ZA STELLA

P.TTA SETTEM BRINI

P.ZA S. ANNA A CAPUNA

PIAZZA CAVOUR

M Cavour

PIAZZA DE NICOLA

PIAZZA PRINCIPE UMBERTO

M P Museo

L.GO DONNAREGINA

Duomo

S. ANDREA D. DAME

L.GO REGINA COELI

PIAZZA SISTO RIARIO SFORZA

P.ZA S. GAETANO

S. Lorenzo Maggiore

P.ZA CALENDA

P.ZA MIRAGLIA

S. Gregorio Armeno

PIAZZA S. MARIA LA SCALA

P.ZA BELLINI

S. Domenico Maggiore

DUOMO

P.TTA UMBERTO

P.ZA S. DOMENICO MAGGIORE

P.TTA SCACCHI

P.TTA S. ELIGIO

Gesù Nuovo

PIAZZA NICOLA AMORE

P.TTA DE OMO.

PIAZZA MERCATO

PIAZZA DEL GESÙ NUOVO

Santa Chiara

CORSO UMBERTO

PIAZZA MASANIELLO

SPACCANAPOLI

P.ZA PORTA-NOVA

NUOVA MARINA

P.TTA PRINCIPESSA MARGHERITA

VIA NUOVA MARINA

P.TTA PORTO

PIAZZA BOVIO

MOLO C. PISACANE

CALATA PORTA DI MASSA

VIA COLOMBO

NUOVA CALATA ALERO

PIAZZA MUNICIPIO

Castel Nuovo

MOLO BEVERELLO

MOLO ANGIOINO

Reggia di Capodimonte

THE HISTORY OF NAPLES

In Greek mythology, Naples was built where the Siren Parthenope was washed ashore after she had been rejected by Odysseus. Greek colonists, perhaps from Rhodes, may have founded a colony at this point as early as the 10th century BC, but this too may be the stuff of legend. What is certain is that Greeks from Cumae built a new city nearby, calling it *Neapolis* (new city), while the original town was renamed *Palaeopolis*, or old city. Neapolis was a leading commercial centre and the Greek language and customs survived even during the Roman period, when it was a favourite area of the elite.

Gorgon, 6th-century BC Cumaean antefix

After the fall of the Roman Empire and a wave of invasions, the city, though it retained some independence, came under Byzantine influence and went through a period of rebirth. In the 10th century the invading Normans succeeded in conquering the whole of Southern Italy, a kingdom initially ruled from Palermo, under Roger II. Norman rule finally came to an end in 1189. With the Angevin (French) and Aragonese (Spanish) dynasties, Naples itself became a capital, and the court began to attract famous artists. The 1400s were a golden era for Naples, but there followed two centuries of direct rule by Spain. The Spanish viceroys were oppressive rulers and the era is remembered for unjust taxation, the Inquisition, plague, overpopulation and the rebellion of Masaniello. Creativity flowered however, despite the widespread poverty.

In 1734 Charles III began the period of Bourbon hegemony. With the exception of the short-lived republican government in 1799 and the subsequent decade of French dominion, the Bourbons ruled Naples until 1860.

Since the unification of Italy the city's problems have become national issues – for example the markedly different level of development between Northern and Southern Italy.

Map of Naples in 1790

◁ *Paquius Proculus and His Wife*, 1st-century AD wall painting from Pompeii

Greco-Roman Naples

Pompeiian cameo

By the 8th century BC, Greeks had founded a settlement at Cumae, one of the earliest Greek colonies in Italy. From there they established a new town on Pizzofalcone hill, known as Parthenope, and trade prospered. Population growth led to the founding of Neapolis, or new city, nearby, and victory over the Etruscans in 474 BC brought further expansion. Neapolis came into contact with the growing power of Rome during the latter's protracted wars with the Samnites, and in the 4th century BC the citizens agreed to become an "allied city" of Rome. In AD 79 an erupting Vesuvius buried a number of ancient Roman cities, including Pompeii.

EXTENT OF THE CITY

| ▨ 8 BC | ▢ Today |

Bedrooms and living rooms

Temple of the Dioscuri
This 16th-century print shows the Roman temple which once stood on the site of San Paolo Maggiore (see p79). The temple façade collapsed in the 1688 earthquake.

Atrium

Via Anticaglia
The "street of ruins" acquired its name from the brick arches connecting the Ancient Roman bath house and the theatre (see p84).

Ornamental basin (impluvium)

TIMELINE

900 BC	600 BC	100 B

1000–900 BC According to Greek myth, city of Parthenope founded

328 BC War with Rome; Naples is defeated but a treaty sanctions the city's freedom

90–89 BC People Campania becor Roman citize

600 BC Greeks from Cumae found *Neapolis* or "new city"

Red-figure vase (5th century BC)

100 BC Tunnel built in Posillipo hill connecting city with Phlegraean Fields area and its trade and military ports

THE HOUSES OF POMPEII

The Roman houses in Pompeii *(see pp150–51)* are among the best-preserved examples of Roman civilization in Campania. This illustration shows a typical patrician house in Pompeii, displaying characteristic features of Roman and Greek domestic architecture. The houses were generally rectangular. To ensure privacy, they faced inwards, as can be seen by the few windows on the outer walls, and the rooms were built around an atrium or courtyard, which was the focal point of domestic life. Wealthier houses were richly decorated.

The garden was surrounded by columns, known as a "peristyle".

The kitchen and dining room (triclinium) were in this part of the house.

The Greek Walls
Made of large tufa blocks, the city walls date from the 5th century BC. Remnants can be seen in present-day Piazza Bellini (see p78).

WHERE TO SEE GRECO-ROMAN NAPLES

Beneath the cloister *of San Lorenzo* (see p80) *layers of the ancient city are still visible.*

Although not much is left of Greco-Roman *Neapolis*, some traces are visible in Piazza Bellini *(see p78)*, around Santa Chiara *(see pp66–7)* and under the Duomo *(see pp82–3)*. Outside the city, Pompeii and Herculaneum are vivid records of ancient Roman life. The Museo Archeologico Nazionale *(see pp86–9)* in Naples houses rich finds. Amphitheatres survive at Pozzuoli *(see p136)* and Santa Maria Capua Vetere *(see p165)*, and Greek ruins at Cumae *(see p138)* and Paestum *(see pp162–3)*.

The Diadumeno Torso from Castel Capuano

Statue of Aphrodite, Museo Archeologico

350–400 Christianity gaining in acceptance

500 Bishop Severus builds the first parish church, now San Giorgio Maggiore *(see p70)*

AD	AD 300	400	500

79 Vesuvius erupts; Pompeii and Herculaneum destroyed

The Siren Parthenope on a Roman coin

476 Romulus Augustulus, last Roman emperor of the West, imprisoned in the *Castrum Lucullanum (see p116)*

536 Byzantine General Belisarius wins Naples, entering city via the aqueduct

From Byzantine Rule to the Aragonese Dynasty

Angevin lily

In the 6th century AD, Naples became part of the Byzantine (Eastern Roman) empire. Despite incursions into Southern Italy by Goths, Lombards and Saracens, it remained a semi-independent duchy, nominally under Byzantine rule, until it became part of the Norman kingdom of Sicily in the 12th century. By the 13th century the French House of Anjou had taken over and Naples became the capital of the Angevin kingdom. Ambitious schemes were begun: land reclamation and building of new castles, churches and monasteries. In 1421 the last Angevin queen, Joan II, named Alfonso V of Aragon as her successor.

GROWTH OF THE CITY

| ■ AD 500 | □ Today |

Tombs in Santa Chiara
The Angevin rulers were buried in Santa Chiara, which contains superbly crafted tombs such as this one by an unknown artist (first half of the 14th century).

Louis of Anjou took vows after refusing the crown of Naples and was canonized in 1317.

Tomb of Ladislas of Durazzo
This tomb is in San Giovanni a Carbonara (see p96), chosen by Ladislas to house the tombs of the Angevin kings.

The Pietrasanta Bell Tower
This is among the few remaining examples of medieval architecture in Naples (see p78).

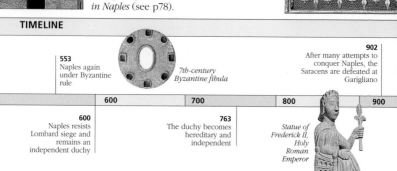

TIMELINE

553 Naples again under Byzantine rule

7th-century Byzantine fibula

902 After many attempts to conquer Naples, the Saracens are defeated at Garigliano

| 600 | 700 | 800 | 900 |

600 Naples resists Lombard siege and remains an independent duchy

763 The duchy becomes hereditary and independent

Statue of Frederick II, Holy Roman Emperor

Frescoes of the Giotto School
Giotto lived in Naples from 1328–33. His influence can be seen in the frescoes in Santa Maria di Donnaregina Vecchia (1332–5).

The crown Louis is placing on the head of his brother Robert legitimized the Angevin dynasty.

ST LOUIS OF TOULOUSE
This Gothic portrait was probably painted in 1317, after Louis of Anjou was canonized. Louis is shown as a Franciscan saint crowning his younger brother Robert King of Naples. Simone Martini's masterpiece is now in the Museo Nazionale di Capodimonte *(see pp98–101)*.

Robert of Anjou

WHERE TO SEE ANGEVIN AND ARAGONESE NAPLES
Evidence of this period is everywhere in Naples, although successive reconstructions have often obscured the original architectural styles. Rather than civic buildings such as Castel Capuano *(see p81)*, it was the churches that changed the face of the city: Santa Chiara *(see pp66–7)*, San Lorenzo *(see p80)*, San Domenico Maggiore *(see p68)*, and Santa Maria di Donnaregina Vecchia *(see p84)* with its wonderful cycle of frescoes painted by the school of Giotto.

Castel Nuovo, *originally Angevin, also has Aragonese elements (see pp54–5).*

King Roger II
The first great king of Naples is depicted in one of the eight statues placed in the niches of the Palazzo Reale façade in 1888 (see pp50–51).

1139 Neapolitans consign city to Roger II, Norman king of Sicily	1194 The city ruled by Henry VI Hohenstaufen, Roger II's son-in-law		1343 Petrarch stays at San Lorenzo	1443 Alfonso of Aragon enters Naples	1496 Threatened by France and Spain, the king cedes Naples to the French
		1224 Frederick II founds the University			

1100	1200	1300	1400

1165 ...el Capuano ...in strategic ... to control ...unications ...ith interior	1266 Charles I of Anjou enters Naples and makes it the capital of the new Angevin kingdom	1279 Construction of Castel Nuovo begins	1421 Joan II, last Angevin sovereign, names Alfonso V of Aragon her heir	1485 The Barons' Conspiracy fails

Bust of Alfonso V

The Spanish Viceroyalty

Masaniello

In 1503 Naples ceased to be an independent kingdom, and became a colony of Spain, ruled by a viceroy. The city began to expand unchecked in the suburbs and beyond the walls. Palazzo Reale was built near Castel Nuovo, and courts assembled at Castel Capuano. With the construction of Via Toledo and the restructuring of Via Chiaia in the mid-1500s, the focus of city development shifted: aristocratic palaces were built along the Riviera and Toledo and the need to accommodate the troops led to the building of the Quartieri Spagnoli district. New churches and monasteries were built. By now Naples was by far the largest city in Italy, with consequent problems of overcrowding and poverty. A famous figure in this period is Masaniello, the evolutionary who was first considered a hero, and then killed by the people who had supported him. Spanish rule came to an end in 1707 when, with the Treaty of Utrecht, the kingdom of Naples was ceded to Austria.

GROWTH OF THE CITY

■ *1500*   □ *Today*

Santa Maria del Carmine *(see p73)*, which gave the square its name.

Don Pedro de Toledo
A controversial figure, Don Pedro was viceroy from 1532 to 1553. He promoted new town planning, but also wanted to bring the Inquisition to Naples, triggering a popular revolt.

Masaniello, born Tommaso Aniello in 1620, was an illiterate fisherman.

TIMELINE

1503 Gonzalo Fernández de Cordóba, sent by the King of Spain, enters the city	**1532–52** The first modern town plan of Naples put into effect	**1600** Construction of Palazzo Reale, by Domenico Fontana	The Eruption of Vesuvius by *Philipp Hackert*
			1631 Eruption of Vesuvius

1500 ———————————————————— **1600**

1510 Failure of the viceroy's attempts to bring the Inquisition to Naples	**1536** Via Toledo opened	**1606–7** Caravaggio in Naples	**1637–60** Construction of Guglia di San Gennaro to thank the patron saint for saving the city from the eruption of Vesuvius

Palazzo Reale

Statue of San Gennaro
The Neapolitans gave their venerated patron saint credit for having stopped the eruption of Vesuvius in 1631.

This memorial stone was to record all the concessions obtained from the viceroy by Masaniello.

MASANIELLO'S UPRISING

This painting by Micco Spadaro depicts Piazza Mercato *(see p73)* during the 1647 riot. A tax levied on fruit sparked the riot which rapidly grew into a fully-fledged uprising against the aristocracy. However, the attempt was soon crushed, as the city's moderates managed to persuade people to rebel against their revolutionary leader. He was killed the same year on 16 July.

Giambattista Vico
The famous philosopher and historian, author of La Scienza Nuova (The New Science), *was born in Naples in 1668, the son of a bookseller.*

WHERE TO SEE VICEROYAL NAPLES

The original 17th-century façade of the Palazzo Reale *(see pp50–51)* has changed little over the centuries. The Cappella del Tesoro di San Gennaro *(see pp82–3)* is one of the richest Baroque monuments in Naples. A short distance from the Duomo is a small area with a wealth of 17th-century treasures: the Guglia di San Gennaro *(see p81)* and Pio Monte della Misericordia *(see p77)*, which houses the canvas that marked a turning point in 17th-century Neapolitan painting – *The Seven Acts of Mercy* by Caravaggio, who stayed in Naples in 1607.

The Certosa di San Martino (see pp108–11) *was extended and decorated in the late 1500s.*

At San Gregorio Armeno (see p80), *the cloister is decorated with this striking fountain.*

1647 Masaniello's uprising

The plague in a painting by Micco Spadaro (detail)

1707 Beginning of Austrian viceroyalty

1723 Pietro Giannone flees to Vienna after publishing his *Civic History of the Kingdom of Naples*, which is banned by the Church

1650   **1700**

1656 Devastating plague epidemic; Naples loses one-third of population

1688 Earthquake damages most of old city

1701 Failure of the Prince of Macchia's conspiracy in favour of the Austrians

1697 Giambattista Vico becomes professor of rhetoric at Naples university

Bourbon Naples

Portrait of Charles III

In 1734 the much-abused kingdom of Naples changed hands once more, with the arrival of the Bourbon king Charles III, who set out to make Naples into a metropolis. He suspended church building in favour of large-scale public works and new industries. He also built a Royal Palace in Caserta modelled on Versailles, which was to be the focal point of an entire city. At the same time, art, antiquities, music and even the *lazzari* (street urchins) attracted travellers making the Grand Tour. The royal schemes lacked a coherent plan, however, and fundamental problems failed to be addressed. Bourbon rule ended in 1860, when Garibaldi arrived in Naples, having won over Sicily and Calabria. In the same year Naples became part of the new kingdom of Italy.

GROWTH OF THE CITY

■ *1700*   □ *Today*

The Palace of Capodimonte

Charles III's Porcelain
The king was so proud of his porcelain factory that when he returned to Spain he closed it down and took his best craftsmen with him.

The Beheading of Ettore Carafa
This relief in the Museo di San Martino depicts the execution of one of the martyrs of the Parthenopean Republic on 17 August 1799.

Antonio Genovesi (1713–69)
A leading figure in the Neapolitan Enlightenment movement, he became the first professor of political economics in Italy in 1754.

TIMELINE

Statuette found in Herculaneum

1738 Beginning of excavations at Herculaneum

Ancient finds at Herculaneum transferred to Palazzo degli Studi

1700

1750

1734 Under Charles of Bourbon Naples becomes an independent kingdom again

1740 Church building suspended

1759 Charles III returns to Spain, his son Ferdinand becomes king

1777 The university moves to the Jesuit College, now a banished society. Ferdinando Fuga turns Palazzo degli Studi into a museum

Cappella di San Gennaro

19th-century Neapolitan painting often featured landscapes and picturesque settings – as seen in this work by Gigante (1806–76), showing the chapel of San Gennaro – as well as the rural scenes of Palizzi (1818–99) and the realism of Morelli (1826–1901).

THE DUKE OF NOJA'S MAP

This was the first modern relief map, the work of Duke Giovanni Carafa di Noja in 1775. The map shows the full extent of the city of Naples and the monumental buildings in the newly developed districts. In this detail the impressive Royal Palace of Capodimonte dominates the city skyline.

Naples appears as a chaotic muddle of buildings here.

WHERE TO SEE BOURBON NAPLES

The most important architectural achievements of the Bourbons are the Teatro San Carlo *(see p53)*, the Palace of Capodimonte *(see pp98–101)* and the Albergo dei Poveri *(see p97)*. Urban projects such as the Foro Carolino and the Villa Reale at Chiaia also date from the Bourbon period. The passion for antiquity inspired collecting and the setting up of the Museo Archeologico *(see pp86–9)*. But Bourbon influence is mainly to be seen outside the city, where kings built hunting lodges as well as royal palaces, such as Caserta *(see pp166–7)*.

The Bourbon court *on a shoot in a painting by Jakob Philipp Hackert (1783)*

The Naples-Portici Railway

The first Italian railway was inaugurated in 1839, when the Bayard locomotive took 9 minutes 30 seconds to travel about 7.5 km (4.5 miles). This painting of the Vesuvio by Fergola is in the Museo di San Martino.

1806 Napoleon gives the role of king of Naples to his brother Joseph Bonaparte

1808 Bonaparte goes to Spain and is replaced by Joachim Murat. The French promote great public works and administrative reforms

1848 Popular revolt restores constitution but it is annulled by Parliament in 1849

Giuseppe Garibaldi

1800

1850

1799 Birth of Neapolitan Republic, overthrown six months later by the counter-revolution. Its leaders are executed in Piazza Mercato

1820 Constitution granted but is repealed the following year

1815 Murat executed at Pizzo Calabro. Ferdinand returns to throne as King of the Two Sicilies

1839 First railway in Italy, Naples-Portici, inaugurated

1860 Garibaldi enters city on 21 October; after plebiscite Naples becomes part of newly united Kingdom of Italy

Naples after Unification

The philosopher Benedetto Croce

In a crowded, densely populated city, the 1884 cholera epidemic brought ancient problems to a head. An attempt to face them was made with the Urban Renewal Plan. Slum clearance was carried out around the port and new districts were created in the centre and towards the hills. However, the Plan failed to solve many basic problems, work took much longer than expected, and triggered a wave of corruption. The Fascist regime contented itself with a new series of public works and the creation of more built-up areas. A leading local figure of the time was the philosopher Benedetto Croce, one of the few Italian intellectuals who openly opposed Fascism.

GROWTH OF THE CITY

☐ *1850*   ☐ *Today*

THE ILVA STEELWORKS IN BAGNOLI

This plant, later known as Italsider, was built near the beach and the ancient hot springs in 1907 *(see p136)*. Renovated for the last time in 1987 and now closed, it has become a symbol of modern development carried out with total disregard for the natural context and scenic beauty of the area.

Santa Chiara
Restoration of Santa Chiara was carried out after the 1943 fire, re-creating its presumed original appearance.

Matilde Serao (1856–1927)
"Naples must be gutted" declared the prominent author on the eve of the Renewal Plan. A few years later, disappointed by the results, she described Corso Umberto I as a "screen" concealing old and new misery.

TIMELINE

The Mount Vesuvius funicular

1880 Inauguration of Vesuvius funicular, which inspires the famous song *Funiculì Funiculà*

1891 First city funicular connecting Vomero with centre becomes operative

1860	1880	1890

1868 Via Duomo begun with first city demolition and finished in late 1800s as part of Urban Renewal Plan

1885 Special law for Urban Renewal Plan: demolition of slum areas begins

1884 Cholera epidemic

The Rettifilo
This eclectic and stately avenue, officially called Corso Umberto I and built after the Urban Renewal projects ended, is a good example of late 19th-century bourgeois Naples.

WHERE TO SEE POST-UNIFICATION NAPLES

The Caffè Gambrinus *(see p52)* was the haunt of Italian avant-garde artists, like the Futurists, as well as such illustrious visitors as Oscar Wilde. During the Urban Renewal period that changed the face of civic Naples, the Art Nouveau style prevailed in the new residential districts and the small villas in Chiaia *(see pp112–19)* and Vomero *(see pp102–11)*. Monumental Fascist architecture is represented by the Palazzo delle Poste e Telegrafi *(see p57)* and the Stazione Marittima (the port). Via Toledo *(see p53)* boasts an important Novecento-style building constructed in 1939 to house the main offices of the Banco di Napoli.

The Caffè Gambrinus *was popular in the early 1900s.*

The Mostra delle Terre d'Oltremare
This huge exhibition and recreational complex was one of the Fascist regime's most notable architectural achievements. Work on the site began in 1937 after the demolition of the Fuorigrotta quarter.

1901 Saredo judicial inquiry reveals government–Camorra rapport

1925–7 Naples incorporates surrounding towns, formerly independent

1940 Mostra delle Terre d'Oltremare, a huge exhibition, recreational and sports complex built by the Fascist regime

Entrance to Mostra d'Oltremare

1900

Benito Mussolini
1920
1945

1899 First stretch of Cumana railway built

1922 On October 24, Fascists meet in Naples on eve of "March on Rome"

1928–41 Rione Carità district replaces old San Giuseppe quarter

1944 Last eruption of Vesuvius

1943 *"Quattro giornate"* uprising: Germans driven out of Naples

Present-day Naples

Eduardo De Filippo

At the end of World War II the city had to cope with the appalling damage inflicted by all the bombardments. The 1950s and 1960s were marked by the large-scale, indiscriminate building activity promoted by politicians who looked only for short-term gain. The closing down of some large factories in the 1980s aggravated the acute unemployment problem. However, Naples has always distinguished itself by its irrepressible vitality and creativity, especially in the fields of music and theatre. Today the city is rediscovering its past, and there is a new commitment to city regeneration, as well as a resurgence of cultural programmes.

GROWTH OF THE CITY

■ *1945*   □ *Today*

Vesuvius
This work by Andy Warhol was produced in 1985 for an exhibition held at the Museo di Capodimonte, where the canvas is now on display. It is the American artist's tribute to the most recurrent artistic motif relating to Naples – an erupting Vesuvius.

San Paolo Stadium
Built in the 1960s, this football stadium has a seating capacity of 80,000. Famous players for Naples include Dino Zoff and Diego Maradona.

TIMELINE

1945 Eduardo De Filippo writes *Napoli milionaria*. Town council approves reconstruction project

1949 Curzio Malaparte's novel *La Pelle*, set in Naples, causes a scandal with its raw descriptions

1952 Shipowner Achille Lauro, leader of the monarchist party, becomes mayor. Period of building speculation begins

Achille Lauro

1962 Centre-left coalition governs city

1963 Francesco Rosi directs film *Hands over the City (see p37)*

1972 Town-planning regulations (still partly in force) protect historic old town, considered a cultural heritage

1975 Inaugura... bypass r... fast traffi... edge of ... town

1950   1960   1970

Posillipo Today

Among the many examples of building malpractice in Naples, Posillipo is one of the most tragic. The hill, known the world over for its ancient history and lovely scenery, has been defaced by unchecked and unscrupulous development.

Skyscrapers are a novelty in Neapolitan architecture.

estrian avenue
etween the
ngs: cars use
ground roads.

CENTRO DIREZIONALE

This district of futuristic administrative office buildings in the heart of the city, near the central railway station, is an example of "rational" modernization. The original plan dates from the 1960s, but in 1982 the famous Japanese architect Kenzo Tange began a new design. The layout of the area is such that traffic, which runs along underground streets, is separated from pedestrians.

The planting of trees softens the stark modern aesthetic and improves the environment for workers.

Montagna di Sale

Mimmo Paladino's Salt Mountain was installed in Piazza del Plebiscito for New Year's Day 1996. The square, restored for the G7 summit and now a pedestrian zone, has become a symbol of the new Naples.

1980 The earthquake in Campania and Basilicata also causes damage in Naples. Reconstruction includes a plan to revive the outskirts

1995–6 Mimmo Paladino's temporary sculpture *Montagna di Sale* is placed in Piazza del Plebiscito

2001 Antonio Bassolino, famous for restoring historic centre of Naples, stands down as mayor. Rosa Russo Jervolino takes over

1990	2000	2010

1982 The new Via Marittima, planned in the 1950s, is completed. Kenzo Tange redesigns the Centro Direzionale

1994 G7 summit opens in July in Naples. First stage of hill metro becomes operative

2001 Thousands of anti-globalisation demonstrators take to the streets while the G8 leaders are in town

2002 Inauguration of Station Art project, through which the work of emerging artists is displayed in city metro stations

NAPLES AT A GLANCE

Naples is filled with evidence of many centuries of occupation blended into the fabric of the present-day city. This complex heritage, from ancient Greeks and Romans to the dukes, kings and queens of the Middle Ages and beyond, has contributed to a rich store of galleries and museums, ancient amphitheatres and ruins, as well as churches, monasteries, royal palaces and monuments. While the *Area by Area* section *(pp44–129)* describes the various places of interest in detail, the following ten pages will provide some background and cultural context. Each corner of Naples has something different to offer, but below is a selection of attractions that no visitor to the city should miss.

NAPLES' TOP TOURIST ATTRACTIONS

Castel Nuovo *See pp54–5*

Santa Chiara *See pp66–7*

Museo di Capodimonte
See pp98–101

Certosa di San Martino *See pp108–11*

Mergellina *See p119*

Castel dell'Ovo *See p116*

Museo Archeologico Nazionale
See pp86–9

Posillipo
See pp124–9

◁ The seafront with its historic hotels, Castel dell'Ovo and the Borgo Marinaro

Naples and the Bay

The Faraglioni of Capri

Formed by an immense crater, the Bay of Naples is both sheltered and exposed; sheltered by the curve of hills to the east which create a natural semi-circular amphitheatre, but open to the sea. The zone is volcanic, shaped by cones and craters of all ages, some submerged, some still bubbling with thermal springs and jets of steam. Now that Vesuvius is quiet (the last smoke trail was seen in 1944), the most active crater in the region is the Solfatara at Pozzuoli *(see p137)*. The living, breathing quality of the land led Homer to choose the coastline as the setting for parts of the *Odyssey*. Chaotic development along the coast has not deterred visitors from seeking out and appreciating the beauty of the bay.

Ischia *has small sandy beaches that are a great tourist attraction.*

Gaiola *is the largest of the three islands facing the Gaiola quarter. The coastline is rocky and precipitous with natural caves.*

Posillipo

Castel dell'Ovo

THE BAY OF NAPLES

Mount Vesuvius stands guard over a bay which owes its beauty and characteristic curves to the violent and often deadly explosions of a series of volcanoes. The conical shape of Monte Epomeo on Ischia still shows its volcanic origin; one submerged crater now does service as the port of Ischia and hot springs abound. Capri, once joined to the mainland, is geologically an extension of the Sorrento peninsula; time has carved beautiful caves along the island's precipitous coastline. Just beyond Punta Campanella are islands known to Homer as the home of the Sirens.

THE BAY FROM MERGELLINA

Vesuvius

Castel dell'Ovo

Sorrento

Punta Campanella

Capri

Ischia

Posillipo

The port of Naples, *once a disembarkation point for transatlantic ships, is now the centre of intense ship, ferry and hydrofoil traffic for tourists along the coast and to the islands of Capri, Ischia and Procida. The Angioino wharf is also important commercially.*

The fertility of the soil *in Naples was proverbial in ancient times. To this day you can still find unexpected pockets of terrace cultivation in built-up areas.*

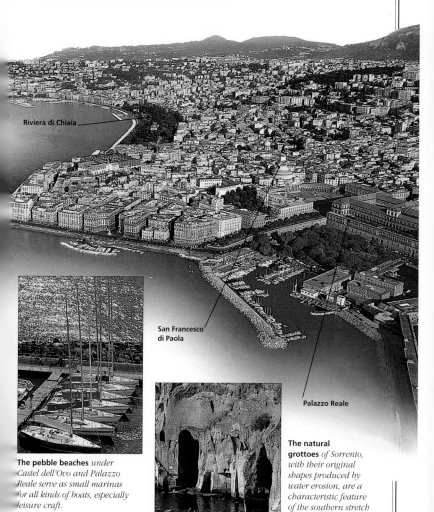

Riviera di Chiaia

San Francesco di Paola

Palazzo Reale

The pebble beaches *under Castel dell'Ovo and Palazzo Reale serve as small marinas for all kinds of boats, especially leisure craft.*

The natural grottoes *of Sorrento, with their original shapes produced by water erosion, are a characteristic feature of the southern stretch of the bay.*

The Architecture of Naples

One feature of the architecture of Naples is
the way in which traces of various epochs
and styles can be seen in one short section of
street, from Roman foundations and remains
to the turn-of-the-century galleria made of
iron and glass. Little remains within Naples of
its Greek heritage, yet in the heart of the city
you can still discern the regular grid layout
adopted in 5th-century BC Neapolis: the three
main streets going east–west – present-day Via
Anticaglia *(see p84)*, Via Tribunali *(see pp76–7)*
and Via San Biagio dei Librai – and the
north–south roads that intersect them at right
angles. Along the waterfront (Lungomare) and
the Riviera di Chiaia, more modern buildings
can be found, elegant palazzi alternating with
villas and splendid luxury hotels.

The ancient grid layout of Neapolis (red
lines) over a plan of the modern city

VIA FORIA

Caserma Garibaldi

VIA DUOMO

1956–7

RIVIERA DI CHIAIA

The wide, elegant Riviera di Chiaia, flanked by fine
buildings, mostly dating from the 18th and 19th centuries

1940–41

LUNGOMARE

1955–6

Faculty of Business Administration,
1934

Hotel Royal, 1956

A MULTI-LAYERED CITY

San Lorenzo Maggiore *(see p80)* is one example of a layered building. Remains of the ancient city are visible under the monastery. The church itself is also the result of a series of reconstructions; the Angevin basilica, built over the ruins of a 6th-century church, was completely rebuilt in the 1700s, and then restored to its original medieval state in the last century. The 18th-century façade still has the original 14th-century wooden doorway.

Gothic church

Roman market

Ground level in Roman times

Ground level in Greek era

Greco-Roman remains

The historic layers of the church

The Galleria Principe di Napoli, built in 1883, the oldest galleria in Naples

San Giuseppe a Chiaia, dating from 1666–73

The Neo-Classical Villa Pignatelli, 1826, designed by Pietro Valente, now a museum *(see p118)*

Hotel Continental

Hotel Vesuvio (reconstruction), 1948

Santa Lucia, 1902

Writers in Naples

Bust of Virgil

The beauty of the Bay of Naples and the fascination of Vesuvius have inspired writers and artists for over 2,000 years. The Greeks wove stories around the landscape, seeing in it a variety of mythological creatures; volcanic activity was regarded as the work of the gods. The poet Virgil so loved Naples that he spent his last years there while writing the *Georgics* and the *Aeneid*. The city's rich Classical inheritance again attracted travellers with the advent of the Grand Tour, over 17 centuries later, when no young man could be considered well educated without a visit to Italy.

Portrait of Giacomo Leopardi

FROM CLASSICAL WRITERS TO THE RENAISSANCE

Before the eruption in AD 79 Vesuvius had been quiet for 1,200 years, but inhabitants were nonetheless aware of the living nature of the land. Pliny the Elder, author of *Naturalis Historia*, died at Pompeii; his curiosity tempted him to go closer to the volcano and he was suffocated by the fumes. His nephew, Pliny the Younger, provides in his letters an eyewitness account of the eruption.

The Renaissance brought a revival of interest in Greek and Latin culture. In the 14th century writers and artists including Boccaccio, Giotto and the great lyric poet and scholar Petrarch were attracted to the court of

Petrarch

Tischbein, *Goethe in the Country* (Museo di San Martino)

Robert of Anjou. Torquato Tasso, a native of Sorrento, worked on his epic poetry at the monastery of Monteoliveto at the end of the 1500s.

TRAVELLERS AND THE GRAND TOUR

The Grand Tour first became a custom in the 16th century and by the 18th century it was English fashion. Young aristocrats were expected to study Europe's Classical past to complete their education and the Tour took them to Rome and Naples. Excavations at Herculaneum in 1711 and at Pompeii in 1733 added to the enormous appeal of this part of Italy. Sir William Hamilton, an archaeologist, collector and envoy to Naples from 1764, entertained Grand Tour travellers at the embassy. The Tour inspired journals, letters and guide books and Goethe, overwhelmed by his visit to the city in 1775 with the painter Tischbein, wrote of Naples in *Italian Journey*.

ROMANTIC NAPLES

Stendhal departed Naples in 1817 smitten with Toledo and Teatro San Carlo, the glories of the "most beautiful city in the universe". In 1812 Alphonse de Lamartine recalled his experiences of Naples in *Graziella*, which featured a girl from Procida,

and the *Gulf of Baia*. In 1828 the American author James Fenimore Cooper was so taken by the city he managed to find good qualities even in its negative aspects. In his description of the Castel Nuovo area he declares: "This was the area of the *lazzaroni*; and it is no easy task to find lovelier or happier vagabonds than the ones here". Charles Dickens' 1844 observations were published in the *Daily News* and in his book, *Pictures from Italy*. The end of Bourbon rule, the unification of Italy and the cholera epidemic of 1884 brought about a decline in the number of visitors to Naples. The foreign traveller remained enchanted by Naples and its Bay, but set off for Pompeii and Paestum, and later, Capri.

TO THE 20TH CENTURY

Poet Giacomo Leopardi (1798–1837) spent the last years of his life in Naples. Neapolitan Matilde Serao wrote vividly of the hectic city and hopes and passions inspired by the lottery in *Il Paese di Cuccagna* (1891). Curzio Malaparte, whose red villa is a landmark on Capri (*see p169*), wrote in *La Pelle* (1948): "Naples is the most mysterious city in Europe. It is the only city of the ancient world that has not perished. …It is not a city: it is a world – the ancient pre-Christian world – which has survived intact on the surface of the modern world".

Naples and the Arts

Silent film stars of 1914

Naples was famous in the 19th century for its spectacular operas and the magnetism of its popular songs, and in more recent times, Neapolitan performers such as Eduardo De Filippo, Totò and Sophia Loren, have all gained worldwide acclaim. The arts scene is still alive today, with creative experiments ranging from variations on the *sceneggiata* to avant-garde theatre, and from traditional song to modern cinema.

OPERA AND THEATRE

Opera may be the preserve of the elite elsewhere, but in Naples passion for opera knows no social boundaries and even permeates street life. Historic Teatro San Carlo *(see p53)* is one of Italy's most prestigious opera houses. The season is well subscribed and performances often sell out. Rossini's opera *Otello* was first performed at the San Carlo, as were two other of his world premieres: *Mosè in Egitto* (1818) and *La Donna del Lago* (1819), based on Sir Walter Scott's *The Lady of the Lake*. Donizetti's *Lucia di Lammermoor* made its debut at the San Carlo in 1835.

Theatre has a broad popularity in Naples. Cinemas forced to close because of dwindling attendance have even been reborn as theatres. Neapolitans are proud of their dialect, used to great effect by beloved comic actors like Eduardo Scarpetta (1853–1924), Totò (1898–1967) and Eduardo De Filippo (1900–84). Comedies by actor-playwrights De Filippo and Raffaele Viviani (1888–1950) affectionately expose the ironies and petty concerns of daily life. They are performed as much today as when they were written.

Experimental theatre has been active in Naples since the establishment of the "Falso Movimento" in 1979. Its founders are now involved in the Teatri Uniti, staging avant-garde plays at the Teatro Nuovo and Galleria Toledo.

Gioacchino Rossini

THE SCENEGGIATA

The *sceneggiata* (popular Neapolitan melodrama) dates from the turn of the 20th century. Simple plots and characters embroiled in tragedy and farce delighted audiences that cheered heroes and booed villains. Music played a vital part in the show and there was always a rousing title song, the *pezzo forte*. This lively genre temporarily fell into disfavour, but was revived in the 1970s and is still performed today.

NEAPOLITAN SONGS

Enrico Caruso remains Naples' most famous tenor, though opera singers from far and wide are lured by the beauty, power and melancholy of Neapolitan songs. The songs' romantic melodies have had a profound influence on the development of Italian music

Massimo Troisi on the set of *Ricomincio da Tre* (1980)

Eduardo De Filippo and Totò

and are familiar worldwide. Best known of all is *O Sole Mio*, composed in 1898 (and modified for Elvis Presley's *It's Now or Never*). Present-day masters of the tradition include Sergio Bruni, who achieved fame with *Carmela*, and Roberto Murolo.

Less well-known traditional forms include the *macchietta* (a comic song routine) and *tammorriate* (dances accompanied by songs).

CINEMA

Although Lombardo Film was founded in the Vomero district in the early 1900s, the first major film produced in Naples was *Assunta Spina* (1915). More familiar however are the films made in the 1950s. Neapolitan stage actors that made the crossover into film included Eduardo De Filippo and Totò. Pozzuoli native Sophia Loren starred in *The Gold of Naples* (1954) and *Marriage Italian Style* (1964). Roberto Rossellini's portrait of the city in *Viaggio in Italia* (1953) is unsentimental, while in the 1960s Francesco Rosi attacked corrupt politicians and developers in *Mani sulla Città*. Despite its flaws, Naples is not easy to leave, as Massimo Troisi showed in *Ricomincio da Tre* and Mario Martone in *L'Amore Molesto*. More recently, Caserta's Royal Palace *(see pp166–7)* was the setting for Star Wars: Episode I (1999) and II (2002), and *Mission Impossible III* (2006).

Symbols of the City

Naples is a city that defies rational explanation, yet visitors have always found a wealth of sights and sounds that sum up aspects of its character. Some are positive: the beauty of the bay, the romantic melodies of Neapolitan songs, the craftsmanship of the cribs in the churches. Others are quite the opposite. Northern Europeans (and Northern Italians) are often shocked by the contrast between the city's general air of *dolce far niente* and its widespread poverty and superstition. All these things have become clichés, making it even harder to distinguish the true nature of Naples.

The pazzariello and his band

Street life: colourful stalls in a city market

FIRST IMPRESSIONS

Naples has always been famous for the vivacity of its alleyways, streets and squares. The zest for life in the Toledo district amazed foreign visitors such as Goethe and Stendhal *(see pp34–5)*. The *lazzaroni* (ruffians) lounging around on street corners made such a strong impression on foreign visitors to Naples in the 18th and 19th centuries, that they became more or less synonymous with the city. Ferdinand I, King of the Two Sicilies from 1759 to 1825, was even nicknamed the *Re Lazzarone*.

Today, many people are struck by the ubiquitous street pedlars. There have been many attempts to regulate their activities, but most have come to nothing.

THE WATER-SELLER

The Neapolitan water-seller *(l'acquaiolo)* was once a very common sight on the streets of the city, offering refreshing drinks to passers-by on torrid summer afternoons. The water often came from the sulphurous springs of Chiatamone, which used to rise near the church of Santa Lucia *(see p116).* It was kept cool in clay jugs, known as *mummere*. If you paid extra, you could have lemon or orange juice added to make a *spremuta*. In some parts of the old city you can still spot a *banco dell'acqua* or water stand with its solid marble counter and decorative citrus fruit. Most, however, have been modernized by the addition of stainless steel and sell cans of Coca-Cola as well as traditional drinks.

Old water-seller's marble stand

THE PAZZARIELLO

A curious and unique figure, sadly now defunct, the *pazzariello* could be seen dressed in an old-fashioned military uniform, wielding a long ceremonial baton with a gold pommel at one end and leading a small marching band. The amusing and immensely popular character, he was originally a town crier, but his duties were later extended to include leading parades on local feast days and advertising goods for sale in a new shop. The *pazzariello* was immortalized by Totò in Vittorio De Sica's film *The Gold of Naples (see p36).*

THE SCUGNIZZO

The stereotype of the cheeky, but basically good, street urchin, plays a major part in the folklore of the city. Living by his wits, ready to run errands for anybody who would give him money or food, he made an indelible impression on the American troops based in Naples during World War II. The true *scugnizzo* no longer really exists. Yet one can perhaps sense his streetwise spirit in the many small boys who now whizz about the city on mopeds.

A *scugnizzo*

PULCINELLA

The character of Pulcinella, stupid, yet at the same time cunning, dogged by chronic bad luck and always hungry, is the stock comic figure of a Neapolitan. One can never be quite sure, as the philosopher Benedetto Croce remarked, whether he represents a faithful portrait, a caricature or an ideal to which Neapolitans aspire. Either as a puppet (he was the model for the English Mr Punch) or in the theatre, Pulcinella has always made people laugh. With his crazy schemes, wild grimaces and the comic effects of his permanently empty stomach, he personifies the city's age-old scourge of famine.

The character of Pulcinella, as we know him today, first appeared in about 1600, but he may well have had a Classical ancestor in the equally hungry Macchus, a character from the ancient farces of Atela, a town northeast of Naples.

Pulcinella

The greatest interpreters of the role within living memory were naturally the two actors who most fully represented the spirit of Naples – Eduardo De Filippo and Totò *(see p37)*. Their performances were especially poignant in the period of famine during and after World War II.

THE CHRISTMAS CRIB

Nobody knows when the custom of representing the nativity of Christ in a sculpted tableau began. One of the earliest examples is the 13th-century sculpture by Arnolfo di Cambio at the Basilica of Santa Maria Maggiore in Rome, but the tradition may well be much older. In Naples it became such an important feature of the Christmas celebrations that people came to think

Detail of historic crib scene at the Museo di San Martino *(see p111)*

of the crib *(il presepe)* as a Neapolitan institution. The traditional local craftsmen, who, in many cases, have produced magnificent works of art *(see p111)*, do not limit themselves to the central figures of the nativity grouped around the baby Jesus in the manger. The scene expands to become a miniature representation of the whole of Naples, with all its characteristic sights and personalities. Look closely at the figures in a modern crib scene and you may spot Pulcinella, Totò or even reality show contestants and unpopular politicians.

THE LOTTERY

The drawing of the lottery, in which a blindfolded child extracts the winning numbers, has remained unchanged, but the lottery is not quite the force it once was. Founded by Ferdinand I

in 1774, *il lotto* can be said, without exaggeration, to have ruled the lives of many 19th-century Neapolitans. It is still very popular and *La Smorfia*, a book that claims to interpret dreams and events to help you choose the winning numbers, has been reprinted many times *(see p71)*.

PIZZA AND PASTA

Ingredients for the topping of a pizza Margherita

The gastronomic symbols of Naples, pizza and pasta, were not always the city's staple foods. Before the population explosion of the 1600s, the poor lived mainly on cabbage and other vegetables. These were then replaced as the staple food by wheat flour, which was less perishable, and the Neapolitans acquired the nickname "macaroni eaters".

Pizza, in its present form, dates from the end of the 18th century. It may not have been a Neapolitan invention, but it was Naples that gave the world the napoletana and the Margherita, its two most enduring varieties.

Period print showing the traditional lottery drawing ceremony

NAPLES THROUGH THE YEAR

There is no single ideal season for visiting Naples; the temperate climate means a pleasant stay at any time of year. However, every season has its particular attractions. In May, an increased number of churches and monuments are open to the public; while July and August are perfect for the beach. The miracle of the city's patron saint San Gennaro is celebrated in May and September. In December, local craftsmen create traditional Christmas crib scenes. In the outlying areas, old traditions, with processions at sea and feasts celebrated in historical costume, are still vital to local life.

SPRING

The mild spring climate is perfect for enjoying drinks at an outdoor café, walking around the town centre, or visiting the surrounding countryside, which is relatively uncrowded during this season compared with summertime. At Easter it may be warm enough to swim in the sea, although traditionally 1 May marks the beginning of the bathing season. The months of March and April can be unsettled, however, and a brief spell of fine weather may be interrupted by a cold snap or even hailstorms. According to a local proverb, the weather experienced in Naples on 4 April will continue for the following 40 days.

San Giuseppe's day *zeppole*

MARCH

Feast of San Giuseppe (19 March). A bird festival is held in Via Medina, with *zeppole* (doughnuts) in every bar, bakery and home. At one time the festival marked the change from winter clothes to the new spring wardrobe.

EASTER

In many outlying districts and in some quarters of Naples there are **Good Friday** processions. One of the most

Madonna dell'Arco, Easter Monday

interesting takes place on the island of Procida. The cortege of priests and parishioners leaves at dawn from the top of Terra Murata and ends up at Marina Grande.

Easter Monday, or "Pasquetta" is the day for outings, when the whole family goes for a meal in a trattoria out of town. For the more traditional, a ceremony is held at the sanctuary of Madonna dell'Arco, near Sant'Anastasia, 15 km (9 miles) east of the city. Barefooted men, known as *fuijenti*, ask for alms, and a statue of the Madonna is carried on flower-laden carts into the countryside. Here the occasion turns into a lively "pagan" feast.

The *Inghirlandata* ceremony

Trotting races at the Agnano racetrack

APRIL

The Agnano racetrack hosts trotting races for the **Gran Premio della Lotteria di Agnano** in April.

MAY

One of the two annual celebrations of the miracle of **San Gennaro** *(see p83)* takes place on the Saturday before the first Sunday in May. The procession starts off at the cathedral with the statue of San Gennaro, patron saint of Naples, being carried from the church. The procession is known locally as the *Inghirlandata* (garlanding) because it was traditionally accompanied by flowered decorations, and the faithful would throw rose petals over the saint's statue.

During May visitors can make the most of the **Maggio dei Monumenti**, when buildings and churches which are normally closed are open to the public. Some offer special tours or concerts too. The scheme, also known as *Napoli Porte Aperte*, was started in 1992 by the Fondazione Napoli '99. Since 1995 it has been sponsored by the Naples city council to encourage the "rediscovery" of historic Naples. May is also the month of the **Vela Longa** regatta, open to any type of sailing boat.

AVERAGE DAILY HOURS OF SUNSHINE

Hours
12
9
6
3
0

Jan Feb Mar Apr May Jun Jul Aug Sep Oct Nov Dec

Sunshine Hours
Naples is famous for its light. The longest days fall in July, when the midday heat can be intense. In autumn the sun can still be quite hot, particularly in the middle of the day.

The Vela Longa regatta is held every May

SUMMER

This season can be quite muggy, especially in July, when the temperature sometimes exceeds 40°C (104°F). However, after mid-August the heat is sometimes interrupted by a brief, heavy and often violent thunderstorm that is known all along the coast as the *tropea*.

Summer nights in the city can be spent at the **Estate a Napoli** festival, which from late July to September features various performance art events and films. The week of the Assumption, or *Ferragosto* (15 Aug), is ideal for those who prefer a semi-deserted, if hot, city.

Outside Naples, interesting cultural events are held at the Pompeii amphitheatre *(see p148)*, and the Vesuvian villas *(see p140)* also host various events. For music-lovers, there are the **Estate Musicale Sorrentina** at Sorrento, and the well-known **Festival Internazionale**, which takes place at Ravello *(see p212)*.

JUNE

The feast of **San Giovanni** (24 Jun), linked to the summer solstice, used to be celebrated with magicians and feasting, and night bathing. Out in the countryside people still gather walnuts to make the traditional walnut liqueur called *nocino* that will be ready by late autumn.

From late June to mid-July, the Mostra d'Oltremare *(see p25)* features the **Fiera della Casa**, when furniture, interior furnishings and local handicrafts are on sale or simply on display. The *fiera* gives you the chance to join the busy crowds and makes a change from sightseeing.

JULY

Piazza Mercato *(see p73)* plays host to the feast of the **Madonna del Carmine** (16 Jul), an ancient tradition. The *Madonna Bruna* is kept inside the church of Santa Maria del Carmine: according to legend she miraculously saved the bell tower from a fire.

Fireworks are used to re-enact the miracle wrought by the Madonna; the ceremony ends with the so-called "burning" of the bell tower.

Sant'Anna is celebrated in Ischia on 26 July with a night procession of illuminated boats and a firework display.

AUGUST

August is the traditional holiday month in Italy and you may find many city restaurants, as well as shops, local services and bars, closed until September. Throughout the region the traditional "fast" held on the Eve of the Assumption (the night of 14–15 August) is helped along by helpings of watermelon, eaten on the beach. At Positano, a ceremony in period costume celebrates the landing of the Saracens.

Feast of the Madonna del Carmine

AVERAGE MONTHLY RAINFALL

Rainfall
The wettest months of the year are November and February. The rainfall does not last for long, but it comes in brief, violent downpours. The driest month is August, but this can also be interrupted by heavy thunderstorms near the end of the month.

AUTUMN

Autumn in Naples is quite mild; with September and October perfect for outings and long hikes in the countryside. The sea is warm enough for swimming well into October and even in early November. Nature lovers and amateur photographers will enjoy the splendid soft autumn light and clear days. Then there are popular local feast days, known as *sagre*, in nearby towns, such as the famous wine festivals (*sagra del vino*), that coincide with the harvesting of the grapes.

Naples itself also comes back to life after the quiet and empty summer months. From September onwards football fans can spend Sunday afternoons in the stadium, following the Neapolitans' favourite sport.

SEPTEMBER

The **Madonna di Piedigrotta** feast is held in the first half of the month. The ancient cave next to the sanctuary (*see p118*), which has been closed for many years, was once the venue for popular rituals. Today, the festival has once again become fashionable. According to an old proverb, the date of the festival of Piedigrotta marks the beginning of the rainy season.

An increasingly popular festival is the **Settembrata Anacaprese**. Throughout the month of September, shows, games and gastronomic contests are held in Anacapri, Capri's second town.

The Piedigrotta feast in a 1930s photograph

The 19th marks the second celebration of the miracle of the blood of **San Gennaro** in Naples' Duomo. For centuries this ceremony, in which the congealed blood of the saint becomes liquid, has attracted scholars, tourists, local worshippers and city authorities.

Also held in September is the **Pizza Fest**, which involves all the best pizza restaurants and a competition is held to decide which is the best pizza.

OCTOBER

The **Classical music season** begins at the Teatro San Carlo.

NOVEMBER

On **All Souls' Day** (1 Nov), also called the Day of the Dead, families take flowers to the graves of their loved ones. This was traditionally followed by a family meal at a trattoria outside town. This is the time of year when confectioners make the delicious *torrone dei morti* almond nougat.

Aerial view of the San Paolo football stadium

AVERAGE MONTHLY TEMPERATURE

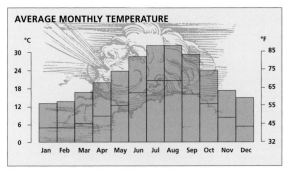

Temperature
This chart gives the average minimum and maximum temperatures for each month. July and August are the hottest months, February the coldest. During the winter, relatively cold days may alternate with a spell of very mild and sunny days.

WINTER

The month of December and the holiday season is rarely accompanied by any snow (except on the mountaintops). However, December and January are not usually cold, and the days can be bright and sunny. February sometimes brings rain and cold. Although the rainfall is not persistent, heavy showers may occur. The "land of the sun" is not in fact warm all year around, as many think, and the few cold days can be really cold.

DECEMBER

The day of the **Immacolata** (Immaculate Conception, 8 Dec) opens the Christmas holiday season. People prepare the *presepe* (nativity scene) in their homes with moss and statuettes of figures such as Mary, the ox and donkey, the Wise Men and Jesus in the crib. The Cardinal and Mayor of the city lay wreaths on the Guglia dell'Immacolata *(see p65)*.

Christmas is celebrated with dinner and presents on Christmas Eve followed by midnight mass. The streets are illuminated and the stands on Via San Gregorio Armeno have crib figures on display *(see p39)*. A few days before New Year's Day the fireworks stalls start to appear and the traditional bagpipers add colour to the street scene.

A bagpipe player, a tradition at Christmas

JANUARY

New Year's Eve is celebrated with an impressive display of fireworks. For an enjoyable midnight outdoors, go and join in the merrymaking in the central Piazza del Plebiscito.

Traditionally the year begins with **Sant'Antuono** (Sant' Antonio Abate, 17 Jan) and in the old centre *cippi* or old things are thrown in bonfires.

On **Epiphany** (6 Jan) the Befana witch arrives in Piazza del Plebiscito. This is a feast for children and stalls sell sweets and "gifts from the Befana", particularly in Via Foria. Naughty children are brought (sweet) "lumps of coal".

FEBRUARY

Masked festivities for **Shrove Tuesday** and **Carnival** are accompanied by lasagna dishes. The **Galassia Gutenberg** book and multimedia fair opens, and the **Mostra d'Oltremare** offers exhibits, lectures and cultural events.

Pulcinella, the protagonist of the Naples Carnival

PUBLIC HOLIDAYS

New Year's Day (1 Jan)
Epiphany (6 Jan)
Easter Sunday and Monday
Liberation Day (25 Apr)
Labour Day (1 May)
Republic Day (2 Jun)
Ferragosto (15 Aug)
All Saints' Day (1 Nov)
Immaculate Conception (8 Dec)
Christmas Day (25 Dec)
Santo Stefano (26 Dec)

A Christmas feast in a square illuminated with fairy lights

NAPLES AREA BY AREA

TOLEDO AND CASTEL NUOVO

Castel Nuovo casts its impressive shadow on an area that is both the commercial and administrative centre of modern Naples and the heart of the old capital. This zone extends as far as the harbour, the boarding point for ferry trips. Centuries of history are concentrated in the area – from the ancient archaeological ruins on the hill of Pizzofalcone to 19th-century buildings such as the Galleria Umberto I. Near the Royal Palace and

Cannonballs at Castel Nuovo

fortress of Castel Nuovo, opposite the basilica of San Francesco di Paola, is the majestic Palazzo Reale, a palace built by the Spanish viceroys. Running north from here is a long and famous 16th-century road, Via Toledo, the main artery of Naples. It is still better known by this name (after the man who built it, Viceroy Don Pedro of Toledo) than its newer, official name, Via Roma. Lining the thoroughfare are elegant buildings, stately churches and shops.

SIGHTS AT A GLANCE

Historic Buildings
Castel Nuovo pp54–5 ⑧
Palazzo delle Poste e Telegrafi ⑭
Palazzo Reale pp50–51 ①
Palazzo Serra di Cassano ⑲

Churches
Santa Brigida ⑫
San Ferdinando ④
San Francesco di Paola ②
San Giacomo degli Spagnoli ⑪
Santa Maria degli Angeli ⑰
Santa Maria Egiziaca a Pizzofalcone ⑱
Santa Maria Incoronata ⑩
Nunziatella ⑳

Historic Streets and Squares
Galleria Umberto I ⑥
Piazza Giovanni Bovio ⑮
Quartieri Spagnoli ⑬
Via Chiaia ⑯
Via Toledo ⑤

Historic Theatres
Teatro Mercadante ⑨
Teatro San Carlo ⑦

Museums
Museo dell'Appartamento Reale (see Palazzo Reale)
Museo Artistico Industriale ㉑
Museo Civico (see Castel Nuovo)

Historic Landmarks
Caffè Gambrinus ③

GETTING THERE
Piazza del Plebiscito and part of Via Toledo are closed to traffic, but a number of city buses run nearby. Route R2 comes from Napoli Centrale railway station, while R3 comes from Mergellina railway station. Bus 24 is on the same route as Capodimonte and the Museo Archeologico. The V1 route links Vomero with the funicular at Montesanto and Toledo. The Alibus or 35 arrive from the airport at Piazza Municipio.

KEY

▨ Street-by-Street map See pp48–9

⚓ Ferry port

🚠 Funicular

◁ Ornate rooms in the Palazzo Reale

0 metres   350
0 yards   350

Street-by-Street: Toledo and Castel Nuovo

Naples is a city of contrasting moods:
the quiet solemnity of Piazza del
Plebiscito, a symbol of the city's rebirth,
is very different from the animation –
you might even call it confusion – of the
surrounding streets. It is a pleasure to
mingle with the crowd in Via Toledo,
drop in at the Caffè Gambrinus or
Galleria Umberto I, pause in the shade
of the historic church of San Francesco
di Paola, or visit the museums at
Palazzo Reale and Castel Nuovo. In
addition to the rich history and art
treasures in this area, Via Toledo is
good for shopping.

Galleria Umberto I
The iron and glass dome was built in the late 1800s by Boubée **6**

Via Toledo
This street, named after a Spanish viceroy, borders the Quartieri Spagnoli **5**

Teatro San Carlo
Richly decorated in gilded stucco, the theatre seats 3,000 and the acoustics are excellent **7**

San Ferdinando
Every year on Good Friday there is a performance of the Stabat Mater *composed by Pergolesi for the confraternity based here since 1837* **4**

PIAZZA TRIESTE TRENT

PIAZZA PLEBISCITO

Caffè Gambrinus
Gabriele d'Annunzio wrote the lyrics to the Neapolitan song "A vucchella" in this café **3**

★ **San Francesco di Paola**
This Neo-Classical church was designed by Lugano architect Pietro Bianchi in 1817 **2**

★ Castel Nuovo
The sculpture on Alfonso of Aragon's triumphal arch stands out between the Mezzo *(middle) and* Guardia *(watch) towers of this palace and fortress, also known as the* Maschio Angioino **8**

LOCATOR MAP
See Street Finder, maps 6–7

This lovely courtyard is the venue for summer events and concerts.

The Palazzo Reale stables

VIA VITTORIO EMANUELE III

VIA SAN CARLO

VIA PARCO DEL CASTELLO

VIA FERDINANDO ACTON

Entrance to Plazzo Reale & library

The Molo Beverello is the passenger terminal of the port built for Charles II in 1302.

0 metres	100
0 yards	100

STAR SIGHTS

★ Palazzo Reale

★ San Francesco di Paola

★ Castel Nuovo

The historic Neapolitan rowing club, Canottieri Napoli, overlooks the gardens next to Palazzo Reale.

EY

– – – Suggested route

★ Palazzo Reale
This palace was begun in 1600 for a visit by Philip III of Spain, which never took place **1**

Palazzo Reale ❶

The layout and size of the Palazzo Reale befit its role as one of the most important royal courts in the Mediterranean. Designed by Domenico Fontana at the request of the viceroy Fernández Ruiz de Castro, construction began in 1600. Building continued for centuries and the palace was only finished in 1843 by Gaetano Genovese. The Ala delle Feste wing, used in the 19th century for entertaining, now houses the Biblioteca Nazionale, the library named after King Vittorio Emanuele III, who donated the wing.

Teatro San Carlo
(see p53)

Maria Carolina's Revolving Lectern
This unusual Neo-Classical piece is based on models from monastery libraries.

The façade, 169m (555 ft) long, was altered in the 18th century by Luigi Vanvitelli, who created the niches which now house statues of Neapolitan kings.

Main Entrance

★ **Teatrino di Corte**
The court theatre was built in 1768 for Maria Carolina of Hapsburg's wedding to Ferdinand IV, and decorated with papier-mâché sculpture.

Public Chambers

State Rooms

MUSEUM OF THE ROYAL APARTMENTS

The 30 rooms in the first-floor Museum of the Royal Apartments (Museo dell' Appartamento Reale) are arranged around a central courtyard. In the west wing are the Court Theatre and the public chambers; in the south are the private chambers. The east wing houses the Cappella Palatina and the Sala di Ercole. The sumptuous decoration, objets d'art and interior furnishing are of the highest quality. The rooms in the State Rooms house 16th- to 19th-century paintings.

A mirror in the Museo

STAR FEATURES

★ Biblioteca Nazionale

★ Teatrino di Corte

Stables
*The original mangers can
still be seen in the stone
construction.*

VISITORS' CHECKLIST

Piazza del Plebiscito. **Map** 7 A3.
Tel *081 40 05 47.* C22,
C25, E3, R2, R3. Centrale: Via
Toledo. **Biblioteca** *by appt
only: call ahead on 081 781 92
31 to book.* **Stables** *closed
except some days in May; phone
for details.* **Appartamento
Reale** *9am–7pm Thu–Tue.*
Wed. *Royal Apartments
only.*
www.pierreci.it

The small garden,
built in the mid-19th
century on the site
of the former stable-
yard, is filled with
exotic plants.

The coach house
is often used for
temporary
exhibitions.

★ **Biblioteca Nazionale
Vittorio Emanuele III**
*This is the most important library in
Southern Italy and one of the best in
Italy; it has about two million books
(including examples which pre-date
1500), manuscripts and a collection
of parchments from Herculaneum.*

The Cappella Palatina
boasts a splendid main altar
created by Dionisio Lazzari
in the 17th century.

Sala di Ercole
*his hall was named after
plaster copies of statues
in the Real Museo
onico (now the Museo
eologico Nazionale) –
including the Farnese
Hercules (see p87) –
h were placed here in
the 19th century.*

KEY

	Royal Apartments (first floor)
	Teatro San Carlo
	Ala delle Feste
	Coach house
	Stables
	Non-exhibition space

19th-century print of a riding competition at San Francesco di Paola

San Francesco di Paola ➋

Piazza del Plebiscito. **Map** 7 A3.
Tel 081 764 51 33. ▦ C22, C25, E3,
R2, R3, 201. ▥ Centrale: Via Toledo.
◷ 8am–noon, 3:30–5:30pm
Mon–Sat; 8am–noon Sun. ✝ ◎

Joachim Murat, Napoleon's brother-in-law, ruled the city of Naples from 1808 to 1815. Dissatisfied with the chaotic jumble of buildings opposite the Palazzo Reale, he decided to rebuild the whole area. The Largo di Palazzo, now called the Piazza del Plebiscito, was meant to play a major role in city life and was used for festivities, ceremonies and military parades.
The first buildings to go up were the palace built for the Prince of Salerno, and the palazzo that is now the home of the Prefecture. Both were laid out symmetrically. Murat did not see the final results of his scheme, only managing to see Leopoldo Laperuta's design for the Doric colonnade and the initial construction work • before the French were driven out of Naples.
In 1815 Ferdinand of Bourbon was reinstated to the throne, and, having fulfilled his vow of reconquering the Kingdom of Naples, completed the project begun

Statue of Charles III by Canova

by Murat. He commissioned the architect Pietro Bianchi to design the central royal basilica, which was dedicated to San Francesco di Paola. Inspired by the Pantheon in Rome, the church has a circular plan with radiating chapels, a large cupola 53 m (174 ft) high and 34m (112 ft) wide, complete with rosettes.
The sculpture and paintings inside the church are almost all Neo-Classical except for the high altar, which was rebuilt in 1835 with semi-precious stones and multi-coloured marble, and lapis lazuli taken from a 17th-century altar in the church of Santi Apostoli *(see p96)*. The cool, formal interior can have a rather chilling effect on visitors. According to architectural historian Renato De

Fusco: "Despite the large size of the interior and the rich marble, stucco and garlanding decoration, the overall impression is not that of Neo-Classical rigour, but rather a lack of harmony between man and the setting, a funereal coldness compared to the exterior". The sobering effect is soon dispelled by emerging into the lovely open space of Piazza del Plebiscito, which is pedestrianized. The two equestrian statues of Charles III and Ferdinand I are the work of Antonio Canova and Antonio Calì.

Caffè Gambrinus ➌

Piazza Trieste e Trento. **Map** 7 A3.
Tel 081 41 75 82. ▦ C22, C25, E3,
R2, R3, 201. ▥ Centrale: Via Toledo.
◷ 8am–1.30am Mon–Fri, Sun;
8am–2.30am Sat. ◎

The café dates from 1860; its walls decorated by the leading Neapolitan painters of the time. It soon became the haunt of politicians, artists and writers, including Guy de Maupassant and Oscar Wilde, as well as the local composers Roberto Murolo and Giovanni Bovio. When the literary café also became popular with opponents of the Fascist regime, the prefect closed it down, initiating a long period of decline and neglect. Fortunately, its lavish Belle Epoque decor has been restored and this historic landmark is once again a favourite. Neapolitans drop in for coffee and cakes, or for iced tea and ice cream.

Interior of the historic Caffè Gambrinus

San Ferdinando

Piazza Trieste e Trento 5. **Map** 7 A3.
Tel 081 40 05 43. C22, C25, E3,
R2, R3, 201. *Centrale: Via Toledo.*
8am–noon, 5–7pm Mon–Sat;
9:30am–1pm Sun.

This church was founded in
1622 as San Francesco
Saverio. In 1769 Ferdinand I
dedicated it to his namesake
saint. The Baroque interior
contains frescoes by Paolo
De Matteis and sculptures by
Vaccaro as well as the tomb of
Lucia Migliaccio, the Duchess
of Floridia. Ferdinand gave
her his estate on the Vomero
hill, which became Villa La
Floridiana *(see p106)*. Until
1919 the square was called
Piazza San Ferdinando.

Gay Odin shop in Via Toledo

Via Toledo ❺

Map 3 A5, 7 A1 (9 B4). C57, E2,
E3, R1, R2, R3, R4, 27, 201.
Centrale: Via Toledo.

In the 1600s travellers were
equally struck by the lively
crowds in the most famous
street in Naples and by its
amazing length. Via Toledo
owes its name to the Spanish
viceroy Don Pedro de Toledo,
who commissioned its
construction alongside the
Aragonese city walls in 1536.
Fine buildings alternate with
shops and churches.

Shopping in Via Toledo
caters to all tastes and budgets.
Locals like to stop at Gay Odin
to sample the exquisite home-
made chocolates and at
Pintauro's for the excellent
sfogliatelle pastry.

The marble floor of the Galleria Umberto I

Galleria Umberto I ❻

Via San Carlo, Via Verdi, Via Santa
Brigida, Via Toledo. **Map** 7 A2.
C22, E3, R2, R3, 201.
Centrale: Via Toledo.

The galleria was built as
part of the Urban Renewal
plan, drawn up after the
cholera epidemic which
struck the city in 1884 *(see
pp26–7)*. The impressive iron
and glass roof and elegant
patterned marble pavement
fill the large open space with
light. The arcade soon
became the favourite haunt
of local composers and
musicians. From the galleria it
was possible to gain entry to
the Salone Margherita, which,
until 1912, was a famous *café
chantant*, and considered the
heart of cabaret entertainment in Naples.

Teatro San Carlo ❼

Via San Carlo 101–3. **Map** 7 A3.
Tel 081 799 23 31. C22, C25, R2,
R3, 24, 201. *Centrale: Via Toledo.*
*Call ahead on 081 66 45 45 to
arrange tour.* 9am–6:40pm Mon–
Fri, 9am–5:40pm Sat & Sun except
during rehearsals, **Season** Oct–Jun.
See **Ent in Naples** *p210, p213.*

This is one of the oldest
remaining opera houses
in the world. Designed by
Giovanni Antonio Medrano
for the Bourbon Charles I, it
was built in a few months
and officially opened on 4
November 1737, 40 years

before La Scala in Milan, on
the king's saint's day. It soon
became one of the most
important opera houses in
Europe, known for its
magnificent architecture and
excellent productions. For
many years, a performance at
the San Carlo was considered
the high point in the career of
a singer or composer.

A fire in 1816 severely
damaged the interior, which
was immediately rebuilt by
Antonio Niccolini, the architect who a few years earlier
had modified the façade by
adding the foyer and balcony.
The focal point of the
magnificent auditorium, with
its six tiers of boxes, is the
royal box, surmounted by the
crown of the Kingdom of the
Two Sicilies.

Many great musical figures,
including Gioacchino Rossini
and Gaetano Donizetti, were
at one time artistic directors
here. The world premieres of
Donizetti's *Lucia di Lammermoor* and Rossini's *Mosè* were
performed here. Founded in
1812, the San Carlo ballet
school vies with La Scala for
the title of the oldest ballet
school in Italy.

**The Teatro San Carlo façade,
remodelled by Niccolini in 1810**

Castel Nuovo ❽

The castle was called *nuovo* (new) to distinguish it from two earlier ones, dell'Ovo and Capuano *(see pp116 and 81)*, which were too small to accommodate the entire Angevin court. Charles I of Anjou began construction in 1279, but the Cappella Palatina is the only part remaining of the original building. Alfonso V of Aragon (who later became Alfonso I, King of Naples and Sicily) began to rebuild it completely in 1443, the year that marked his triumphant entry into Naples. To celebrate this event, Alfonso later ordered the construction of the superb Arco di Trionfo, one of the most significant expressions of early Renaissance culture in Southern Italy. The castle, with its five impressive cylindrical towers, is designed on a trapezoidal plan facing onto a beautiful central courtyard. From here you can gain access to the most famous chamber in the castle, the Sala dei Baroni (Barons' Hall), now used by the town council. Since 1990 a small but fine art collection, the Museo Civico, has occupied three floors of the west wing.

The Renaissance doorway of the Cappella Palatina

Cappella Palatina

This is the only surviving part of the 13th-century building. An elegant Renaissance doorway leads to the chapel, which is dedicated to St Barbara. The portal itself is crowned with an elaborate rose window typical of the Catalan style of its creators. The portal is also adorned with a Madonna executed by Francesco Laurana (c.1425–1502) in 1474.

The walls inside the chapel were once decorated with frescoes by Giotto and his workshop; today, only small fragments on the splays of the lofty Gothic windows remain.

Sala dei Baroni

Next to the chapel, the Barons' Hall, which is reached by means of an outer stairway, owes its name to the grim events that took place there in 1486. Then, the great barons who had plotted a conspiracy against Ferdinand I of Aragon, were arrested and subsequently executed.

The imposing Castel Nuovo, with its stunning Renaissance triumphal arch

TIMELINE

		1443–68 Building of Arco di Trionfo	1547 Popular revolt against the Inquisition	1647 Signing of pact between the viceroy and Masaniello after popular uprising	
1279 Charles I of Anjou begins construction of Castel Nuovo	**1443** Alfonso V's total rebuilding plan				
1200	**1300**	**1400**	**1500**	**1600**	**1700**	**1800**
	1329 Giotto and his assistants paint the Cappella Palatina frescoes	**1486** The Barons' conspiracy	**1509–37** Reconstruction of the defence system with new battlements and moats		The Barricades at San Ferdinando during the 1848 uprisings *(detail of a painting in the Museo Civico)*

Sala dei Baroni: the splendid Spanish Gothic vault

This elegant, yet grand and austere hall, 26 m (85 ft) wide and 28 m (92 ft) high, was built by the Spanish craftsman Guglielmo Sagrera, who was summoned to Naples for the purpose in 1446. It is now the main meeting room of the town council. Its principal features are the magnificent Catalan-inspired ribbed vault with intersecting ribs in the shape of a huge star, the monumental fireplace, and the large rectangular "cross windows".

19th-century Neapolitan painting, Museo Civico

Museo Civico

A large part of the west wing of Castel Nuovo and part of the Cappella Palatina are occupied by the Museo Civico (civic museum). Before visiting the museum, do not miss the opportunity to take in the splendid panoramic views of the Bay of Naples and Mount Vesuvius from the upper floors of the castle.

The museum houses paintings, sculptures and objets d'art that come from the castle itself, from neighbouring churches and other Neapolitan monuments. These works date from the 14th to the 19th century, but by far the largest section consists of 19th-century Neapolitan paintings. Some of these – such as Vincenzo

Caprile's *Vecchia Napoli* (Old Naples), depicting the famous Zizze fountain in its original state – offer views of a city that no longer exists.

Arco di Trionfo

The combination of white marble against the grey volcanic stone of Castel Nuovo is immediately striking to the visitor, as is the contrast between the ornamental reliefs and the severe geometric form of the towers. The structure, with its two superimposed arches, takes its inspiration from ancient Roman architecture.

The monumental gateway of the *Arco di Trionfo* (Triumphal Arch) was built in 1443 in honour of Alfonso V of Aragon. The bas relief depicting the *Trionfo di Alfonso* (Triumph of Alfonso) lies above the lower section, while the upper arch, which was once intended to house a statue of the sovereign, now holds allegorical figures representing the Four Virtues (looking from left to right, Temperance, Justice, Fortitude and Magnanimity). On the tympanum, supporting two large symbolic statues of rivers, stands a figure

Upper section of Arco di Trionfo

of the archangel St Michael. A number of Italian artists contributed to the final building of the arch, the most significant among them being the Neapolitan artist Francesco Laurana, who also worked on the Cappella Palatina and sculpted the statues of Justice and the bas relief of Alfonso I on his chariot. Another artist of note was Laurana's pupil and assistant Domenico Gagini.

Castel Nuovo in a painting by Antonio Joli

Teatro Mercadante ❾

Piazza Municipio 74. **Map** 7 B2.
Tel 081 551 33 96. ▦ C22, C25, R2,
R3, R4, 201. ▦ Centrale: Via Toledo.
See **Ent in Naples**, p210, p213.

Built in 1778 to a design by
Francesco Securo, this
theatre was originally known
as *"del Fondo"* because money
for its construction came from
a fund created by the sale of
confiscated Jesuit property.
The three-tier façade, with
eight caryatids supporting the
cornice, was added in 1892.
The theatre opened in 1779
with *L'Infedeltà Fedele* by
Cimarosa, a leading
Neapolitan composer.

**Late 19th-century façade of the
Teatro Mercadante**

Santa Maria Incoronata ❿

Via dell'Incoronata. **Map** 7 B2. ▦ C22,
C57, R2, R3, R4, 24, 201. ▦ Centrale:
Via Toledo. ◯ 8–10:30am Mon–Sat;
11am, 12:30pm, 6:30pm Sun & hols.

It is immediately obvious that
this church is at a lower level
than Via Medina. The reason
goes back to the 16th century,
when Charles V built the new
moats for Castel Nuovo. Earth
had been dug out to make
room for the ditches and
when it was tipped nearby
it partially buried this
small mid-14th century
church. Santa Maria
Incoronata was origi-
nally built for Joan I of
Anjou to celebrate her
coronation and also to
house a fragment of
Jesus's crown of thorns.
The two fresco cycles
in the first bay of the
main nave, for years
attributed to Giotto, are
in fact the work of his
pupil Roberto Oderisi.

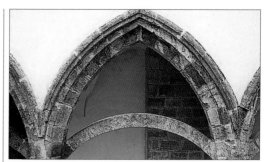

Detail of the portico of Santa Maria Incoronata

San Giacomo degli Spagnoli ⓫

Piazza Municipio. **Map** 7 B2. **Tel** 081
552 37 59. ▦ C22, C25, C55, C80,
C85, R2, R3, R4, 201. ▦ Centrale:
Via Toledo. ◯ 7:30–11am Tue–Sat,
11am–2pm Sun. ✝ ▣

Part of the 19th-century
Palazzo San Giacomo (now
the town hall), the church of
San Giacomo dominates Piazza
Municipio. In 1540 Don Pedro
Alvarez de Toledo, the viceroy responsible for the present
appearance of the city centre,
built the church and adjoining
hospital for the Spanish
community. This was the
church of the local aristocracy
and although rebuilt in 1741,
it still belongs to the Real
Hermandad de Nobles
Hespanoles de Santiago, a
confraternity founded more
than four centuries ago.
    San Giacomo contains tombs
of Spanish nobles, including
that of Don Pedro and his
wife Maria. They were never
buried in their sumptuous
tomb however: Don Pedro
died in Florence and is buried
there in the cathedral.

**The marble tomb of Don Pedro Alvarez de
Toledo in San Giacomo degli Spagnoli**

Santa Brigida ⓬

Via Santa Brigida 1. **Map** 7 A2.
Tel 081 552 37 93. ▦ C57, E2, R2, R3,
24, 201. ▦ Centrale: Via Toledo. ◯
8am–12:30pm, 5–7pm daily. ✝ ▣

The curious aspect of this
17th-century church is the
dome, which could not be
more than 9 m (30 ft) high
because it would have
obstructed artillery fire from
Castel Nuovo. However, the
fresco of a vivid sky created by
Luca Giordano (1632–1705)
on the cupola makes the
most of boldly conceived
perspective and creates a
feeling of immense space.
    The artist, nicknamed Luca
Fapresto (Luca the Swift)
because he worked so rapidly,
painted the dome in exchange
for his tomb, which can be
found in the left transept.

Quartieri Spagnoli ⓭

Map 7 A1. ▦ E2, E3. ▦ Centrale:
Via Toledo.

The Spanish Quarter is one of
the city's working class districts; densely populated and
rather run-down (tourists
should take care when visiting
the area). Built in the 17th
century to the west of Via
Toledo to house Spanish
troops, its origins live on in the
name, but today it is difficult
to appreciate the original grid
layout. Alleys are festooned
with laundry, shielding the
streets from the light.
    Despite the state of neglect,
there is still some fine architecture, such as the church of
Montecalvario (founded in

A stall laden with fish in the atmospheric 17th-century Quartieri Spagnoli district

1560), which gives its name to one of the area's districts, and Santa Maria della Concezione, a Baroque masterpiece by Domenico Antonio Vaccaro.

The great Italian poet Leopardi once lived at No. 24 Via Santa Maria Ognibene, and the local playwright Eduardo De Filippo *(see p37)* used the area as a setting for his plays.

Entrance to the Palazzo delle Poste e Telegrafi

Palazzo delle Poste e Telegrafi ⓮

Piazza Matteotti 3. **Map** 7 B1 (9 B5). *Tel* 081 428 95 85. 🚌 C57, E2, E3, R1, R4, 24, 149, 201. ⏲ 8am–6:30pm Mon–Fri, 8am–12:30pm Sat. 📷

The post office building was designed in 1935 by Giuseppe Vaccaro as part of an Urban Renewal and Development plan that resulted in the demolition of the San Giuseppe quarter. The bombastic style of the civic architecture of this period (also found in

the police headquarters, the tax office and the provincial administration building) is typical of buildings constructed during the Fascist era. The Post Office combines these emphatic features with other innovative elements of the European Modern Movement.

The curvilinear façade and broad staircase make this one of the most interesting examples of 20th-century Neapolitan architecture. In striking contrast to the Post Office is the nearby cloister of Monteoliveto *(see p64)*, sadly now very dilapidated.

Piazza Giovanni Bovio ⓯

Map 7 B1 (9 C5). 🚌 C25, C55, R1, R2, R4.

Neapolitans call this square Piazza della Borsa after the former Stock Exchange *(Borsa)* that dominates it. Built in 1895 when taste was eclectic, the old exchange is reminiscent of 16th-century

buildings in the Veneto. It is now the home of the Chamber of Commerce. Incorporated into the left side of this building is the small church of Sant'Aspreno al Porto, originally medieval but totally rebuilt in the 1600s.

The square marks the beginning of Corso Umberto I, also known as the *Rettifilo*. This grand avenue was built after slum clearance around the harbour, to connect the city centre and the central railway station, giving a new look to early 20th-century Naples *(see pp28–9)*. The 17th-century Fountain of Neptune has been moved, temporarily, to the corner of Piazza Municipie and Via Medina. Frequently altered, the fountain was moved several times before finding its final home in Piazza Bovio in 1898. It was the work of three artists: the statue of Neptune was sculpted by Michelangelo Naccherino, the balusters and lions were by Cosimo Fanzago, and the monsters at the base by Pietro Bernini.

The Fountain of Neptune

Via Chiaia ⑯

Map 7 A3. 🚇 C22.

In Neapolitan dialect, *chiaia* means "beach", and in fact this street was opened in the 16th century to connect Largo di Palazzo (now Piazza del Plebiscito) with the coast. Together with Via Toledo (*see p53*), Via dei Mille (*see p113*) and Via Calabritto this is one of Naples' smartest shopping streets. While browsing, it is worth stopping to see the Ponte di Chiaia, a 17th-century gateway restored in the 1800s. Nearby is Palazzo Cellamare, built in the 16th century and enlarged in the 18th century, when it became known for the magnificent banquets and receptions held there. The impressive portal was designed by Ferdinando Fuga. Near the Ponte, a lift affords easy access to Piazza Santa Maria degli Angeli and the Pizzofalcone hill.

The portal of the church of Santa Maria degli Angeli

Santa Maria degli Angeli ⑰

Piazza Santa Maria degli Angeli. **Map** 6 F2. **Tel** 081 764 49 74. 🚇 C22, E3. ⏰ 7:30–11:30am, 5–7pm Mon–Sat; 8:30am–1:30pm, 6–7pm Sun. 🔲 📷

Construction of this church began in the 17th century on land donated to the devout Theatine religious order by Donna Costanza del Carretto Dira, the Princess of Melfi. The building was designed by the Theatine cleric Francesco Grimaldi, and it is clearly visible from any point overlooking the city. The three-nave interior is so well designed that

Via Chiaia and Ponte di Chiaia

Francesco Milizia, the author of an 18th-century guide to Naples, said that it "is perhaps the most well-proportioned church in the city".

The frescoes on the vaults, which depict episodes from the life of the Virgin Mary in vivid and luminous colour, are the work of Giovan Battista Beinaschi (1638–88).

Santa Maria Egiziaca a Pizzofalcone ⑱

Via Egiziaca 30. **Map** 7 A3. **Tel** 081 764 51 99. 🚇 C22, E3. ⏰ 5:30–7:30pm daily. 🔲 📷

The portal on Via Egiziaca opens out onto the area in front of this Baroque church.

Its construction began in 1661 at the request of the closed order of nuns who lived nearby in the Sant'Agostino convent. The building's design was entrusted to Cosimo Fanzago (1593–1678), a Lombard architect and sculptor who was to become one of the most prestigious creators of the local Baroque style. Its octagonal plan was greatly admired by contemporaries of Fanzago. The paintings in the main chapels are by Paolo De Matteis (1662–1728), while the sculptures are by Nicola Fumo. The high altar is in pure Rococo style.

Palazzo Serra di Cassano ⑲

Via Monte di Dio 14–15. **Map** 6 F2. **Tel** 081 764 26 52. 🚇 C22, E3. ⏰ certain days in May. 📷

The main doorway to Prince Aloisio Serra di Cassano's palace is no longer the main entrance to one of the most beautiful examples of 18th-century Neapolitan civic architecture. To express his grief over the execution of his son Gennaro – one of the leaders of the 1799 revolution in Naples – the prince ordered the original entrance (at No. 67 Via Egiziaca) to be

Interior of the cupola of Santa Maria Egiziaca a Pizzofalcone

The impressive double staircase in Palazzo Serra di Cassano

this was the school where young artists were educated following past examples. The most important works of art are the ceramics. Among these are two large ceramic tile panels designed by the important 19th-century Neapolitan artists Domenico Morelli and Filippo Palizzi.

Façade of the Museo Artistico with its decorative tiles

closed that same year. The originality of this building, which was designed by one of the leading architects of the time, Ferdinando Sanfelice (1675–1748), lies in the majestic staircase with its double flight of steps. Set in the entrance hall that opens on to the courtyard, it is decorated with white marble that contrasts beautifully with the building's imposing, grey volcanic stone.

The *piano nobile* (upper floor) of the palazzo is now the home of the Istituto Italiano per gli Studi Filosofici, a leading international cultural institution.

Nunziatella **⑳**

Via Generale Parisi. **Map** 7 A4.
Tel 081 764 15 20. C22.
phone Mon–Fri and ask for Secretaria
to book.

The façades of the church and former convent of the Nunziatella, which has been occupied since 1787 by the military college of the same name, converge at a right angle to form a beautiful little square. At the beginning of the 18th century, the Jesuits at the Nunziatella asked architect Ferdinando Sanfelice – who was working on the nearby Palazzo Serra di Cassano at the time – to build the church and restore the convent, which dates from the 16th century.

Entering the little church, the first thing to strike the visitor is the harmonious balance Sanfelice established between the architectural space and the pictorial and sculptural decorative elements. The most important frescoes were painted by Neapolitan artist Francesco de Mura (1696–1782); in the apse is the *Adoration of the Magi*, the *Assumption of the Virgin* is on the ceiling, and on the inside of the façade is *Rest during the Flight to Egypt*. The altar, the work of Giuseppe Sanmartino (1720–93), is one of the most important examples of Neapolitan Baroque in existence.

Museo Artistico Industriale **㉑**

Piazzetta Demetrio Salazar 6. **Map** 7
A3. **Tel** 081 764 74 71. C22, E3.
Mon–Sat by appointment only.
ask at Art Institute.

Founded in 1878 by Gaetano Filangieri, who also founded the Filangieri Civic Museum *(see p70)*, and Demetrio Salazar,

Scroll decoration on the Nunziatella façade

THE BIRTHPLACE OF PARTHENOPE

Ancient ruins on Pizzofalcone

In the 7th century BC, Greek colonists from Rhodes founded the first urban settlement in Naples on the hill of Pizzofalcone: Parthenope, renamed Palaepolis (old city) three centuries later when Neapolis (new city) was founded to the east. The old city was later abandoned and by the Middle Ages the area had reverted to farmland. The site of ancient Naples was revived however in the 16th century, when it became a residential neighbourhood favoured by aristocrats and important officials, who were attracted by the beauty of the site and its proximity to the Royal Palace. In the 18th century Via Monte di Dio was one of the most important residential streets in Naples, and to this day it retains some of its original character.

SPACCANAPOLI

The straight street called Spaccanapoli corresponds to the lower *decumanus*, one of the three main thoroughfares in Greco-Roman Naples; the other two being present-day Via Anticaglia *(see p84)* and Via dei Tribunali *(see pp76–7)*. At the end of the 13th century, after the construction of Castel Nuovo *(see pp54–5)*, the administrative hub of the city began to shift towards the seafront. Commercial activity developed in the Piazza Mercato zone,

Bust-reliquary of San Bartolomeo, Santa Chiara

while in the old centre there was a concentration of churches and convents, notably Santa Chiara. When the city expanded around the newly built Via Toledo *(see p53)* during the era of the Spanish viceroyalty, the area which is now Piazza del Gesù Nuovo became the junction point between the old and modern cities. Subsequent development in the 19th century, including the opening up of Corso Umberto I, led to the demolition of part of the city's medieval fabric.

SIGHTS AT A GLANCE

Historic Buildings
Archivio di Stato **17**
Monte di Pietà **14**
Palazzo Carafa Santangelo **13**
Palazzo Filomarino **7**

Churches
Cappella Sansevero **10**
Gesù Nuovo **3**
Gesù Vecchio **20**
Sant'Angelo a Nilo **11**
Sant'Anna dei Lombardi **2**
Santissima Annunziata **23**
Santa Chiara pp66–7 **5**
San Domenico Maggiore **9**
Sant'Eligio Maggiore **25**
San Giorgio Maggiore **15**
San Giovanni dei Pappacoda **22**
Santi Marcellino e Festo **19**
Santa Maria del Carmine **24**
Santa Maria La Nova **1**
Santa Marta **6**
Santi Severino e Sossio **18**

Historic Streets and Squares
Corso Umberto I **21**
Piazza San Domenico Maggiore **8**

Spires and Statues
Guglia dell'Immacolata **4**
Statue of the Nile **12**

Museums
Museo Civico Filangieri **16**

GETTING THERE
Spaccanapoli is partly closed to traffic. The red bus lines R1 (from Vomero), R2 (from the central railway station), R3 (from the Mergellina station) and R4 (from Capodimonte) stop in Via Toledo, a short walk away from the district. Piazza Mercato can be reached by trams 1 and 4. You can also get to Spaccanapoli by underground (Montesanto, Dante and Cavour/Museo stations) and, from Vomero, via the Centrale and Montesanto funicular railways.

KEY
Street-by-Street map
See pp62–3
M Metro station
Funicular

0 metres   350
0 yards   350

◁ **View over Spaccanapoli, once a major thoroughfare in ancient Naples**

Street-by-Street: Spaccanapoli

The long street commonly known as Spaccanapoli is divided into seven sections bearing different names. Because of its rich array of churches, squares and historic buildings it has been called an "open-air museum", like nearby Via dei Tribunali. It is also one of the most lively and atmospheric places in Naples, with shops, crafts and cafés. Piazza San Domenico, near the University, is always crowded with young people. Those with a sweet tooth can enjoy the excellent pastries at the Scaturchio pasticceria.

Piazza San Domenico
An unusual siren with two tails is sculpted on the base of the spire **8**

San Domenico Maggiore
This church was built in 1283 by Charles I of Anjou **9**

★ Gesù Nuovo
The rusticated façade of the church was once part of Palazzo Sanseverino **3**

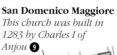

PIAZZA DEL GESÙ NUOVO

VIA S. SEBASTIANO

VIA BENEDETTO CROCE

VIA S. CHIARA

CALATA TRINITÀ MAGG.

Palazzo Filomarino
The philosopher Benedetto Croce died here in 1952 **7**

Sant'Angelo a Nilo
The interior houses the tomb of Cardinal Brancaccio, sculpted by Donatello and Michelozzo **11**

Guglia dell'Immacolata
Erected in the 1700s, this spire was named after the statue of the Virgin at its pinnacle **4**

★ Santa Chiara
Robert of Anjou was responsible for building this church. The tiled cloister was designed by Domenico Antonio Vaccaro in 1742 **5**

Santa Marta
This small church dates from the 15th century **6**

★ Cappella Sansevero
This moving Veiled Christ *is the only work of art by a Neapolitan artist (Giuseppe Sanmartino) in the di Sangro family chapel* ⑩

LOCATOR MAP
See Street Finder, maps 4, 5, 7

Statue of the Nile
This statue, erected in honour of the Egyptian god Nile, gives its name to the square in which it stands ⑫

Ospedale delle Bambole, the dolls' hospital, is a unique place where dolls and puppets are repaired.

Palazzo Marigliano

San Nicola a Nilo

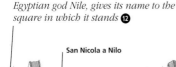

VIA S. BIAGIO DEI LIBRAI

VIA GRANDE ARCHIVIO

VIA PALADINO

Palazzo Carafa Santangelo
Diomede Carafa designed this palazzo in the 15th century ⑬

Archivio di Stato
The state archive contains documents dating back to the Angevin period ⑰

Museo Civico Filangieri
Prince Filangieri's art collection in elegant Palazzo Como includes detailed mosaic floor tiles like these ⑯

O MAGNVM PIETATIS OPVS

Monte di Pietà
This majestic building and the adjoining chapel were designed by Giovan Battista Cavagna ⑭

| 0 metres | 100 |
| 0 yards | 100 |

KEY

- - - Suggested route

STAR SIGHTS

★ Gesù Nuovo

★ Santa Chiara

★ Cappella Sansevero

Santa Maria La Nova ❶

Largo Santa Maria La Nova 1. **Map** 7 B1 (9 C5). *Tel* 081 552 32 98. 🚌 *C25, C57, CD, E1, E3, R1, R3, R4, 24, 201.* 🚇 *Centrale: Via Toledo.* Ⓜ *Dante, Cavour-Museo.* ◯ *9:30am–1pm Fri–Sun.* **Cloisters** ◯ *9am–6:30pm daily.*

In order to make room for Castel Nuovo *(see pp54–5)* a Franciscan church devoted to the Virgin Mary had to be demolished. In exchange, Charles I of Anjou gave the friars a nearby plot of land and had a new church built at his own expense, Santa Maria La Nova. The richly decorated wooden ceiling was painted by the leading artists of the time (Santafede, Curia, Imparato and Corenzio), creating a gallery of 16th- and 17th-century Neapolitan painting. In the fourth chapel on the right is Giovanni da Nola's altarpiece of Sant' Eustachio. Other chapels contain works by Caracciolo, Teodoro d'Errico and Santacroce. In the former monastery, now the seat of the provincial government, there are two cloisters; the smaller one (No. 44) has Renaissance frescoes and marble tombs, while the other (No. 43) contains a garden. Nearby, at 11 Piazza Tommaso Monticelli, is the 15th-century façade of Palazzo Penna.

Sant'Anna dei Lombardi ❷

Piazza Monteoliveto 3. **Map** 7 A1 (9 B5). *Tel* 081 551 33 33. 🚌 *C25, C57, CD, E1, E3, R1, R3, R4, 24, 201.* 🚇 *Centrale: Via Toledo.* Ⓜ *Dante, Cavour-Museo.* ◯ *9am–12.30pm Tue–Fri.* 🕆

Founded in 1411 as Santa Maria di Monteoliveto, this was the favourite church of the Aragonese kings, who summoned the leading artists of the time to decorate it. Its name changed when it was assigned to the Confraternity of Lombards (to whom it still belongs), whose church had collapsed in the 1805 earthquake. The roof was damaged during World War II and has not been restored, but the interior contains some examples of Renaissance sculpture.

Cappella Piccolomini, altarpiece decoration

The marble altarpiece in the Cappella Piccolomini, by Antonio Rossellino (1475), has dancing angels on the top, the work of Benedetto da Majano. The latter also executed the altarpiece in the Terranova chapel (1489). The Tolosa chapel was decorated by the della Robbia workshop in Florence. To the right of the presbytery is Guido Mazzoni's *Lamentation over the Dead Christ* (1492), an amazingly realistic tableau of eight life-size terracotta figures surrounding Christ. Their grief-stricken faces are said to be modelled on the Aragonese kings.

At No. 3 Via Monteoliveto is the 16th-century Palazzo Gravina, now occupied by the Faculty of Architecture.

Detail of the reliquary in Gesù Nuovo

Gesù Nuovo ❸

Piazza del Gesù Nuovo 2. **Map** 3 B5 (9 B4). *Tel* 081 551 86 13. 🚌 *C57, CD, E1, E3, R1, R3, R4, 24, 201.* Ⓜ *Dante, Cavour-Museo.* 🚇 *Montesanto.* ◯ *7am–12:30pm, 4–7:30pm daily.* 🕆

The façade, covered in diamond point rustication, was once part of 15th-century Palazzo Sanseverino. It was retained by the Jesuits when they bought the building and in 1584 transformed it into the large church seen today. The 17th-century doorway incorporates the original Renaissance entrance to the palazzo. The Baroque interior is richly decorated with multi-coloured marbles and ornate works of art including statues, a reliquary and vivid frescoes.

The smaller cloister in the former monastery of Santa Maria La Nova

In the chapel of St Ignatius of Loyola, founder of the Society of Jesus, are two of Cosimo Fanzago's finest works: the sculptures of *David* and *Jeremiah*. The cupola, frescoed by Lanfranco, collapsed in the 1688 earthquake; the only survivors were the corbels showing the four Evangelists in flight. Above the main entrance is Francesco Solimena's huge fresco, *Expulsion of Heliodorus from the Temple* (1725). The statue of the Virgin, on a lapis lazuli globe above the altar, dates from the mid-19th century. The second chapel on the right houses the remains of San Giuseppe Moscati, canonized in 1987.

Façade of Gesù Nuovo

Guglia dell'Immacolata ❹

Piazza del Gesù Nuovo. **Map** 3 B5 (9 B4). ▦ C57, CD, E1, E3, R1, R3, R4, 24. Ⓜ Dante, Cavour-Museo. Ⓜ Montesanto.

The Jesuits commissioned this gigantic marble spire as a symbol of devotion to the Virgin Mary, and as a tangible sign of the their power. The monument, modelled on ancient Egyptian obelisks and designed by Giuseppe Genuino, was begun in 1743. The complex stone ornamentation, depicting the Jesuit saints and stories of Mary, was sculpted by Francesco Pagano and Matteo Bottigliero and is regarded as a key work of 18th-century Neapolitan sculpture. The statue of the Madonna is the centre of festivities on the Feast of Immaculate Conception.

Guglia dell'Immacolata

Santa Chiara ❺

See pp66–7.

Santa Marta ❻

Via San Sebastiano 42. **Map** 3 B5 (9 B3). **Tel** 081 726 04 95. ▦ C57, CD, E1, E3, R1, R3, R4, 24. Ⓜ Dante, Cavour-Museo. Ⓜ Montesanto. ◯ 8:30am–noon Sun. ✝

This small church was founded by Margherita di Durazzo in the 15th century and became the headquarters of one of the city's most important confraternities, whose members included kings, viceroys and high-ranking officials. The church stands opposite the bell tower of Santa Chiara *(see pp66–7)*. The doorway still retains its original depressed arch structure. On the high altar is a painting by Andrea and Nicola Vaccaro (1670), depicting Santa Marta, to whom the church is dedicated. The *Codice di Santa Marta (Codex of St Martha)*, with its valuable miniatures, came from this church and is now kept in the Archivio di Stato, or state archive *(see p70)*. You can get to the underground cemetery from the room next to the sacristy.

Palazzo Filomarino ❼

Via Benedetto Croce 12. **Map** 3 B5 (9 C5). ▦ C57, CD, E1, E3, R1, R3, R4, 24. Ⓜ Dante, Cavour-Museo. Ⓜ Montesanto. **Library** ◯ 9am–12 noon Tue, Fri.

This is the first of many noble buildings you will see in the Spaccanapoli and Decumano Maggiore areas. These mansions and palaces are often in a bad state of preservation yet have retained an air of splendour and stateliness, and still bear traces of the lives of the generations of aristocrats who built and lived in them. The original Palazzo Filomarino dates back to the 14th century, but the building was substantially altered in the 16th century. It then underwent restoration in the following century after being damaged during Masaniello's uprising *(see p73)*. The 18th-century doorway is the work of the architect Sanfelice. Philosopher Benedetto Croce, a leading figure in Italian culture and politics in the first half of this century *(see p26)*, lived in this palazzo in the latter part of his life. The Italian Institute of Historical Studies, founded by Croce, takes up the whole of the first floor with its 40,000-volume library. At No. 45 on the same street is the impressive Baroque doorway of Palazzo Carafa della Spina.

The library of philosopher Benedetto Croce on the first floor of Palazzo Filomarino

Santa Chiara ❺

In 1310 Robert of Anjou laid the first stone of the convent and church that the Angevin rulers later chose as the site for their tombs. Santa Chiara was where the kingdom's assemblies were held, as well as ceremonies, such as the one celebrating the miracle of San Gennaro's blood *(see p40)*. In the mid-1700s, the church's Gothic lines were obscured by the addition of elaborate Baroque ornamentation. After the church was totally destroyed by fire in 1943, restoration work tried to recover as much as possible of the original; the present interior is simple and austere, typical of a Franciscan church. Near the apse are the fine sculpture groups of the royal Angevin tombs; a beautiful wooden 14th-century crucifix executed by an unknown artist is on the altar. The lovely cloisters are an oasis of calm and a convenient meeting place for Neapolitans.

★ **Poor Clares' Choir**
Built by Leonardo Di Vito, this choir is one of the best examples of Neapolitan Gothic. It was frescoed by Giotto and his assistants, but only fragments of the original have remained intact.

The bell tower still has its original base, with Gothic inscriptions describing the foundation of the church.

Marble pavement by Vaccaro

The rose window tracery consists of six marble circles.

The main gateway is a 14th-century portal with a large jutting vault.

Projecting Porch
This massive structure in piperno stone stands out against the yellow tufa façade. On the marble portal is the coat-of-arms of Queen Sancia of Majorca, the wife of Robert of Anjou.

Tertiaries' Cloister

TIMELINE

1340 Santa Chiara consecrated and declared royal church	**1742** Building of the tiled cloister		**1943** 4 Aug: fire caused by bomb destroys church	**1995** Museo dell'Opera opens to the public

Detail of the cloister

1300	1700	1900
1310 Robert of Anjou lays the first stone	**1343** Giovanni and Pacio Bertini sculpt Tomb of Robert of Anjou	**1769** Church totally rebuilt in Baroque style　　**1953** 4 Aug: restored church reopens for worship

Royal Tombs
The tombs of Charles of Calabria (shown here) and his wife Mary of Valois are by Tino da Camaino (c.1285–1337). In the centre of the rear wall is the tomb of Robert of Anjou, one of Italy's greatest medieval funerary monuments.

VISITORS' CHECKLIST

Via Benedetto Croce. **Map** 3 B5.
Tel 081 552 62 09. C25, CD,
E1, E3, R1, R3, R4. M Dante,
Cavour-Museo, Montesanto.
Church 6:45am–1pm,
4–8pm; **Cloister & Museum**
9:30am–6:30pm Mon–Sat;
9:30am–2:30pm Sun and hols.
museum only.

★ **Museo dell'Opera**
This museum houses objects, decorative ornaments and sculptures from Santa Chiara. In the section devoted to archaeology, you can see the ruins of a Roman bathhouse that extend outside the museum. There are also sections on History, Ancient Marbles and Reliquaries. This last boasts Giovanni da Nola's Ecce Homo (1519).

The Roman baths, which once marked the city's western limit, lie between the first two rooms of the Museo dell'Opera and the outer courtyard.

The Tomb of Philip of Bourbon, the idiot son of Charles III who died in 1777, is found in the last chapel on the right. Designed by Ferdinando Fuga, it is one of the few 18th-century works that survived the fire in 1943.

★ **Tiled Cloister**
The simple arches of the 14th-century cloister frame the garden redesigned by Domenico Antonio Vaccaro in 1742. The 72 octagonal pillars are punctuated by seats at intervals, and every surface is decorated with majolica tiles painted by Donato and Giuseppe Massa.

STAR FEATURES

★ Royal Tombs

★ Poor Clares' Choir

★ Tiled Cloister

★ Museo dell'Opera

Guglia di San Domenico

Piazza San Domenico Maggiore ⓧ

Map 3 B5 (9 C3). CD, E1, R2. Dante, Cavour-Museo, Montesanto. Montesanto.

This piazza was the result of a rare Renaissance town-planning project in Naples. In the 1500s the area, once crossed by the Greek city walls, was still being used for kitchen gardens. Rebuilding by the Aragonese rulers transformed the zone into a setting appropriate for the church of San Domenico, which had been chosen to house the royal tombs. They also wanted to improve the area around the statue of the Nile, the aristocratic residential district. The top of the piazza is dominated by the apse of San Domenico; next to this is the lovely 14th-century portal of the church of Sant'Arcangelo a Morfisa. Imposing buildings line the other sides of the square. Opposite the church (at No. 17) is the 17th-century Palazzo Sangro di Casacalenda; to the left (No. 3) is Palazzo Petrucci with its 15th-century portal; to the right (Nos. 12 and 9) are Palazzo Corigliano and Palazzo Sangro di Sansevero. In the centre stands the Guglia di San Domenico, built in gratitude for release from the plague of 1656. The spire was designed by Cosimo Fanzago and finished only in 1737 by Domenico Antonio Vaccaro.

San Domenico Maggiore ⓨ

Piazza San Domenico Maggiore 8/a. **Map** 3 B5 (9 C3). **Tel** 081 459 188. CD, E1, R2. Dante, Cavour-Museo, Montesanto. Montesanto. 8:30am–noon, 4:30–7pm daily.

In 1283 Charles I of Anjou ordered the construction of a new church and monastery for the powerful Dominican order. The Gothic three-nave building was built onto the medieval church of Sant'Arcangelo a Morfisa, whose 14th-century doorway still remains. The appearance of today's church is the result of radical reconstruction. In 1506 a fire almost totally destroyed the basilica. In 1850–53 Federico Travaglini rebuilt the interior in Neo-Gothic style, removing much of the original spirit of this monument. However, in the second chapel on the right there are 14th-century frescoes ascribed to Pietro Cavallini, a pupil of Giotto. The tombs of 45 rulers and

Corradini's *Modesty* in the Cappella Sansevero

dignitaries at the Aragonese court are arranged along a balcony in the sacristy. The ceiling fresco was painted by Francesco Solimena in 1706.

Cappella Sansevero ⓩ

Via Francesco de Sanctis 19. **Map** 3 B5 (9 C3). **Tel** 081 551 84 70. CD, E1, R2. Dante, Cavour-Museo, Montesanto. Montesanto. 10am–5:40pm Wed–Mon (10am–1pm Sun). limited.

The lavish decoration in the family chapel was planned by Raimondo di Sangro, Prince of Sansevero, in the second half of the 18th century. In each sculpture group a member of the powerful family is represented by an allegorical figure. Antonio Corradini's *Modesty* (to the left of the altar) is set on the tomb of the prince's mother. On the tomb of his father, said to be a dissolute man who later repented his ways, is Francesco Queirolo's *Deception* (to the right of the altar). The focal point of the chapel is the extraordinary *Veiled Christ,* the masterpiece of Neapolitan sculptor Giuseppe Sanmartino (1720–93). Sculpted from a single block of marble, the recumbent figure of Christ lies draped with the thinnest of translucent veils. In the chapel crypt, two "anatomical machines", perhaps creations of the mysterious Raimondo di Sangro himself, are on display. The stories about the famous prince – inventor, alchemist, lover of science and the occult, and Masonic Grand Master – have engendered legends depicting him as a demon or a sorcerer.

Fresco by Francesco Solimena in the sacristy of San Domenico Maggiore

For hotels and restaurants in this area see pp178–9 and pp192–3

Sant'Angelo a Nilo

Piazzetta Nilo. **Map** 3 B5 (9 C3). **Tel** 081 551 62 27. CD, E1, R2. Dante, Cavour-Museo, Montesanto. Montesanto. 8:30am–1pm, 4:45–7pm Mon–Sat; 8:30am–1pm Sun.

Built in the late 1300s by Cardinal Brancaccio next to his family palace, this church was remodelled four centuries later by Arcangelo Guglielmi-nelli. It houses the earliest Renaissance work in Naples: the cardinal's funerary monument, sculpted in Pisa by Donatello and Michelozzo in 1426–7 and sent to Naples by ship. On the front of the sarcophagus, in the bas relief representing the *Assumption of the Virgin*, Donatello created one of the first examples of his revolutionary "stiacciato" technique – the relief receding gradually from the foreground to give the illusion of depth. From the church you can visit the courtyard of Palazzo Brancaccio where, thanks to the family's patronage, the first public library in Naples was founded in 1690.

Statue of the Nile

Largo Corpo di Napoli. **Map** 3 B5. CD, E1, R2. Dante, Cavour-Museo, Montesanto. Montesanto.

An 18th-century inscription informs the reader that the Alexandrian merchants who worked in this area of the Greco-Roman city had this statue sculpted in honour of the Egyptian god Nile. The statue disappeared after the merchants left Naples; and although it was found in the 1400s, its head was missing. At that time the recumbent putti next to the god, symbols of the many tributaries of the river god, were interpreted as babies at their mother's breast, so

The frescoed ceiling in the Monte di Pietà chapel

that the sculpture was called "the Body of Naples", the mother-city suckling her children. The statue has kept this name despite the addition of a bearded head in the 17th century.

Palazzo Carafa Santangelo

Via San Biagio dei Librai 121. **Map** 3 C5 (10 D3). CD, E1, R2. Dante, Cavour-Museo, Montesanto. Montesanto. 7am–1pm, 4–7pm Mon–Sat.

This important example of Neapolitan Renaissance architecture is known as Palazzo della Capa di Cavallo because of the terracotta copy of a horse's head (now in the courtyard). This was a gift from Lorenzo de' Medici to his friend Diomede Carafa in 1471 to em- bellish his new palace. The original sculpture, a Roman bronze, has been in the Museo Archeologico (see pp86–9) since 1809.

The marble portal, similar to that of Palazzo Petrucci in Piazza San Domenico (see p68), and the façade with its shallow rustication are examples of the new Renaissance style. In late 15th-century Naples this look merged with the late Gothic style, as can be seen in the form of the arches and pilasters and the inlay in the wooden doors with the Carafa family coats of arms. Opposite the palace is the animated Baroque façade of the church of San Nicola a Nilo, which is also the site of a second-hand dealer's stall.

Monte di Pietà

Via San Biagio dei Librai 114. **Map** 3 C5 (10 D3). **Tel** 081 551 70 74. CD, R2. Dante, Cavour-Museo, Montesanto. Montesanto. 9am–2pm Sat & Sun.

This majestic building was built in the late 1500s for the charitable institute set up to grant loans to people in debt to moneylenders. The Cappella della Pietà at the end of the courtyard has a late Renaissance façade with sculptures by Pietro Bernini (at the sides of the entrance) and Michelangelo Naccherino (on the tympanum). The church interior was frescoed by Belisario Corenzio and the young Battistello in the early 1600s.

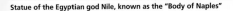

Statue of the Egyptian god Nile, known as the "Body of Naples"

San Giorgio Maggiore ⑮

Via Duomo 237/a. **Map** 3 C5 (10 E3).
Tel 081 28 79 32. ▦ C5, C55, E1,
R2. ◯ 8:30am–noon, 5–7pm
Mon–Sat; 8:30am–1pm Sun. ✚

San Giorgio Maggiore,
originally an early Christian
basilica, is one of the city's
oldest churches. It was
completely rebuilt in the
mid-1600s to a design by
Cosimo Fanzago. The only
surviving part of the original
church is the semi-circular
apse with Corinthian columns
at the entrance of the 17th-
century church, originally
built facing a different
direction. The right-hand nave
of the rebuilt church was
demolished in the late 19th
century to make room for the
extended Via Duomo. The
frescoes in the third chapel
are by Francesco Solimena.
Before visiting the church,
pause for a moment at
Palazzo Marigliano (at No. 39
Via Duomo). Though run-
down, it is one of the most
important examples of 16th-
century Neapolitan civic
architecture.

Museo Civico Filangieri ⑯

Via Duomo 288. **Map** 3 C5 (10 E3).
Tel 081 20 31 75. ▦ E1, R2, C5,
C55. ◉ for restoration until 2007.

The building now occupied
by the Civic Museum was
built in the late 15th century
as the Como family residence
in the Florentine Renaissance

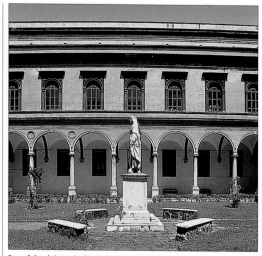
One of the cloisters in the Archivio di Stato

style. It became a monastery
in the late 1500s, was demolished during work on Via
Duomo (1879) and then faith-
fully rebuilt 20 m (66 ft) from
its original site.
　In 1882 Prince Gaetano
Filangieri established his fine
art collection there and
donated it to the city in 1888.
Much of the collection was
scattered during World War II
and was reassembled through
private donations. Today it
consists of objects from
various sources, including
weapons, furniture, paintings,
medallions, porcelain, coins
and costumes. The spiral
staircase leads from the
ground floor to the Sala Agata
(named after the founder's
mother), which in turn leads
to the prince's library via a
suspended passageway.

Archivio di Stato ⑰

Piazzetta Grande Archivio 5. **Map** 3
C5 (10 E3). **Tel** 081 563 81 11. ▦
C5, C55B, CD, E1, R2. ◯ 10:30am–
noon Mon–Sat.

In 1835 Ferdinand II
decided to use the former
Benedictine monastery of
Santi Severino e Sossio to
house the enormous quantity
of documents relating to the
administration of the kingdom
that had accumulated since
the Angevin period. The old
monastery, built in the 9th
century and enlarged in 1494,
was remodelled to allow for
its new function.
　The huge complex has four
cloisters and a number of
rooms containing numerous
works of art. One cloister is
known as the *Chiostro del
platano*, named after an
ancient plane tree (felled in
1959 because it was dying)
which, according to tradition,
had been planted by St
Benedict himself. The mid-
16th century frescoes
depicting the life of the saint
are the work of Antonio
Solario, known as Lo Zingaro
or "gypsy". The State Archive
contains over a million files,
registers, documents and
parchments, and is one of the
most important in Europe.
　By the entrance to the
former monastery is the 17th-
century Fontana della Selleria.

The Sala Agata in the Museo Civico Filangieri, Palazzo Como

Santi Severino e Sossio ⓲

Via Bartolomeo Capasso 22. **Map** 3 C5
(10 D4). *Tel* 081 563 81 11. 🚌 C5,
C55B, CD, E1, R2. 🕐 8–10am
Mon–Sat; 9am–12:30pm Sun. ✝

Marco Pino, *Adoration of the Magi*

Founded in the 9th century
together with the adjoining
monastery (which became the
Royal Archives in 1835), this
church was rebuilt from the
late 1400s on, and finished in
1571. The façade is the result
of restoration effected after
the 1731 earthquake. In the
interior there are some
excellent works of art. Among
the paintings are beautiful
canvases by the Sienese painter
Marco Pino (first, third and
sixth chapels on the right). The
sculptures include the tomb of
Andrea Bonifacio (who died at
the age of six), a masterpiece
by the Spanish sculptor Bartolomeo Ordoñez, in the vestibule
of the sacristy. The cloister
opening times vary slightly and
they are not open on Sundays.

Santi Marcellino e Festo ⓳

Largo San Marcellino 10. **Map** 3 C5
(10 D4). *Tel* 081 551 61 77. 🚌 C5,
C55B, CD, E1, R2. 🕐 8am–8pm
Mon–Fri; 8am–2pm Sat (not strictly
open to public but can take a look).

The two adjacent monasteries
of Santi Marcellino e Pietro and
of Santi Festo e Desiderio, date
from the 8th century. In the

A NUMBER FOR EVERY OCCASION

At noon every Saturday life
stands still for a few minutes
in the streets and alleyways
of Old Naples in anticipation
of an important event – the
lottery draw. In the hall of
the lottery office
(Ufficio Lotto e
Lotterie) at No. 17
Via del Grande
Archivio, a crowd
will be waiting
impatiently for the
result. Devised in
Genoa in the 16th
century, the
lottery was
legalized the
following century
and grew rapidly
in popularity in
the 1800s. Neapolitans were
immediately hooked. As
Matilde Serao wrote in the
late 19th century: "Even
Neapolitans who can't read
know *La Smorfia* by heart

**The lottery in a
19th-century print**

and immediately apply it to
any dream or real-life
event whatsoever". *La
Smorfia* is a guide to the
significance of numbers
and is the lottery "bible".
It can be found in
any Lotto office.
There are about
60,000 entries in
alphabetical order,
and each entry has
a corresponding
number. The book
was first published
in the 19th century
and is regularly
updated in order
to offer readers
interpretations of
even the most
modern events and
dreams. For example,
should you dream of
owning a computer, you
will find that the number to
choose is 45.

---

mid-15th century they were
combined to create a single
large complex. The church,
built the following century, is
adorned with refined 18th-
century marble inlay. Unfortunately, it is now in a state of
almost total abandon and has
been closed to the public for
many years. The spacious
cloister with piperno stone
arches has a pretty garden in

the centre; from the south-
facing side there is a splendid
panoramic view of the Bay of
Naples. By royal decree, the
complex became the property
of the University of Naples in
1907. The building next to the
church is occupied by the
Museum of Palaeontology,
which has a fine painted
majolica floor and over
50,000 artefacts on display.

The airy cloister of the San Marcellino monastery

Courtyard of Gesù Vecchio, part of the University of Naples

Gesù Vecchio ⑳

Via Giovanni Paladino 39. **Map** 3 C5 (10 D4). **Anthropology Museum, Zoology Museum, Mineralogy Museum Library Tel** 081 253 51 63. C5, CD, E1, R2. 9am–6:45pm Mon–Fri. **Museums** 9am–1:30pm, 3–5pm Mon & Thu; 9am–1:30pm Tue, Wed & Fri; 9am–1pm Sat–Sun. www.musei.unina.it

The home of the University of Naples since 1777, this late 16th-century building was the first Jesuit college in the city. In the late 19th century, thanks to the Urban Renewal plan (see pp24–5), the University expanded with the addition of a large factory building looking out over Corso Umberto I. One part remaining of the original college is the lovely Cortile delle Statue (courtyard of statues), from which you can visit the upstairs rooms occupied by the university library since 1808, and home to 850,000 volumes. In 1801 the large

hall that was once the Jesuits' library was turned over to the Mineralogy Museum, the most important in Italy and one of the most famous in the world. Other sections house the Anthropology Museum and the Zoology Museum, founded in 1811 by Joachim Murat, then ruler of Naples.

Back in Via Paladino, look out for the sumptuous Baroque interior of the college church (at No. 38), begun in 1564, and containing works by Solimena and Fanzago.

Corso Umberto I ㉑

Map 4 D5 & 7 C1 (10 E4). C5, C55B, CD, E1, R2.

This wide straight street, known to Neapolitans as the Rettifilo, connects the central railway station (Stazione Centrale) with the city centre and Piazza Giovanni Bovio (see p57). It was built in the late 19th century as part of the Urban Renewal plan (see pp26–7). The most important building is the University of Naples, with its impressive Neo-Renaissance façade.

Cappella Pappacoda ㉒

Largo San Giovanni Maggiore. **Map** 7 B1 (9 C4). **Tel** 081 552 69 48 (Istituto Universitario Orientale). C5, CD, C55B, E1, R2. not strictly open to public; used by university Mon–Fri.

In the early 15th century Artusio Pappacoda, Grand Seneschal and councillor in the Angevin court, founded

this small church. The original late Gothic doorway, like marble embroidery on the austere tufa façade, is the work of Antonio Baboccio (1351–1435), a sculptor, architect and goldsmith who also sculpted the main portal of the cathedral (see pp82–3). The campanile is particularly interesting because of the colour contrast created by the different materials – marble, tufa and piperno. The church is now deconsecrated and is used as the Great Hall by the nearby Istituto Universitario Orientale (Oriental Institute).

Portal of Cappella Pappacoda

Santissima Annunziata ㉓

Via dell'Annunziata 35. **Map** 4 D4 (10 F3). **Tel** 081 28 90 32. C5, C55B, CD, E1, R2. 8am–4pm Mon–Sat.

The Santa Casa dell'Annunziata was a charitable institution that existed as long ago as the

The façade of the University in Corso Umberto I after expansion of the site

Painting of the *Madonna Bruna* in Santa Maria del Carmine

PIAZZA MERCATO

Thanks to their position near the harbour, the churches of Sant'Eligio and Santa Maria del Carmine and the area around them became the focal point of commercial life in late 13th-century Naples. The lively market quarter around Piazza Mercato in the heart of Naples was also the setting for significant events in the city's history. In 1268, Corradino, the last Hohenstaufen king of Naples, was beheaded at the tender age of 16 in front of the Carmine church and the new Angevin rulers

View of Piazza Mercato, with Santa Maria del Carmine

decreed that in future all executions were to be carried out in the square. In 1647 the uprising against the Spanish headed by Tommaso Aniello d'Amalfi, known as Masaniello *(see pp22–3)*, began here. Ten years on, the square was used for the graves of those who had died during the plague epidemic. But the most dramatic events occurred in 1799, when the short-lived, glorious Parthenopean Republic was crushed and all its leaders were executed in Piazza Mercato.

early 1300s to offer help to abandoned children. The church was destroyed by fire in 1757 and rebuilt by Luigi and Carlo Vanvitelli, who designed the cupola and light-filled, one-nave interior with 44 Corinthian columns and three chapels on each side. Among the parts untouched by the fire is the sacristy, with frescoes by Corenzio (1605) and 16th-century inlaid wooden cupboards. To the left of the church, an impressive marble doorway leads to the former foundling hospital, now used as a hospital.

Santa Maria del Carmine ❷

Piazza del Carmine. **Map** 4 E5.
Tel 081 20 11 96. 🚋 1, 2.
🚌 C82. ⏱ 6:45am–noon, 4:30–7:30pm Mon–Sat; 6:45am–1pm, 4:30–7:30pm Sun. 🚹

Neapolitans are devoted to this church because of its many works of art but in particular because of the *Madonna Bruna*, a 14th-century painting kept behind the altar. This famous effigy, the object of deeply felt veneration, is celebrated annually on 16 July at the feast of the Madonna del Carmine *(see p41)*, during which the miracle of the Madonna is re-enacted.

Except for the cross dome in the presbytery, little remains of the original Angevin construction. Instead the church displays typical 18th-century architectural forms

both inside and out. The interior was decorated by Tagliacozzi Canale; the ceiling, destroyed in World War II, has been completely rebuilt in keeping with the original. To the left of the nave is the tomb of Corradino, Duke of Swabia, who was beheaded in 1268 in Piazza Mercato opposite the church *(see above)*. The medieval wooden crucifix placed in a tabernacle under the triumphal arch is also the object of devout worship. There are frescoes and canvases by Solimena in the wings of the transept. The 75-m (246-ft) campanile, completed by Fra Nuvolo in 1631, is the tallest in Naples.

The campanile of Santa Maria del Carmine (1631)

Sant'Eligio Maggiore ❷

Largo Sant'Eligio. **Map** 4 D5 (10 F4).
Tel 081 553 84 29. 🚋 1, 2. 🚌 C82.
⏱ 8:30am–12:30pm Mon–Wed; 5–7pm Thu–Sat; 9:30am–2pm Sun. 🚹

The history of Sant'Eligio has parallels with Santa Chiara *(see pp66–7)*. This church, the first to be founded by the Angevin dynasty in Naples, was destroyed in World War II and in the process of reconstruction none of the later Baroque additions was restored. Go through the side doorway with the pointed arch to enter the austere Gothic three-nave interior with its impressive raised transept. The left-hand nave leads to a cross-vaulted area decorated with 14th-century frescoes by artists of the Giotto school.

DECUMANO MAGGIORE

In the heart of Greco-Roman Naples, part of the ancient grid plan with three parallel east-west roads (Roman *decumani*), intersected at right angles by the north-south *cardines*, is present-day Via dei Tribunali. It was once called Decumano Maggiore (or Massimo) because it was so vital a part of the city structure. In the late 13th and early 14th centuries the area was significant for its

One of the lions at the Duomo entrance

Gothic religious architecture. Today, the churches of San Lorenzo, San Pietro a Maiella and especially the Duomo (cathedral), reveal this past. The Duomo is a stupendous blend of art and architectural styles from the 4th to 19th centuries. Outside the city walls, past 18th-century Piazza Dante, lies the Museo Archeologico Nazionale, home of one of the world's richest Classical archaeological collections.

SIGHTS AT A GLANCE

Historic Buildings
Accademia di Belle Arti ⓴
Castel Capuano
  and Porta Capuana ⓮
Palazzo Spinelli di Laurino ❺
Pio Monte di Misericordia ⓭

Churches
Cappella Pontano ❸
Duomo pp82–3 ⓫
Gerolamini ❿
Santa Caterina a Formiello ⓯
San Gregorio Armeno ❾
San Lorenzo Maggiore ❽
Santa Maria delle Anime
  del Purgatorio ad Arco ❻
Santa Maria di
  Donnaregina Nuova ⓱
Santa Maria di
  Donnaregina Vecchia ⓰
Santa Maria Maggiore
  della Pietrasanta ❹
San Paolo Maggiore ❼
San Pietro a Maiella ❷

Historic Streets and Squares
Piazza Bellini ❶
Piazza Dante ㉑
Via Anticaglia ❶

Spires
Guglia di San Gennaro ⓬

Museums
*Museo Archeologico
  Nazionale pp86–9* ⓳

GETTING THERE
Via dei Tribunali allows limited traffic and no buses cross it. The red bus lines R1 (from Vomero), R2 (from the Centrale railway station), R3 (from the Mergellina railway station) and R4 (from Capodimonte) stop in Via Toledo, Via Diaz and Via Monteoliveto. The R2 bus runs along Corso Umberto I, which crosses Via Duomo at Piazza Nicola Amore. R1 passes by the Museo Archeologico Nazionale. You can take the Metro (Montesanto station) and, from Vomero, the Montesanto funicular. The Metro goes to the Museo Nazionale (Cavour/Museo stations) and Piazza Dante.

KEY

Street-by-Street map
See pp76–7

Ⓜ Metro station

◁ Interior of the Duomo, with its Mannerist paintings set into the carved, gilded wooden ceiling

0 metres 500
0 yards 500

Street-by-Street: Via dei Tribunali

Via dei Tribunali was named after Castel Capuano, visible in the distance at the end of this long avenue, when it became the home of the civil courts *(tribunali)* in the 1500s. One of the streets crossing the Decumano Maggiore is Via San Gregorio Armeno, among the loveliest streets in Old Naples, where art and handicrafts flourish. The craftsmen in San Gregorio Armeno still carve shepherds and other figures for the traditional Neapolitan nativity scenes *(see p39)*, just as they did four centuries ago – to the delight of visitors and Neapolitans alike.

San Paolo Maggiore
The sacristy was frescoed by Solimena in 1689–90 ❼

Piazza Bellini
This is one of the liveliest spots in the centre ❶

Sant'Antoniello a Port'Alba Monastery

Croce di Lucca

Palazzo Firrao

VIA S. M. DI COSTANTINOPOLI

PIAZZA BELLINI

VIA S. PIETRO A

PIAZZA MIRAGLIA

VIA NILO

VIA S. SEBASTIANO

Greek walls

Santa Maria delle Anime del Purgatorio ad Arco
Funerary motifs adorn the area in front of the church and its interior ❻

Santa Maria Maggiore della Pietrasanta
This church was rebuilt in the Baroque era by Fanzago over the ruins of an early basilica ❹

San Pietro a Maiella
The Gothic church was greatly altered by rebuilding work ❷

Cappella Pontano
This chapel was built for the humanist Pontano ❸

Palazzo Spinelli
Created in the 1700s by merging two 16th-century palaces, Palazzo Spinelli has an original oval courtyard with stuccoes ❺

STAR SIGHTS

★ San Lorenzo Maggiore

★ San Gregorio Armeno

★ Duomo

Guglia di San Gennaro
The spire was erected to thank the saint for saving the city from Vesuvius in 1631 ⑫

LOCATOR MAP
See Street Finder, maps 2–4

Gerolamini
The façade of the monastery church was designed by Ferdinando Fuga ⑩

Statue of San Gaetano

VICO CINQUESANTI

★ Duomo
The cathedral was built over the ruins of two early Christian basilicas ⑪

VIA DUOMO

VIA DEI TRIBUNALI

VIA S. GREGORIO ARMENO

Santa Maria della Colonna

Pio Monte di Misericordia
A portico was built onto the façade to shelter the needy ⑬

★ San Lorenzo Maggiore
San Lorenzo contains many layers of history: an 18th-century façade, Gothic interior and ancient ruins under the cloister ⑧

★ San Gregorio Armeno
The lavish decoration of this monastery is immediately apparent in the vestibule ⑨

KEY

– – – Suggested route

0 metres	100
0 yards	100

Piazza Bellini ❶

Map 3 B5. 🚏 C5, C57, CD, E1, R3, R4. Ⓜ Dante, Cavour-Museo, Montesanto. 🚇 Montesanto.

This square, at the southern end of Via Santa Maria di Costantinopoli, is one of the most interesting places in Old Naples. The area now occupied by the piazza and street lay outside the city proper until the mid-16th century, when the viceroy Pedro de Toledo extended the city walls. The remains of part of the ancient Greek walls of Neapolis were brought to light in the piazza after excavations carried out in 1954. The walls are visible in the middle of the square, at the foot of the monument to the composer Vincenzo Bellini. Overlooking the square is the monastery of Sant'Antonio a Port'Alba, which incorporates the 15th-century Palazzo Conca. On the opposite side is Palazzo Firrao (No. 99 Via Santa Maria di Costantinopoli), an important example of 17th-century Neapolitan civic architecture. The façade is adorned with busts of the Spanish royal family.

San Pietro a Maiella ❷

Via San Pietro a Maiella 4. **Map** 3 B5. **Tel** 081 45 90 08. 🚏 C5, C57, CD, E1, R3, R4. Ⓜ Cavour-Museo, Montesanto. 🚇 Montesanto. ⏱ 8am–noon Mon–Thu; 8am–noon, 5:30–7:30pm Fri; 8am–noon, 5:30–9pm Sat; 9am–1pm Sun. ✝

The founder of this church, the nobleman Pipino da Barletta, dedicated it to Pietro da Morrone, the hermit friar from Maiella who became Pope Celestine V in 1294. The original Gothic architecture, modified by the numerous additions over the centuries, was restored between 1888 and 1927. The restoration uncovered some 14th-century frescoes in two of the chapels.

An outdoor café in Piazza Bellini

The removal of the Baroque decoration also revealed splendid gilded wooden ceilings in the nave and transept with paintings by Mattia Preti (1656–61), regarded as among the supreme examples of 17th-century Neapolitan painting.

Since 1826 the monastery (at No. 35) annexed to the church has housed one of Italy's music conservatoires.

Cappella Pontano ❸

Via Tribunali (no street number, opposite No. 376). **Map** 3 B4. 🚏 C5, C55, CD, E1, R3. Ⓜ Dante, Cavour-Museo, Montesanto. 🚇 Montesanto. ⏱ 9am–1pm Mon–Sat.

The famous humanist Giovanni Pontano, secretary to King Ferdinand of Aragon, commissioned this small, elegant chapel in 1492. Based on a design for a pagan temple, the harmonious proportions make it one of the most significant works produced in Renaissance Naples. The chapel contains a frescoed triptych by Francesco Cicino da Caiazzo – restored in 1792 – and a 15th-century pavement of coloured tiles, which is in a good state of preservation. The numerous Latin epigraphs were written by Giovanni Pontano himself.

Bust of Giovanni Pontano

Santa Maria Maggiore della Pietrasanta ❹

Via Tribunali. **Map** 3 B5. 🚏 C5, CD, E1, R3. Ⓜ Cavour-Museo, Montesanto. 🚇 Montesanto. 🔴 for restoration.

The interior of Santa Maria Maggiore della Pietrasanta

The church was named after a holy stone (pietrasanta) with an inscribed cross, which was kept here until recently and was popular with worshippers. This majestic, centrally planned church was built by Cosimo Fanzago over the ruins of an early Christian basilica. Traces of the original church have been discovered in the crypt. The campanile (see p20) also belonged to the basilica; dating from the 10th–11th centuries, it is the sole example of early medieval architecture in Naples. Many fragments of even older buildings, from the Roman age on, were inserted into the lower part of the campanile. In the Middle Ages the road was lower and passed under the bell tower arch.

Palazzo Spinelli di Laurino ❺

Via Tribunali 362. **Map** 3 B5. 🚌 *C5, CD, E1, R2, R3.* Ⓜ *Dante, Cavour-Museo, Montesanto.* 🚋 *Montesanto.* ◯ *8am–7pm Mon–Sat.*

In the 18th century, the architect Ferdinando Sanfelice carried out radical changes to this 16th-century palazzo. He also created the oval courtyard and the building beyond, where the chatter from the crowded Via dei Tribunali could be clearly heard by the dukes of Laurino. The double-flight monumental staircase is another of Sanfelice's designs. Similar examples can be seen in the Palazzo Serra di Cassano *(see p58)*, Palazzo dello Spagnolo and Palazzo Sanfelice *(see p94)*.

Santa Maria delle Anime del Purgatorio ad Arco ❻

Map 3 B4. *Via Tribunali 39.* 🚌 *C5, CD, E1, R2, R3.* Ⓜ *Dante, Cavour-Museo, Montesanto.* 🚋 *Montesanto.* **Church** ◯ *9:30am–1pm daily.* **Cemetery** 🕯️ *every 30 mins 10am–12:30pm Sat.* ✝️

This church still belongs to the confraternity of the same name founded in 1604 to collect alms to pay for the masses for the souls of the dead. Evidence of the importance attached to worship of the dead in 17th-century Naples is shown by the many skulls, bones and other funerary motifs on the small stone columns in front of the façade, on the façade itself, and in the interior. The church has a single nave and lavish Baroque decoration. In the apse area here is a disturbing relief with a winged skull by Cosimo Fanzago, who also designed the church. Steps lead to the underground cemetery, which is still used for the worship of

Interior of the church of Purgatorio ad Arco

souls in Purgatory, a ritual not altogether appreciated by the Christian church.

San Paolo Maggiore ❼

Piazza San Gaetano. **Map** 3 C4. **Tel** *081 45 40 48.* 🚌 *C5, CD, E1, R2, R3.* Ⓜ *Dante, Cavour-Museo, Montesanto.* 🚋 *Montesanto.* ◯ *9am–1pm, 3–6pm Mon–Sat.*

In Greco-Roman Naples, present-day Piazza San Gaetano was the site of the Greek *Agora* and later, of the Roman Forum. The Romans built a Temple of the Dioscuri here, which was converted into a Christian basilica in the 8th century. This ancient church was then remodelled from 1583 to 1603 by Francesco Grimaldi. The new church,

with a three-nave Latin cross plan, also incorporated the pronaos of the pagan temple; but only two Corinthian columns of the latter survived the 1688 earthquake.

In the richly decorated interior there are fine frescoes by Massimo Stanzione on the vault over the central nave. Sadly, they were damaged by water seepage and bombardments during World War II. The Cappella Firrao, on the left side of the apse, has many 17th-century tombs, sculptures and frescoes. The marvellous paintings in the sacristy are by Francesco Solimena (1689–90). A stairway leads down to the crypt (also accessible from outside the church).

Façade of San Paolo Maggiore

UNDERNEATH THE CITY

Underneath Naples there is another world to be explored, just as fascinating as the city above. Since its early days the city has been built out of material quarried from the ground – the local yellow tufa is excellent for building. Over the years, caves and tunnels were left in this way, and became catacombs, aqueducts, passageways, and escape and shelter areas during

Entrance to underground Naples

World War II bombing raids. The caves were extended to their current size during Spanish rule *(see pp22–3)*, when it was forbidden to import raw material for building houses and palazzi. Today you can descend into the bowels of Naples: on the left-hand side of San Paolo Maggiore is one of the entrances to *Napoli Sotterranea (see p219)*.

San Lorenzo Maggiore ❽

Via dei Tribunali 316. **Map** 3 C4 (10 D3). **Tel** 081 290 580. 🚋 E1. Ⓜ Dante, Cavour-Museo, Montesanto. 🚇 Montesanto. **Church** ◯ 9am–1pm, 3–6pm daily. **Excavations** ◯ 10am– 5pm Mon–Sat; 10am–1:30pm Sun. ● Aug. ⬆

The construction of one of Naples's oldest and richest monumental complexes was begun in 1265, for Charles I of Anjou, on the site of a 6th-century church (see p35). The façade was totally rebuilt by Sanfelice in 1742, but the large 14th-century portal and original wooden doors are intact. The single-nave Gothic interior has an apse, designed by French architects, with nine chapels placed around the ambulatory. Here is the tomb of Catherine of Austria, a fine sculpture by Tino da Camaino (c.1323) and, in the sixth chapel from the right, frescoes by a Neapolitan pupil of Giotto. It was in this church that the writer Boccaccio first saw the girl he celebrated in his writings as Fiammetta.

To the right of San Lorenzo is the monastery, where you can visit the cloister, the chapterhouse and the refectory which, from 1442 on, was the assembly hall of the royal Parliament. The cloister affords access to the excavation site that has revealed important remains of the Greco-Roman city. These include a *macellum* (market) and a vast area

The Baroque interior of the church of San Gregorio Armeno

below this where you can see the building that housed the *aerarium* (public treasury) and a street of workshops.

San Gregorio Armeno ❾

Convent: Piazzetta San Gregorio Armeno 1; **Church**: Via San Gregorio Armeno 44. **Map** 3 C5 (10 D3). **Tel** 081 552 01 86. 🚋 E1. Ⓜ Dante, Cavour-Museo, Montesanto. 🚇 Montesanto. **Convent and Church** ◯ 9:30–12 noon daily. **Cloister** 🈺 ⬆

This is one of the most important religious sites in Naples. San Gregorio was founded in the 8th century by a group of nuns who had fled Byzantium with the relics of St Gregory to escape religious persecution. The monastery was rebuilt in the 1500s and enlarged during the following

century. The lovely campanile was erected in 1716 on a footbridge that connected two parts of the complex. The decoration of the sumptuous Baroque interior – a "room of Paradise on Earth", as Carlo Celano wrote in his guide to Naples – was designed in the mid-18th century by Niccolò Tagliacozzi Canale. Notable works include the late 16th-century wooden ceiling, the two organs and, above the entrance, Luca Giordano's frescoes of *The Embarkation, Journey and Arrival of the Armenian Nuns with the Relics of St Gregory* (1671–84).

There is a lovely fountain in the cloister with a statue of Christ and the Samaritan, sculpted in 1733 (see p23). From here you can visit the Cappella della Madonna dell'Idria, decorated by Paolo De Matteis in 1712.

Gerolamini ❿

Church: Piazza Gerolamini 107; **Cloisters, Library & Gallery**: Via Duomo 142; **Cappella dell'Assunta**: Via Duomo 144. **Map** 3 C4 (10 D2). **Tel** 081 29 44 44. 🚋 CD, E3, R3. Ⓜ Dante, Cavour-Museo, Montesanto. 🚇 Montesanto. **Church, Cloisters, Library & Gallery** ◯ 9am–2pm Mon–Fri; 9am–noon Sat. 📷 ✏

The monastery of the Gerolamini was founded in the late 16th century by th Oratorio di San Filippo Neri congregation, also called "de Gerolamini" because they

Cloister of San Lorenzo Maggiore

The cloister in the Gerolamini

came from San Girolamo alla Carità in Rome. The church was built in Tuscan Renaissance style; the interior was rebuilt in the early 1600s, and the façade was modified by Ferdinando Fuga in 1780. Luca Giordano, Pietro da Cortona and Guido Reni decorated the Baroque interior.

Alongside the church there are two cloisters. The first, designed by Giovanni Dosio, shares features with the cloister he created at the Certosa di San Martino (see pp108–11). There are fine paintings in the Quadreria (art gallery). The 60,000-volume library has 18th-century furnishings and decoration.

Duomo ⓫

See pp82–3.

Guglia di San Gennaro ⓬

Piazza Riario Sforza. **Map** 3 C4 (10 D2). C5, C57, CD, E1, R2. Dante, Cavour-Museo.

This sculpted marble spire is dedicated to San Gennaro, the patron saint of Naples, for having protected the city during the 1631 eruption of Vesuvius. The guglia, the oldest of the three spires in Naples, was designed by Cosimo Fanzago in 1636, the same artist who later worked on the Guglia di San Domenico (see p68). The bronze statue at the top of the spire was sculpted by

Guglia di San Gennaro

Tommaso Montani. Behind the spire in the small square you can glimpse the stairway of the side entrance to the Duomo (see pp82–3) and, higher up, the dome of the Cappella di San Gennaro.

Pio Monte di Misericordia ⓭

Via Tribunali 253. **Map** 3 C4. **Tel** 081 44 69 44. C5, C57, CD, E1. Cavour-Museo. **Church** 9:30am–1:30pm Mon–Sat. **Art gallery** 9:30am–1:30pm Tue, Thu & Sat. by appt.

The Seven Acts of Mercy, a masterpiece by Caravaggio

Pio Monte is one of the most important charitable institutions in Naples. It was founded in 1601 to aid the poor and ill and to free the Christian slaves in the Ottoman Empire. The entire complex was designed by Francesco Antonio Picchiatti in the second half of the 17th century. After passing through the five-arch loggia (where pilgrims could shelter) decorated with sculptures by Andrea Falcone (1666–71), you enter the church. The eye is immediately drawn to the extraordinary altarpiece, The Seven Acts of Mercy, a masterpiece by Caravaggio (1571–1610), one of Italy's greatest artists. The art gallery on the first floor of the building houses the

fine Pio Monte collection. Pio Monte is still active as a charitable institution today.

Castel Capuano and Porta Capuana ⓮

Piazza Enrico De Nicola and Via Concezio Muzy. **Map** 4 D4 (10 F2). **Tel** 081 223 72 44. C5, C57, CD, E1, R2. Cavour-Museo. **Cappella Sommaria** by appt.

A palace and fortress built by the Normans in 1165 to defend the nearby city gateway, Castel Capuano remained a royal residence for the Angevin and Aragonese rulers even after the construction of Castel Nuovo (see pp54–5). In 1540 Don Pedro de Toledo turned the castle into law courts, a function it maintains to this day. On the first floor is the huge frescoed Court of Appeal, which leads to the splendid Renaissance Cappella della Sommaria, decorated by the Spanish painter Pietro Roviale.

A short distance away from the courts stands the gateway of Porta Capuana. Although much older in origin, its present appearance is the result of late 15th-century reconstruction by Giuliano da Maiano. The two towers, called Honour and Virtue, enclose the marble arch, repeating the pattern established in the Arco di Trionfo in Castel Nuovo.

The marble arch of Porta Capuana, rebuilt in the 1400s

Duomo ⓫

This great cathedral was built for Charles I of Anjou in the late 1200s–early 1300s. The church incorporated older Christian buildings and has been altered substantially over the centuries. The left-hand nave leads to the early medieval basilica of Santa Restituta, radically changed in the 17th century, and the San Giovanni in Fonte baptistry. The Cappella Minutolo has retained its original Gothic structure and decoration; the mosaic pavement and 13th-century frescoes are by Montano d'Arezzo. The Crypt of the Succorpo was built under the apse in the 1500s to house the relics of San Gennaro, until then in the Montevergine sanctuary. In the early 1600s the Cappella di San Gennaro was erected after the ending of the 1527 plague epidemic.

The bust of San Gennaro

★ **Baptistry**
This is the oldest baptistry in the Western world, built around AD 550. The mosaics date from the same period.

The archaeological area, which can be entered from the left-hand nave, reveals layers of buildings from three successive periods: Greek, Roman and early Middle Ages.

★ **Santa Restituta**
The structure of the early Christian basilica was changed in the Angevin period (when it became a side chapel in the new cathedral) and its decoration was replaced in the late 1600s. In the last chapel on the left is the beautiful mosaic Madonna and Saints Gennaro and Restituta, executed by Lello da Orvieto in 1322.

The three portals were the work of Antonio Baboccio da Piperno (1407); the middle one still bears two 14th-century lions and Tino da Camaino's *Virgin and Child* in the lunette.

Entrance to Museo del Tesoro di San Gennaro

TIMELINE

c.450 The Santa Restituta and Santa Stefania basilicas built	**1300** Duomo built on the site of the two basilicas	**1497** Work begins on crypt to house relics of San Gennaro		**1876** The façade is rebuilt in Neo-Gothic style	**1969** Digs begin in archaeological area
400	**1300**	**1500**	**1600**		**1900**
	c.550 The San Giovanni in Fonte baptistry added to Santa Restituta	**1349** An earthquake destroys the façade of the Duomo	**1608–37** Cappella di San Gennaro erected	**1621** Old ceiling replaced by present-day one in gilded wood	

Over 100 ancient columns are used s facing or the ave illars.

The Crypt of the Succorpo, with three naves, was decorated with Renaissance statues by Tommaso Malvito and assistants.

Font
The basin is made of Egyptian basalt. There are Greek sculptures and a 14th-century episcopal throne in the right-hand nave.

Cappella Minutolo

MIRACLE OF THE BLOOD

On the Saturday preceding the first Sunday in May and on 19 September *(see pp40–42)* the blood of San Gennaro, kept in two phials, turns to liquid. This ritual dates from the late 1300s and in Naples is the equivalent of an oracle: if the miracle does not occur, catastrophes are imminent.

Guglia di San Gennaro *(see p81)*

★ **Cappella di San Gennaro**
The dome with its depiction of Paradise was frescoed by Lanfranco in 1641–3. The reliquary bust of San Gennaro, a masterpiece of Gothic craftsmanship, is displayed in the Museo del Tesoro di San Gennaro.

STAR FEATURES

★ Cappella di San Gennaro

★ Baptistry

★ Santa Restituta

The monumental façade of Santa Maria di Donnaregina Nuova

Santa Caterina a Formiello **⑮**

Piazza Enrico De Nicola. **Map** 4 D4
(10 F1). **Tel** 081 44 42 97. C5,
E1, R2, 201. Ⓜ Cavour-Museo. ○
9am–1pm Mon–Sat. ● Sun.

The dome of Santa Caterina
a Formiello dominates the
surrounding area. The church
was called *formiello* because
it was built next to *formali*,
the ancient city aqueducts.
The 16th-century building has
delightful Baroque decoration
in the interior. Luigi Garzi and
Guglielmo Borremans executed
the frescoes (1695–1709). The
marble tombs of the Spinelli
family are in the apse area.

Santa Maria di Donnaregina Vecchia **⑯**

Vico Donnaregina 25. **Map** 3 C4
(10 D1). **Tel** 081 44 18 06. C5,
E1, R2, 201. Ⓜ Cavour-Museo.
○ 9am–noon Sat by appt.

The monastery and the
church of Santa Maria di
Donnaregina Vecchia were
founded in the 8th century
and then totally rebuilt in
1293, at the request of Marie
of Hungary, wife of Charles II
of Anjou. The interior of the
church, with one nave that

ends in a pentagonal apse, was
built on two levels to create a
separate area for nuns. The
lower part boasts an elegant
marble tomb of the queen who
founded the complex, sculpted by Tino da Camaino in
1325–6. In the upper section –
reached via a stairway to the
right of the entrance – is the

**Detail of the 13th-century fresco
cycle in Donnaregina Vecchia**

largest 14th-century cycle of
frescoes in Naples, which was
painted by Roman artists and
local pupils of Giotto from
1332 to 1335 *(see p21)*.

Santa Maria di Donnaregina Nuova **⑰**

Largo Donnaregina 7. **Map** 3 C4
(10 D1). **Tel** 081 44 18 06. C5,
E1, R2, 201. Ⓜ Cavour-Museo.
○ by appt.

In the early 1600s the Poor
Clares in the Santa Maria
Donnaregina convent decided
to build a new church, incorporating part of the old church
in the new construction. The
two churches, connected by
the apse areas, were separated during restoration work
in 1928–34. The original 14th-
century features were redis-
covered and the plan of the
17th-century construction was
modified. The single-nave
interior is richly decorated in
multi-coloured marble with
floral motifs, and there are fine
frescoes by Francesco Solimena
(1657–1747) in the nuns' choir.

Via Anticaglia **⑱**

Map 3 C4 (10 D2). C5, E1, R2,
201. Ⓜ Cavour-Museo.

The third, northernmost
decumanus (east–west
major road) in Greco-Roman
Naples today has four official
sections (Via Sapienza, Via
Pisanelli, Via Anticaglia and

The elegant interior of the pharmacy in the Ospedale degli Incurabili

Foro Carolino, present-day Piazza Dante, the 18th-century palace and hemicycle designed by Luigi Vanvitelli

Via Santi Apostoli), as does Spaccanapoli, the lower *decumanus (see p61)*.

The name "Anticaglia", meaning ruins, derives from the remains of the brick walls of a Roman building in this stretch of the street. These walls connected the ancient theatre, on the left as you go towards Via Santa Maria di Costantinopoli, and the bath-house on the opposite side of the street. The theatre, where Emperor Nero is known to have acted, had a seating capa-city of about 8,000. Nearby was the *odeion*, or ancient roofed theatre, used for concerts and poetry readings.

On the corner of Via Duomo and the third *decumanus*, there is a fine marble and piperno double stairway – from here you can visit the atrium of the church of San Giuseppe dei Ruffi, which was added in the early 18th century. Once past the Roman ruins, a right-hand turn at Via Armanni takes you to the Ospedale degli Incurabili. Inside is the unusual *Farmacia* (pharmacy) with about 400 brightly coloured majolica vases on shelves of inlaid wood – a positive art gallery of Neapolitan ceramics. However, visits are allowed only during the month of May for the "Maggio dei Monumenti" *(see p40)*.

Museo Archeologico Nazionale ⓳

See pp86–9.

Accademia di Belle Arti ⓴

Via Vincenzo Bellini 36. **Map** 3 B4 (9 B2). **Tel** 081 551 05 47. 🚌 C5, C57, R1, R4, 24, 149, 201. Ⓜ Dante, Cavour-Museo, Montesanto. 🕐 10am–2pm daily (by appointment). 🖼

Architect Enrico Alvino transformed the 18th-century convent of San Giovanni delle Monache into the Academy of Fine Arts in the 1840s. The Neo-Renaissance style reflects the prevailing fashion of the time. A broad staircase with plaster casts of ancient sculptures leads to the first floor. There is an important collection of modern painting, especially works by 19th-century Neapolitan and southern Italian artists.

The Accademia di Belle Arti staircase

Piazza Dante ㉑

Map 3 A5 (9 B3). 🚌 C5, C57, E1, R1, R4, 24, 149, 201. 🚋 Ⓜ Dante.

The names given to this square over the centuries sum up its history. Until the 1700s it lay outside the city walls and was used as a marketplace, hence the name Largo del Mercatello. In the

18th-century print of Largo del Mercatello

second half of the 18th century it took on its present form and was called Foro Carolino, after King Charles III, who commis-sioned the new layout. The semicircular façade with its colossal columns was designed by Luigi Vanvitelli as a setting for the king's statue, which was intended for the central niche but was never sculpted. The 26 figures on the cornice are allegories of the sovereign's qualities. Following the unification of Italy, a statue of Dante was placed in the middle of the square, hence its present name. To the left of the piazza is Port'Alba, the gate-way built in 1625 to connect the city with outlying districts.

Museo Archeologico Nazionale ⑲

This building, housing one of the world's most important archaeological museums, started life in the late 1500s as the home of the royal cavalry and was rebuilt in the early 17th century as the seat of Naples university. In 1777, when Ferdinand IV transferred the university to the former monastery of Gesù Vecchio (see p72), the building was again adapted to house the Real Museo Borbonico and library. In 1860 it became public property. Restoration and reorganization of exhibits still continue in the museum.

Sacrifice of Iphigenia
In this Pompeiian fresco, Iphigenia, daughter of Agamemnon, is about to be sacrificed to Artemis, who saves her by taking a deer instead.

Bust of "Seneca"
Found in the Villa dei Papiri (see p144) in Herculaneum, this 1st-century BC bronze head was long thought to represent the philosopher Seneca the Elder. Today, however, its identity is less certain.

★ The Battle of Alexander
The splendid mosaic from the House of the Faun in Pompeii (see p150) depicts Alexander the Great's victory over Persian emperor Darius III (333 BC).

The Secret Cabinet
The erotic works from Pompeii and Herculaneum housed here caused embarrassment at the time of the Bourbons. Visitors may book a viewing: ask at the information desk on arrival.

KEY TO FLOORPLAN

- ☐ Basement
- ☐ Ground floor
- ☐ Mezzanine
- ☐ First floor
- ☐ Second floor
- ☐ Non-exhibition space

Key to Symbols *see back flap*

Blue Vase
This wine vessel found in a Pompeii tomb was made with the so-called glass-cameo technique: a layer of opaque white paste was placed over coloured glass and then engraved with decorative motifs.

Spring Fresco
The fresco removed from the Villa Stabia in the Varano plain is a masterpiece of grace and elegance; the female figure rendered with soft, delicate colours.

96

83
84 82
81 79
80 78
75 76
74 73
68 72
67 71
69 70
56
57 55
52 53 54
24 16
27 26 25 17 15
14 18
13 19
12 20
8 21
11 22
9 10 23
7 157
1 156
2 155
3 4 5 6 154
153
152
151
150
31

Stairs down to Egyptian Collection

★ Farnese Bull
Excavated in the Baths of Caracalla in Rome, this is the largest sculptural group (c.200 BC) to have survived from antiquity. The best-known piece in the Farnese Collection, it shows the punishment of Dirce who, having ill-treated Antiope, was tied to an enraged bull by the latter's sons.

★ Farnese Hercules
Made by Glykon of Athens, this statue is an enlarged copy of a sculpture by the Greek master Lysippus. Napoleon is said to have regretted leaving it behind when he removed his booty from Italy in 1797.

...porary
...ance

STAR EXHIBITS

★ The Battle
  of Alexander

★ Farnese Hercules

★ Farnese Bull

Exploring the Museo Archeologico

The real Museo Borbonico, as the museum was known, held the Farnese Collection of paintings, ancient artefacts and books, and archaeological finds from sites in Campania and Southern Italy. In 1925 the books moved to the Palazzo Reale *(see pp50–51)* and in 1957 the Farnese Collection paintings returned to Capodimonte *(see pp98–101)*. The remaining material consisted of ancient finds, and the museum became the Archaeological Museum.

Wild goat from Edessa

The impressive Farnese Collection and sculpture from Herculaneum, Pompeii and other Campanian cities can be seen on the ground floor, the mezzanine level, and the first floor. Pompeiian mosaics, on the mezzanine level, and domestic items, weapons and murals, on the first floor, show daily life in the ancient cities. A lower ground floor level houses the Egyptian Collection. The arrangement aims to display the exhibits in context.

Funerary stela of the scribe Huy

SCULPTURE

The fine collection of Greco-Roman sculpture consists mostly of works found in excavations around Vesuvius and the Phlegraean Fields, as well as the treasures from the Farnese Collection. The sculptures – most of which are the only existing Roman copies of lost Greek originals – are displayed on the ground floor. Among the numerous fine works are the statues of *Harmodios and Aristogeiton*, or the "tyrannicides", young Athenians who killed the 6th-century BC tyrant, Hipparchos, and the bronze and alabaster *Artemis of Ephesos*, whose many breasts symbolize fertility. The *Doryphoros* carrying a spear is a copy of a famous Greek original, as is the impressive *Farnese Hercules*. The *Farnese Atlas*, holding up the world, is a Hellenistic statue, while the huge *Dioscuri* statues, discovered in the Roman baths of Baia *(see p137)*, and the harmonious *Farnese Flora* are copies by Roman sculptors.

The Farnese Flora

Cameo with Dionysus and satyr

INCISED GEMS

This precious collection, begun by Cosimo de' Medici, contains Greek, Roman and Renaissance gems. The highlight is the veined sardonyx *Farnese Cup*, a large and beautiful cameo carved in Egypt around the 2nd and 1st centuries BC. Another stunning agate and sardonyx cameo shows the infant Dionysus playing with a satyr.

THE EGYPTIAN COLLECTION

Valuable works of Egyptian art from the Ancient Kingdom (2700–2200 BC) to the Roman age are exhibited here. The black basalt *Farnese Naophorous*

represents a kneeling official. These were the intermediaries between men and gods. The limestone funerary stela of Huy (1320–1200 BC) retains some of its original colouring.

As well as human and animal mummies, the Egyptian section includes Canopic vases, containers for the internal organs of the deceased with lids in the shape of animal heads. The collection of *shabti* comprises wood, stone and faience statuettes representing workers for the deceased in the afterlife.

MOSAICS

The majority of the mosaics on display in the museum come from Pompeii, Stabiae, Herculaneum and Boscoreale and date from the 2nd century BC to AD 79. The realistic images, such as the female portraits from Pompeii, are particularly fascinating.

Mosaic of a female from Pompeii

Among the many pavement mosaics made of tiny tesserae and often derived from Greek paintings, is *La Fattucchiera* (the Sorceress). This interesting example of the Hellenistic tradition depicts a scene from *Synaristoi*, a comedy by the Greek playwright Aristophanes. Another masterpiece is the *Battle of Alexander* found at Pompeii. This large, detailed mosaic was based on a Hellenistic painting and depicts Alexander the Great leading his cavalry against Darius III, the Persian Emperor, seen fleeing in his chariot.

Some rooms in the museum have reconstructions of large mosaic paved floors.

observatory. A large sundial *(meridiana)*, decorated with the signs of the zodiac, was created for the spacious hall which had originally been destined to be the Bourbon library (Biblioteca Borbonica).

The idea of the observatory, however, was discarded when experts realized that the location of the building meant that it was impossible to have a total view of the sky. A few years later the observatory was built elsewhere *(see p97)*. As originally planned, the Salone della Meridiana was opened to the public in 1804 as a library.

There are also numerous fragments of frescoes which depict landscapes, portraits and mythological scenes and characters, such as the *Sacrifice of Iphigenia*. These show the variety and quality of Roman painting from this period.

TEMPLE OF ISIS

Head of Isis

The paintings, sculptures and furnishings from the Temple of Isis in Pompeii are presented in such a way as to recreate the sanctuary as it appeared to the first archaeologists in 1764. *The Portrait of Io at Canopos* was uncovered on 18 November of the same year in the presence of King Ferdinand IV, and shows the nymph Io being welcomed to Egypt by Isis. The marble head of the goddess, to whom the temple was dedicated, dates from the 1st century AD.

VILLA DEI PAPIRI

This villa in Herculaneum *(see p140)*, still partly buried today, was an art gallery in its own right. The rich array of artworks found here during the excavations in 1750–61 are exceptional: this ancient private collection has been handed down to us intact. A map of the villa shows where every object was found.

Among the pieces on display are life-size statues and small sculptures in marble and bronze, such as the *Dancing Faun* which greeted visitors in the atrium of the villa. Most of the pieces were inspired by Greek figurative art. A vast library of around 1,700 papyrus scrolls was also found in the villa. An apparatus used to unroll the charred scrolls is on display. The original scrolls are now kept in the Biblioteca Nazionale *(see p51)*.

Statue of a faun, Villa dei Papiri

FRESCOES

Most of the frescoes in the collection were removed from buildings in cities buried by the eruptions of Vesuvius, and assembled here from the mid-1700s onwards. The most important came from the Basilica in Herculaneum (such as the painting of *Achilles and Chiron*). Others were taken from the Villa di Fannio Sinistore at Boscoreale, where one wall was decorated with illusionistic architectural perspective, and from the extensive landed property of Julia Felix in Pompeii *(see p147)*. The frieze from her house, with a still life of apples and grapes and scenes from the forum, gives a fascinating glimpse of everyday life in a 1st-century AD city.

THE MODEL OF POMPEII

Model of Pompeii

Paper, cork and wood were all used in the making of this extensive scale model of the Pompeii excavations. The archaeologist Giuseppe Fiorelli had the original idea and the model was constructed in various stages between 1861 to 1879. The extraordinarily exact reproduction of every detail found in the ruins (including paintings and mosaics done in watercolour), make this an extremely important historical document. In some cases, when detailed records of Pompeiian decoration are needed, this model is the only useful source that remains.

SALONE DELLA MERIDIANA

When the building was being reorganized and fitted out as a museum in the late 18th century, the architects had the idea of adding an

The famous fresco *Achilles and Chiron* from Herculaneum

CAPODIMONTE AND I VERGINI

Although the Spanish viceroys had forbidden construction outside the city walls, from the 17th century onwards suburban development continued. In the early 19th century, building began in the northern suburbs. The avenue leading to the Capodimonte palace, now the home of one of Europe's most important museums, was created as an extension of Via Toledo. The

Porcelain at Capodimonte

square next to the Museo Archeologico was redesigned and Via Foria, on which the Botanic Garden and, from 1751, the huge Albergo dei Poveri were being built, was widened. The old Sanità, Vergini and Fontanelle districts are a lively working quarter in which visitors need to exercise caution. On the streets leading to the early Christian cemeteries, tenements alternate with historic churches and buildings.

SIGHTS AT A GLANCE

Churches and Cemeteries
Cimitero delle Fontanelle **6**
Santi Apostoli **8**
San Gennaro Catacombs **12**
San Giovanni a Carbonara **7**
Santa Maria degli Angeli alle Croci **9**
Santa Maria della Sanità and San Gaudioso Catacombs **5**
San Severo and Catacombs **4**

Historic Buildings
Albergo dei Poveri **11**
Osservatorio Astronomico **14**
Palazzo Sanfelice **3**
Palazzo dello Spagnolo **2**

Historic Gate
Porta San Gennaro **1**

Museums and Galleries
Museo Nazionale and Park of Capodimonte pp98–101 **13**

Parks and Gardens
Orto Botanico **10**

GETTING THERE
The Capodimonte museum and Catacombs of San Gennaro can be reached via bus routes 24 and R4, which start from Piazza del Municipio and Piazza Bovio. You can walk to the Vergini and Sanità districts from the Metro station at Piazza Cavour. Many buses run along Via Foria. Bus C51 serves the Fontanelle.

| 0 metres | 250 |
| 0 yards | 250 |

KEY

Street-by-Street map
See pp92–3

Ⓜ Metro station

⌐ Caravaggio's *Flagellation of Christ* (1610), on display in the Museo di Capodimonte

Street-by-Street: North of the Ancient Walls

The area north of the city walls has been used for burials and worship of the dead since it was first inhabited. A visit to the catacombs (which were underground cemeteries and not hiding places), first created in the early Christian era, is an unforgettable experience. The area outside the walls was also used to dump rubbish. The district known today as Via San Giovanni a Carbonara was once called the Fosso Carbonario (literally, "coal ditch"), and this is how the street and the beautiful 14th-century church acquired their current names.

The church of Santa Maria dai Vergini, built in the 14th century, was badly damaged in World War II.

San Severo
This church was built on the burial site of St Severus, Bishop of Naples from 364 to 410 ❹

★ Palazzo Sanfelice
This staircase in the smaller courtyard was the prototype for another one designed by Ferdinando Sanfelice in San Giovanni a Carbonara (see p96) ❸

★ Santa Maria della Sanità
The high altar was built in a raised position so that the entrance to the San Gaudioso catacombs could be seen ❺

Palazzo dello Spagnolo
This monumental gateway is one entrance to the double-flight staircase, the highlight of this palazzo, which was designed by Sanfelice in 1738 ❷

KEY

‒ ‒ ‒ Suggested route

0 metres   50
0 yards   50

★ **San Giovanni a Carbonara**
The double-flight winding staircase here was designed by Ferdinando Sanfelice. The magnificent sculptures inside make this one of the most important churches in Naples **7**

LOCATOR MAP
See Street Finder, maps 2–4

CAPODIMONTE AND I VERGINI
DECUMANO MAGGIORE
SPACCANAPOLI

The Padri della Missione Church was designed by Vanvitelli.

VIA FORIA
VIA DOMENICO CIRILLO
P. ZZETTA SETTEMBRINI
VIA SS. APOSTOLI
EI VERGINI VIA CROCELLE
VIA DUOMO
VIA FORIA
PAGANO
PIAZZA CAVOUR

San Carlo all'Arena
is so-named because in the 1600s the street nearby was covered in sand *(arena)*.

Santi Apostoli
This church was founded in the 5th century, perhaps on the site of an ancient temple. It was rebuilt from the late 1500s to the mid-1600s. The Paradise in the dome was painted by Giovanni Battista Beinaschi in 1680 **8**

Santa Maria Succurre Miseris
was founded in the 14th century and rebuilt in the 1700s by Ferdinando Sanfelice, using Baroque motifs throughout.

Porta San Gennaro
In the mid-15th century the city walls were extended and this gateway was rebuilt in its present location **1**

STAR SIGHTS

★ Palazzo Sanfelice

★ Santa Maria della Sanità and San Gaudioso Catacombs

★ San Giovanni a Carbonara

The double-flight staircase in Palazzo dello Spagnolo

feasts, organized by the court in order to win the Neapolitans' favour. This theatrical aspect of his work can be clearly seen in the two palazzi he designed for the Sanità district.

Once through the majestic doorway of the Palazzo dello Spagnolo, you will notice a feature taken from the Palazzo Sanfelice: the magnificent double-flight external staircase. This type of staircase, which effectively separates the main courtyard from the smaller one, is one of the most notable features of Neapolitan palaces.

trademark. His contemporaries likened it to a large bird with outspread wings, and it became known as a stair *ad ali di falco* – a "falcon's wing" staircase.

The best way to grasp the beauty of the design is to walk up the steps; from the first landing you can see the garden behind. On the far side of the second courtyard (at No. 2 Via Sanità), which has unfortunately lost its original decoration, there is yet another elliptical staircase.

Porta San Gennaro ❶

Map 3 C3. C5, CD, 47, 110. M Cavour-Museo.

This gateway was named after San Gennaro, the patron saint of Naples, because it marked the beginning of the street that leads to the catacombs where he was buried *(see p97)*. After the plague of 1656, Mattia Preti painted a fresco on each city gate as an *ex voto* from those who survived. Porta San Gennaro is the only one that still has traces of the artist's work. On the inner façade is a bust of San Gaetano with a dedication and the date – 1658.

Palazzo dello Spagnolo ❷

Via Vergini 19. **Map** 3 B3. C5, C51, C52, CD, 47, 110. M Cavour-Museo. 7:30am–2pm, 3:30–8pm Mon–Fri; 7:30am–1pm Sat.

Built in 1738 by Ferdinando Sanfelice (1675–1748) for the Marquis Nicola Moscati, this building became the property of the Spanish nobleman Tommaso Atienza in the 19th century and was renamed the Palace of the Spaniard. In addition to his work as an architect, Sanfelice also designed temporary staging and scenery for outdoor

Palazzo Sanfelice ❸

Via Sanità 2–4. **Map** 3 B3. C5, CD, 47, 110. M Cavour-Museo. 8am–1pm, 3–7pm Mon–Fri; 8:30am–1pm Sat (by appointment).

Ferdinando Sanfelice built this large palazzo for his own family in 1728, as can be seen in the inscription on the top of the right-hand doorway. It is one of the finest palazzi in Naples and it was here that the famous Neapolitan architect first created the unusual external staircase he subsequently adopted, with some variations, in Palazzo dello Spagnolo ten years later. This type of strikingly original staircase became Sanfelice's

Painting by Giovan Battista Spinelli in San Severo

San Severo and Catacombs ❹

Piazza San Severo 81. **Map** 3 B2. **Tel** 081 544 13 05. R4. M Cavour-Museo. for restoration. by appt only.

Fresco of *San Pietro* in the catacombs of San Severo

San Severo was the Bishop of Naples from 364 to 410. This site was chosen for his tomb and, as was the usual practice among early Christians, a large underground cemetery grew up around it. The basilica over the catacombs was abandoned in the 9th century when the saint's relics were transferred to San Giorgio Maggiore *(see p70)*. The building was only restored in the 16th century and again more comprehensively in the late 17th century. In the third chapel on the left is the entrance to the catacombs. In the same chapel there is a cell with three arched niches hewn out of the stone to house sarcophagi. The niches are decorated with frescoes which, despite their poor condition, are good examples of catacomb painting.

Central nave of Santa Maria della Sanità

Santa Maria della Sanità and San Gaudioso Catacombs ❺

Piazza Sanità 124. **Map** 3 A2. *Tel* 081 544 13 05. Ⓜ Cavour-Museo. ⬤ 8:30am–12:30pm, 5–8pm daily (except Sun pm). 🔺 **Catacombs** ☑ every 45 mins 9:30–12:30am daily. 📷

View of Santa Maria Sanità from the Ponte della Sanità

The heart of the working-class Sanità quarter is the basilica of Santa Maria. Confusingly, the church is also known as the church of San Vincenzo because it houses a much revered image of the popular saint, known locally as *'o munacone* (the big monk). Designed by Fra Nuvolo, the church was built on a Greek cross plan in 1603–13, with 24 columns supporting one central dome and 12 lateral domes (a reference to Christ and the Apostles). The central tiled dome is overlooked by the 19th-century Ponte della Sanità, linking the city centre to Capodimonte.

Inside, the main altar was raised to allow worshippers to see the space that serves as a kind of atrium for the underground cemetery. The entrance to the catacombs can be clearly seen.

Tradition has it that in 452, the African bishop Settimio Celio Gaudioso died in exile in Naples, and was buried in the Sanità valley. The catacombs grew up around his tomb and were named after him. The many corridors still bear traces of frescoes and mosaics (4th–6th centuries AD). The catacombs remained in use for centuries. Evidence for this includes some rather gruesome early 17th-century tombs, each with a skeleton drawn on the wall. The catacombs are also open in the afternoon for groups.

Cimitero delle Fontanelle ❻

Via Fontanelle 77. **Map** 3 A3. 🚌 C52. Ⓜ Cavour-Museo. ⬤ to public except for tours (ask at tourist office).

A walk along Via Fontanelle, through a poor area that is more like a country village than a city district, leads to the church of Maria Santissima del Carmine. Tours sometimes run to the nearby Fontanelle cemetery *(cimitero)*. The huge rock-hewn caverns on the hill of Materdei were already being used as the city ossuary when they were selected as the final resting place for the victims of the devastating 1836 cholera epidemic. Some people may find the place upsetting, as did the tourist played by Ingrid Bergman in Rossellini's film *Viaggio in Italia*, which made the cemetery famous. Controversy over "adoptions" of skulls to bring good luck has made this a sensitive site.

The ossuary of the Fontanelle Cemetery

San Giovanni a Carbonara **❼**

Via San G a Carbonara 5. **Map** 3 C3. *Tel* 081 29 58 73. 🚌 201 ○ 9am–1pm daily.

Cappella Caracciolo di Vico, San Giovanni a Carbonara

The imaginative double-flight staircase designed by Ferdinando Sanfelice in the early 1700s leads to the 14th-century Chapel of Santa Monica. Left of the chapel is the doorway to San Giovanni a Carbonara. Founded in 1343 by Augustinian monks, this church was restored and enlarged at the end of the century by King Ladislas to make it a worthy burial site for the Angevin rulers.

    When the king died in 1414, his tomb, the work of anonymous Tuscan and Lombard sculptors *(see p20),*was erected at the request of his sister, Joan II, who succeeded him to the throne. The grandiose funerary monument, with seated statues of Ladislas and Joan, dominates the single-nave interior. Through a small doorway beneath the monument is the circular Cappella Caracciolo del Sole, built in 1427 and paved with coloured Tuscan tiles. Behind the altar is the tomb of Ser Gianni Caracciolo, Joan's lover and Grand Seneschal at the court, who died in 1432.

    To the left of the presbytery is the harmonious Cappella Caracciolo di Vico, built in the Renaissance style in 1517 by Giovan Tommaso Malvito following a design by Bramante. Another work by Malvito is the richly decorated tomb of the Miroballo family opposite the entrance of the church.

Santi Apostoli **❽**

Largo Santi Apostoli 9. **Map** 3 C4. *Tel* 081 29 93 75. 🚌 CD, E3, 201. Ⓜ Cavour-Museo. ○ 9am–12:45pm daily (also eves, but too dark to view frescoes).

To reach the church of Santi Apostoli you have to go along a short stretch of Via Pisanelli, which turns into Via Anticaglia *(see p84).* The church was founded in the 5th century and restructured at the beginning of the 17th century by Francesco Grimaldi (1610) and, after 1627, by Giovanni Conforto. The church is best known for a wonderful fresco cycle by Giovanni Lanfranco (1638–46). This masterpiece influenced artistic development in Naples. The artist also frescoed the cupola of the Cappella del Tesoro di San Gennaro *(see pp82–3).*

Santa Maria degli Angeli alle Croci **❾**

Via Veterinaria 2. **Map** 3 C2. *Tel* 081 44 07 56. 🚌 E1, 47, 201. Ⓜ Cavour-Museo. ○ 7–11:30am, 5–8pm daily. 🚫

The name of this church refers to the Stations of the Cross, once marked by wooden crosses *(croci)* alongside the ascent to the church. Santa Maria was founded at the end of the 16th century by Franciscans and rebuilt in 1638 by Cosimo Fanzago. The façade is simply decorated with white and grey marble.

The white and grey marble façade of Santa Maria degli Angeli alle Croci

This plain design was a daring shift from the usually lavish architecture of Neapolitan Baroque. The interior houses a magnificent marble pulpit sculpted by Cosimo Fanzago. The eagle supporting it symbolizes St John the Evangelist. The extraordinary bas relief of the dead Christ on the altar was sculpted by Carlo Fanzago, Cosimo's son.

Cactus plants in the Orto Botanico

Orto Botanico **❿**

Via Foria 223. **Map** 4 D2. *Tel* 081 44 97 59. 🚌 47, 201. Ⓜ Cavour-Museo. ○ 9am–2pm Mon–Sat; Sun & hols by appt.

Established in 1807 by Joseph Bonaparte, the "Royal Plant Garden" is today one of the leading Italian botanical gardens for the high quality of its collections as well as its sheer size, covering 12 hectares (30 acres). It has a rich stock of tree and shrub specimens from all latitudes and examples of many plant species, as well as several glasshouses with varying climatic conditions. The temperate house is an early 19th-century Neo-Classical building. The collections of citrus trees, desert plants and tree ferns are particularly interesting. Even though you may not be a botanical enthusiast, a walk along the paths of this green oasis, in the heart of one of the busiest areas in Naples, can make a very pleasant break from the city.

Albergo dei Poveri ⓫

Piazza Carlo III. **Map** 4 E2.
🚌 47, C55B. Ⓜ Cavour-Museo.

The enormous building you see today is only one-fifth of the large-scale complex that King Charles III wanted to build to provide a refuge for "the poor of the entire kingdom". Construction of the "Hotel of the Poor" began in 1751 according to a design by Ferdinando Fuga. Work continued until 1829. In reality, the building was hated by the poor, including orphans, who were compelled to live and work there, without hope of leaving. After many years in a state of neglect, restoration work is now underway.

San Gennaro Catacombs ⓬

Via Capodimonte 13. **Map** 3 A1.
Tel 081 741 10 71. 🚌 R4, 24.
🎫 9am, 10am, 11am, noon Tue–Sun. 🎥 📷

The original nucleus of this large subterranean cemetery may have been the tomb of a pagan aristocrat donated in the 2nd century to the growing Christian community. The catacombs began to grow in importance in the 3rd century after acquiring the tomb of Sant'Agrippino, but it was as the burial site of the saint, bishop and martyr Gennaro, brought here in the

The Neo-Classical façade of the Osservatorio Astronomico

5th century, that the catacombs became famous. The cemetery also housed the tombs of Neapolitan bishops up to the 11th century. The vast size and two-level layout of this holy site distinguish it from other catacombs of the same era and make it the most important complex in Southern Italy. Remains of precious 2nd- to 10th-century mosaics and frescoes (including the oldest known portrayal of San Gennaro, dating from the 5th century) adorn the walls of the catacombs. Don't miss the Bishops' Crypt on the upper floor and the Sant'Agrippino Oratory and baptistry on the lower level. The basilica of San Gennaro extra Moenia was erected over the catacombs in the 5th century but was greatly modified by subsequent rebuilding in the 11th century and then again in 1932.

Watercolour of the Catacombs of San Gennaro by Giacinto Gigante

Museo Nazionale and Park of Capodimonte ⓭

See pp98–101.

Osservatorio Astronomico ⓮

Salita Moiariello 16. **Map** 3 B1.
Tel 081 557 51 11. 🚌 24.
🕐 Mon–Fri by appt.

Situated in the middle of a large park on top of the hill of Miradois, 150 m (490 ft) above sea level, the observatory benefits from a splendid vantage point with fine panoramic views of the city and the bay. Founded in 1819 by Ferdinand IV, this was the first scientific facility of its kind in Europe. The Bourbon court had always been keenly interested in astronomic studies, and it was Charles III who established the first university chair of astronomy in Naples in 1735. The observatory was originally planned for the Museo Archeologico, and in fact construction of a new observatory began there in 1791 (see p89), but the project was discarded. A few years later the elegant Neo-Classical building that now houses the observatory was built by the Gasse brothers. Today part of the observatory is occupied by a museum with a fine collection of clocks, telescopes and old scientific instruments.

Museo Nazionale and Park of Capodimonte ⑬

From the beginning Capodimonte was both a royal palace and a museum because Charles III wanted a home for the works of art he had inherited from his mother Elizabeth Farnese. Construction began in 1738 under architect Antonio Medrano, but the palace was only completed a century later, despite the fact that a large part of the Farnese Collection had been on display there since 1759. The collection was dispersed after the French occupation in 1799 *(see p25)*, but following the Bourbon restoration in 1815, was enlarged considerably.

In 1860 Capodimonte became the property of the House of Savoy and was the residence of the Dukes of Aosta until 1947. The museum was opened to the public again in 1957.

In 1996, after restoration, the first floor was reopened, and in 1997 the Neapolitan and contemporary art collections were arranged on the second floor (not shown here).

Pietà
This painting by Annibale Carracci, which dates from around 1600, drew inspiration from Michelangelo and is one of the masterpieces of Carracci's monumental style.

Main Entrance

THE PARK OF CAPODIMONTE

Charles III was drawn to Capodimonte because of hunting, his favourite pastime, and he decided to build an important hunting lodge here. The first section of this large park (over 120 hectares/300 acres), with numerous ancient trees, was laid out by Ferdinando Sanfelice in 1742 into five broad radiating roads, lined with holm-oaks. The buildings used for various court activities can be found in the woods.

The rooms in the Royal Apartments on the first floor reveal the two-fold function as royal palace and museum that Capodimonte fulfilled from the outset.

Ferdinand IV at Capodimonte by Antonio Joli

KEY

- Farnese Gallery
- Borgia Collection
- De Ciccio porcelain collection
- Farnese and Bourbon Armoury
- Maria Amalia's Porcelain Parlour
- Royal apartments
- Non-exhibition space

Neapolitan Craftsmanship
This is a multi-purpose piece of early 19th-century furniture made in a Neapolitan factory: the lower part contains a glass bowl, which serves as an aquarium, and a table with a bird cage, which serves as a jardinière. The rotating figure of Fortune is perched on top.

Café

First Floor

VISITORS' CHECKLIST

Via Miano 2 (Porta Piccola), Via Capodimonte (Porta Grande). **Map** 3 B1. *Tel* 081 749 91 11.
🚌 R4, 24. **Museum** ☐ 8:30am–7:30pm Thu–Tue. **Park** ☐ 8am–1 hr before sunset. 🅿 museum only. 🚫 👶 ♿ 🖥 📷 🛍
www.capodimonte.selfin.it

★ Danaë *(c.1545)*
Golden light bathes this canvas by Titian, in which the mythical god Jupiter disguises himself as a shower of gold in order to seduce Danaë, daughter of the king of Argos.

★ Crucifixion *(1426)*
In this early Renaissance painting by Masaccio, the emotional intensity of faces and gestures emphasizes the drama. The panel was part of an altarpiece for a church in Pisa, now dismantled and scattered in various museums.

★ Maria Amalia's Porcelain Parlour
This room was built in 1757–9 for the Royal Palace at Portici (see p140); then dismantled and moved here in 1866. The walls and ceiling of the queen's parlour are tiled with about 3,000 pieces of finest Capodimonte porcelain.

STAR EXHIBITS

★ Crucifixion by Masaccio

★ Danaë by Titian

★ Maria Amalia's Porcelain Parlour

Exploring the Museo di Capodimonte

The Farnese Collection, which is the core of the Art Gallery, features the major Italian and European schools of painting hfrom the 15th to the 17th centuries. When the Real Museo (now the Museo Archeologico Nazionale, *see pp86–9*) was created in Palazzo degli Studi in the early 1800s, the paintings were transferred from Capodimonte and returned in 1957, along with other works purchased since the 19th century by the Bourbon rulers and the Italian government. Following the completion of recent restoration and rearrangement of the collections, 13th–19th century Neapolitan painting and sculpture is now displayed on the second floor. The 19th-century collection is located in the mezzanine, while the first floor is devoted to the Farnese Collection and the Royal Apartments.

Antea (1531–35) by Parmigianino

PAINTING FROM THE 13TH TO THE 16TH CENTURIES

The Farnese Collection did not focus on medieval works, so that paintings from this period are later purchases or come from churches in the Naples region. For example, the beautiful *Santa Maria de Flumine* (c.1290) came from a church of the same name in Amalfi. The most important 14th-century painting is the large altarpiece painted by Simone Martini in 1317 on the occasion of the canonization of St Louis of Toulouse (*see pp20–21*), *St Louis of Toulouse Crowning Robert of Anjou King of Naples.*

The 15th century is also represented by a superb canvas – Masaccio's *Crucifixion*, actually the upper part of a dismantled polyptych taken from the church of the Carmine in Pisa. The other panels are in Pisa, London, Berlin and Malibu.

Transfiguration by Giovanni Bellini

Giovanni Bellini's masterpiece, *Transfiguration* (c.1480–85), has been considered one of the gems of the Farnese Collection since the 1600s. The *Tavola Strozzi* panel is an extraordinary "snapshot" of 15th-century Naples.

The focal point of the 16th-century paintings are the splendid Titians: *Portrait of Pope Paul III*, *Pope Paul III with His Grandchildren*, and *Danaë* (*see p99*), which exemplify the Venetian genius's masterly use of colour. Artists from the region of Emilia Romagna, the home of the Farnese family, are well represented. Major works are Correggio's

masterpiece *Mystic Marriage of St Catherine* and the *Antea* by Parmigianino, a portrait of a young woman with elegant dress and a marten stole. An important group of canvases by the Carraccis includes Annibale Carracci's *Pietà*, inspired by the strong sculptural forms of Michelangelo, and his large allegorical work, *Hercules at the Crossroads*, in which the mythical hero has to choose between pleasure and virtue.

PAINTING FROM THE 17TH TO THE 20TH CENTURIES

Among the 17th-century works in the museum, Bartolomeo Schedoni's *Charity* (1611) is one of the most famous, and is greatly admired for its expressive intensity. The myth of *Atalanta and Hippomenes* is depicted in Guido Reni's canvas, which the Bourbon rulers bought in 1802 because they lacked a major work by the Bolognese master.

The astounding *Flagellation of Christ* by Caravaggio (*see p90*) was painted in stages from 1607 to 1609–10, and hung in San Domenico Maggiore until its move to Capodimonte. It is regarded as the linchpin of all 17th-century Neapolitan painting, which is represented here by many leading artists, such as Battistello Caracciolo, Luca Giordano and Mattia Preti. No less astounding is Artemisia Gentileschi's painting of

The *Tavola Strozzi*, a representation of 15th-century Naples (detail)

Judith and Holofernes, a subject she made her own. The artist, who favoured rather violent themes, was an exceptionally gifted painter and remarkably independent for a woman of her times.

Portrait of Ferdinand IV as a Youth was painted by the German artist Anton Raphael Mengs in 1760; the young king, whose luxurious clothes are rendered in great detail, was nine at the time. In addition, there are some fine landscapes by Ferdinand IV's court painter, Jakob-Philipp Hackert.

Capodimonte also has a large body of 19th-century Neapolitan paintings, including works by Anton Pitloo, the Dutch painter who settled in Naples *(see p36)*, and Giacinto Gigante. Don't miss the latter's famous painting of the Cappella del Tesoro in the Duomo. Among the modern works, Andy Warhol's *Mount Vesuvius (see p28)* was painted in 1985 for an exhibition at the museum in the same year.

Francesco Solimena's *Study of a Young Man's Face* **(1728)**

Vatican. Perforations (which can still be seen) were made with a needle, and powder was sprinkled over the holes to transfer the lines to the wall where the fresco was to be painted.

Solimena's *Study of a Young Man's Face* is a charming study for a later painting. Another important cartoon is Raphael's *Moses before the Burning Bush*, a preparatory drawing for a detail of a fresco in the Stanza di Eliodoro in the Vatican.

THE DECORATIVE ARTS

The major section in the fine Decorative Arts collection is the armoury, which has about 4,000 weapons and is one of the most important of its kind. Many of the objects here

come from the Naples Royal Arms Factory, founded in 1734 by Charles III. There are also over 4,000 ceramic pieces in this part of the museum, including the De Ciccio majolica collection and examples of the superb porcelain manufactured in Naples at the instigation of Charles III. A fine example of this craftsmanship is Queen Maria Amalia's Porcelain Parlour *(see p99)*.

Other decorative arts include objects made of ivory, amber and rock crystal, as well as medallions, semi-precious stones and other pieces such as the 17th-century gilded silver table trophy of Diana by Jacob Miller.

***Diana on a Deer*, table trophy**

***Judith and Holofernes* by Artemisia Gentileschi (1597–1651)**

THE COLLECTION OF DRAWINGS AND PAINTINGS

Among the museum's huge inheritance there are about 2,500 drawings and watercolours and 22,000 prints and engravings. One of the most famous works is a cartoon (a preparatory drawing made with charcoal or chalk) made by Michelangelo around 1546. It was drawn for part of the fresco of *The Crucifixion of St Peter* in the Cappella Paolina in the

THE ROYAL PORCELAIN FACTORY

King Charles III promoted and fostered the manufacture of decorated porcelain in Naples. The "soft-paste" porcelain, produced with the aid of leading chemists and mineralogists in the Kingdom of Naples, allowed the Real Fabbrica to vie with top European manufacturers such as Meissen. A new pavilion for the Royal Factory was opened in the royal park of Capodimonte in

The Biscuit Vendor (1750–51)

1743, and the fame of Neapolitan porcelain continued to grow. By 1759, when the king returned to Spain, the factory had become so important to him that he had it dismantled and took it, as well as its staff, with him. The factory was reopened in 1771 by Ferdinand, and production of top-quality pieces began again. Today the Royal Factory is the home of the Institute for the Porcelain and Ceramics industry.

VOMERO

I n 1885 the Town Council of Naples approved a plan for a new district to be developed "in the rise between Castel Sant'Elmo, the village of Vomero and Antignano", which, once completed, would accommodate 30,000 inhabitants. So began the story of the district of Vomero, which soon became famous for its scenic beauty and healthy climate. These qualities have

Detail of the cloister, Certosa di San Martino

since been partly ruined (especially since World War II) by chaotic, uncontrolled property development with total disregard for the natural surroundings. Yet, some interesting areas are preserved. At the top of the hill is one of the most important monuments in Naples, the Certosa di San Martino, with its splendid Baroque church, fine museum and the elegant residence called the Quarto del Priore.

SIGHTS AT A GLANCE

Historic Buildings
Castel Sant'Elmo ❹
Certosa and Museo Nazionale di San Martino pp108–11 ❺

Parks and Gardens
Villa La Floridiana ❷

Streets and Squares
Pedamentina ❻
Via Luigia Sanfelice ❼
Via Scarlatti ❶

Museums and Galleries
Museo Nazionale della Ceramica Duca di Martina ❸

GETTING THERE
The fastest way to reach Vomero is via the funiculars: the Chiaia route from Parco Margherita, the Centrale from Via Toledo and the Montesanto from the historic centre. To get to Castel Sant'Elmo and the Certosa you can also take the circle bus line V1 from Piazza Fuga, which connects with the Centrale funicular.

KEY

▩	Street-by-Street map *See pp104–5*
Ⓜ	Metro station
⊞	Funicular

Street-by-Street: Vomero

Take one of the funicular railway lines up the hill to Vomero for fine views of the city centre and the Bay of Naples. Art-lovers will find that Neapolitan masters are well represented in the museums of the Certosa di San Martino and Villa La Floridiana (the Duca di Martina). Meanwhile, a walk along the atmospheric streets in the heart of the district reveals an eclectic range of shops and goods, including the Daniele pasticceria in Via Scarlatti, known for its delectable cakes. In Via Luigia Sanfelice is the villa of the Neapolitan comic Eduardo Scarpetta.

Eduardo Scarpetta

Montesanto funicular

Vanvitelli

Via Scarlatti
This street is the main thoroughfare through Vomero ❶

Centrale funicular

Chiaia funicular

Museo Nazionale della Ceramica Duca di Martina
This is one of Italy's most important collections of decorative arts ❸

★ Villa La Floridiana
The villa, rebuilt by Antonio Niccolini in the early 19th century, now houses the Duca di Martina museum. It stands in a large park filled with pine, holm-oak, plane and cypress trees ❷

KEY

‒ ‒ ‒ Suggested route

LOCATOR MAP
See Street Finder, maps 1, 2, 5, 6

0 metres	100
0 yards	100

In Via Tito Angelini are some turn-of-the-century houses, such as Villino Maria (below), which have survived the wave of property development since World War II.

★ **Certosa and Museo Nazionale di San Martino**
After the unification of Italy, this impressive complex – built in the 14th century but drastically restructured later on – became state property and was turned into a museum ❺

The section of the Museo di San Martino given over to Neapolitan painting and sculpture of the 19th century includes Vincenzo Gemito's expressive *Head of a Peasant Woman.*

★ **Castel Sant'Elmo**
The patriots of the Parthenopean Republic (see p25) conquered the castle in 1799, but when the revolution was crushed they were imprisoned there ❹

STAR SIGHTS

★ Certosa and Museo Nazionale di San Martino

★ Villa La Floridiana

★ Castel Sant'Elmo

Via Scarlatti ❶

Map 2 D5. 🚇 *Centrale: Piazza Fuga; Chiaia: Via Cimarosa.* 🚌 *V1.*

The most elegant street in Vomero is lined with tall plane trees and descends from Piazza Vanvitelli towards Via Cilea. Now closed to traffic, Via Scarlatti is the perfect place for a pleasant walk interrupted by the odd break for shopping. If you lift your gaze above the line of shops you will note the striking contrast between the 19th-century buildings and those constructed in the last 30 years in the wave of property development that has radically altered the face of Vomero.

Villa La Floridiana ❷

Via Domenico Cimarosa 77, Via Aniello Falcone. **Map** 2 C5. **Tel** *081 578 84 18.* 🚌 *C28, V1.* 🚇 *Centrale: Piazza Fuga; Chiaia: Via Cimarosa.* **Park** ⚪ *9am–1 hr before sunset daily.* **Villa** ⚪ *8:30am–4pm daily.*

In 1817 Ferdinand I acquired an estate on the Vomero hill as a present for his second wife Lucia Migliaccio, the Duchess of Floridia, whom he had married shortly after the death of Maria Carolina of Austria. The estate, which was named La Floridiana in honour of the duchess, included a park with a magnificent view

Looking across the Floridiana park

of the city. There were two buildings on the property. The Villa La Floridiana was rebuilt as a summer residence in the Neo-Classical style by Antonio Niccolini in 1817–19. It now houses the Duca di Martina Ceramics Museum *(see below).* There was also a "Pompeiian" coffee-house, later called Villa Lucia, also designed by Niccolini, which became private property.

The Italian government purchased the Villa La Floridiana in 1919.

Museo Nazionale della Ceramica Duca di Martina ❸

Villa Floridiana, Via Domenico Cimarosa 77, Via Aniello Falcone 171. **Map** 2 C5. **Tel** *081 229 21 10.* 🚇 *Centrale: Piazza Fuga; Chiaia: Via Cimarosa.* 🚌 *C28, V1.* 🕐 *8:30am–1:15pm Wed–Mon.* 🚫 💷 🚻

Placido de Sangro, the Duke of Martina and member of an illustrious noble family, was an avid, passionate collector of decorative art objects, especially porcelain and ceramics. When he died in 1891, his valuable collection of about 6,000 pieces was inherited by his grandson Placido, who donated them to the city of Naples in 1911.

Since the mid-1920s Villa La Floridiana has been the home of the Duca di Martina National Ceramics Museum, where curators aim to reproduce as closely as possible the arrangement and spirit of the collections in the De Sangro residence. The pleasant and unusual atmosphere of a home-cum-museum has remained unchanged, despite additions and later donations.

The porcelain pieces come from the most important Italian and other

Interior of the Duca di Martina ceramics museum

European factories, while the collection of Oriental art – consisting mostly of 18th- and 19th-century porcelain – is one of the best in Italy.

The museum also contains 15th-century ivory pieces, majolica, Limoges enamel, leather and tortoiseshell objects and drawings by 17th- and 18th-century Neapolitan artists, including Solimena, Giordano and De Matteis.

Castel Sant'Elmo ❹

Via Tito Angelini. **Map** 2 E5. **Tel** *081 578 40 30.* 🚌 *V1.* 🚇 *Montesanto: Via Morghen.* ⚪ *8:30am–6:30pm Thu–Tue.* ⚫ *Mon.* 🚫 📷 🚻 *partial.*

In the 1330s the Angevin rulers instigated a flurry of building on the Vomero hill west of Naples – the construction of the Certosa di San Martino and the enlargement and reconstruction of the nearby fortified residence of Belforte, which had been inhabited by Charles I of Anjou's family since 1275.

In the 16th century Pedro Scriba, a leading military architect of the time, completely transformed the 14th-century castle into its present six-pointed star configuration.

Because of its strategic position, Castel Sant'Elmo under viceroy Pedro de Toledo became the focal point of the new defence system for Naples. For centuries it was used as a prison; among its illustrious "guests" were the great Renaissance philosopher Tommaso Campanella, the 1799 revolutionaries and patriots involved in the 19th-century Risorgimento.

The entrance bears Charles V's coat of arms and a fine epigraph. The complex, which also contains a large lecture hall, has been the venue for temporary exhibitions and cultural events since 1988. From the castle walls there is a spectacular 360-degree view of Naples and the bay.

Castel Sant'Elmo on the top of Vomero hill

Certosa di San Martino ❺

See pp108–11.

Pedamentina ❻

Map 2 F5. 🚇 *Montesanto: Via Morghen, Corso Vittorio Emanuele.* 🚠 *C16, V1.*

The steps connecting Castel Sant'Elmo and the city sprawling below still make for a delightful walk "descending towards the sea amidst the green slopes", as old guidebooks put it, even though the landscape has changed considerably in the meantime. Descent being easier than ascent, you may choose to go down rather than climb the 414 steps from San Martino to Corso Vittorio Emanuele and take in the glimpses of beautiful panoramic views that change at every stage. The route downwards passes by dilapidated buildings and slum housing, but the views of the bay are very rewarding.

Via Luigia Sanfelice ❼

Map 2 D5 & 2 E5. 🚇 *Centrale: Piazza Fuga; Chiaia: Via Cimarosa.*

Should you ask for the "Santarella", people will point to Via Luigia Sanfelice. The key to this riddle lies in a curve in the road where there is a villa with a curious nameplate: "Qui rido io" (this is where I laugh). This was the home, built in 1909, of the well-known Neapolitan author and comic actor Eduardo Scarpetta (the father of Eduardo De Filippo) *(see p37)*, whose best-known work is *Na santarella*. In Via Luigia Sanfelice and nearby Via Filippo Palizzi there are a number of elegant houses which are interesting examples of Neo-Renaissance or Art Nouveau styles.

Nameplate at the villa of comic actor and author Eduardo Scarpetta

---

FROM THE "FERROVIA DI DELIZIA" TO THE FUNICULAR RAILWAY

In 1875 the engineers Bruno and Ferraro designed a rail system to take passengers up the Vomero hill along the Chiaia and Montesanto slopes, using two funiculars, connected so that the ascent of one line caused the descent of the other. The "train of delights", as it was called, allowed travellers to admire stupendous views of the bay while crossing the hill, in those days a rural area. The initial scheme gradually evolved into two independent funicular railways which ran through a tunnel, providing a rapid and efficient means of transport between Vomero and the city centre. The Chiaia funicular was opened in 1889, Montesanto in 1891. In order to improve connections with what in the meantime had become the most rapidly expanding district in the city, the Centrale funicular was built in 1928. Centrale was the longest of the three; from its starting point in Via Toledo it reaches a point halfway between the other two. There is also a fourth line, the Mergellina funicular, which connects the seafront with Via Manzoni.

The present-day funicular railway

Certosa di San Martino ❺

Procession
tray

In 1325 Charles Duke of Calabria began construction of what is one of the richest monuments in Naples. The Carthusian monks were forward looking, and from the 16th to the 18th centuries the greatest artists of the time worked at the Certosa (charterhouse) of San Martino. The original look of San Martino was gradually altered by Mannerist and Baroque rebuilding. The most radical redecoration and enlargement was carried out by the architects Giovanni Antonio Dosio, at the end of the 16th century, and Cosimo Fanzago, who took over in 1623. The 17th and 18th centuries brought further changes.

The French deconsecrated the monastery in 1806, and since 1866 it has housed the San Martino museum, with displays of Neapolitan art and history.

Chiostro dei Procuratori
This cloister was built in the late 16th–early 17th century by Giovanni Antonio Dosio.

Nativity section

Historical section

The Prior's garden

★ **Quarto del Priore**
The Prior's Residence was richly decorated and had a splendid panoramic view over the bay of Naples (see p111).

TIMELINE

1300		1600		1800	
1325 Construction begun under Charles of Anjou	**1578** Decoration and enlargement by Dosio and Conforto	**1631–56** Complex rebuilt and redecorated by Cosimo Fanzago		**1807** The last monks forced to leave the monastery	*Chain of the Order of the Two Sicilies*
	1368 Consecration of the church.	**1623** Cosimo Fanzago begins work on the Chiostro Grande	**1799** Monastery damaged during Parthenopean revolution	**1866** The Certosa becomes state property and part of it is turned into a museum	

★ **Church and its Subsidiary Rooms**
Sumptuous Baroque decoration and alterations such as the large round windows in the façade were successfully incorporated into the original Gothic church.

VISITORS' CHECKLIST

Piazzale San Martino 5. **Map** 2 F5. *Tel* 081 558 59 42. Montesanto: Via Morghen. V1. 8:30am–7:30pm Thu–Tue.

Entrance

Central Nave
In 1580 Giovanni Antonio Dosio closed the aisles and built six side chapels. The vaults of the original 14th-century nave are still visible.

★ **Chiostro Grande**
The main cloister, with its 64 marble columns, was designed by Giovanni Antonio Dosio at the end of the 16th century and later remodelled by Cosimo Fanzago. The latter also designed the seven corner marble doors supporting figures of Carthusian saints.

19th-century Neapolitan art

Monks' cemetery

STAR FEATURES

★ Church and its Subsidiary Rooms

★ Chiostro Grande

★ Quarto del Priore

Exploring the Certosa di San Martino and the Museum

From the outset the Carthusian monks intended San Martino to be a storehouse for Neapolitan history and civilization. The collections document the rich and varied forms of artistic expression found in Naples from the 15th to 19th centuries: from paintings to coral jewellery, traditional crib scenes *(presepi)*, porcelain, prints and ivory carvings. There is also a fascinating collection of maps. Other parts of the museum are devoted to Neapolitan costumes, festivals and theatre. The minor arts section contains an interesting collection of glass from Venice and other European sources. Although a large part of the collections in the San Martino Museum is closed to the public as a result of restoration work, the beauty of the church, the Quarto del Priore (Prior's Residence), the cloisters and the gardens will more than make up for what you miss.

Detail of the inlaid wood panelling in the sacristy (1587–98)

THE CHURCH AND ITS SUBSIDIARY ROOMS

At the end of the 14th century, the prior Severo Turboli set up an elaborate plan for the complete restructuring of the San Martino charterhouse. The original Angevin church was enlarged and modernized and its Gothic structure almost completely disappeared under the multitude of frescoes, stucco-work and marbles produced by leading artists of the time.

The most radical changes to the building were carried out in the 17th century by architect and sculptor Cosimo Fanzago, who worked at San Martino from 1623 to 1656. He designed the interior of the church and its lavish decoration. Coloured marble adorns the nave and chapels, such as in the Cappella di San Bruno. The rooms adjacent to the church are also richly ornamented. In the sacristy the panels of the beautiful inlaid walnut wardrobes contain 56 intarsia scenes with striking perspective effects (16th century). The fresco of *The Triumph of Judith* on the vault of the brightly-lit Cappella del Tesoro was painted by Luca Giordano in 1704.

HISTORICAL SECTION

These interesting rooms dedicated to the history of the Kingdom of Naples are temporarily closed to the public. Paintings, furnishings, sculptures, medallions, arms and memorabilia recreate the key moments in the political, social and cultural history of Naples, from the Aragonese to the Bourbon dynasties. The importance of this valuable collection is exemplified in two famous works that combine historical and artistic

Statue of Charles III of Spain (1754)

The Cappella di San Bruno, designed by Cosimo Fanzago (1631)

For hotels and restaurants in this area see pp179–80 and p194

documentary significance:
The Revolt of Masaniello (see pp22–3), painted in 1647, and *Piazza del Mercatello during the 1656 Plague*, both painted by Micco Spadaro. These dramatic compositions tell the story of two important events in the history of 17th-century Naples. They are also an accurate and useful representation of what the city looked like at that time.

THE NATIVITY SCENES

Only towards the end of the 19th century did the *presepe* or nativity scene start to be considered an artistic genre in its own right, worthy of a museum. This section of the San Martino museum has one of the most important public collections of its kind, with displays of entire nativity scenes as well as individual figures, such as Mary and Joseph, the Three Kings or the shepherds. Animals and accessories, such as the crib, are also displayed.

Among the most important nativity scenes is a creation by the Neapolitan playwright, Michele Cucinello. Many of the

Panorama of Naples Viewed from the Conocchia, by Giacinto Gigante

statuettes were executed by famous Neapolitan artists. *Blind Beggar with Cataracts* (c.1780), in the Perrone Collection *(see p39)*, is by the artist Giuseppe Sanmartino, who sculpted the *Veiled Christ* in the Cappella Sansevero *(see p63)*.

Blind Beggar with Cataracts by Giuseppe Sanmartino

NINETEENTH-CENTURY NEAPOLITAN ART

This collection of paintings and sculpture also displays pieces that are significant from both an artistic and historical standpoint. The collection consists of purchases made

by the Italian government but owes its strength primarily to donations of important private Neapolitan collections.

All the schools of painting that flourished in this area during the 19th century are represented here. A recurring theme was the Campania landscape, a favourite with local artists. The paintings usually depict a serene and beautiful landscape, such as in Giacinto Gigante's *Panorama of Naples Viewed from the Conocchia*. Among the pieces of sculpture, those by Vincenzo Gemito are not to be missed. *Il Malatiello* (The Sick Child) and *Testa della Popolana* (Head of a Peasant Woman) portray the expressive intensity characteristic of this artist's work.

THE QUARTO DEL PRIORE

The prior, the only person who was allowed contact with the outside world, governed the life of the monastery from his apartments. This was a fabulous residence, rich with artistic treasures and opening onto lush gardens overlooking Naples and the sea.

Built in the 17th century and enlarged the following century, the luxurious quarters have undergone scrupulous restoration. Originally, this part of the complex was used to exhibit the rich art collection of the Carthusian monks. Following the restoration, an attempt

Triptych by Jean Burdichon (c.1414) in the art gallery of the Quarto del Priore

has been made to recreate the Quarto del Priore as it was when inhabited by the prior, with paintings, sculpture, fabric and furniture adorning the rooms.

The art collection and high-quality furnishings reflect the refinement and great artistic sensitivity of the Carthusian monks as well as their ability to keep abreast of the latest artistic and architectural developments.

With its stunning decor, works of art and sculpture and spectacular panoramic views over the city, the Quarto del Priore is one of the highlights of a visit to the Certosa di San Martino.

The Borgo Marinaro and Castel dell[...]

SIGHTS AT A GLANCE

CASTEL DELL'OVO AND CHIAIA

The Chiaia area grew to its present extent in the 19th century, although there had been buildings along the seafront outside the city walls since the 16th century. In the late 18th century the construction of the Villa Reale (now called the Villa Comunale) along the Riviera di Chiaia changed the face of this part of Naples.

In the meantime, the city was becoming popular with tourists: 8,000 per year were reported by 1838, which is a significant number of

Decorative detail in the Stazione Zoologica

visitors for that time. In the second half of the 19th century, the development of the Amedeo quarter and the elegant streets that radiate from Piazza Amedeo made this the favourite residential area of the upper middle class. The Chiaia area also bears traces of the distant past: Castel dell'Ovo, the fortress jutting into the sea in front of Santa Lucia, and the oldest castle in Naples, and the Parco Virgiliano in Mergellina, said to be the place where the Roman poet Virgil was buried.

GETTING THERE

The fastest way to get to this area is by metro (Mergellina station for Mergellina and the seafront area; Piazza Amedeo station for the Chiaia area). The funicular from the Parco Margarita station takes you from Chiaia to Vomero, while the Mergellina funicular takes you from Mergellina to Via Manzoni. The R3 bus route, tram 1 and bus 140 run along the Riviera di Chiaia and skirt the Villa Comunale. The circular bus routes C24, C25 and C28 link the whole area.

KEY

Street-by-Street map
See pp114–5

Ⓜ Metro station

⛴ Ferry port

🚟 Funicular

Street-by-Street: Lungomare

Besides being a pleasant way of spending the time, walking along the seafront is a tradition handed down over generations of Neapolitans. However, the sea is not just something to look at here: in the summer, despite the many "no bathing" signs, it is filled with bathers and every day of the year huge quantities of fish are sold on the seafront and in Mergellina, and served in the many neighbouring restaurants. At the Villa Comunale you can combine a walk in the park with a visit to Europe's oldest aquarium. Nearby Villa Pignatelli has stupendous rooms with 19th-century furnishing and decoration.

San Pasquale was built for Charles III in 1749, on the occasion of the birth of his first son.

Villa Comunale
The kiosk, known as the Cassa Armonica or sound box, was built in the gardens during the 19th-century restoration of the villa **5**

Palazzo Pignatelli

VIA RIVIERA DI CHIAIA

VIA FRANCESCO CARACC

Stazione Zoologica
This aquarium was founded in 1872 as a centre for marine studies **6**

Santa Maria in Portico
The church is built on a Latin cross plan with one nave and its dome is covered with multi-coloured tiles **8**

KEY

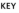 Suggested route

0 metres	200
0 yards	200

★ Villa Pignatelli
Originally called Villa Acton, this house was modelled on an ancient Pompeiian design, with the side facing the sea consisting of a loggia supported by Doric columns **7**

For hotels and restaurants in this area see pp180–81 and pp194–5

Santa Lucia
*There are shrines all
over Naples, such as this
one in Via Santa Lucia,
dedicated to St Lucy* ❶

LOCATOR MAP
See Street Finder, maps 5–7

Borgo Marinaro is a
characteristically lively
place to wander around,
with its small harbour,
cafés and trattorias.

Piazza dei Martiri
*The lovely façade of Palazzo
Calabritto enlivens this
popular square* ❹

★ Castel dell'Ovo
*The unmistakable
bulk of the castle
dominates the
surrounding area* ❷

STAR SIGHTS
★ Castel dell'Ovo
★ Lungomare
★ Villa Pignatelli

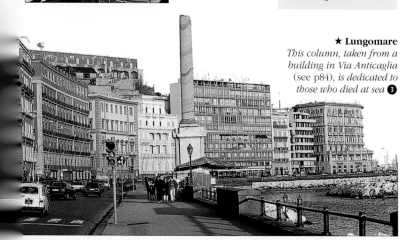

★ Lungomare
*This column, taken from a
building in Via Anticaglia
(see p84), is dedicated to
those who died at sea* ❸

Santa Lucia ➊

Map 7 A4. 🚌 C25, 140.

One of the most famous streets in Naples, Santa Lucia exemplifies the city's striking contrasts. Luxury hotels that were built for the elite in the 19th century and imposing buildings for the regional government rub shoulders with the Pallonetto di Santa Lucia slum area where the poor eke out a living. This quarter is named after the church at the beginning of the street, Santa Lucia a Mare, whose history goes back to the 9th century. It has been rebuilt several times. Before you reach the seafront, on the right, you will see the tall rocky face of the hill of Pizzo-falcone, the site of the oldest part of Naples *(see p59)*.

Castel dell'Ovo with its tall tufa curtain walls

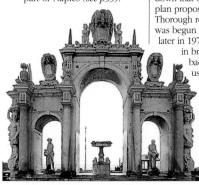

The Immacolatella Fountain

Castel dell'Ovo ➋

Borgo Marinaro. **Map** 7 A5. *Tel 081 41 50 02.* 🚌 C25, 140. 🕐 8:30am–7pm Mon–Sat; 8:30am–2pm Sun.

The oldest castle in Naples is built on the islet of Megaris, once the site of a villa owned by the Roman patrician Lucullus. Later, in the 5th century, a community of monks founded the San Salvatore monastery, the only remaining part of which is the church. The oldest part of the castle dates from the 9th century. Under the Norman, Hohenstaufen, Angevin and Aragonese rulers, the castle underwent continuous changes according to the requirements of each dynasty. The present

appearance is the result of the rebuilding carried out after 1503, the year the fortress was almost destroyed during a siege by Ferdinand II of Spain.

Despite the rebuilding, there followed a period of decline that lasted until 1871, at which point the castle was so run-down that one urban renewal plan proposed its demolition. Thorough restoration work was begun just over a century later in 1975, and succeeded in bringing the site back to life. It is now used for cultural events. Around the castle is the pic-turesque Borgo Marinaro quarter, built at the end of the 19th century for the fishermen of Santa Lucia. It is a popular place with visitors because of its restaurants, cafés and lively atmosphere.

Lungomare ➌

Map 5 & 6.
🚌 C25, 140.

A walk along the road skirting the coast from Santa Lucia to Mergellina is another experience you must not miss while in Naples. The view of the city and the bay is breathtaking. The first stretch of the seafront – which corresponds to Via Nazario Sauro and Via Partenope – was built in the 19th century, as a result of reclamation along Via Santa Lucia and Via Chiatamone. The two ends of this long and pleasant seafront promenade are marked by two beautiful 17th-century fountains: the Immacolatella, which was built by Michelangelo Naccherino and Pietro Bernini in 1601, and the Sebeto fountain, which was the work of Cosimo Fanzago (1635–7).

THE LEGEND OF THE EGG

Opinions vary as to the origin of the curious name given to Castel dell'Ovo, or Castle of the Egg, which first appears in 14th-century documents. One possible explanation is the shape of the castle. However, popular tradition has it that the name derives from a magic egg hidden in the castle which determined its fate and that of the entire city: as long as the egg remained intact, both would be protected from catastrophes. The magic spell was supposed to have been originally cast on the ancient egg by the Latin poet Virgil, who, according to medieval legends, possessed super-natural powers and the gift of divination.

The castle in the 1800s

Piazza dei Martiri ➍

Map 6 F2. 🚌 C25.

The Square of Martyrs is the heart of the "chic" commercial centre of Naples. Its focal point is the Monumento ai Martiri Napoletani designed by Enrico Alvino in 1866–8, with four lions at the base symbolizing the anti-Bourbon uprisings of 1799, 1820, 1848 and 1860. Palazzo Calabritto (No. 30), built by Luigi and Carlo Vanvitelli, dominates the square on the seaward side.

Along the streets that radiate from the square, historic palazzi alternate with elegant shops and cafés. Palazzo Portanna (No. 58), built in the 18th century by Mario Gioffredo, was rebuilt by Antonio Niccolini for Lucia Migliaccio, the morganatic wife of Ferdinand IV. Among the Neo-Renaissance and Liberty style buildings along Via Filangieri and Via dei Mille, Palazzo Mannajuolo (No. 36 Via Filangieri) is worth seeing for its beautiful inner staircase. In nearby Via Poerio and Via San Pasquale are the Lutheran and Anglican churches, founded in 1861–2.

19th-century statue at the Villa entrance

Villa Comunale ➎

Map 6 E2. **Tel** 081 761 11 31. 🚌 C18, C19, C24, C28, R3, 140. 🚋 1. 🕐 7am–10pm Mon–Sat; 7am–midnight Sun & public hols.

The first design for this park area dates from 1697, during the rule of viceroy Luis de la Cerda, but it was Ferdinand IV who, almost a century later, asked architect Carlo Vanvitelli and landscape gardener Felice Abate to lay out the Real Passeggio di Chiaia as a public park.

The Villa Reale, later the Villa Comunale, was completed in 1781, and was enlarged in the following century. Among the pine, monkey puzzle, palm and eucalyptus trees there are 19th- and early 20th-century sculptures and several fountains, including the so-called *Paparelle*, which in 1825 replaced the famous *Farnese Bull* sculpture group, which is now in the Museo Archeologico *(see p86)*. The park, which extends from the Riviera di Chiaia to Via Caracciolo, also boasts the Neo-Classical Stazione Zoologica and the iron and glass kiosk known as the Cassa Armonica, designed in 1877 by Enrico Alvino. Today the park hosts children's activities such as pony riding and bicycle hire.

Façade of the Stazione Zoologica

Stazione Zoologica ➏

Villa Comunale. **Map** 6 E2. **Tel** 081 583 31 11. 🚌 C18, C19, C24, C28, R3, 140. 🚋 1. 🕐 9am–5pm Tue–Sat; 9am–2pm Sun. 📷 ♿

This institute, run by the Consiglio Nazionale delle Ricerche (National Research Council), is one of the oldest and best known of its kind in the world. It was established in 1872–4 by the German scientist Anton Dohrn to study marine environments. The building, which was designed by Adolf von Hildebrandt, was enlarged and remodelled in 1888, 1904 and again in 1957. It contains research labs, a small exhibition and the oldest aquarium in Europe, with specimens from the Bay of Naples. The frescoes depicting marine and rural scenes in the reading room of the library were painted by Hans von Marées in 1873.

The park area of Villa Comunale with the Riviera di Chiaia along the seafront

Museo Diego Aragona Pignatelli Cortes and Museo delle Carrozze in Villa Pignatelli **❼**

Riviera di Chiaia 200. **Map** 6 D2.
Tel 081 761 23 56. C18, C19,
C28, R3, 140. 1. 8:30am–
1:30pm Wed–Mon.

The Neo-Classical villa was built in 1826 by Pietro Valente for the illustrious Acton family. The Rothschilds became the new owners 20 years later and changed the furnishings and interior decoration. Prince Diego Aragona Pignatelli Cortes then purchased the villa, which is named after him, and in 1952 his granddaughter donated it to the Italian state. The loveliest rooms are the red hall in Louis XVI style, the smoking room with leather-lined walls and the ballroom with its large, elegant mirrors and magnificent chandeliers. Villa Pignatelli is often used for temporary exhibitions, concerts and other cultural events. A small building nearby is occupied by the **Museo delle Carrozze** (Carriage Museum), which has an interesting collection of Italian and French coaches dating from the late 1800s to the early 1900s.

The façade of Santa Maria in Portico

Presbytery and apse of the Chiesa dell'Ascensione a Chiaia

Santa Maria in Portico **❽**

Via Giuseppe Martucci 17.
Map 6 D2. *Tel 081 66 92 94.*
C18, C19, C28, R3, 140. 1.
Amedeo. Chiaia: Parco
Margherita. 7–11am,
5–8pm daily.

In 1632 the Duchess of Gravina Felice Maria Orsini donated some of her property to the Padri Lucchesi della Madre di Dio congregation so they could build a monastery and church. The name "in Portico" refers to the Roman church of Santa Maria in Campitelli al Portico d'Ottavia, where the Lucca Fathers came from. For years the façade in piperno was attributed to Cosimo Fanzago, but is now known to be the work of Arcangelo Guglielminelli. The interior is decorated with fine 18th-century canvases and stuccoes by Domenico Antonio Vaccaro, who also designed the high altar. There is a crib with 17th-century figures in the sacristy. A short walk down nearby Via Piscicelli takes you to the **Chiesa dell'Ascensione a Chiaia**, with fine paintings by Luca Giordano. The 14th-century church was rebuilt in the 1600s by Cosimo Fanzago.

Santa Maria di Piedigrotta **❾**

Piazza Piedigrotta 24. **Map** 5 B3.
Tel 081 66 97 61. C16, C24.
1. Mergellina. 7am–noon,
5pm–8pm Mon–Sun.

This church is mentioned in a letter written by Giovanni Boccaccio in Neapolitan dialect in 1339, in which he mentions the "Madonna de Pederotta". Much altered over the years, Santa Maria di Piedigrotta is commonly believed to have been rebuilt in 1353 to replace a church founded in 1207. It was again rebuilt in the mid-1400s and in the early 1500s. The orientation of the church, which had faced the "grotta" (cave), was altered the following century. The present façade is the

Fresco by Belisario Corenzio in Santa Maria di Piedigrotta

result of 19th-century restoration by Enrico Alvino. Gaetano Gigante decorated the vault. Inside is the 15th-century wooden panel *Descent from the Cross*, by an unknown Neapolitan artist.

The church's great popularity is linked to a beautiful 14th-century wooden sculpture of the *Madonna and Child*, made by the Siena School, which dominates the church from a high tabernacle. The worship of the Piedigrotta Madonna culminates in the 7 September feast *(see p42)*. In the past, even the royal family took part in the solemn procession. Worshippers, however, did not appreciate the statue's restoration in 1976 to its original state, because the Virgin's large blue mantle and luminous halo were removed.

Parco Vergiliano ❿

Via Salita Grotta 20. **Map** 5 A2. *Tel 081 66 93 90.* C16, C24. 1. Ⓜ *Mergellina.* 8am–1 hr before sunset.

View of the Parco Virgiliano

Myth, legend, traces of the past and natural beauty are what make this park one of Naples's most intriguing sites. It officially became a park after restoration work in 1930. In 1939 a monument to the poet Giacomo Leopardi was erected, and his remains were transferred here from Recanati, his home town.

The park is famous mostly because, according to legend, the poet Virgil is buried here. However, the so-called Tomb of Virgil is in fact an anonymous Roman funerary monument and has nothing to do with the great poet.

Another legend involving Virgil is that with a single gesture he created the *Crypta Neapolitana*, a tunnel about 700 m (2,300 ft) long; but this too is belied by historical facts: it was built by the Roman architect Cocceius in the 1st century BC to connect Neapolis and Puteoli. In the 1920s the tunnel caved in and is now inaccessible. The entrance, however, with its medieval frescoes and epigraphs, can still be seen from the park.

Mergellina ⓫

Map 5 B4. C16, C21, C24. Ⓜ *Mergellina.*

The fishermen's quarter that developed over the inlet at the foot of Posillipo hill, and was hailed by poets and writers for its beauty, was a popular place for pleasure trips from the Angevin age on. The harmony of the landscape was broken by 19th-century land reclamation that extended the coastline further into the sea. However, Mergellina is still enjoyable to walk around. The numerous cafés, called *chalet* by the locals, offer excellent ice cream and fresh fruit.

St Michael and the "Mergellina devil"

Hydrofoil boats for the islands and other destinations in the bay depart from the quays in the harbour.

Santa Maria del Parto ⓬

Via Mergellina 21. **Map** 6 B4. *Tel 081 66 46 27.* C16, C24. 1. Ⓜ *Mergellina.* mornings by appt only.

The history of the church of Santa Maria del Parto is closely linked with the figure and works of Jacopo Sannazaro (1458–1530), the famous Neapolitan humanist and poet in the service of the Angevin court. The church was built in the 1520s, upon the initiative of Sannazaro, on a plot of land donated by Frederick of Aragon and was named after one of the poet's works, *De Partu Virginis*. Behind the high altar is the tomb of the poet himself, a fine marble group sculpted by Giovan Angelo Montorsoli and Francesco del Tadda in 1537, and probably designed by Sannazaro himself. Before leaving, don't forget to look at the "Mergellina devil" depicted in a wooden panel by Leonardo da Pistoia on the right-hand altar. The panel shows St Michael, who has just vanquished the devil – the devil has assumed the guise of a beautiful woman.

The small harbour of Mergellina, filled with fishing boats and pleasure craft

TWO GUIDED WALKS

Naples is a city of contradictions: on the one side there are narrow, labyrinthine streets in the historic centre, full of revving scooters and the pungent aroma from fish stores; on the other there are wide avenues lined with chic shops, frequented by bejewelled ladies in fur coats. These two walks explore both sides of Neapolitan life. The first moves from the military district of Pizzofalcone to the elegant shopping streets of the Chiaia region, offering a complete change of atmosphere with just the short ride down the Ponte di Chiaia lift. The second walk takes you from the Fascist-era buildings of Piazza Matteotti, and then through the Montesanto district and the bustling Pignasecca market with its wide variety of food and clothing stalls crammed in between rows of discount houseware shops and *tripperie* (tripe shops). Day-to-day life is on constant display here – mothers and babies, hawkers and shoppers all mingle on the streets together. Montesanto also skirts a claustrophobic but characteristic grid of tiny streets you might wish to venture into for a true experience of local life, complete with wafting cooking odours and rows of laundry flapping from balconies in the breeze.

Scroll decoration on the Nunziatella façade

CHOOSING A WALK

The Two Walks
This map shows the location of the two guided walks in relation to the main sightseeing areas of Naples.

Grand façade of Palazzo di San Giacomo (*p123*)

Capodimonte and I Vergini

Decumano Maggiore

Spaccanapoli

Vomero

Chiaia
(*p121*)

Toledo and
Castel Nuovo

Castel dell'Ovo
and Chiaia

Montesanto
(*pp122–3*)

0 km   1

0 mile   0.5

KEY

···· Walk route

A 45-Minute Walk through Chiaia

This walk balances hidden architectural gems with elegant window shopping as it winds its way through one of Naples' most glamorous neighbourhoods.

Baroque Naples

Start at Piazza Trieste e Trento ① and head west on Via Chiaia to the lift under the 17th-century Ponte di Chiaia ② *(see p58)*. Take the lift up to Piazza Santa Maria degli Angeli for the church of the same name ③ *(see p58)*. This Baroque church was erected by Francesco Grimaldi in the early 17th century and boasts frescoes by Beinaschi. Head south on Via Monte di Dio and pop into the Palazzo Serra di Cassano ④ *(see p58)*, today the home of the Italian Institute of Philosophical Studies and an example of one of Naples' many hidden architectural treasures, particularly its spectacular staircase. At the end of Via Monte di Dio, turn a short right for the Nunziatella ⑤ *(see p59)*, Italy's famous military academy. Founded in 1787 by Ferdinand IV, the Nunziatella takes its name from the nearby Annunziata, a Baroque church noted for its frescoes and paintings by Francesco de Mura as well as for its 17th-century crypts, the final resting places for the era's Neapolitan nobility.

Walk round the square until you are on back on Via Monte di Dio, turn right and then left onto Via Egiziaca a Pizzofalcone and left again on Via G. Serra, which will bring you back to the lift. Take the lift down again and continue

A view of Via Chiaia seen from the Ponte di Chiaia ②

west on Via Chiaia. Follow the curve of Via Santa Caterina to the church of Santa Maria della Mercede ⑥, built in the 17th century by the Spanish Mercedari fathers. Turn right on Via Filangieri, a street full of chic clothing stores. Gran Caffè Cimmino at No. 12 ⑦ is a good spot for refreshment.

Baroque painter Luca Giordano. Turn left onto Via Bausan, dotted with Spanish restaurants. Turn left onto Via Santa Teresa a Chiaia ⑪ for some window shopping at its high-class boutiques. Pass through Piazza Rodinò ⑫, then head for a bite to eat at the L.U.I.S.E snack bar on Piazza dei Martiri ⑬.

Art and boutiques

Take the stairs on your right where Via Filangieri meets the elegant Via dei Mille, and walk up to Palazzo Cellamare ⑧ *(see p58)*, a Bourbon-era building once known for its royal revelries. Head back down to Via dei Mille and stroll past the Palazzo delle Arti Napoli, the contemporary art museum ⑨, to the church of Santa Teresa a Chiaia ⑩ with its two altarpieces by the

The double staircase in Palazzo Serra di Cassano, decorated with white marble ④

KEY

···· Walk route

Ⓜ Metro station

TIPS FOR WALKERS

Starting point: Piazza Trieste e Trento

Length: 2 km (1 mile)

Getting there: C22, C25, E3, R2, R3 and 201 bus lines stop in front of the Piazza Trieste e Trento

Safety tips: Petty crime is a problem in Naples: leave valuables in your hotel safe and carry cash in a money belt.

A 90-Minute Walk through Montesanto

A visit to Naples would not be complete without a stroll through at least one of its fascinating open-air markets. This walk begins on the wide shopping street Via Toledo and winds its way past the imposing Fascist structures of Piazza Matteotti and through the Pignasecca in the Montesanto district. Though officially a *mercatino* (little market), the Pignasecca is a favourite among Neapolitans. In addition, several atmospheric churches here make for welcome havens from the jostling and haggling crowds.

Fish stall on Pignasecca ⑬

Renaissance to Facism

Start the walk at the Funicolare Centrale ①, then turn left onto Via Toledo *(see p53)* heading northwards. Turn right shortly afterwards onto Via Santa Brigida. The 17th-century church of Santa Brigida ② *(see p56)* will be ahead of you, attached to the north side of Galleria Umberto I *(see p53)*. Its interior, particularly the paintings by Luca Giordano, is its real treasure. Beyond the church turn left, right and then left into Via Vittorio Emanuele III and up to Piazza Municipio. Turn right onto Via Cervantes, home to the Palazzo San Giacomo with its church of San Giacomo degli Spagnoli ③ *(see p56)*, erected in 1540 by Viceroy Pedro of Toledo. The church was built in typical Mannerist style, and behind the main altar stands Giovanni da Nola's magnificent High Renaissance marble monument to the viceroy. The palazzo has been Naples'

municipal headquarters since the Italian Unification in 1861.

Continue along Via Cervantes until you reach Piazza Matteotti ④ and its circle of stark Fascist-era buildings. The Palazzo delle Poste e Telegrafi ⑤ *(see p57)* is the square's main attraction, the monumental curving edifice being an emblem of 1930s rationalist architecture. Take Via C. Battisti to Piazza Carità and the Istituto Nazionale Assicurazioni ⑥, erected in 1938. In front of the building stands the monument dedicated to Salvo d'Acquisto ⑦, the one-time Vice Brigadier of the *carabinieri* (the military arm of the Italian police) and a noted World War II hero. Born in Naples in 1920, d'Acquisto sacrificed himself to the Germans in 1943 in order to save the lives of 22 innocent Italians who were falsely accused of

setting off a bomb that killed two German soldiers.

Art and Architecture

Across Via Toledo, still in Piazza Carità but along Via San Liborio, there are two striking 18th-century buildings, the Palazzo Mastelloni ⑧, with its fine staircase, and Palazzo Trabucco ⑨, both built by Nicolò Tagliacozzi Canale, one of the three architects to renovate the beautiful Certosa of San Martino in

Nave of San Giacomo ③

Imposing Piazza Dante, a popular meeting place ⑯

Vomero *(see pp108–11)* over the course of three centuries. Continue north on Via Toledo until you reach the church of San Nicolà alla Carità ⑩. The highlight here is the nave that features an enormous landscape painted over two centuries by several Neapolitan artists including Francesco Solimena and Alessio d'Elia.

From Via Toledo turn left onto Vico San Nicolà alla Carità and continue until you reach Via Pignasecca. This busy and lively street is a great place to watch animated Neapolitans' haggle for goods. Stop for tasty,

mostly fried snacks at Friggitoria Florenzano ⑪, then continue to the bustling Pignasecca *mercatino* in Piazza Pignasecca ⑫. Take the left fork onto Via Portamedina. On the right is the Ospedale Pelligrini, the courtyard of which hides the

Wide thoroughfare of Via Toledo

church of SS Trinità dei Pellegrini ⑬, built in the 16th century for religious pilgrims. Via Portamedina ends at Piazza Montesanto where the church of Santa Maria di Montesanto ⑭ stands.

From the church, follow Via Montesanto and turn left onto Vico Spezzano. Turn right and walk along to the impressive Palazzo Spinelli di Tarsia ⑮, one of

Naples' largest and finest noble residential complexes. It was built by the architect Domenico Antonio Vaccaro for the aristocratic Spinelli family in the 1700s.

Lively piazzas

Head down Via Tarsia and turn left to Piazza Dante ⑯ *(see p85)* and the church of San Michele Arcangelo ⑰. This church is considered a jewel of 18th-century late Baroque Neapolitan architecture and is another work by Vaccaro. Piazza Dante has been pedestrianized since its days as a car park and now serves as a general meeting point for students, a rest spot for elderly Neapolitans, and an unofficial football arena for the young. Pause for a fine lunch at Trattoria 53 ⑱ situated on the square.

After lunch leave Piazza Dante by the north end and follow the road round to the right to Port'Alba and spend an hour or so at this pedestrianized lane lined with bookshops and outdoor book stalls. The walk ends at Piazza Bellini ⑲ *(see p78)*, an ideal spot for a refreshing apéritif. Return to Piazza Dante where the metro will take you to your next point of interest.

KEY

···· Walk route

Ⓜ Metro station

🚠 Funicular

0 metres 200
0 yards 200

PIAZZA MATTEOTTI ④
DIAZ
VIA CERVANTES DE SAAVEDRA
VIA MEDINA
VIA S. BARTOLOMEO
PIAZZA MUNICIPIO ③
VIA G. ②
VERDI
VIA S. CARLO
V. VITTORIO EMANUELE III

Impressive double staircase of Palazzo Mastelloni ⑧

TWO TRIPS AROUND POSILLIPO

The peninsula that juts into the sea, separating the Bay of Naples from Pozzuoli, was called *Pausilypon* ("respite from pain") by the ancient Greeks, because of the great beauty of the site. As can be seen by the many ruins along the coast, in Roman times a huge settlement grew up along the westernmost edge of what is now called Posillipo, and was connected to the neighbouring Phlegraean Fields (*see pp136–9*). Posillipo was occupied by religious communities and suburban villages during the Middle Ages, and became the favourite holiday resort of the Spanish aristocracy in the 17th century, when

Sant'Antonio campanile

luxurious seaside villas and aristocratic palaces were built here. In the following century, the area began to decline, and it was only in the early 19th century that it regained its former popularity. This was partly as a result of improved access, thanks to the new coastal road opened in 1812 by Joachim Murat, ruler of Naples from 1806. However, from the 1950s on (during the era when Achille Lauro, *see pp28–9*, was mayor of Naples), the upper part of the hill between Via Orazio, Via Petrarca and Via Manzoni was overtaken by unregulated, unscrupulous property development that has sadly ruined an area of unsurpassed scenic and historic beauty.

GETTING AROUND

The best way to take in the fascination and beauty of the Posillipo coast is by boat; however, excursions can only be made in the summer (for information: **Ascultur Campania**, Via F Galiani 20, **Tel** *081 557 35 95*). Other-wise take bus 140 down Via Posillipo and Via Santo Strato and then walk towards the sea along Via Ferdinando Russo and Via Marechiaro.

SIGHTS AT A GLANCE

Capo Posillipo ③
Marechiaro ④
Palazzo Donn'Anna ①
Parco Virgiliano ⑥
Santa Maria del Faro ⑤
World War I Memorial ②

Naples

Nisida

KEY

• • • Land trip (*pp126–7*)

• • • Sea trip (*pp128–9*)

0 metres 500

0 yards 500

ISOLA LA GAIOLA

◁ **View of the rocky Posillipo coastline**

Posillipo by Land

If you decide to explore Posillipo by land, bear in mind that the complete itinerary shown here would make a very long walk. The best way to get around is, in the following order, by scooter, taxi (you are advised to agree on the fare beforehand), Citysightseeing Napoli tour bus *(see p224)*, bus (routes 140, C27 and C31) or, least popular because of traffic and parking problems, a rented car. Many of the old villas, which are now privately owned, are hidden from view and only a few of them can be seen from the road. However, the views are stupendous and the routes down to Capo Posillipo and Marechiaro, though demanding, are very rewarding.

Palazzo Donn'Anna ①

Palazzo Donn'Anna on the seafront

In 1637 the Spanish viceroy Ramiro Guzman, Duke of Medina, married the Neapolitan princess Anna Carafa. To celebrate, Don Ramiro asked the architect Cosimo Fanzago to build the large Palazzo Donn'Anna at the water's edge. Construction began in 1642, but the building was never completed and was never used by the couple. The viceroy returned to Spain in 1644 and Donn'Anna died soon after.

The palazzo was damaged during the 1647 uprising and again as a result of the 1688 earthquake. It was partly restored in the early 1700s but decades later it was still being described in tourist guides as a building in a state of total neglect.

Its air of mystery gave rise to the rumour that in its past the palace had been used by Queen Joan II for secret assignations with her lovers. Popular belief has it that after these men had served their purpose, they were thrown into the sea below the palace.

Palazzo Donn'Anna suffered further damage in the early 19th century when part of the façade was demolished to build the Via Posillipo. In 1870 attempts were made to turn it into a hotel, but the idea was abandoned.

Despite its tormented history and the damage wrought by time and neglect, the massive tufa palace with its cavernous vaults is still majestic, and one of the city's celebrated sights.

World War I Memorial ②

From Piazza San Luigi you can see how property development has spoilt the view of the hill. Beyond the piazza stands the Ara Votiva or War Memorial, situated in a small park. The middle of the park is dominated by the large Egyptian-style mausoleum that Matteo Schilizzi began building in 1883 as a tomb for his brother Marco. This impressive monument was purchased and finished in 1923 by the Naples city council, in order to house the remains of soldiers who had died in World War I.

Capo Posillipo ③

After Piazza Salvatore di Giacomo, a square with a small garden in the middle, go down Via Ferdinando Russo towards the bay of Capo Posillipo and Villa Volpicelli. The villa, first built in the 17th century, was rebuilt in the 19th century by Raffaele Volpicelli and gives the impression of a castle floating on the sea.

The Neapolitans call the area around the Villa Volpicelli the Riva Fiorita, or flowered shore. In summer the little harbour, the beach and the cliff area opposite hum with life. Cafés and the famous restaurant Giuseppone a Mare *(see p194)* lend atmosphere to this area at all times of the year. To reach the fishing village of Marechiaro, take the road that curves down to the left.

The 17th-century Villa Volpicelli, built on the water's edge

For hotels and restaurants in this area see p181 and p195

The Bay of Naples viewed from Posillipo in a 1920s photograph

Marechiaro ④

A famous Neapolitan song says that this coastline is so romantic, even the fish make love in the moonlight. Going down Via Marechiaro by day, you will see elegant villas surrounded by greenery and beautiful panoramic views of the countryside.

Towards the sea is a small square with the remains of a Roman column from the so-called Temple of Fortune. Further down, in the pretty fishing village of Marechiaro, there are bars, cafés, restaurants and bathing facilities. The village has been made famous by a song of the same name by Salvatore di Giacomo.

Santa Maria del Faro ⑤

This church, recorded in documents as far back as the 1300s, was probably built over the remains of an ancient Roman lighthouse (*faro* in Italian). It was restored by Sanfelice in the 18th century but the façade dates from the 19th

Santa Maria del Faro

century. From here you can walk down the Calata del Ponticello, which brings you close to the sea.

Parco di Posillipo ⑥

After going back up Via Marechiaro along Via Boccaccio, you will arrive at the beautifully planted Parco di Posillipo, which is also known as Parco Virgiliano or Parco della Rimembranza. It occupies the top of the hill overlooking the sea and offers a spectacular view from the Bay of Naples to Mount Vesuvius and the Sorrento peninsula on one side, and the Bay of Pozzuoli and the Phlegraean Fields on the other. Below are the island of Nisida, formed from an ancient volcanic crater, and the remains of the now-restored ILVA steelworks. At sunset, the views towards Ischia are stunning.

THE VILLAS OF POSILLIPO

The northern stretch of Via Posillipo is dominated by **Villa Doria D'Angri**, built in 1833 by Bartolomeo Grasso for Prince D'Angri and now the Istituto Santa Dorotea. Further down, on the seaward side, is 17th-century **Villa Quercia**, painted a typically

Villa Rosebery, now state property

Pompeiian red. A hunting lodge built by the Duke of Frisio in the 1700s was bought at the end of the 19th century by Count **Pavoncelli**, who gave the villa at No. 43 his name. **Villa Grottamarina** (No. 33) was the home of Maria Anna, sister of King Philip IV of Spain, in the 1630s. The French engineer Alfredo Cottreau built the **Villa Cottreau** (No. 35) in the late 1800s; several wings on different levels descend towards the sea. Pompeiian red is again the colour of the **Villa Bracale** (No. 37), whose original 17th-century structure is almost unrecognizable today. The pagoda-shaped **Villa Roccaromana** (No. 38a) was built in 1814 for Prince Caracciolo. **Villa d'Abro** (No. 46) was named after the nobleman Aslan d'Abro, who bought it in 1870 and had it restored in Neo-Romantic style. Beyond Capo Posillipo is **Villa Rosebery** (No. 26 Via Russo), the Neapolitan residence of the President of the Italian Republic. It was here, on 9 May 1946, that King Vittorio Emanuele II abdicated and the crown passed to his son Umberto. At No. 27 Via Russo is the 17th-century **Villa Emma**, the summer residence of the German painter Jakob Philipp Hackert who depicted the excavations of Pompeii. Fringed palms give a tropical feel to the **Villa Gallotta**, built close to the water's edge.

Villa Gallotta

Viewing Posillipo from the Sea

From the sea, Naples and the bay can be viewed in all their splendour. To the west of the city, from Castel dell'Ovo north to Nisida and beyond, as far as the Phlegraean Fields, the coast is dotted with grottoes and inlets. Beyond Capo Posillipo you can see the fishing village of Marechiaro, Roman ruins, and the small islands of Gaiola and Nisida. Bars and bathing beaches lure visitors here in summer. In winter the dramatic coastline can still be admired from a hydrofoil or ferry on an excursion to Procida and Ischia *(see pp170–73)*.

Neapolitan *gozzo* boat

Cala di Trentaremi
The tufa cliffs of Cala di Trentaremi are reflected in the sea, which gleams blue and green. This cove is particularly sheltered and is a favourite with bathers.

Nisida
The ancients called this place Nesis, or little island. It was here that Brutus and Cassius, in the former's villa, plotted to kill Caesar in 44 BC. The Angevin building that dominates the island became a prison under the Bourbons.

← Nisida

Punta Pennata

Harbour of Gaiola

Posillipo Park
A well-equipped sports centre is one of the attractions in the park of Posillipo, on the Coroglio summit.

Gaiola
The presence of ruined ancient buildings between the tufa island of Gaiola and the village of Marechiaro has led scholars to suggest that a complete Roman city once existed here.

Marechiaro

The original name for the water by this fishing village was Mare planum (calm sea), which was translated literally in Italian as "Marepiano". With usage it became "Marechiaro", the name now used for the area as a whole. At weekends Neapolitans love to come and eat out here (see p194).

DIRECTORY

Bagno Elena
Via Posillipo 14.
Tel 081 575 50 58.

Bagno Ideal
Via Posillipo 18.
Tel 081 575 36 17.

Bagno Sirena
Via Posillipo 357.
Tel 081 575 12 55.

Bagno Rocce Verdi
Via Posillipo 68.
Tel 335 602 96 00.

Bagno Marechiaro
Discesa Marechiaro.
Tel 081 769 12 15.

Marinella Beach, with its parks and lido, is one of the area's most popular resorts.

Church of Santa Maria del Faro

Palazzo degli Spiriti
The remains of the "palace of the spirits" are visible only from the sea. This name was given to the three-storey Roman ruins because of their mysterious appearance.

SWIMMING AND RELAXING

If sightseeing in Naples in midsummer becomes too much, take a break at one of the *stabilimenti balneari* (bathing spots) along the Posillipo coast. Rent a deckchair and an umbrella and swim in the sea or the pool provided. Neapolitans started the habit in the 19th century at the **Bagno Elena**, first opened 150 years ago. A short distance away are the **Bagno Ideal** and the **Bagno Sirena.** For those who prefer cliffs to sand, there are the **Bagno Rocce Verdi**, with two seawater pools, and **Bagno Marechiaro** *(see p188)*, with its restaurant overlooking the waters of the bay.

The rocks at Posillipo

The picturesque village of Atrani, Amalfi Coast ▷

POMPEII & THE AMALFI COAST

POMPEII & THE AMALFI COAST

To the north of Naples, fertile plains sweep down to the town of Santa Maria Capua Vetere, home to one of the largest remaining Roman amphitheatres in Italy. The remote hinterland to the east is wild, mountainous and lonely country. To the south is the breathtaking Amalfi coast and the dramatic seaboard of the Cilento. Buried Roman towns and Greek ruins reveal the region's ancient history.

From the 17th century onwards Naples was an increasingly crowded and often tormented metropolis. By contrast, the countryside around the city managed to retain its charm and attracted visitors, especially foreigners, many of whom made Campania their home. "A brief sojourn in Naples", the German historian Gregorovius wrote in the mid-1800s, "is enough to demonstrate that not all life is concentrated in the city but flows mightily into the surroundings".

Today, a visit to Pompeii, buried by an erupting Vesuvius in AD 79, is a high priority for tourists, but this was not always so. Travellers on the Grand Tour in the 1600s and early 1700s preferred the volcanic phenomena of the Solfatara crater and the Phlegraean Fields to the west of Naples. Even in the late 18th century Goethe described the area around Paestum, southeast of Naples, as "anything but picturesque", populated by "buffaloes that look like hippopotami, with wild, bloodshot eyes". Only when the first archaeological digs unearthed the remains of Paestum and the buried cities around Mount Vesuvius, did a tour of the ancient ruins become popular.

The beautiful colour, light and atmosphere found on the islands of Capri and Ischia, and the Sorrento peninsula began to interest landscape painters in the 19th century. The southern flank of the peninsula – the Amalfi coast – remained isolated, and regarded by many as barren, until the mid-1960s, when it attracted visitors in search of an alternative, remote lifestyle. Ironically, the Amalfi coast has since become a very popular holiday area.

Paestum, south of Naples; in the background are the temples of Neptune and Hera

◁ The fishing harbour of Corricella on the island of Procida

Exploring the Coast

The main centre from which to explore Campania is Naples itself, well situated in the middle of the bay. Road and rail links are generally good in the region, with both state railways (FS) and privately run lines serving a variety of destinations. The Circumvesuviana railway connects all the sights in the area of Vesuvius, including Pompeii. The islands in the bay are accessible by hydrofoil (half an hour) or ferry (one hour) from Mergellina and Beverello. Services also run from Sorrento, Positano, Amalfi and Salerno.

Castello Aragonese in Ischia

SIGHTS AT A GLANCE

KEY

▬▬	Motorway
▬▬	Major road
▬▬	Secondary road
▭▭▭	Minor road
▬▬	Scenic road
▬▬	Main railway
──	Minor railway
▲	Summit

0 kilometres   20

0 miles   20

SEE ALSO

• **Where to Stay** pp181–7

• **Where to Eat** pp196–201

• **Shopping in Campania** pp208–9

View of the Phlegraean Fields at Cuma

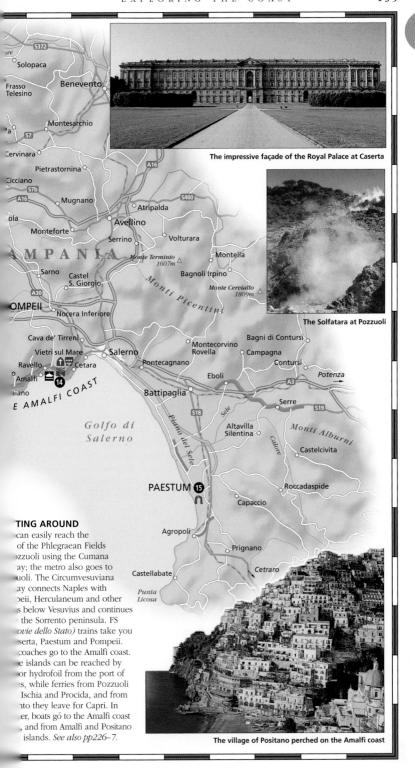

The impressive façade of the Royal Palace at Caserta

The Solfatara at Pozzuoli

TING AROUND

can easily reach the
of the Phlegraean Fields
ozzuoli using the Cumana
ay; the metro also goes to
uoli. The Circumvesuviana
ay connects Naples with
peii, Herculaneum and other
s below Vesuvius and continues
the Sorrento peninsula. FS
ovie dello Stato) trains take you
serta, Paestum and Pompeii.
coaches go to the Amalfi coast.
e islands can be reached by
or hydrofoil from the port of
s, while ferries from Pozzuoli
Ischia and Procida, and from
nto they leave for Capri. In
er, boats go to the Amalfi coast
, and from Amalfi and Positano
islands. *See also pp226–7.*

The village of Positano perched on the Amalfi coast

Bagnoli ❶

Road map C3. 🚌 C1, F9. 🚉
Cavalleggeri Aosta. 🚇 *Cumana: Bagnoli.*

The area west of Naples, beyond Posillipo, is called "de' Bagnoli" because of the fumaroles and hot springs there. In 1907 the ILVA steelworks was built here *(see pp26–7)*, blighting a beautiful natural setting. The factory has since been closed down. Today part of the site is taken up with the **Città della Scienza** (Science City), first opened in 1996. A series of itineraries features education through games involving science, aimed at both children and adults.

🏛 Città della Scienza
Via Coroglio 104. **Tel** 081 372 37 28. ◯ 9am–5pm Tue–Sat; 10am–7pm Sun. 🌐
🅿 📷 📹 ♿

Pozzuoli ❷

Road Map C3. 🏛
77,000. ℹ️ *Azienda Autonoma di Soggiorno e Turismo, Via Campi Flegrei 3.* **Tel** 081 526 14 81/24 19; *Largo Matteotti 1.* **Tel** 081 526 66 39. Ⓜ 🚉 *Cumana: Pozzuoli.* ⛴ *to Ischia & Procida.*

The *macellum* at Pozzuoli, commonly known as the Temple of Serapis

The amphitheatre stage entrance

◯ 9am–6pm Sat & Sun. 📷 11am, noon, 4pm & 5pm Sat & Sun; call ahead on 848 800 288 to book. 🌐

Around the 7th century BC, the Greek colony of Dicearchia was founded on this site overlooking the port. By 194 BC Roman Puteoli was a flourishing trade centre with luxurious villas. The town later became the Rione Terra quarter. A Roman temple can still be seen under the San Procolo cathedral. The amphitheatre, one of the most ancient in Italy, shows how important the city of Pozzuoli once was.

⚱ Anfiteatro Grande
Via Terracciano 75. **Tel** 081 526 60 07. ◯ 9am–1 hr before sunset Wed–Mon. 🌐

The amphitheatre had a seating capacity of 40,000. The underground area was used for the caged animals and the equipment to lift them up to the arena, as well as a sophisticated drainage system to collect rainwater.

⚱ Temple of Serapis
Piazza Serapide. **Tel** 081 44 01 66. 🚫 to public but visible from road.

The so-called Temple of Serapis (2nd century AD),

The Anfiteatro Grande at Pozzuoli, with three tiers of seats

The Solfatara in Pozzuoli, known as *Forum Vulcani* in ancient times

actually the *macellum* or food market, is all that remains of the ancient port district.

🦅 Solfatara
Via Solfatara 161.
Tel 081 526 23 41.
⬜ 8:30am–4:30pm daily.🖼

This volcanic crater was an obligatory stop for those making the Grand Tour. It is now dormant, but you can see phenomena created by the still molten underground magma and water seepage: fumaroles and sulphur fumes.

🦅 Riserva degli Astroni Oasi WWF
Bypass (tangenziale; 1 km from Agnano exit). **Tel** 081 588 37 20.
⬜ 9:30am–2pm. 🖼 *holidays & holiday eves; groups by appt.*

This wildlife reserve lies in an extinct crater covered with trees. It was once an Aragonese hunting ground.

Baia and Bacoli ❸

Road Map B3. 🏘 *27,000.*
🚉 *Cumana: Baia, Bacoli.*

Along the coast between Pozzuoli and Capo Miseno there are many places that were well-known in antiquity. Baia boasted sumptuous Roman villas with terraces overlooking the sea, famous therapeutic springs (still in use in the Middle Ages) and an Aragonese castle, now an archaeological museum.

Bacoli lies along the coast and runs into the modern town of Miseno, which developed over the site of the Roman town of Bauli. At the time of the Emperor Augustus the port of Miseno was connected to Lake Miseno in the interior. The port was

The Bath of Mercury at Baia

planned so as to avoid silting from volcanic movement, and replaced Porto Giulio (*see p139*), the headquarters of the Roman navy. The Arco Felice, which in the 1st century AD was the gateway to Cumae (*see pp138–9*), stands on the peninsula protecting the Bay of Pozzuoli.

Beaches and clubs make this area a summer favourite.

⛪ Casino Vanvitelliano del Fusaro
Via Fusaro 162, Baia. *Tel* 081 868 76 35. 🚉 *Cumana: Baia.*
⬜ 10am–1pm Sun.

In 1794 Vanvitelli built a Casino or hunting lodge on an island in Lake Fusaro for Ferdinand IV. This is the only non-volcanic lake in the area.

🏛 Parco Archeologico di Baia
Via Fusaro 35, Baia. **Tel** 081 868 75 92. 🚉 *Cumana: Baia.* ⬜ *9am–1 hr before sunset Tue–Sun.* 🖼

The large domes at this archaeological site were once thought to be temples, but are now known to be the remains of a spa that included baths named after Venus and Mercury and the so-called Temple of Diana.

This monumental complex was built from the late 2nd century–early 1st century BC, on two levels, with terraced land descending to the sea.

The site is now used to exhibit excavation finds from the Phlegraean Fields area.

🏛 Museo Archeologico dei Campi Flegrei
Via Castello, Baia. *Tel* 081 523 37 97. 🚉 *Cumana: Baia.*
⬜ 9am–1 hr before sunset Tue–Sun. 🖼

The Castello di Baia was

View of the city of Baia; in the foreground, the Roman ruins

Hall in the Museo Archeologico

once an Aragonese fortress. It was totally rebuilt in the 1600s. It is now an Archaeological Museum, with finds from the Phlegraean Fields *(Campi Flegrei)*. Also on display are the Roman plaster casts of Greek statues found in Baia. From the northwest tower you can see the reconstructed Sacello degli Augustali, used for worship of the emperor, found near the Forum at Miseno. The zone is now partly under water.

Piscina Mirabilis
Via A Greco, Bacoli. **Tel** 081 523 31 99. 9am–1 hr before sunset, but call ahead to confirm.
This enormous reservoir, divided into five longitudinal sections supported by pillars, collected water brought by Roman aqueduct from the River Serino, then supplied to the fleet stationed at Miseno.

Cento Camerelle
Via Cento Camerelle 165, Bacoli. **Tel** 081 523 31 99. Call ahead to check opening hours.
The tunnels dug out of the tufa contained a series of cisterns placed at different levels. They originally supplied a villa dating back to the Republican era.

The *Piscina Mirabilis* at Bacoli

Cumae ❹

Road map B3. Cumana: Fusaro. from Fusaro (10 mins to Cumae).

Founded in the 8th century BC, probably by Greeks stationed on Ischia, Cumae is one of the oldest colonies of Magna Graecia. A powerful port for centuries, Cumae resisted the Etruscans but succumbed to the Romans in the 3rd century BC and became a Roman colony. A village grew up over the ruins of the upper city in the 5th–6th centuries but was utterly destroyed by the Saracens in 915. The ancient settlement has not yet been completely excavated.

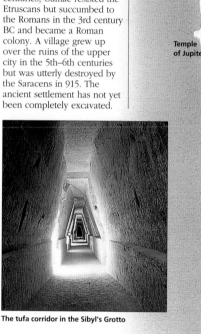

The tufa corridor in the Sibyl's Grotto

The best-known areas are the acropolis on the rise to the northwest and the necropolis in the plain. The acropolis walls, partly rebuilt, and two huge temples are well preserved. The Temple of Apollo lies on the lower terrace, the Temple of Jupiter on the upper one; both were rebuilt in the age of Augustus and the pre-Christian era. At the foot of the acropolis is the entrance to the so-called Sibyl's Grotto.

The lower city, inhabited at a later period, is still being excavated and studied. There is a forum, various baths and an amphitheatre. There are also remains of different epochs: the Samnite age forum conceals the more ancient *agora*, or Greek city centre. In recent years a sanctuary dedicated to Isis,

destroyed with the rise of Christianity, has been discovered in the port area.

Archaeological Park
Via Acropoli. **Tel** 081 854 30 60. 9am–1 hr before sunset.

Temple of Apollo
Most of the finds from the Temple of Apollo date from the Roman era, when a terrace overlooking the city was added on. In the early Christian period the temple was turned into a basilica and burial pits were hewn out of the ancient foundations.

The Sibyl's Grotto
According to myth this was where to find the Cumaean Sibyl, the oracle consulted by Aeneas. The tufa passageway, trapezoid in section, is illuminated by narrow

ARCHAEOLOGICAL PARK

Acropolis

Temple of Jupiter

View of the Archaeological Park, the site of the excavations revealing ancient Cumae

Temple of Jupiter
This ancient sanctuary became an early Christian church and remains of the altar and baptistry are still visible today.

Roman Crypt
The part visible is the last stretch of a long tunnel that begins at Via Sacra and goes through the hill of Cumae.

Map labels:
- Roman crypt
- Temple of Apollo
- Necropolis
- Thermae
- Forum
- Arco Felice
- Sibyl's Grotto
- Tomb of the Sibyl
- Amphitheatre
- To the station

0 metres 500
0 yards 500

THE PHLEGRAEAN LAKES

The wide arc of land around the bay of Pozzuoli has been known for centuries as the Campi Flegrei, or Burning Fields, because of the constant volcanic activity. Mud still bubbles from the clay bed of the Solfatara and in places the ground is still hot. Over time some of the Phlegraean craters have become lakes. **Lake Averno**, in ancient times thought to be the entrance to hell, owes its name (*a-ornon* in Greek: "without birds") to the once-suffocating vapours. At the end of the 1st century BC, its almost sacred character declined after the construction of Porto Giulio, a system of channels that connected the sea and the lakes. Ships first reached the outer port in **Lake Lucrino** and then the inner basin of Lake Averno, connected to Cumae by the tunnel through Monte Grillo. The port was abandoned when it silted up and trade was transferred to Miseno. Lake Lucrino again became a pleasure area. Its extent was greatly reduced by the 1538 eruption that created **Monte Nuovo**.

Lake Averno

fissures and ends in a vaulted chamber. Despite its undoubted fascination, there is no proof of the tunnel ever having had a religious function. It seems more likely that the tunnel was part of a network of underground routes used for military purposes. The complex system includes the Roman crypt and the Grotto of Cocceius, which connected Cumae to Lake Averno.

Portici and the Vesuvian Villas **5**

Road Map C3. 🏛 68,000. ℹ *Ente Ville Vesuviane Napoli, Piazza del Plebiscito.* **Tel** *081 40 53 93.* FS 🚉 *Circumvesuviana: Portici.* 🚌 *city buses.*

The coast east of the city, up to the foot of Mount Vesuvius, has always been dotted with rural estates, owned by the nobility but used for agriculture as much as rural retreats. The luxurious villas now known as the Ville Vesuviane were built in the early 1700s, when the value of land in the area rose because of the interest in the archaeological excavations around the volcano. Prince d'Elboeuf, who discovered Herculaneum in 1709, built a villa here. A few decades later, after the building of the Royal Palace at Portici, these aristocratic villas grew in number, transforming the road between Resina and Torre del Greco into what became known as the **Miglio d'Oro**, or Golden Mile. The presence of the Bourbon palace and the location of these villas, with fine views of, and often access to, the countryside and sea, made this area a favourite resort among the aristocracy. A port was built here in 1773.

Over 100 of the villas are of considerable architectural interest; unfortunately, only a few can be visited. Many are either inhabited or in a state of decay. Some are well worth a stop, if only to see the decorations on the façade or the magnificent gardens that have survived massive urbanization.

⛪ Reggia di Portici
Via Università 100, Portici. **Tel** *081 775 51 09.* ⭘ *by appt.*
The Royal Palace *(reggia)* was built between 1738 and 1742 in the centre of a splendid park at the foothills of Vesuvius and overlooking the sea.

The Royal Palace in Portici

Two villas had occupied the site and a road still crosses the large inner courtyard and continues towards Herculaneum. Originally, finds from the site at Herculaneum and the other archaeological sites in the area were kept in Maria Amalia's

Porcelain Parlour in the palace, but these have since been transferred to the museum at Capodimonte *(see p99)*.

The palace did not have a mooring, so the sovereigns bought the Villa d'Elboeuf for this purpose. Designed by Ferdinando Sanfelice, the villa incorporates some splendid stucco-work and a magnificent circular staircase. The villa was separated from the sea by the Naples-Portici railway *(see p25)* in 1839.

In 1873, the Royal Palace and its park became the home of the Faculty of Agriculture of the University of Naples. It hosts an antiques fair annually in March.

⛪ Villa Campolieto
Corso Resina 283, Ercolano. **Tel** *081 732 21 34.* ⭘ *10am–1pm Tue–Sun.*

Built in 1755–75 first by Gioffredo and then by Vanvitelli, this is the only Vesuvian villa that has been completely restored. A monumental staircase links the ground floor and upper floor. Vanvitelli's elegant portico hosts the Festival delle Ville Vesuviane *(see p41)* each summer, and the villa sometimes stages events.

⛪ Villa Favorita
Corso Resina 291, Ercolano. ⭘ *to the public.*

This villa, set in an extensive park, was designed by Ferdinando Fuga in 1768 as a royal residence. Ferdinand IV decorated it with paintings, silk from San Leucio *(see p165)* and a mosaic removed from the Villa Jovis in Capri *(see p169)*. His son Leopold supervised the layout of the park and stables. The villa was restored in 1854.

⛪ Villa Prota
Via Nazionale 1009, Torre del Greco. ⭘ *to the public.*

This is one of the most spectacular of the Vesuvian villas. Through the large portal, built with balconies and a gateway, you can see the driveway and park. The main wing was built to one side so as not to obstruct the views from the villa.

Vanvitelli's curved portico in Villa Campolieto

Torre Annunziata ❻

Road Map D3. 👥 *51,000.* 🛈 *Pro Loco Ufficio Informazioni Turistiche: Via Sepolcri 16.* **Tel** *081 862 31 63.* 🚉 *Circumvesuviana: Torre Annunziata.*

The town was built over the ruins of ancient Oplontis, which was destroyed in the eruption of Vesuvius in AD 79. Its name derives from a watch-tower *(torre)* built to warn the populace of any imminent Saracen raids, and a chapel consecrated to the Annunziata (the Virgin Mary), around which the town grew up.

In the 18th century Charles III founded an arms factory here, designed by a pupil of Vanvitelli and finished by Ferdinando Fuga. In the late 1700s and early 1800s Torre Annunziata became a centre for pasta production. Towards the sea are the spas, Terme Vesuviane Nunziante, named after the general who discovered the ruins of a Roman baths complex here in 1831. He was responsible for the present-day structure, which is still in operation.

⋔ Oplontis Excavations

Via Sepolcri 1. **Tel** *081 857 53 47.* ⬜ *Apr–Oct: 8:30am–7:30pm daily (last adm 6pm); Nov–Mar: 8:30am–5pm daily (last adm 3:30pm).* 📷

The excavation area includes the villas of Craxus and Poppaea (the latter was Nero's second wife). Brought to light in 1964, the complex reflects the elegant taste of its owners. As well as large gardens and porticoes, the private baths of the house can also be seen, complete with *calidarium* (the hot room) and *tepidarium* (the warm room). Also interesting are the 1st century BC–1st century AD wall paintings. These frescoes depict still lifes or scenes combining architecture and figures, in some cases with illusionistic effects around the doorways or windows. Many amphoras were found in the rooms of the Villa of Craxus, which were used as storerooms or shops.

The harbour at Torre Annunziata

Torre del Greco ❼

Road Map C3. 👥 *104,000.* 🛈 *Via Procida 2a.* **Tel** *081 881 46 76.* 🚉 *Circumvesuviana: Torre del Greco.*

The name derives from a watch-tower built by Frederick II and from the vineyards which produce wine from a grape variety called Greco. Torre del Greco is mainly known for its fine coral manufacture. The old town, rebuilt several times after the various eruptions of Vesuvius, lines the coast, while the newer districts, with villas surrounded by gardens, lie on the slopes of the volcano itself. Don't miss Palazzo Vallelonga in Via Vittorio Emanuele and the Camaldoli alla Torre monastery, both 18th-century buildings. The poet Giacomo Leopardi lived in the Villa delle Ginestre (on a road crossing Via Nazionale) and wrote his last poems there, including *La Ginestra* (The Broom).

The imperial villa of Poppaea Sabina at Torre Annunziata

THE RED GOLD AT TORRE DEL GRECO

By the 15th century the main trade in Torre del Greco was coral fishing. Over the centuries the town became a collection point for coral, as other coastal towns followed suit. The first factories were established by foreigners during the course of the 1800s and the Bourbon rulers then set up their own. Local designs were at first inspired by classical models, and subsequently influenced by the Art Nouveau style. As well as coral, there are mother-of-pearl, turtle shell and ivory pieces. The *coralline* boats that went out to collect the coral have been modernized and re-equipped, but today most of the raw material comes from Japan. Admirers of red gold can visit the numerous workshops *(see pp208–9)* in town or the museum at No. 6 Piazza Palomba.

Carved piece of coral

Mount Vesuvius ❽

Carbonized eggs from Pompeii

In ancient times Vesuvius was simply "the mountain", covered with vegetation and vines. The first person to understand its volcanic nature was the Greek geographer, Strabo (AD 19), who suggested that its rocks had been burned by fire. In AD 79 an almighty eruption smothered the cities on its foothills and greatly altered the surrounding landscape. Ash and debris showered Pompeii, and Herculaneum was buried by a landslide of thick mud. Pliny the Younger recorded the cloud of black smoke that rose "like an umbrella pine" from the mountain. His uncle, Pliny the Elder, was suffocated by the gaseous vapours that engulfed the area. Today, the volcano inspires both fear and fascination and it is constantly monitored for activity.

Layers of ash alternate with lava flow, settle on the sides of the volcano and gradually build up the cone.

Vineyards
The land around volcanoes, rich in alkali and phosphorus, is extremely fertile. On the slopes of Vesuvius, the grapes grown make Lacrima Christi, once considered one of Italy's best wines.

Layers of lava

Magma (molten rock from the earth's mantle) wells upwards and forms a reservoir beneath the earth's surface.

HISTORY OF THE VOLCANO

These sections show the changes in the structure of Vesuvius following the most significant eruptions, from prehistoric times to the formation of the present-day cone.

First eruptions began 35,000 years ago

Further ash and lava flows built up a second cone

8th century BC: Monte Somma is a single cone

After AD 79: Monte Somma is an open caldera

Today's cone, Vesuvius, formed in the old caldera

Vesuvius Observatory
The observatory on the slopes of Vesuvius was built by Ferdinand II in 1841–5. The Neo–Classical building has a well-stocked library and an interesting collection of minerals. There is a splendid panoramic view from the square. Today it is only used as a base for recording data; the research section has been transferred to Naples.

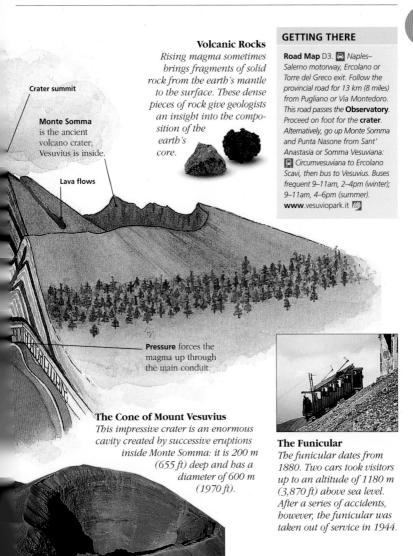

Volcanic Rocks

Rising magma sometimes brings fragments of solid rock from the earth's mantle to the surface. These dense pieces of rock give geologists an insight into the composition of the earth's core.

Crater summit

Monte Somma is the ancient volcano crater; Vesuvius is inside.

Lava flows

Pressure forces the magma up through the main conduit.

GETTING THERE

Road Map D3. *Naples–Salerno motorway, Ercolano or Torre del Greco exit. Follow the provincial road for 13 km (8 miles) from Pugliano or Via Montedoro. This road passes the* **Observatory.** *Proceed on foot for the* **crater.** *Alternatively, go up Monte Somma and Punta Nasone from Sant' Anastasia or Somma Vesuviana: Circumvesuviana to Ercolano Scavi, then bus to Vesuvius. Buses frequent 9–11am, 2–4pm (winter); 9–11am, 4–6pm (summer).* **www**.vesuviopark.it

The Cone of Mount Vesuvius

This impressive crater is an enormous cavity created by successive eruptions inside Monte Somma: it is 200 m (655 ft) deep and has a diameter of 600 m (1970 ft).

The Funicular

The funicular dates from 1880. Two cars took visitors up to an altitude of 1180 m (3,870 ft) above sea level. After a series of accidents, however, the funicular was taken out of service in 1944.

TIMELINE (1600–Present Day)

1694 Another eruption, with lava flow from the crater

1794 Torre del Greco destroyed

1906 Another eruption: the crater widens by 300 m (985 ft)

1933 A series of shocks shows the volcano is active once again. Lava appears on 3 June

1600 — 1700 — 1800 — 1900

1631 On 16 December the lava claims 600 victims. Naples is saved and thanks San Gennaro by building the Guglia in Piazza Sforza *(see p62)*

1767 The lava reaches San Giorgio a Cremano and approaches Naples

1880 The funicular opens to public

1944 After a final violent explosion, the trail of smoke disappears

Herculaneum ❾

Silver disc of Apollo

Ancient Herakleion fell under Greek influence around the 5th century BC and then under Samnite rule. In 89 BC the town became part of the Roman Empire, a residential *municipium* and resort. The town's quiet existence was brought to an abrupt halt in AD 79, when the eruption of Vesuvius that buried Pompeii covered Herculaneum with a deep layer of lava and mud. Excavations began in the 18th century, and uncovered Roman houses built around a rectangular plan. Perhaps the best known is the Villa dei Papiri, the inspiration for the J Paul Getty museum in Malibu, Los Angeles. Sculptures found in the villa are now in the Museo Archeologico Nazionale (*see pp86–9*).

The city baths, built in 10 BC, are divided into two sections. The one for men is larger and decorated, and includes a gymnasium; the women's section is smaller and better preserved.

Decumanus Maximus

★ Trellis House
A characteristic example of an inexpensive Roman multi-family dwelling, the Trellis House has wood and reed laths in the crude tufa and lime masonry.

0 metres   50
0 yards   50

Villa dei Papiri

House with the Mosaic Atrium
This house has a famous mosaic floor with geometric patterns, as well as living rooms, and a portico and terrace facing the sea.

★ House of the Stags
The name derives from the beautiful sculpture groups of stags found here. The house is one of the more elaborate: the inner porticoed garden connects the northern section (entrance, indoor triclinium and smaller rooms) to the southern side, which has bedrooms and an arbour with a sea view.

★ House of the Neptune and Amphitrite Mosaic

This mosaic is in the summer dining room. The building and a shop, with wooden shelves for amphoras, are among the best preserved.

VISITORS' CHECKLIST

Road Map C3. **FS** *Portici-Ercolano.* *Circumvesuviana: Ercolano-Scavi.* **Tel** 081 739 09 63. ☐ Apr–Oct: 8:30am–7:30pm (last adm 6pm); Nov–Mar: 8:30am–5pm (last adm 3:30pm). 📷 **Villa dei Papiri** 📅 Sat & Sun. www.arethusa.net

Entrance

Decumanus Inferiore

House of the Bicentenary

This patrician residence, excavated 200 years after digging began, had mosaic floors and wall paintings.

STAR SIGHTS

★ House of the Neptune and Amphitrite Mosaic

★ House of the Stags

★ Trellis House

The Excavation Area

The site of ancient Herculaneum is well below the level of the modern town. The area is still being excavated. The recently restored Villa dei Papiri contains frescoes, mosaics and the skeleton of a horse. It can be visited on a tour.

The House of Telephus contains a 1st-century BC relief narrating the myth of Achilles and Telephus.

The House of the Gem is named after a cameo portrait from the era of Claudius that was found here.

Pompeii ❿

An earthquake in AD 62, which shook Pompeii and damaged some of its buildings, was merely a prelude to the tragic day in AD 79, when Vesuvius erupted, engulfing the city and its inhabitants with a terrible storm of cinders and ash.

"Samovar" from Pompeii

When the remains of Pompeii were discovered around 1750 it looked as though a spell had been cast to freeze all life. The bodies of people were unearthed along with their houses, temples, works of art and everyday objects. The first archaeologists removed the most important finds, which became part of the royal collection and were then transferred to the Museo Archeologico Nazionale *(see pp86–9).*

The House of the Golden Cupids *(see pp150–51)* is named after the delightful images, reproductions of the originals, in the bedroom.

House of the Faun *(see p150)*

★ House of the Vettii
This is one of the most famous places in Pompeii (see p150). It has rich wall decoration dating from the last Pompeiian period after AD 62. The array of themes includes Daedalus and Pasiphaë, shown here.

The Forum
Originally the market place, the Forum (see p148) became the focus for the most important civic functions, both political and religious.

Temple of Apollo *(see p148)*

Porta Marina entrance

Macellum
The macellum was the covered meat and fish market. Fronted by a portico with two moneychangers' kiosks, it opened onto the Forum near the weights and measures office and the Forum Holitorium vegetable market.

Forum *(see p148)*

Basilica *(see p148)*

Temple of Venus *(see p148)*

STAR SIGHTS

★ House of the Vettii

★ Via dei Sepolcri

Fresco from a Lupanare
Most of the guests at the inn – called hospititium *or* caupona *– were gladiators, as important visitors were put up in private homes. Here and in the* lupanares, *or brothels, paintings and graffiti depict this world and the services offered by waitresses and prostitutes, as well as boys, to satisfy their clients and lovers.*

VISITORS' CHECKLIST

Road Map C3. ⓕⓢ *Pompei-Scavi.* 🚆 *Circumvesuviana: Pompei-Villa dei Misteri.* **Digs:** *Porta Marina, Piazza Esedra, Porta Anfiteatro, Piazza Immacolata.* **Tel** *081 857 53 47.* ⭘ *Apr–Oct: 8:30am–7:30pm (last adm 6pm); Nov–Mar: 8:30am–5pm (last adm 3:30pm).* 🚻 ♿ *check: path is under construction* ℹ *AAST, Via Sacra 1.* **Tel** *081 850 72 55.* www.pompeiisites.org

Modesto's Bakery, where carbonized bread was found, is one of several bakeries in Pompeii with wood-fired ovens and millstones.

The Stabian Baths *(see p149)*, the oldest in the city, had separate sections for men and women.

Plaster Casts
Since 1863, plaster cast techniques have enabled researchers to re-create body shapes. Many were killed by the toxic fumes while engaged in everyday tasks.

Small Theatre *(see p149)*

The Large Theatre *(see p148)* was built in the hollow of a hill for good acoustics.

Gladiators' courtyard and barracks *(see p149)*

THE ARCHEOLOGICAL SITE
The illustration shows the western section of Pompeii. For a map of the entire area see p151.

Triangular Forum *(see p149)*

0 metres		50
0 yards		50

★ Via dei Sepolcri
"Twenty steps wide, 500 long, the entire length still furrowed by the ancient carriage wheels, completely furnished with pavements like ours, and lined throughout, at left and right, with funerary monuments." This is how an awestruck Alexandre Dumas described Via dei Sepolcri, outside the northwest city wall, which was discovered in the first digs.

Exploring Pompeii

Thanks to its strategic position near the Sarno River, Pompeii was a centre of commerce for inland areas. The first town plan (6th century BC) was irregular but, from the 4th century BC on, building developed on a Greek-inspired grid plan. Slabs of old lava from Vesuvius were used to pave the roads. Large villas and houses of different periods and styles, made of brick, stone and cement and often richly decorated, offer an unparalleled view of ancient domestic architecture *(see pp150–51)*. Furthermore, the streets, workshops and public areas are in an excellent state of preservation. Finds such as furnishings, tools, jewellery and even food and drink reveal how the people of Pompeii lived, from the ruling class down to the slaves.

The Forum viewed from the Temple of Apollo

with the fate of Pompeii, her temple was badly damaged in the earthquake of AD 62, then totally devastated by Vesuvius.

The Basilica, Pompeii's ancient judicial seat opening onto the Forum

THE FORUM

The Forum, a rectangular paved area, was the centre of public life, and the oldest part of Pompeii, built on the highest spot. Arranged around it are a number of important administrative and religious institutions. To the south is the Basilica, or law court, while opposite are the temples of Apollo, Jupiter and Vespasian, and the Sanctuary of the Lari. The imposing Eumachia building was perhaps used by the wool merchants' guild or, more probably, for commercial transactions. On the other side of the Basilica is the site of the Temple of Venus. The goddess was the protectress of the city, but in tandem

TRIANGULAR FORUM

Surrounded by columns and built on a steep-sided lava mass, the Triangular Forum was the focal point for leisure activities. In front of the Doric temple is a well and also a curious building that scholars think was revered by Pompeiians as the sanctuary of the mythical founder of the city. The sacred area was perhaps dedicated to the gods Hercules and Athena.

THEATRES

The large theatre (2nd century BC) was rebuilt several times in its history and in modern times has again been used as the venue for summer cultural events. It was built to seat about 5,000 people. The quadrangular portico behind the stage, originally designed as a space

The Forum, with Vesuvius in the background

The gladiators' barracks, part of the Large Theatre complex

for the audience to stroll in during intermissions, was turned into a barracks for the gladiators after AD 62. Skeletons, including one of a baby, have been excavated here.

Next door is the indoor theatre, or Small Theatre, used for music concerts. Behind this is the Temple of Isis, the goddess worshipped locally.

VIA STABIANA

This avenue, passing through the Porta di Stabia, to the south, was a major thoroughfare used by carriages travelling between Pompeii and the port and coastal districts.

On the west side of the avenue are the Stabian Baths, the most ancient in Pompeii; the original structure dates from the 4th century BC. Behind the baths, in the alley, is the best preserved of the city's many brothels. It is the only one with two storeys, two entrances and an independent stairway – all designed to ensure greater privacy for clients. Erotic wall paintings and a dish of pasta were found in this building. At the junction with Via di Nola are the central baths,

which were under construction at the time of Vesuvius' devastating eruption.

Near Porta Vesuvio you can see the remains of an aqueduct. This channelled water from the Serino River aqueduct, built in the era of Augustus, into three conduits that served both private homes and public fountains. The aqueduct fell into disuse after being damaged by the earthquake of AD 62.

An inn in Via dell'Abbondanza

AMPHITHEATRE AND GREAT GYMNASIUM

The Amphitheatre (80 BC) and the Augustan era Great Gymnasium, with a

swimming pool in the middle, are in an outlying area between the Nocera and Sarno gateways. The amphitheatre was used for gladiatorial combat and is the oldest one of its kind in existence. The stone tiers were separated into different sections for the various social classes. A large cloth canopy (velarium) shaded spectators from the sun.

VIA DELL'ABBONDANZA

A public fountain in Via dell'Abbondanza

The liveliest street in Pompeii was lined with private homes (see pp150–51) and shops selling a wide range of goods. The buildings and contents present a vivid picture of everyday life, down to the cart tracks in the street. You can visit the shop of VeArecundus, who made felt and tanned hides; Stefano's well-preserved laundry, where urine was used as a cleaning agent; or the bakery run by Sotericus, where bread was baked but not sold retail. Among the inns, the most famous belonged to Asellina, whose obliging foreign waitresses are depicted in graffiti on the wall. The inn (thermopolium) still has the record of the proceeds of that fateful day in AD 79: 683 sesterces.

The Houses in Pompeii

Many large houses of great historical value and
architectural interest are concentrated in the area
between Via di Mercurio (the most elegant *cardo*,
reserved for pedestrians, in the northwest of Pompeii)
and Via Stabiana, and along Via dell'Abbondanza.
Wealthy residents had houses with courtyards, living
rooms and gardens (*see pp18–19*), often with decorated
walls. A typical Pompeiian house was constructed
around two open courts: the atrium, an Italic feature,
and the colonnaded garden, a feature of Greek origin.
The layout of suburban farmsteads was different; the
Villa of the Mysteries is one of the most famous.

Bronze statue, House of the Faun

HOUSE OF THE VETTII

The lari shrine, House of the Vettii

The owners of the House of
the Vettii were freedmen
who had become rich mer-
chants. The house has been
carefully restored, and its
interior walls are adorned
with splendid paintings and
friezes featuring mythological
themes. In the atrium of the
more rustic part of the house
is the altar of the lari – the
deities who protected the
place. This depicts the
ancestral spirit of the *pater
familias* with two lari and,
below, a serpent.

On the north side of the
house is a kitchen, with a
small room decorated with
erotic scenes.

HOUSE OF THE FAUN

The name comes from a
bronze statue in the
middle of the impluvium
(pond) in one of the atria.
The original is in the Museo
Archeologico Nazionale, as
are many of the mosaics,
including the famous *Battle of
Alexander* (*see pp86–9*). Built
in the 2nd century BC, this is
one of the largest private
dwellings here.

HOUSE OF THE TRAGIC POET

The entrance has a mosaic
of a dog with a "beware
of the dog" inscription, but
many frescoes are in the
Museo Archeologico. The
name derives from a mosaic
showing a drama rehearsal.

HOUSE OF THE GOLDEN CUPIDS

This house, owned by the
family of Poppaea, Nero's
second wife, was decorated
with the elegant taste
characteristic of Nero's era.
It is not large and is built on
an irregular plan because of
the limited space. The name
derives from the cupids
(*amorini*) in gold leaf that
decorate the bedroom.
Gardens were an important
feature at that time, and this
garden was well tended and
lavished with sculptures,
hanging disks (*oscilla*),
theatre masks, marble tables
and a swimming pool.

HOUSE OF THE CITARISTA

Named after the bronze
statue of *Apollo the Lyre
Player* found in the central
peristyle and now in the
Museo Archeologico (*see
pp86–9*), this was really two
houses. It is distinguished by
the number of open courts:
two atria and three peristyles.

HOUSE OF MENANDER

The wealth of decoration
and the grandeur of its
atrium, peristyle and the
rooms facing east make this
one of Pompeii's most
interesting houses. The walls
of this home were decorated
with lovely paintings,
including a portrait of the
Greek playwright after whom
it has been named, and

The peristyle in the House of the Golden Cupids

PLAN OF POMPEII

0 metres 100
0 yards 100

House of the Golden Cupids

Villa of the Mysteries

House of the Vettii

VIA DI NOLA

House of Julia Felix

House of the Faun

VIA DI MERCURIO

VICOLO DI MERCURIO

VIA DELLA FORTUNA

VIA STABIANA

VIA DELL'ABBONDANZA

House of the Tragic Poet

Porta Marina entrance

PIAZZA ANFITEATRO

Entrance

KEY

☐ See pages 142–143

House of the Citarista

House of Menander

House of the Cryptoporticus

---

images of Ulysses in the Trojan War. A treasure trove of 115 silver objects was also found here in 1930. The bath is quite unusual; it lies on the western side of the peristyle, around a porticoed atrium which still has traces of a fresco portraying divine and mythological figures. The dressing room affords access to the frescoed *calidarium* (warm room).

On the same street is the Samnite period **House of the Labyrinth**. This has two atria and a spacious peristyle with a mosaic on the floor representing *Theseus and the Minotaur in the Labyrinth*.

HOUSE OF THE CRYPTOPORTICUS

The "hidden portico" that characterizes this house lies under the garden. In AD 79 the owner was probably converting it into a wine cellar, as can be seen by the store of amphoras. The showcases in the corridor contain plaster casts (*see p146*) of the inhabitants who had taken shelter in the *cryptoporticus* during the eruption, but who suffocated from the ashes that made their way in through a vent.

In the *triclinium* (dining room) you can still see frescoes and traces of the rich stuccowork on the vault.

HOUSE OF JULIA FELIX

The patrician villas in Pompeii were usually built outside the town centre. The House of Julia Felix occupies an entire block, divided into the owner's quarters and rented dwellings and shops. An inscription with the rental regulations was found here. The house also had baths that were rented and open to the public, who probably flocked here after the Forum Thermae had been damaged by the AD 62 earthquake. The clients waited for their turn in the vast porticoed courtyard, where you can still see the seats. From here they went to the outdoor pool and then to the baths proper, with a *frigidarium* (cold pool) and *tepidarium* (warm pool).

VILLA OF THE MYSTERIES

This large villa outside the city walls on Via dei Sepolcri was built in the early 2nd century BC. It was converted from an urban dwelling into an elegant country house. The architecture and paintings make it one of the most famous houses in Pompeii. It contains a well-known cycle of frescoes with 29 brightly coloured life-size figures against a red background, who represent a bride's initiation to the Dionysian mysteries or a postulant's initiation to the Orphic mysteries. Some scholars say this subject was depicted because the owner was a priestess of the Dionysian cult, which was widespread in Southern Italy.

Scene from the famous fresco cycle in the Villa of the Mysteries

Sorrento Peninsula ⓫

Lemons at Sorrento

The peninsula created by the Lattari hills rises steeply out of the sea and forms a boundary between the bays of Naples and Salerno. The softer northern side has been inhabited for centuries, and is dotted with ancient as well as modern villas. The coast between Vico Equense and Sorrento *(see pp154–5)* is especially built up, though spectacular views across the Bay of Naples abound. The rugged coastline is wilder and more precipitous on the southern side *(see pp158–61)* after Punta della Campanella, which was almost inaccessible by land until the 19th century. Today tourism is the most important industry but inland, olive groves and citrus trees are still tended and out of season many of the small coastal communities regain their fishing village atmosphere.

Vico Equense

CASTELLAMMARE DI STABIA

Road map D4. 🏙 *69,000.*
🚈 *Circumvesuviana: Castellammare.*
ℹ️ *Azienda Autonoma di Soggiorno e Turismo, Piazza Matteotti.*
Tel *081 871 13 34.*

Castellammare was totally rebuilt in the 9th century along with the castle used to defend the most important of its many sources of therapeutic waters. The old **thermal baths** that made it a holiday resort in ancient times are still in use today. The Bourbon rulers built major shipyards here that were later abandoned. **Ancient Stabiae**, an agglomeration of villas and farmsteads, lies outside the modern town on the Varano plain. Stabiae was destroyed by the Vesuvius eruption of AD 79, and was only partly excavated in the 18th century. After World War II more ancient houses were found along the coast and in the interior. Many of these villas were richly decorated and placed in splendid scenic positions. The oldest is the **Villa di Arianna** on the Varano hill, with a 1st-century BC nucleus and 13 rooms overlooking the bay. **Villa San Marco** on the same site has the remnants of a Roman swimming pool but fewer frescoed decorations.

🛁 Thermal Baths
Piazza Amendola. **Tel** *081 871 44 22.* 🔘 *for renovation until 2008.*

🏛 Villa di Arianna and Villa San Marco
Via Passeggiata Archeologica. **Tel** *081 871 45 41.* 🕗 *8:30am–1 hr before sunset.*

🏔 Monte Faito

A cable car, which departs from the Circumvesuviana train station (April to October), takes visitors up to the wooded slopes of Monte Faito. From the cable-car station those with a head for heights can climb even higher to the church of San Michele, 1,280 m (4,195 ft) above sea level.

TOUR AROUND THE SORRENTO PENINSULA

Castellammare di Stabia ①
Massa Lubrense ⑦
Monte Faito ④
Punta della Campanella ⑧
Sant'Agata sui due Golfi ⑨
Sorrento *(pp154–5)* ⑥

Stabiae ②
Vico Equense ⑤
Villa di Arianna & Villa San Marco ③

1131 m
(3710 ft)

KEY

━━ Suggested route

▲ Peak

0 kilometres   5

0 miles   3

The picturesque village of Marina di Lobra, Massa Lubrense

VICO EQUENSE

Road map D4. 🏠 *20,000.*
🚉 *Circumvesuviana: Scraio, Vico Equense.* 🛈 *Via San Ciro 16.*
Tel 081 879 93 51 or 081 879 88 26.

On a rocky spur with precipitous cliffs, this town of Etruscan origin, famous in antiquity for its wine, is now a tourist resort with popular bars and restaurants. With its steep antique streets, piazzas and castle, and its pizza by the metre, Vico Equense retains its independence from the coastal sprawl. The Vescovado quarter is built on a Roman street plan and has striking medieval buildings including **Castello Giusso**, which can be seen from the outside but is not open to the public.

The gothic church of **Santissima Annunziata** was built in the 14th century. From the front of this former cathedral (reached by passing under the arch of the bell-tower) there is a sheer drop to the sea far below allowing for dramatic panoramas.

Pizza a Metro *(see p201)* claims to have invented the idea of selling pizza by the metre and Neapolitans come here to test how much they can munch their way through.

🔒 Santissima Annunziata
Via Vescovado. ⏱ *Mon–Sat 9–10:30am; Sun 9:30am–12:30pm.*

MASSA LUBRENSE

Road map C4. 🏠 *12,000.*
🛈 *Viale Filangieri 11.* **Tel** *081 808 98 56.* 🛒 *Fri.*

Massa is a market town and bathing resort on the western end of the peninsula. Its 16th-century church, **Santa Maria delle Grazie** dominates Piazza Largo Vescovado. Just below the square there are dazzling views across the sea to Capri *(see pp168–9)* and a steep path winds down past the tiled dome of **Santa Maria di Lobra** to the pretty village of **Marina di Lobra**, where a scattering of restaurants face the beach and fishing boats are left abandoned on the sand.

PUNTA DELLA CAMPANELLA

Road map C4.

The coastline and turquoise waters around the south-westerly tip of the Sorrento Peninsula are protected as a maritime area. Wild and rocky, steep cliffs with improbably perched trees rise from small coves. A paved path (Bassa Via dei Monti Lattari) leads from Termini out to the point. Alternatively ramblers can follow the ridge path from Nerano *(see p158).*

Santa Maria delle Grazie, Massa Lubrense

SANT'AGATA SUI DUE GOLFI

Road map C4.

Perched inland with beautiful vistas north and south, Sant'Agata is famous for the Don Alfonso restaurant *(see p201)* and a favourite with Neapolitans. On a hill high above the town, with the most stunning views of all, is the vast 17th-century building of **Il Monastero del Deserto**, which was built as a Carmelite monastery. It is now inhabited by Benedictine nuns who occasionally open it up for visitors.

🔒 Il Monastero del Deserto
Tel *081 878 01 99.* ⏱ *3–6pm daily (phone to check).*

Breathtaking views from Monte Faito

Sorrento ⑫

On the cliffs at the southern end of the Bay of Naples, Sorrento has been a popular resort town since the 1700s: Casanova and Goethe both stayed here as guests of the British envoy, Sir William Hamilton, and his wife Lady Hamilton. The town has ancient origins though and you can still distinguish the original Greek town plan in the centre of Sorrento to the west of Piazza Tasso, and just out of town there are Roman remains at Punta del Capo. In the summer the laid-back town fills with wandering tourists taking in the views or relaxing at cafés. Down at the water's edge both Marina Grande and Marina Piccola have small beaches but the town is dominated more by boats than by sand as ferries arrive and depart for the Amalfi Coast, Naples and the islands. Lemons, a reminder of the fertility of the surrounding countryside, also dominate, as both flavouring and decoration.

Torquato Tasso statue

🌿 Villa Comunale
🕐 dawn–dusk.
One of Sorrento's most tranquil spots, the Villa Comunale is a thin stretch of tree-lined park overlooking Marina Piccola and the Bay of Naples beyond. The views are especially spectacular when the colours change at sunset, and it is easy to while away the time watching the comings and goings far below. Steps from the park lead down to the sea.

🏛 San Francesco
Piazza San Francesco 8-9.
🕐 7am–9:30pm daily.
Vibrant bougainvillea flowers tumble down around the beautiful and peaceful 14th-century cloisters attached to

the church of San Francesco. The architecture is a mixture of styles and periods: rounded arches on two sides and interlaced Arabic ones on the other two.

🏛 Museo Correale di Terranova
Via Correale 50.
Tel 081 878 18 46.
🕐 9am–2pm Mon, Wed–Sat; 9am–1pm Sun. ⬤ Tue and public hols. 📷
The Museo Correale di Terranova is Sorrento's most important museum. Housed in an attractive ancient villa, the collections consist of 17th–19th-century objets d'art including furnishings, china, ceramics and glassware, as well as paintings by Neapolitan and international artists. Archaeological finds from the local and surrounding areas are also on display.

🍋 Cataldo Lemon Orchard
Corso Italia 267. **Tel** 081 870 40 40,
🕐 9am–7pm daily.
www.igiardinidicataldo.it
Lemons are everywhere in Sorrento: the distinctively large, thick-skinned fruit hang outside shops, decorate ceramics and flavour the local tipple, limoncello. In the centre of town is the Cataldo Lemon Orchard – a traditional citrus grove typical of the kind found all over the region.

Thriving citrus groves, Cataldo Lemon Orchard

Owned by the town council and run by a local farm, visitors can wander around the orchard and buy a variety of lemon-based products as well as other liqueurs including mandarin and liquorice.

🏛 Piazza Tasso
The hub of Sorrento, Piazza Tasso is also the most attractive part of town, with narrow streets following the layout of Roman Surrentum. The statue here is of Torquato Tasso, the 16th-century Renaissance poet who was born in the town. The square is also the popular starting and finishing place for the evening *passeggiata*, or stroll.

Fresh fruit and vegetable market stalls lining Sorrento's narrow streets

🏛 Sedile Dominova
Via P R Giuliani. ⬤ to the public.
The Sedile Dominova, in the piazza of the same name, is a 15th-century building once used as an assembly hall for the nobility. Its external frescoes, including the coats of arms of local families, can still be seen in its arches, though the building is now used as a working men's club.

🏛 Duomo
Via Santa Maria della Pietà 44.
Tel 081 878 22 48. 🕐 9:30am–noon, 4:30–8:30pm daily.
The Duomo is of ancient origin and was rebuilt in the 1400s and then remodelled several times. Its façade was reconstructed in the early 20th century. Inside the cathedral is the archbishop's marble throne, sculpted in 1537, and fine *intarsia-* (inlaid wood) decorated choir stalls.

The colourful harbour at Marina Grande

🏛 Museobottega della Tarsialignea

Palazzo Pomarici Santomasi,
Via San Nicola 28.
Tel 081 877 19 42. ⬜ *Apr–Oct:
9:30am–1pm, 4–8pm Tue–Sun;
Nov–Mar Tue–Sun: 9:30am–1pm, 3–
7pm;* ⬤ *Mon and public hols.* 📷
☑ ℹ www.*alessandrofiorentino
collection.it*

Sorrento's tradition of inlaying wood, instances of which can be seen in its cathedral, is on display at this private museum. The collection includes plenty of fine examples of the art, including furniture and natural and stained wooden objects from the 17th–20th century. Don't miss the impressively decorated ceilings in two of the rooms.

Marina Grande

Fishing boats bob gently in the calm water at picturesque Marina Grande, to the west of the town centre. The colourful, if somewhat shabby houses that face the waterfront add to its charm. Nearby, the deep waters at Marina Piccola make for a hectic port. Boats leave here for Naples, Capri, and in summer for the Amalfi Coast. Both harbours have small stretches of sand, most of which you must pay to access.

⚓ Bagno della Regina Giovanna

Punta del Capo descent (Calata).
West of the town, a cobbled lane leads from Capo di Sorrento down to Punta del Capo, where you can visit the so-called Bagno della Regina Giovanna, Roman ruins of what was probably the home of the wealthy citizen, Pollius Felix. Close to the water's edge, the archaeological site is surrounded by trees, and the sea enters a small, rocky cove through an arch, making it a sheltered swimming spot. Above this, Roman walls and the remains of an under-floor heating system are all that is left of the ancient villa.

Marina di Puolo

Beyond Punta del Capo a path and a road descend to Marina di Puolo, a small, secluded cove and one of the best beaches in the Sorrento area. Sunbathers share the sand and pebbles with small boats and a row of pretty fishermen's cottages line the edge of the beach.

SORRENTO

0 metres   250
0 yards   250

Ferry Terminal
Hydrofoil Terminal
Marina Piccola
Museo Correale di Terranova ③
Marina Grande ⑨
Villa Comunale ①
San Francesco ②
Cataldo Lemon Orchard ④
PIAZZA LAURO
VIA MARINA GRANDE
VIA VITTORIO VENETO
VIA S. PAOLO
VIA ACCADEMIA
VIA S. CESAREO
PIAZZA S. ANTONINO
VIA DEGLI ARCHI
PIAZZA TASSO ⑤
VIA CORREALE
CORSO   ITALIA
VIA CAPASSO
STRETTO S. VINCENZO
Museobottega della Tarsialignea ⑧
VIA FUORO
VIA S. TASSO
⑥ Sedile Dominova
VIA PIETA
⑦ Duomo
CORSO ITALIA
VIA SERSALE
VIA MARZIALE
VIA FIORIMONTE
VIA DEGLI ARANCI
Stazione Circumvesuviana
VIA MARZIALE
⑩
⑪
VIA DEGLI ARANCI

Key to Symbols *see back flap*

Along the Sorrento Coast ⑬

A boat trip

The best way to take in all the beauty of the bay is by sea – to discover the isolated beaches, villages perched on the hillsides and ancient watch-towers. From Amalfi, Sorrento and Capri you can rent a launch or a slow *gozzo* boat. In the summer the major centres offer organized excursions on larger boats with a guide, but you cannot stop where you like. A favourite excursion is from the Amalfi coast to Capri (or vice versa), an all-day trip with evening meal at one of the coastal restaurants; the return in the moonlight is an unforgettable experience.

Sorrento Peninsula
An enjoyable way of seeing the coast from the sea is to take a fast motorboat and travel the full length of the Sorrento coastline, rounding Campanella point.

Marina del Cantone is an excellent place to stop for lunch: the local speciality is pasta with courgettes. The small Recommone restaurant in the nearby cove is also good.

Sorrento

Punta della Campanella
An ancient temple of Minerva stood on this rocky cliff; before then the site was possibly dedicated to the cult of the Sirens, after whom Sorrento, or Surrentum (see p153), may have been named. The road to the top is narrow and in poor condition.

Marina di Massa Lubrense, a pictures-que fishing harbour, is now a popular resort.

Capri
The island of Capri (see pp168–9) is also associated with the Sirens, as the promontory of Marina Piccola is called Scoglio delle Sirene. Those who want to stroll on the "blue island" can alight here, otherwise take a boat trip around the island, or simply stop for lunch at one of the many restaurants along the coast (see pp196–7).

0 kilometres   4

0 miles   2

VISITORS' CHECKLIST

At **Positano** *you can hire a boat from* **Lucibello** *on the large beach* **Tel** *089 87 50 32; or* **Grassi**, *on Fornillo beach.* **Tel** *089 81 16 20. At* **Capri**, *from* **Sercomar**, *Piazza Fontana 64.* **Tel** *081 837 87 81; from* **Banana Sport**, *Via Marina Grande 12.* **Tel** *081 837 51 88; and from* **Whaels**, *Via Colombo 17.* **Tel** *081 837 88 94.*

Positano

The square, pastel-coloured houses of Positano (see pp158–9) cling to the steep slopes of Monte Sant'Angelo a tre Pizzi and Monte Comune overlooking the sea. Lush gardens and bougainvillea fill the terraces of these charming houses. This is one of the most popular resorts on the Amalfi coast, famous for its bright, patterned textiles.

Isca

Just offshore is the small island of Isca, where the Neapolitan actor and playwright Eduardo De Filippo (see p37) lived. The house now belongs to his son Luca.

The Li Galli Archipelago

These islands, known as the Sirenuse until the 19th century, were once considered to be the home of the mythical Sirens who lured sailors onto the rocks. The clear water between the three crags, Gallo Lungo, La Rotonda and Castelluccia, makes swimming irresistible.

The Amalfi Coast

Portal of Amalfi Duomo

Suspended between sea, sky and earth, state road 163, which twists and turns along the full length of the Amalfi coast, offers stunning views at every corner. Until the 19th century, this stretch of the "divine coast" was isolated and could only be reached by going up difficult mountain paths on mules. By the early 1900s, this very isolation had become the main appeal and the coast began to attract travellers, artists and writers. Visitors of all kinds were drawn to steep-stepped Positano, clinging to tall cliffs; Amalfi with its glorious past as a marine republic; and Ravello, which Wagner chose as "the magic garden of Klingsor", the setting for his opera *Parsifal*. The limestone islands called Li Galli, southwest of Positano, are traditionally the home of the Sirens made famous by Homer in his accounts of the trials of Odysseus. Exploring by boat *(see pp156–7)* enables you to appreciate this astonishing coast at closer quarters.

A stretch of state road 163

NERANO

Road Map D4. ▥ *Sita.*
The first stop on the Amalfi coast road is the quiet village of Nerano, administratively part of Massa Lubrense. The road to Nerano goes upwards from Sorrento and cuts across the end of the peninsula near the small village of **Termini**. The sea sparkles in the distance, and the panoramic views are stunning. You can even see Capri and the rocky islands of Li Galli *(see p157)*.

Nerano is perched on a ridge; below is the beach and the town of **Marina del Cantone**, popular mostly because of its small seafront restaurants, some supported by stilts. Walkers can descend on foot among the olive trees to the bay of **Ieranto**.

POSITANO

Road Map D4.
▨ *3,700.* ▥ *Sita.* ▧ *from Capri & Naples.* ▤ *AAST, Via Saraceno 4.*
Tel *089 87 50 67.*
In 1953 John Steinbeck wrote that Positano "bites deep. It is a dream place that isn't quite real when you are there and becomes beckoningly real after you have gone". The town climbs the hill in steps, with the oldest houses in the upper part of Positano, either faded red or pink, decorated with Baroque stuccoes. The traffic-free street going down to the sea, Via Pasitea, penetrates the atmospheric heart of town with its narrow stepped alleys, houses with vaulted roofs, terraces and tiny gardens that defy the rock. The brightly coloured articles Positano is famous for – such as cloth bags and beachwear – on display inside and outside the many shops, blend well with the pastel-coloured houses, and the local craftsmen are only too happy to make sandals for you while you wait.

Near the beach is the small church of Santa Maria dell'Assunta, whose cupola is covered with yellow, blue and green majolica tiles. The descent ends at Marina Grande, a pebble beach used by fishing boats, lined with bars and restaurants.

If you want to go to inlets inaccessible by land, or to the little islands of **Li Galli**, or take a trip along the coast, boats are always available. If you prefer to go on foot, you can always swim at Ciumicello, Arienzo or take the easy path to Fornillo beach, with its two watch-towers. There are also craggy grottoes in the inlets, including La Porta, where

Typical Amalfi scenery, with sheer cliffs overlooking the sea

For hotels and restaurants in this region see pp181–7 and pp196–201

there are Palaeolithic and Mesolithic ruins. From Montepertuso, a village above Positano, you can walk along a splendid scenic path to **Nocelle**. For those who love good food, there are plenty of bars and restaurants, including Buca di Bacco (*see p199*), which is famous for its delicious *arancini* rice croquettes.

The beach at Marina di Praia

PRAIANO

Road map D4. 🏘 *1,900.* 🚌 *Sita.*
This fishing village is perched on the ridge of Monte Sant'Angelo and stretches towards Capo Sottile. The church of San Luca, with 16th-century paintings by Giovan Bernardo Lama, lies in the upper part. In an inlet just outside Praiano is **Marina di Praia**, a small beach surrounded by fishermen's houses. On the road from Positano there are more delightful beaches; just before Praiano is **Vettica Maggiore** and further on, Conca dei Marini. The views are splendid from the terraced square of Vettica Maggiore, by the church of San Gennaro. Before you reach Amalfi, the road widens into an open space where you can go down (by lift) to the **Grotta dello Smeraldo**, where stalagmites and stalactites merge to form great columns in the emerald-green water.

⚓ Grotta dello Smeraldo
State road 163, km 264 (via lift or stairs); boat from Amalfi.
⏱ 9:30am–4pm daily. 📷

AMALFI

Road map D4.
🏘 *6,000.* 🚌 *Sita.* ℹ️
AAST, Corso Roma 19/21.
Tel *089 87 11 07.*
Tucked in between mountains and sea, Amalfi is a perennial favourite with visitors for its scenic beauty and original architecture. It also has a

The rocky Amalfi coastline

glorious history as a powerful maritime republic – in the 11th century Amalfi was a rival to the ports of Venice and Genoa.

Little remains to show for the colourful trading history of this small town, whose inhabitants once numbered 60,000. Amalfi's cathedral, the **Duomo di Sant'Andrea**, founded in the 9th century, was rebuilt in Romanesque style in the 11th century and then altered several times. The façade and atrium date from the late 1800s, but the carved bronze doors were cast in Constantinople around the year 1000, and the campanile (1276) is decorated with Arabic-like interlaced arches typical of southern Italian Romanesque. Left of the porch, the Chiostro del Paradiso (Paradise cloister) was built in around 1266 for Bishop Augustariccio as a cemetery for prominent citizens. The garden is surrounded by an ornate colonnade with interlaced arches supported by paired columns and with fragments of sculpture from different periods. Near Piazza Duomo is the Arsenal; you can still see the ruins of two naves and the vault. Heading inland from Amalfi, you can visit the Valle dei Mulini (Valley of the Mills), famous for its traditional paper production and the **Museo della Carta** or Paper Museum.

🏛 Duomo di Sant'Andrea
Piazza Duomo.
⏱ 9am–1pm, 3–8pm daily.

🏛 Museo della Carta
Valle dei Mulini.
⏱ Mar–Oct: 10am–6:30pm daily; Nov–Feb: 10am–3:30pm Tue–Sun.

Piazza Duomo in Amalfi and the wide steps leading to the cathedral

RAVELLO

Road map D4. 🏛 *2,500.* 🚌 *Sita.*
🚌 *AAST, Piazza Duomo 10.*
Tel *089 85 70 96;*
*Ente Provinciale di Turismo, Piazza
Vescovado 1.*
Tel *089 85 76 57.*

Ravello's history is entwined
with that of Amalfi: the
former became part of the
Duchy of Amalfi in the 9th
century. The period of
greatest splendour was the
13th century, when trade with
Sicily and the Orient was at
its height. Somewhat off the
beaten track, Ravello is for
those who love peace and
quiet and stupendous views.

The **Duomo** is dedicated to
San Pantaleone, the town's
patron saint, and the blood of
the saint is kept here. The
church dates from 1086 and
its bronze doors from 1179.
Inside is a splendid raised
pulpit, the work of Niccolò di
Bartolomeo da Foggia in
1272. The twisted columns,
patterned with mosaics, rest
on sculpted lions.

Walking around the town,
Moorish details are evident in
the buildings, in the inner
courtyards and gardens and
the many churches. The
narrow streets and pathways
offer occasional, often
unexpected, glimpses of
marvellous coastal views.
Two highlights are Villa
Rufolo and Villa Cimbrone.

The view from the terrace at Villa Cimbrone

Villa Rufolo, originally built
for the Rufolo family, is a mixture of 13th- and 14th-century
constructions. It was remodelled in the 19th century by a
Scottish enthusiast, who preserved the Arabic elements. It
is famed for the courtyard with
double arches and even more
for the tropical gardens, which
inspired Wagner's *Parsifal.*
The annual Ravello Festival
now stages concerts here.

On Via San Francesco,
which takes you to Villa
Cimbrone, are the churches
of San Francesco, of Gothic
origin but rebuilt in the 18th
century, and Santa Chiara, the
only one on the coast that
has retained its *gynaeceum*
(women's gallery).

Villa Cimbrone was built
in the late 1800s by the
Englishman Lord Grimthorpe.
An assortment of ancient
architectural elements were

incorporated in the house.
From the villa's clifftop terrace
there is a spellbinding view of
the coast to Punta Licosa and
the Paestum plain. Villa
Cimbrone is now a small
hotel *(see p181).*

Another place well worth
visiting is the church of San
Giovanni del Toro, in the
square of the same name,
with its three tall semicircular
apses and beautifully
decorated domes.

🏛 **Duomo**
Piazza Duomo. **Tel** *089 85 83 11.*
🕐 *9am–1pm, 4–7pm.*

🏛 **Villa Rufolo**
Piazza Duomo. **Tel** *089 85 76 57.*
🕐 *Summer: 9am–8pm; winter:
9am–6pm.* 🖼

🏛 **Villa Cimbrone**
Via Santa Chiara 26.
Tel *089 85 80 72.* 🕐 *9am–1 hr
before sunset.* 🖼

The picturesque village of Cetara; standing out among rooftops is the dome of San Pietro

MAIORI, MINORI AND CETARA

Road map D4 & E4.
Maiori: 6,000; Minori: 3,100; Cetara: 2,500. Sita.
i Maiori: AAST, Corso Regina 71. **Tel** 089 87 74 52;
Cetara: Pro Loco, Via San Francesco 15. **Tel** 089 26 14 74.

Ancient *Reginna Minor* and *Maior* are now two popular seaside resorts with a long and noble history. **Minori**, where the Amalfi Maritime Republic arsenals were situated, dates back to Roman times. Near the seafront is the basilica of Santa Trofimena, built in the 12th–13th centuries and then rebuilt in the 1800s. The church houses the relics of the ancient patron saint of Amalfi.

Maiori is like an amphitheatre at the end of the Tramonti valley. It was founded in the 9th century but is today a modern town, rebuilt after a flood in 1954. The fine beaches and good bathing facilities have made it one of the most visited towns on the coast. The 18th-century campanile on 12th-century Santa Maria a Mare towers over the Maior stream.

After the lovely beach of Erchie, **Cetara** was the easternmost possession of Amalfi. At the end of the 9th century it was also a stronghold for the Saracens, who anchored their ships at Cala di Fuenti cove. The name perhaps derives from the Latin *cetaria*, or tuna-fishing net; the fish, salted and sold in ceramic pots, is a typical local product.

A characteristic ceramics shop in Vietri

VIETRI

Road map E4. *10,000.* Sita.
The majolica-decorated dome and bell tower of San Giovanni Battista (1732) have almost come to symbolize this town overlooking the Bay of Salerno. Vietri is famous as a seaside resort and especially for its ceramics. Cooking utensils, plates, vases and tiles have been manufactured here since the 1400s. In the mid-18th century, Vietri became known as the majolica-makers' district, a suburb of the Cava de' Tirreni (see below). The most original items made were the extremely popular tiles painted with religious

Majolica plate made in Vietri

subjects. You can still see these tiles in streets, private homes and churches.

Today you can find ceramics of all kinds, either traditional or experimental in colour and shape, catering for all tastes. The green donkey used as the logo of local production is a relatively recent invention, inspired by the 1930s creations of Dutch and German ceramicists. The Villa Guarigli park is home to the **Museo della Ceramica** (Ceramics Museum) featuring local items from the 1600s to the present.

🏛 Museo della Ceramica
Torretta di Villa Guariglia, Via Nuova Raito. **Tel** 089 21 18 35. ◻ May–Sep: 9am–1pm, 4–7pm Tue–Sun; Oct–Apr: 9am–1pm, 3–6pm Tue–Sun.

CAVA DE' TIRRENI

Road map E4.
53,000. Sita.

Lying in a valley in the interior, Cava de' Tirreni is the only town in Southern Italy to have streets lined with porticoes. Go and see the 11th-century abbey of Santissima Trinità and the old Scacciaventi quarter, whose winding streets block the wind (*scacciaventi* means "wind-chaser").

View of Vietri, with the dome and campanile of San Giovanni

Paestum

Ancient Poseidonia, founded along the Sele River by Greek colonists from Sybaris around 600 BC, became the Roman colony of Paestum in 273 BC. The town began to decline in the 1st century BC due to malaria. Seismic distur-bance and deforestation (the

Red-figure lekythos

local pines made excellent raw material for building ships) had gradually turned the area into marshland. The inhabitants tried to combat the rising water level; they raised their streets and homes, or went to live on higher ground. It was at this time that the Temple of Hera was made into a church by the converted population. Eventually, however, Paestum was abandoned for the nearby town of Capaccio.

This ancient site was first unearthed in the 18th century during the building of a road, but most of it remained undiscovered until the 1950s.

★ **Temple of Ceres**
This temple was built around 500 BC and dedicated to Athena. For centuries, until a votive offering was found nearby, it had been attributed to Ceres.

Temple of Neptune
The name of this temple has been a subject of debate. It was probably dedi-cated to Apollo or Zeus, but it is commonly known as the Temple of Neptune. Built in 450 BC, it is one of the most complete Greek temples in Europe.

THE THREE TEMPLES AT PAESTUM

These plans compare the structure of the 3 main temples at Paestum. The Temple of Hera (6th century BC) has 9 front columns, 18 side columns and 2 aisles divided by a row of columns. The Temple of Ceres (6th century BC) has 6 fluted columns at the front, 13 lateral ones and an un-divided *cella*. The largest, Temple of Neptune (5th cen-tury BC), has 6 front columns, 14 side ones and its *cella* is divided into 3 aisles by 2 rows of 2-tier columns.

Temple of Ceres

Temple of Hera

Temple of Neptune

STAR SIGHTS

★ Temple of Ceres

★ Temple of Hera, the "Basilica"

★ Tomb of the Diver (funerary fresco in Paestum Museum)

Paestum
Museum

VISITORS' CHECKLIST

Road map F5. *Via Magna Grecia.*
FS *Napoli–Salerno: Paestum.*
Site ◯ *9am–2 hrs before sunset.*
Tel *0828 81 10 23.*
Museum ◯ *9am–7pm daily.*
◯ *1st & 3rd Mon of month.*
ℹ️ *AAST, Via Magna Grecia 887.*
Tel *0828 81 10 16.*
*www.*infopaestum.it

Metope with Dancing Girls
*This metope, on display in the Paestum Museum, comes
from one of the two temples in the sanctuary of Hera
Argiva at the mouth of the Sele River. Founded by the
first colonists, the complex was discovered in 1934–40
after almost two centuries of searching.*

The amphitheatre
(1st century BC–1st
century AD) has only
been partly excavated.

Forum

Baths

★ Tomb of the Diver
*The frescoed slabs of the
Tomb of the Diver, which
date from about 480 BC,
were discovered in 1968
about 1 km (half a mile)
from Paestum. The image
of the diver on the lid
symbolizes the passage to
the afterlife. These unique
examples of Greek
funerary painting can be
seen in the site's museum.*

★ Temple of Hera, the "Basilica"
*The absence of religious features
led the first archaeologists to believe
this was a civic building, when in
fact it is the oldest temple in
Paestum, built around 530 BC.*

Antonio Joli, The Temples of Paestum (1758)
*Temple ruins had a profound effect on local landscape painters,
who often used them in their art. Antonio Joli's painting shows the
Basilica, the Temple of Neptune and, beyond,
the Temple of Ceres.*

Hoardings and shop signs in present-day Caserta

Caserta ⑯

Road map C2. 🚈 70,000. 🚉
Caserta. 🛈 *Ente Provinciale per il Turismo, Palazzo Reale.* **Tel** *0823 32 22 33.*

Caserta was once known as the village of La Torre, named after a medieval tower of the Acquaviva family. It was only from the middle of the 18th century, when Charles III, Bourbon king of Naples, chose the plain at the foot of the Tifatini mountains as the site for his new centre of administration, that the town began to flourish and expand. It was at this time that it took the name of the nearby medieval village of Caserta Vecchia.

Present-day Caserta is a modern agricultural town that reflects the major rebuilding carried out in the 1950s. A few older buildings remain, such as the church and monastery of Sant'Agostino in Via Mazzini and the former residence of the Acquaviva family in Piazza Vanvitelli. However, the main reason to visit Caserta is the Royal Palace *(see pp166–7).* Conceived by Charles III as the heart of his new administrative centre, the palace was to be a leading European court, modelled on Versailles and linked to the capital and other cities by radial roads and protected by the fortress at Capua. This plan to move

Façade of the cathedral of San Michele, Caserta Vecchia

power away from the capital city was influenced by the apparent vulnerability of the Palazzo Reale on the Naples seafront *(see pp50–51),* a fact that came to light in 1742 when the English fleet had threatened to attack. Once this danger had passed, however, attention was turned to the style of the palace. The king summoned Luigi Vanvitelli, technical adviser at the Vatican, to draw up designs. The palace and the new city were begun in 1752.

When Charles III became king of Spain and returned to Madrid in 1759, construction on the Royal Palace languished. Supervision of the costly and interminable works was handed over to his son Ferdinand IV and in particular, his minister Tanucci. The new king concentrated on the magnificent park and bothered little about the unfinished palace.

Some further work was carried out, but as the two semicircular buildings at the entrance to the grounds illustrate, these were poor substitutes for the splendid buildings proposed in Vanvitelli's original designs.

ENVIRONS
🏛 Caserta Vecchia
Road map C2.

The fascination of Caserta Vecchia, 10 km (6 miles) along a winding road northeast of Caserta, does not lie in the individual monuments but the town itself, which has a remarkably well-preserved medieval character. This small hilltop town was probably founded by the Lombards in the 8th century and then came under Norman rule. When Charles III designed his new palace, activity in this lively community moved into the new town in the plains.

Caserta Vecchia revolves around the main square where the cathedral of San Michele stands. Nearby is the Gothic church of Annunziata with a marble portal opening onto a 17th-century portico. On the eastern side of the village are the ruins of a 13th-century castle, dominated by a 30-metre (98-ft) turret.

🔒 Cathedral of San Michele
🕐 *9am–1pm, 3–7:30pm daily.*
The cathedral in Caserta Vecchia was completed in 1153. The faded yellow and grey tufa façade is simple, with three marble portals. Columns on the triangular tympanum above the middle portal are supported by lions.

Caserta Vecchia, dominated by the cathedral of San Michele

The 14th-century dome has the interlaced Arabic arches often seen on Romanesque buildings in Southern Italy.

The interior of the church is lined with irregular columns and stunning majolica tiles. A starlit sky is represented in the dome, with grey stone for the night and white marble stars.

To the right of the cathedral stands the dark stone bell tower, added a century later, with an archway over the road.

🏠 Village of San Leucio
Road map C2.
This area, 3 km (2 miles) northwest of Caserta was purchased by Charles III in 1750. Five years later Ferdinand IV built a royal lodge here, Casino di Belvedere. In 1789, he founded a progressive community with enlightened laws and based on the production of silk. An existing building was designed as a silk factory to be used by the local artisans. All you can see today of the ambitious project are the workmen's dwellings and the Belvedere lodge on the slopes of the hill. The royal lodge was also the residence of the silk factory management.

The Belvedere lodge, San Leucio

🏛 Sant'Angelo in Formis
Road map C2. ⬜ daily (ask the caretaker in house opposite). 📷
The small, Romanesque church of Sant'Angelo in Formis lies 10 km (6 miles) northwest of Caserta. Built on the ruins of an ancient temple to Diana, Roman goddess of the forest, it was reconstructed in 1073. Many features of the temple were incorporated into the church such as the delicate Corinthian columns on the portico, and the church floor. Inside, a cycle of 11th-century frescoes, painted in Byzantine style by artists from the School of Montecassino, depict stories from the Bible.

THE IDEAL VILLAGE OF SAN LEUCIO

Pretty street in the village of San Leucio

San Leucio was founded in 1789 by Ferdinand IV as a village for workers of the local silk factory. The aim of this social experiment was to create a community dedicated to the pursuit of happiness instead of personal profit. The community had its own laws, attributed to the king but in fact written by Antonio Planelli. These were based on reason and morality, included compulsory education, equal inheritance rights for men and women (who, however, had to marry within the community), the abolition of the dowry and medical assistance for the aged and disabled. The 1799 revolution brought about the end of the most ambitious project of the founders, the creation of an entire model city, Ferdinandopoli, although the designs survive. San Leucio is famous for its silk manufacture and the articles produced here are still very much in demand.

🏛 Roman Amphitheatre
Piazza Adriano, Santa Maria Capua Vetere. **Tel** 0823 79 88 64.
⬜ 9am–1 hr before sunset. 📷
The amphitheatre at Santa Maria Capua Vetere, 6 km (4 miles) west of Caserta, dates from the 1st century BC. Restored by Hadrian and Antonius Pius, it is still well preserved today, especially its underground structure. Second in size only to the Colosseum in Rome, it had four "storeys": the first three were travertine arches with busts and statues of the gods, while the last was blind and decorated with pilasters. Statues of Eros, Venus and Psyche found here are on display in the Museo Archeologico Nazionale (see pp86–9).

🏠 Ponti della Valle
This viaduct, 2 km (1 mile) from Maddaloni, is over 500 m (1640 ft) long and is supported by three arches. It was built in 1753–8 by Vanvitelli to bring water to the Royal Palace at Caserta.

Ruins of the amphitheatre at Santa Maria Capua Vetere

Royal Palace of Caserta

Statue on a fountain

In his memoirs, the architect Vanvitelli says it was the king who designed the Royal Palace. This may have been adulation, or perhaps Charles III knew what he wanted – to emulate his favourite models, the Buen Retiro in Madrid and Versailles in France. Vanvitelli drew inspiration from the former for this quadrangular, 1,200-room structure, which was finally completed in 1852. The lower ground floor now houses a museum, with photos and exhibits relating to the palace and Caserta culture.

First floor

★ Eighteenth-century Royal Apartments
The Halberdiers Hall connects the upper vestibule and the 18th-century Royal Apartments. The ceiling is adorned by Domenico Mondo's fresco The Triumph of the Bourbon Arms *(1785).*

The upper Vestibule is a grand, imposing space, with its marble-lined walls and an inlaid floor.

★ Throne Room
This is one of the large 19th-century salons – in contrast with the smaller 18th-century rooms – in the palace. It was decorated by Gaetano Genovese in 1844–5 and was once filled with elegant French furniture.

STAR FEATURES

- ★ Eighteenth-century Royal Apartments
- ★ Throne Room
- ★ Court Theatre

For hotels and restaurants in this region see pp181–7 and pp196–201

Great Staircase
The staircase is positioned to one side so as not to interrupt the splendid view of the park from the main doorway.

VISITORS' CHECKLIST

Road map C2. Piazza Carlo III.
Tel 0823 44 80 84. **Apartments**
⬜ *8:30am–7:30pm Wed–Mon.*
Park ⬜ *8:30am–6pm (2:30pm winter).* **Museo dell'Opera** ⬜
8:30am–1 hr before dusk. 🚻 📷

KEY (UPPER FLOOR)

⬜	18th-century Royal Apartments
⬜	19th-century Royal Apartments
⬜	*Terraemotus* exhibition
⬜	Cappella Palatina
⬜	Biblioteca Palatina
⬜	Art Gallery
⬛	Non-exhibition space

Art Gallery
Among the portraits in the Art Gallery is that of Maria Carolina, Ferdinand IV's wife, who occupied four elaborate rooms in the 18th-century apartments.

★ **Court Theatre**
The theatre is on the ground floor. The rear of the stage could be opened to the air, creating a natural backdrop.

THE PARK

Luigi Vanvitelli designed this famous park, one of the last examples of the fashion for a regimented garden in the Italian or French style. The long central axis is designed on descending levels, creating a remarkable effect with pools and fountains ornamented with splendid sculptures. The play of flowing water culminates in the **Grande Cascata** waterfall, almost 80 m (260 ft) high, also known as the Fountain of Diana. Next to this is the English Garden, perhaps the first of its kind in Italy. The idea was suggested to Queen Maria Carolina by her friend Lord Hamilton and landscaping work began in 1768.

Flowing water with fountains and waterfalls, the park's central feature

Capri **⑰**

Excursion taxi

The first illustrious residents in Capri were the Roman emperors Augustus and Tiberius. For the last decade of his life, Tiberius ruled Rome from Capri, and the ruins of his luxurious villa can still be seen today. Despite this noble history, the island saw few visitors until the 19th century, when a poet named August Köpisch found the Grotta Azzurra, which was known to locals but not to travellers on the Grand Tour. Tourism began to flourish, and Capri became the haunt of foreign politicians, artists and intellectuals, Alexandre Dumas and Oscar Wilde among them. The singer Gracie Fields and the writer Norman Douglas, author of *Siren Land*, made the island their home.

Marina Grande
Capri's main harbour is a colourful village with seafood restaurants and some Roman and Byzantine remains. A funicular takes you to central Capri in a few minutes.

Rocky Beaches
Sunloungers are set up among the rocks on this island with few sandy beaches.

The Grotta Azzurra, or Blue Grotto, owes its name to the blue colour of the water, the result of light refraction.

| 0 metres | 1000 |
| 0 yards | 1000 |

Anacapri
On the slopes of Monte Solaro (see p173) is the second town on the island, Anacapri. Here you can visit the church of San Michele, the Villa San Michele (home of the Swedish physician Axel Munthe), the excavations at the imperial villa of Damecuta and, of course, appreciate the magnificent view from the top of the hill.

Villa Jovis
The retreat built by Emperor Tiberius stands on the mountain named after him. Excavations have unearthed baths, apartments and "Tiberius's drop", from which his victims were supposedly thrown into the sea.

Writer Curzio Malaparte gave this villa, shaped like a hammer with a sickle on the roof, to the Chinese government in 1957.

I Faraglioni, Capri's most striking offshore rocks, soar up to 109 m (360 ft) out of the sea.

Tragara

The Certosa di San Giacomo, founded in 1371, is now occupied by a school and the Diefenbach Museum which has paintings and historical objects.

Marina Piccola

VISITORS' CHECKLIST

Road Map C4.
Capri 8,000; Anacapri 5,400.
from Naples & Sorrento.
AAST: **Capri**, Via Marina Grande/Piazza Umberto I.
Tel 081 837 06 34 or 081 837 06 86; **Anacapri**, Via Orlandi 19a. **Tel** 081837 15 24.
Grotta Azzurra: from Marina Grande. from Anacapri, 9am–1 hr before sunset. if the sea is particularly rough.
Certosa di San Giacomo: Viale della Certosa, Capri. **Tel** 081 837 62 18. 9am–2pm Tue–Sun. **Villa Jovis:** Via A Maiuri, Capri. 9am–1 hr before sunset daily.
Villa San Michele: Via Capodimonte 34, Anacapri.
Tel 081 837 14 01.
Nov–Feb: 9am–3:30pm daily; Mar: 9am–4:30pm daily; Apr, Oct: 9am–5pm daily; May–Sep: 9am–6pm daily.
Monte Solaro: Anacapri. Chair lift from Via Caposcuro.
Tel 081 837 14 28.
Mar–Oct: 9:30am–1 hr before sunset daily; Nov–Feb: 10:30am–3pm daily. in adverse weather conditions.
www.capritourism.com

The "Piazzetta" in Capri
In the heart of town the famous "Piazzetta", officially Piazza Umberto I, is an outdoor living room, crowded day and night, packed with café tables buzzing with gossip and animated discussion. Excursions around the island also start from here. Overlooking the scene is the Baroque dome of Santo Stefano.

Via Krupp
Commissioned by the German industrialist Krupp, this famous road makes its vertiginous descent towards the sea in a series of hairpin bends.

Ischia ⑱

Bougainvillea

The hot springs on the volcanic island of Ischia were renowned in antiquity and still draw visitors today. Ancient Pithecusa was founded here in the 8th century BC by the same Greek traders who later founded Cumae on the mainland *(see pp138–9)*. Repeated attacks in the early 1300s forced people to take refuge on the small offshore island which the Aragonese later turned into a castle. A favourite with Bourbon royalty, Ischia also enchanted landscape painters and visitors such as the Irish philosopher Berkeley and the French poet Lamartine. The island is green and rugged, and each coast has a different character, offering beaches or steep hills, busy nightlife or quiet seclusion.

Fungo di Lacco Ameno
This "mushroom" rock is a prominent landmark outside Lacco Ameno, where the Greek colonists first landed.

Lacco Ameno is home to the Muse Archeologico di Villa Arbusto whe items from th Greek settl ment are hel

Forio

The beach at Citara is generally considered the most beautiful in Ischia.

Santa Maria del Soccorso
This small sanctuary in the town of Forio combines elements of Gothic, Renaissance and Baroque, and is known for its collection of votive offerings from sailors. The English composer Sir William Walton lived just north of here, at La Mortella.

0 kilometres   2

0 miles   1

Sant'Angelo
Originally a fishing village and now a thermal spa resort, Sant'Angelo lies west of the long Maronti beach. Here "taxi boats" can be hired to take you to coves otherwise inaccessible by land. Nearby are the Nitrodi hot springs.

Monte Epomeo
(see p173) is an extinct volcano. According to mythology, the eruptions and quakes were caused by the wails and sighs of the giant Typhoeus, imprisoned under the island.

Casamicciola Terme
*Despite the damage caused by the 1883 earthquake,
the spa town of Casamicciola has retained its
atmosphere and some Art Nouveau architecture.
The Norwegian writer Ibsen wrote* Peer Gynt *here.*

Ischia Porto is the
island's main town
where ferries dock.

Ischia Ponte
*This village is connected to
the small offshore island of
Castello Aragonese by a
causeway built in 1438.*

Castello Aragonese
*Different architectural styles can be
seen inside the fortified walls of the
island: the Angevin cathedral of the
Assunta, a monastery and the church
of San Pietro a Pantaniello. There is a
lovely view from the Carta-
romana belvedere.*

Maronti beach

Procida ⑲

Road map B3. 👥 *11,000.* 🚢 🚢
from Naples & from Pozzuoli.
ℹ️ *Azienda Autonoma di Soggiorno
e Turismo, Via Roma, Stazione
Marittima 1.* **Tel** *081 810 19 68.*

Much smaller than Capri and Ischia and also much less affected by tourism, the third island in the Bay of Naples is a favourite with those who love the simplicity and traditions of the local culture. This is the enchanting world that author Elsa Morante, recollecting her many visits here, evoked in *Isola di Arturo* (Arthur's Island). Procida's economy is sustained not only by tourism but, to a large extent, by the money its emigrants send back home to their families.

Deeply rooted local traditions are evident in the various festivals; for example, the Good Friday procession *(see p40)* that descends to the modern port from so-called Terra Murata – the rise dominated by the Abbey of San Michele – or the Graziella celebration that takes place in the port in mid-August.

The multi-coloured houses resting against the tufa rock make the island architecture one of the most distinctive in the region. Unique to

The fortified rise of Terra Murata with the Abbey of San Michele

*Map labels:*
Capo Bove
Punta di Mezzogiorno
Vivara Nature Reserve
Chiaiolella
Centane
Punta Solchiaro

0 metres 1000
0 yards   1000

the island are the vaulted buildings; originally built as winter boat shelters and later enlarged, acquiring among other things façades with arches and half-arches that frame the doors and windows, terraces, loggias and long external staircases. You can see this type of architecture, albeit in a partially modernized version, on your arrival in Procida in Marina Grande new the area

View of Marina Grande

Marina Grande

Punta della Lingua

Marina Corricella

Terra Murata

Punta di Pizzaco

Typical Procida architecture

WALKING ON THE ISLANDS

While Procida is almost flat – the highest point, Terra Murata, is 91 m (300 ft) above sea level – Capri and Ischia are steep-sided. On Capri (*see pp168–9*), the path connecting Monte Solaro (589 m, 1930 ft)) to Anacapri is delightful and practicable even for lazy visitors, though there is always the option of the chairlift. Walkers will be well rewarded by the striking view and the 14th-century Santa Maria di Cetrella monastery on Marina Piccola (a detour halfway up). Experienced hikers come back down by the "Passetiello" path which includes a stretch directly above the sea and leads to Capri.

The highest mountain in the bay is the extinct Epomeo volcano (788 m, 2580 ft) on Ischia (*see pp170–71*). A climb up the cone traditionally starts off at night from Fontana so as to admire the view at dawn. The view takes in the island itself, the Bay of Naples and the Tyrrhenian coast up to Roccamonfina and the Pontine Islands. A rough dirt track leads to the church of San Nicola (1459) and the adjoining monastery, both hewn out of the tufa rock. On your way down you can choose the road to Forio or Casamicciola.

Looking out over Capri from the Monte Solaro chairlift

built up in the 17th and 18th centuries, and at the small, popular Chiaiolella port on the other side of the island. The Abbey of San Michele, dominating Terra Murata, dates back to 1026, though it has since been rebuilt. Marina Corricella, at the foot of Terra Murata, has been virtually untouched by modern times; the soil is very fertile and the gardens here are filled with lemon trees. You can also visit the luxuriant **Vivara Nature Reserve**, a small island connected to Chiaiolella by a bridge, with examples of Mediterranean flora and an ornithological centre. It was here that intriguing remains of a late Bronze Age Mycenean settlement were found a few years ago.

🔒 **Abbey of San Michele**
Via Terra Murata. *Tel* 081 896 76 12.
⏰ 9am–12:30pm, 3:30–7pm daily.

🦋 **Vivara Nature Reserve**
⏰ ask the Protezione Civile (which manages the park) for permission.
Tel 081 896 74 00.

Monte Solaro (589 m) (1930 ft)

Capri

Monte Epomeo (788 m) (2580 ft)

Ischia

Terra Murata (91 m) (300 ft)

Procida

TRAVELLERS'
NEEDS

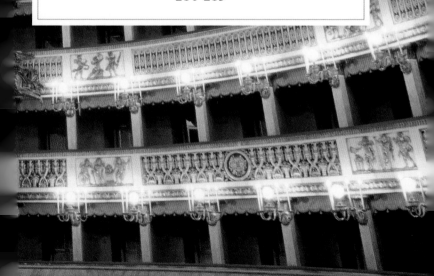

WHERE TO STAY

The fascination and enchantment of Naples and the surrounding countryside have drawn visitors here for many centuries. Kings and queens, revolutionaries in exile, poets, writers and composers are among the host of celebrities who have wintered at the foot of Mount Vesuvius since the 18th century. Hotels and pensioni in the centre of Naples tend to be fairly expensive, but efforts are being made to widen the range of facilities available. Along the Amalfi coastline, around Sorrento and on the islands, traditional holidaying areas, the range of accommodation is much wider. Choices on offer cover all price categories, from simple pensioni to a grand luxury hotel with pools and magnificent views along the coast. This section and the lists of hotels on pages 178–87 will help you make your choice.

PRESTIGE
hotels

Logo of the
Prestige hotels

The 5-star Excelsior *(see p180)* overlooking the seafront

WHERE TO LOOK

Outside Naples there is no lack of choice of hotels, from luxury chains to cheaper, family-run pensions. The latter are clean and comfortable, and often have fine panoramic views. In Naples itself, the range is fairly limited, although more bed and breakfasts are now appearing. Hotels sometimes offer poor value for money. The most exclusive hotels are usually located on hills or on the seafront with superb views.

If you plan to spend a lot of time visiting museums, churches and galleries, it is best to stay in the centre of Naples. You will be within easy reach of the most important sights, and you can go back to your hotel to relax between spells of sightseeing. For those who don't mind the walk, a hotel in the commercial district is ideal; it may not have the characteristic charm of an older establishment but will be modern and comfortable. The Prestige hotel chain, such as the Grand Hotel Vesuvio, the Excelsior and the Majestic, offer excellent service to an international clientele, and include 42 suites and 22 conference halls. The information bureaux of the Ente Provinciale per il Turismo (**EPT**, the Italian Tourist Board – *see p219*) publishes lists of hotels, pensioni and camp sites. For further information you can also make inquiries at the **Associazione Albergatori Napoletani** (Neapolitan Hotel Owners' Association).

PRICES AND GRADING

Italian hotels are classified by a star-rating system, from one, the lowest, to five stars. Prices including taxes are displayed inside each room. Breakfast is often not

Breakfast on the terrace of the Executive Hotel *(see p178)*

included, and may be an expensive item compared with a coffee and croissant in the nearest local bar. In Naples there is no difference between low and high season, but it is always worth asking about discounts, particularly off season. It is often possible to negotiate special rates for groups or longer stays. On average, single rooms cost two-thirds of the double room rate; rooms without a bathroom may cost up to 30 per cent less. In holiday resorts prices differ in low and high season; during the peak summer months you may be expected to take half-board.

HOTEL FACILITIES

Almost all the middle-range and luxury hotels in Naples underwent refurbishment some years ago and now provide a high level of comfort, including sound-proofing. The cheaper hotels (one or two stars) tend to have clean but simple rooms, often with shared bathroom. Hotels outside Naples usually offer better facilities for less money.

The Hotel Pension Pinto Storey *(see p180)*, opened in 1878

The elegant foyer in Parker's *(see p180)*

BOOKING AND PAYING

You should book well in advance if you have special requests such as a room with a good view. During July and August, the peak holiday season, hotels along the coast and on the islands get very full, so once again you must book ahead of time. Naples can also get busy, particularly if there are special events scheduled, and advance booking is recommended. If you do need to find a hotel on arrival, the local tourist offices will advise you.

When booking, you will probably be asked to pay a deposit, which can be done by credit card or international money order. When you arrive at your hotel, the reception will ask for your passport; this is to register travellers with the police, a legal formality. By law, the hotel must give you a receipt when you check out.

Telephone calls from the room and drinks from the mini-bar can be very expensive, so it is advisable to check beforehand.

BUDGET ACCOMMODATION

If you are on a tight budget you can stay in a hostel. The **AIG** (Associazione Italiana Alberghi per la Gioventù – Youth Hostel Association) has lists of hostels. In Naples, the Ostello Mergellina, near the Mergellina railway station and a stone's throw from the Parco Vergiliano *(see p119)*, is highly recommended. Rooms have washing facilities and breakfast is included. There are also inexpensive family-run pensions with clean, basic rooms, but in general bathrooms are communal.

Interior of Il Nido hotel in Sorrento *(see p187)*

Associazione Albergatori Napoletani
Piazza Carità 32.
Tel 081551 49 02.
www.napleshotels.na.it

AIG Ostello Mergellina
Salita della Grotta 23.
Tel 081 761 23 46.

Camping
Camp sites are usually open from April to October, and are often near the sea. Small brown road-signs indicate the nearest site. The one closest to Naples is the **Vulcano Solfatara**. *It is easily reached by metro (Pozzuoli stop), and has bungalows with 2–4 beds as well as a restaurant, swimming pool and a minimarket. Along the coast, at Meta di Sorrento is the* **Bleu Village**, *while Sorrento offers* **Nube d'Argento**, *in the middle of an orange grove, and* **Campogaio**, *directly overlooking the sea. On Ischia the* **Eurocamping dei Pini** *is about 1 km (half a mile) from the centre. A good alternative for those who want to be at the sea is the* **Mirage**, *on Maronti beach. On Procida a good camp site is the* **Punta Serra**.

Bleu Village
Via Alimuri 7 (Sorrento).
Tel 081 878 65 57.

Campogaio
Via Capo 41 (Sorrento).
Tel 081 807 35 79.

Eurocamping dei Pini
Via delle Ginestre 28 (Ischia).
Tel 081 98 20 69.

Mirage
Spiaggia dei Maronti
(Barano, Ischia).
Tel 081 99 05 51.

Nube d'Argento
Via Capo 21 (Sorrento).
Tel 081 878 13 44.

Punta Serra
Via Flavio Gioia (Procida).
Tel 081 896 95 19.

Vulcano Solfatara
Via Solfatara 161 (Pozzuoli).
Tel 081 526 23 41.

View from the terrace of the Poseidon in Positano *(see p185)*

Choosing a Hotel

The hotels in this guide have been carefully selected for their quality of service and location. They are listed by area. For more detailed information on exact locations in Naples, see the Street Finder on pages 228–43; for towns and islands in the rest of the region, see the Road Map on the inside back cover.

PRICE CATEGORIES
The following price ranges are for a standard double room and taxes per night during the high season. Breakfast is not included, unless specified.

€ Under €80
€€ €80–€140
€€€ €140–€180
€€€€ €180–€260
€€€€€ Over €260

NAPLES

TOLEDO AND CASTEL NUOVO L'Appartamento Spagnolo ⬜ €€
*Via Nuova Santa Maria Ognibene 30, 80120 **Tel** 081 1956 58 35 or 335 629 27 60 **Rooms** 3* **Map** 2 F5

This stylish bed and breakfast, on the second floor of a *palazzo* owned by an interior designer, is located in the Quartieri Spagnoli, one of Naples' most colourful areas. High ceilings and antiques harmonize with more modern furnishings and the owner's tasteful colour palette. Minimum two-night stay. **www.bohemienbeb.com**

TOLEDO AND CASTEL NUOVO Chiaia B&B ⬜⬜📶⬜ €€
*Via Palasciano 17, 80122 **Tel** 081 1957 3004 **Fax** 339 718 40 97 **Rooms** 3* **Map** 6 D2

Opposite Da Dora (*see p195*), one of the city's finest fish restaurants, this little bed and breakfast has charming rooms, as well as some apartments. A short walk from the Riviera di Chiaia and the seafront, it is owned by a helpful family of sailing aficionados and boat excursions are available. Breakfast on the terrace. **www.chiaiabaiabb.it**

TOLEDO AND CASTEL NUOVO Chiaia Hotel de Charme ⬜ €€€
*Via Chiaia 216, 80121 **Tel** 081 41 55 55 **Fax** 081 42 23 44 **Rooms** 14* **Map** 6 F2, 7 A3

Set on the first floor of a *palazzo* on the pedestrian shopping street of Via Chiaia, this lovely, intimate hotel is only two minutes' walk from Piazza Plebiscito. All rooms are soundproofed and individually furnished with antiques; seven have whirlpool baths. Deservedly popular, with charming and professional staff. **www.hotelchiaia.it**

TOLEDO AND CASTEL NUOVO Mercure Angioino ⬜⬜ €€€
*Via Depretis 123, 80133 **Tel** 081 552 95 00 **Fax** 081 552 95 09 **Rooms** 85* **Map** 7 B2

Located between the university and the port, the Mercure Angioino is convenient for ferries to the islands and visiting Castel Nuovo. Mainly a business hotel, it provides modern and comfortable facilities. The clean, tastefully decorated bedrooms are soundproofed to block out street noise. Nearby public car park. **www.mercure.com**

TOLEDO AND CASTEL NUOVO Palazzo Alabardieri ⬜📶 €€€
*Via Alabardieri 38, 80121 **Tel** 081 41 52 78 **Fax** 081 197 22 10 **Rooms** 33* **Map** 6 F2

This hotel was built within the former convent of the church of Santa Maria di Chiaia, just off Piazza dei Martiri, one of the city's most prestigious squares. All rooms are elegant. Superior rooms are spacious and generally have parquet floors. The junior suites are particularly stylish. Motor launch available for excursions. **www.palazzoalabardieri.it**

SPACCANAPOLI Ginevra ⬜ €
*Via Genova 116, 80143 **Tel** 081 28 32 10 **Fax** 081 554 17 57 **Rooms** 10* **Map** 4 F4

Ideal for a short visit or for those on a budget, the Ginevra is conveniently located for the station in a pleasant area – the nearby morning market around Via Nazionale is excellent. All rooms are modern, clean and comfortable, with TVs and phones. Superior rooms have fridges. Friendly staff. **www.hotelginevra.it**

SPACCANAPOLI Garden ⬜🕴⬜📶⬜ €€
*Corso Garibaldi 92, 80143 **Tel** 081 28 43 31 **Fax** 081 553 60 69 **Rooms** 35* **Map** 4 E4

At the far end of Piazza Garibaldi, this is a well-run, moderate-range hotel, with a panoramic roof terrace and a bar. Bedrooms are comfortable. The Garden is within walking distance of the sights of central Naples, and handy for trips to Pompeii, Sorrento and beyond. Several good bars and restaurants are nearby. **www.hotelgardenapoli.it**

SPACCANAPOLI Il Convento ⬜⬜📶⬜ €€€
*Via Speranzella 137a, 80132 **Tel** 081 40 39 77 **Fax** 081 40 03 32 **Rooms** 14* **Map** 7 A1

Standing next to the old convent of Santa Maria di Francesco delle Cinque Piaghe, this hotel nevertheless has a fairly modern interior. Bedrooms are airy, decorated in soothing colours and attractively furnished. The larger rooms and suites have their own tiny flower-filled roof terraces. Convenient central location. **www.sea-hotels.com**

SPACCANAPOLI Executive Hotel ⬜🕴⬜📶⬜ €€€
*Via del Cerriglio 10, 80134 **Tel** 081 552 06 11 **Fax** 081 552 81 63 **Rooms** 19* **Map** 7 B1, 9 C5

Occupying part of the pretty monastery of Santa Maria la Nova, the Executive enjoys a central location yet is away from the bustle of busy roads. It is managed by a local hotel chain, in an efficient and friendly way. Public rooms are filled with antiques and bedrooms are attractive too. There is a gym and a lovely roof terrace. **www.sea-hotels.com**

Key to Symbols *see back cover flap*

SPACCANAPOLI Hotel Mediterraneo

€€€

Via Nuova Ponte di Tappia 25, 80133 **Tel** *081 551 22 40* **Fax** *081 552 58 68* **Rooms** *223* **Map** *7 A2*

Part of the Marriott chain, this hotel has a lovely location just off Via Toledo – close to the historical sights, shops, restaurants and port. Bedrooms and suites display an understated elegance and many offer fine views. Breakfast is served in the panoramic roof restaurant. Piano bar and cocktail bar. **www.mediterraneonapoli.com**

SPACCANAPOLI Starhotel Terminus

€€€

Piazza Garibaldi 91, 80142 **Tel** *081 779 31 11* **Fax** *081 20 66 89* **Rooms** *145* **Map** *4 E4*

Moments from the central railway station at Piazza Garibaldi, this large hotel caters mainly for the business market and offers facilities such as Wi-Fi throughout. Bedrooms are stylish and comfortable and there is a charming roof terrace and bar. Executive rooms are designed with business guests in mind. **www.starhotels.it**

SPACCANAPOLI Suite Esedra

€€€

Via A Cantani 12, off Corso Umberto I, 80133 **Tel** *081 553 70 87* **Fax** *081 28 74 51* **Rooms** *17* **Map** *10 F3*

Set back off Corso Umberto on its own little square, Suite Esedra is conveniently located midway between the historic centre and the main railway station. Each of its attractive rooms has a quirkily different astrological theme. The mini-penthouse suite has a tiny hot tub on a private terrace with a view. **www.sea-hotels.com**

DECUMANO MAGGIORE Alloggio dei Vassali

€€

Via Donnalbina 56, 80134 **Tel** *081 551 51 18* **Fax** *081 551 51 18* **Rooms** *5* **Map** *9 B5*

This appealing bed and breakfast is on the second floor of Palazzo Donnalbina, which dates from the 18th century. Wooden beams, stucco work and antique furniture are among its smart features. All rooms have private bathrooms, DVD players and computers with Internet access. Next to the hotel there is a day spa. **www.bandbnapoli.it**

DECUMANO MAGGIORE Donna Regina

€€

Via Luigi Settembrini 80, 80139 **Tel** *081 44 67 99* **Fax** *339 781 92 25* **Rooms** *3* **Map** *10 D1*

Formerly the mother superior's quarters in the 14th-century Donna Regina monastery, this lovely bed and breakfast overlooks two churches. It is filled with both heirlooms and modern art (the owner is a painter). Bedrooms are all en suite and utterly charming. Dinner is available on request. **www.discovernaples.net/donnaregina.htm**

DECUMANO MAGGIORE Hotel des Artistes

€€

Via Duomo 61, 80138 **Tel** *081 44 61 55* **Fax** *081 211 04 03* **Rooms** *9* **Map** *3 C4, 10 D1*

Close to the Duomo, the ferry port and the main railway station is this welcoming, old-fashioned place decked out with antique furniture and chandeliers. Bedrooms are large and decorated in warm, comforting colours; they face onto either the street or the inner courtyard. All have modern bathrooms. **www.hoteldesartistesnaples.it**

DECUMANO MAGGIORE Neapolis

€€

Via F Del Giudice 13 (Via Tribunali), 81038 **Tel** *081 442 08 15* **Fax** *081 442 08 19* **Rooms** *19* **Map** *3 B5, 9 C3*

Beside the church of the Pietrasanta, on the ancient Decumano Maggiore, this third-floor hotel is within easy striking distance of all the major sights. It is above a good trattoria that has a lovely patio – great for summer dinners alfresco. Internet access is available in the smart, spacious bedrooms. **www.hotelneapolis.com**

DECUMANO MAGGIORE Palazzo Doria D'Angri

€€

Piazza VII Settembre 28, 81038 **Tel** *081 790 10 00* **Rooms** *11* **Map** *3 A5, 9 B4*

Garibaldi declared Italy's unification from the balcony of this beautiful palace, designed by Vanvitelli, the architect behind the Royal Palace of Caserta. The location is ideal, close to Piazza Dante and Via Toledo. While public rooms have exquisite frescoes by Fidele Fischetti, bedrooms are much simpler. **www.albergosansevero.it**

DECUMANO MAGGIORE Costantinopoli 104

€€€€

Via S Maria di Costantinopoli 104, 80138 **Tel** *081 557 10 35* **Fax** *081 557 10 51* **Rooms** *13* **Map** *9 B2, 3 B4*

This Liberty (Art-Nouveau) villa has beautiful stained glass, a courtyard and a garden with palm trees, a sun terrace and a small pool. It is an oasis from the chaos beyond, located in the historic centre just five minutes from the Archaeological Museum, on a street of antiquarian shops and booksellers. **www.costantinopoli104.it**

CAPODIMONTE AND I VERGINI Casa Totò B&B

€

Via Antonio de Curtis 1b, 80137 **Tel** *081 45 00 71* **Fax** *333 588 61 14* **Rooms** *3* **Map** *10 D1*

This friendly bed and breakfast is close to the end of Via Duomo, on the street where Neapolitan comedy legend Totò (*see p37*) was born and lived: his house-museum is nearby. Every room is en suite and has a corner kitchen and guests can relax in the charming courtyard. Breakfast is served on geranium-filled balconies. **www.bnbnapoli.com**

VOMERO Hotel Cimarosa

€€

Via Cimarosa 29, 80127 **Tel** *081 556 70 44* **Fax** *081 578 28 52* **Rooms** *19* **Map** *2 D5*

A step away from the funicular station at Piazza Fuga, from which you can ride down to Via Toledo, this hotel occupies the top floor of a genteel *palazzo*. It has recently been upgraded from a *pensione* to a hotel and some bedrooms are en suite. Rooms are immaculate, with views over the bay towards Capri. **www.hotelcimarosa.it**

VOMERO San Francesco al Monte

€€€€

Corso Vittorio Emanuele 328, 80135 **Tel** *081 423 91 11* **Fax** *081 251 24 85* **Rooms** *31* **Map** *5 B1*

Once a Franciscan monastery, this hotel has a spectacular roof terrace and pool perched high on Vomero hill, giving views over Naples, Vesuvius and the sea. Each of the rooms – former monks' cells – is beautifully and individually furnished. Bathrooms are luxurious. There is a terrace restaurant in summer. **www.hotelsanfrancesco.it**

VOMERO Parker's   €€€€€

Corso Vittorio Emanuele 133, 80121 **Tel** *081 761 24 74* **Fax** *081 66 35 27* **Rooms** *83*   **Map** *5 C1*

Built by an English marine biologist over a century ago, this imposing pile has an air of hushed luxury. Bedrooms are large and the public rooms are decorated with Neo-Classical furniture and paintings. A beautiful view of the Bay of Naples can be had from the panoramic bar and restaurant. There is also a spa/gym. **www.grandhotelparkers.com**

CASTEL DELL'OVO AND CHIAIA Le Fontane al Mare   €

Via N Tommaseo 144, 80121 **Tel** *081 764 38 11* **Fax** *081 764 34 70* **Rooms** *21*   **Map** *6 F3*

This *pensione*, located on the upper floor of a building on the Santa Lucia seafront, shares the views of nearby five-star hotels, but costs a fraction of the price. Rooms are charming and very clean, but not all are en suite; those without bathrooms have the sea views. Every room has a washbasin. Popular, so it is wise to book ahead.

CASTEL DELL'OVO AND CHIAIA Ausonia   €€

Via F Caracciolo 11, 80122 **Tel** *081 68 22 78* **Fax** *081 66 45 36* **Rooms** *20*   **Map** *5 B3*

The Ausonia occupies a house on the seafront, just steps away from the harbour of Mergellina. A lovely family-owned hotel, it offers nautically-themed rooms and is, appropriately, run like a tight ship. Views are of an internal courtyard. Staff go out of their way to be helpful. **www.hotelausonianapoli.com**

CASTEL DELL'OVO AND CHIAIA Cappella Vecchia   €€

Via Santa Maria a Cappella Vecchia 11, 81021 **Tel** *081 240 51 17* **Rooms** *6*   **Map** *6 F2*

This small guesthouse is in a charming area, on a tiny street off Piazza dei Martiri in Chiaia. Convenient for exploring the city, it is near the Piazza Vittoria bus terminus, the Piazza Amedeo metro station and plenty of shops. The bedrooms are modern and cheerful, and the owners are very helpful. **www.cappellavecchia11.it**

CASTEL DELL'OVO AND CHIAIA Pinto Storey   €€

Via G Martucci 72, 80121 **Tel** *081 68 12 60* **Fax** *081 66 75 36* **Rooms** *16*   **Map** *6 D1*

A *pensione* in an elegant part of town, the Pinto Storey is within easy walking distance of the seafront, opposite the metro and near the funicular to Vomero. On the fourth floor of a Liberty (Art-Nouveau) villa. The pretty lobby is filled with antiques, while the bedrooms have more modern fittings. No reception at night. **www.pintostorey.it**

CASTEL DELL'OVO AND CHIAIA Rex   €€

Via Palepoli 12, 80132 **Tel** *081 764 93 89* **Fax** *081 764 92 27* **Rooms** *36*   **Map** *7 A4*

One street back from the seafront, this hotel is well located and offers reasonable rates. While facilities are minimal, bedrooms are large and comfortable – ideal for families. Some have little balconies with pleasant views. Breakfast is served in your room. Rooms can be a little noisy as the windows are not soundproofed. **www.hotel-rex.it**

CASTEL DELL'OVO AND CHIAIA Terrazza Pignatelli B&B   €€€

Via Ascensione 8, 80121 **Tel** *081 40 83 51* **Fax** *333 665 01 65* **Rooms** *3*   **Map** *6 D2*

A delightful spot, away from the crowds of the historic centre, with a little terrace where you can enjoy breakfast and plan your day. Near the Lungomare (seafront) and the Villa Communale park, it is a pleasant stroll to the shops and the area's sights. Rooms are stylishly decorated in warm colours and with antiques. **www.terrazzapignatelli.com**

CASTEL DELL'OVO AND CHIAIA Palazzo Turchini   €€€€

Via Medina, 80133 **Tel** *081 551 06 06* **Fax** *081 552 14 73* **Rooms** *27*   **Map** *7 B2*

A venerable institution, this former royal orphanage and music conservatory dates from the 1700s. Facing the Fountain of Neptune and beside the parish church, La Incoronotella, it boasts a roof terrace and a winter garden. Bedrooms have parquet floors and elegant furnishings; some have private terraces. **www.palazzoturchini.it**

CASTEL DELL'OVO AND CHIAIA Royal Continental   €€€€

Via Partenope 38-44, 80121 **Tel** *081 245 20 68* **Fax** *081 764 57 07* **Rooms** *403*   **Map** *7 A4*

The only hotel on Santa Lucia harbour with a roof-top pool and spa: its 1950s exterior belies its stylish interior. Bedrooms and the restaurant have fine views over Castel dell'Ovo. All bedrooms are smart, but modernists will love the Gio Ponti floor with its 24 rooms conceived by the design pioneer. **www.hotelroyal.it**

CASTEL DELL'OVO AND CHIAIA Santa Lucia   €€€€

Via Partenope 46, 80121 **Tel** *081 764 06 66* **Fax** *081 764 85 80* **Rooms** *107*   **Map** *7 A4*

Directly facing the harbour of the same name, the Santa Lucia is one of Naples' historic seafront hotels. Built over a century ago, it has elegant Neo-Classical furnishings. Bedrooms are airy, stylish and filled with antiques; the nicest are a good size and have wonderful sea views. Many of the bathrooms have whirlpool baths. **www.santalucia.it**

CASTEL DELL'OVO AND CHIAIA Excelsior   €€€€€

Via Partenope 48, 80121 **Tel** *081 764 01 11* **Fax** *081 764 97 43* **Rooms** *136*   **Map** *7 A4*

Easily the best located of the cluster of luxury hotels along Santa Lucia, the Excelsior has front and side views of Vesuvius and Castel dell'Ovo. The roof-top terrace is disarmingly beautiful and the restaurant is a real treat, serving excellent food. Comfortable bedrooms and sumptuous decor throughout. Helpful staff. **www.excelsior.it**

CASTEL DELL'OVO AND CHIAIA Miramare   €€€€€

Via N Sauro 23, Via Partenope, 80132 **Tel** *081 764 75 89* **Fax** *081 764 07 75* **Rooms** *31*   **Map** *7 B4*

This lovely Art-Nouveau hotel, standing on the seafront along from Santa Lucia towards the port, is crammed with antiques and has a charming proprietor. There is a beautiful terrace with fine views towards Vesuvius. Bedrooms vary, but all are soundproofed. It pays to upgrade to a room with a sea view. **www.hotelmiramare.com**

Key to Price Guide *see p178* **Key to Symbols** *see back cover flap*

CASTEL DELL'OVO AND CHIAIA Vesuvio

€€€€€

Via Partenope 45, 80121 **Tel** *081 764 00 44* **Fax** *081 764 44 83* **Rooms** *171*   **Map** *7 A4*

Arguably one of Naples' most luxurious hotels, Vesuvio is found in Santa Lucia. The penthouse suite is famously spectacular, the choice of visiting royalty, politicians and footballers. All bedrooms are sumptuous, however, and full of antiques. Many have a terrace or balcony. Other facilities include a spa, gym and roof-top restaurant. **www.vesuvio.it**

POSILLIPO Relais Posillipo

€€

Via Posillipo 69, 80123 **Tel** *081 248 31 93* **Fax** *081 57 56 22* **Rooms** *11*   **Map** *5 A4*

This glass-walled boutique hotel is set high on Posillipo's prestigious hill, with spectacular views. Spacious public and guest rooms are decorated to a blue-and-white scheme; some bedrooms have Jacuzzis and terraces. It is an easy bus ride to the centre and Vomero, while the Parco Virgiliano and Marechiaro are nearby. **www.relaisposillipo.com**

POSILLIPO Hotel Paradiso

€€€€

Via Catullo 11, 80122 **Tel** *081 247 51 11* **Fax** *081 761 34 49* **Rooms** *74*   **Map** *5 A4*

Part of the Best Western chain, this hotel has gorgeous views across the bay and a roof-top bar and restaurant. Rooms are spacious and elegant, with parquet floors. A little isolated for those without their own transport, although it is only a short walk to a funicular, which takes you down to Mergellina port. **www.hotelparadisonapoli.it**

POMPEII & THE AMALFI COAST

AMALFI La Conchiglia

€€

Via Matteoti 5, 84011 **Tel/Fax** *089 87 18 56* **Rooms** *11*   **Road Map** *D4*

On the far side of Amalfi, near the sea, this small hotel has large and airy rooms, some with private terraces and sea views. La Conchiglia has a well-known restaurant that opens in summer, offering excellent home cooking. A warm welcome awaits guests, who can also take advantage of a private beach. Excellent value for money.

AMALFI Hotel Amalfi

€€

Via dei Pastai 3, 84011 **Tel** *089 87 24 40* **Fax** *089 87 22 50* **Rooms** *40*   **Road Map** *D4*

Tucked away in a quiet spot in old Amalfi, this family-run hotel occupies a former pasta factory. From the lovely terrace, there are views of the Duomo across the roof tops. A patio and a restaurant are also available for guests. Ask ahead for a room with a geranium-decked balcony. Bedrooms are large and comfortable. **www.hamalfi.it**

AMALFI Hotel Antica Reppublica

€€

Vico dei Pastai 2, 84011 **Tel** *089 873 63 10* **Rooms** *10*   **Road Map** *D4*

Recently renovated, this small hotel has a roof terrace where breakfast is served. Overlooking the main square, it is also close to the seafront. Rooms are cheerful, with terracotta floor tiles and pastel coloured walls with stencilling. Junior suites have whirlpool baths and four-poster beds. Friendly owners. **www.anticareppublica.it**

AMALFI Hotel Lidomare

€€

Largo Duchi Piccolomini 9, 84011 **Tel** *089 87 13 32* **Fax** *089 87 13 94* **Rooms** *15*   **Road Map** *D4*

A stylish, old-fashioned and extremely comfortable family-run hotel in the heart of Amalfi. Rooms are large and quiet with majolica-tiled floors, heavy old furniture and modern bathrooms. Some have private balconies with sea views. The entrance is tucked away upstairs, down an alley opposite the Duomo. **www.lidomare.it**

AMALFI Luna Convento

€€€€

Via P Comite 33, 84011 **Tel** *089 87 10 02* **Fax** *089 87 13 33* **Rooms** *45*   **Road Map** *D4*

A beautiful convent building, dating from 1222, houses this hotel on the coastal road leaving Amalfi. A romantic Moresco cloister and a lovely pool and sun terrace built around a Saracen look-out tower are among its charms. Bedrooms, originally monastic cells, are individually styled and there are two suites. **www.lunahotel.it**

AMALFI Miramalfi

€€€€

Via Quasimodo 3, 84011 **Tel** *089 87 15 88* **Fax** *089 87 12 87* **Rooms** *49*   **Road Map** *D4*

This getaway boasts a magical setting just outside Amalfi, perched on the cliff side above a sea-water pool and a beach reached by a lift. The facilities are modern, though the decor is a little dated. Each bedroom has its own terrace and is spacious, light and airy. A panoramic terrace restaurant completes the picture. **www.miramalfi.it**

AMALFI Santa Caterina

€€€€€

SS Costiera Amalfitana 9, 84011 **Tel** *089 87 10 12* **Fax** *089 87 13 51* **Rooms** *70*   **Road Map** *D4*

In the family since 1880, this luxury hotel is one of the Amalfi Coast's finest. Poised on a promontory high over Amalfi, it has extensive gardens and terracing. Bedrooms and suites are lavish, with antiques, majolica tiles and balconies. Facilities include a spa, a private lido and an excellent restaurant. **www.hotelsantacaterina.it**

BAIA Agriturismo Il Casolare

€

Via Selvatica 12, Contrada Coste dei Fondi di Baia, Bacoli, 80070 **Tel** *081 523 51 93* **Rooms** *4*   **Road Map** *B3*

This deservedly popular *agriturismo* provides delicious food and rustic accommodation. It is set amid lush vegetation that thrives in the fertile soils of a 10,000-year-old extinct volcano. The owner, will collect guests from Lucrino railway station. The shared kitchenette is ideal for families. Wonderful views and a sun terrace. **www.datobia.it**

CAPRI Agriturismo Maruzella   €€   Road Map C4/5

Via Lo Funno 15, Anacapri, 80071 **Tel** *081 837 27 68* **Fax** *081 837 27 68* **Rooms** *3*

At Capri's first *agriturismo* guests are surrounded by orchards, vegetable gardens, vines and farm animals. With just three rooms, those who stay here feel very much part of the family. Dining is at a communal table and there is also a terrace. Bedrooms are comfortable. The hosts organize gastronomic evenings and boat trips.

CAPRI La Prora   €€   Road Map C4/5

Via Castello 6, Capri, 80073 **Tel** *081 837 02 81* **Fax** *081 837 02 81* **Rooms** *8*

A brief stroll from the Piazzetta, up the steps past the church, this lovely old-style place is run by three sisters. Dating from the 1800s, the hotel was built by a retired naval officer in a nautical style (La Prora means prow). Bedrooms are cool and simple; some have private patios. Charge for air conditioning. **www.albergolaprora.it**

CAPRI La Reginella   €€   Road Map C5

Via Matermania 36, Capri, 80073 **Tel** *081 837 05 00* **Fax** *081 837 05 00* **Rooms** *10*

Up in the hills outside Capri Town, overlooking Marina Piccola, La Reginella offers spectacular views over the bay, the Faraglioni islands and Monte Solaro. This family-run hotel has an attractive sitting room, terrace and garden. The restaurant upstairs is air conditioned in the summer. Bedrooms offer old-fashioned comfort. **www.hotellareginella.it**

CAPRI Villa Krupp   €€   Road Map C5

Via G Matteoti, Capri, 80073 **Tel** *081 837 03 62* **Fax** *081 837 64 89* **Rooms** *12*

Built by German industrialist Friedrick Krupp, the villa was once home to Maxim Gorky and a notorious former guest was Lenin. Incredible views are to be had from the terraces, which face the Faraglioni islands and the Roman gardens of Augustus (donated to Capri by Krupp). Meals are served on the terrace. Ask for a room with a sea view.

CAPRI Villa Mimosa B&B   €€   Road Map C5

Via Nuova del Faro 48a, Anacapri, 80071 **Tel** *081 837 17 52* **Fax** *081 837 17 52* **Rooms** *3*

Not far from the centre of Anacapri, in a lovely spot with sea views, this bed and breakfast has cool, elegant rooms with delightful individual furnishings. Sunny flower-filled terraces adjoin each room. Only a short stroll away from the bus terminal. Friendly hosts make for an intimate, relaxing break. **www.mimosacapri.com**

CAPRI Biancamaria   €€€   Road Map C5

Via G Orlandi, Anacapri, 80071 **Tel** *081 837 10 00* **Fax** *081 837 20 60* **Rooms** *25*

Right in the heart of Anacapri, this small family hotel is convenient for exploring the whole island. The decor of the cool, airy rooms is traditional and they are spotless and comfortable. Small patios give views to Monte Solaro or the roadside. Rooms at the back of the hotel are quieter. Charge for air conditioning. **www.hotelbiancamaria.com**

CAPRI Il Mulino   €€€   Road Map C5

Via La Fabbrica 9, Anacapri, 80071 **Tel** *081 838 20 84* **Fax** *081 838 21 32* **Rooms** *6*

Set in lower Anacapri, down towards the Blue Grotto, is the lovely Il Mulino. It is a 15-minute walk to town or you can take a bus. This former farm has gardens and terraces amid olive groves, citrus trees and tumbling geraniums. Rooms are comfortable, with modern facilities, and each has a terrace. Delicious breakfasts. **www.mulino-capri.it**

CAPRI San Michele   €€€   Road Map C5

Via G Orlandi 1, Anacapri, 80071 **Tel** *081 837 1427* **Fax** *081 837 1420* **Rooms** *60*

This delightful rose-coloured villa in central Anacapri is finished in Neo-Classical style and has a timeless family feel. There is a tempting pool and a garden affording wonderful views. Some bedrooms have terraces or balconies with views. Not all have air conditioning. The restaurant terrace is impressive. **www.sanmichele-capri.com**

CAPRI Weber Ambassador   €€€   Road Map C5

Via Marina Piccola, Capri, 80073 **Tel** *081 837 01 41* **Fax** *081 837 88 66* **Rooms** *44*

Perched above Marina Piccola, Capri's most spectacular beach, with fine views over the Faraglioni islands, this yellow-painted hotel has flower-filled terraces shaded by blue canopies. There is a roof garden and a lovely terrace for breakfast (expensive, but generous). Sea-view rooms and suites cost more. **www.hotelweber.com**

CAPRI Gatto Bianco   €€€€   Road Map C5

Via V Emanuele 32, Capri, 80073 **Tel** *081 837 02 03* **Fax** *081 837 80 60* **Rooms** *41*

Very close to the Piazzetta, this hotel boasts elegant public rooms, charming service and pretty gardens. Furnished with antiques, the bedrooms are cool and spacious; some offer balconies or terraces. A white cat was found during the hotel's construction, hence the name. Beauty treatments available. **www.gattobianco-capri.com**

CAPRI La Minerva   €€€€   Road Map C5

Via Occhio Marino 8, Capri, 80073 **Tel** *081 837 70 67* **Fax** *081 837 52 21* **Rooms** *19*

This pretty five-storey hotel offers flower-filled terraces, sea views and attractive architectural details. Superior rooms have terraces; deluxe rooms have whirlpool baths and private sea-facing terraces. La Minerva is located in a quiet, picturesque spot not far from the centre of Capri Town. **www.laminervacapri.com**

CAPRI Capri Palace Hotel & Spa   €€€€€   Road Map C5

Via Capodimonte 2b, Anacapri, 80073 **Tel** *081 978 01 11* **Fax** *081 837 31 91* **Rooms** *93*

One of Capri's most beautiful hotels, located in quiet Anacapri. Bedrooms, some with balconies, overlook Monte Solare or the sea. Suites have private terraces and pools. Lovely main pool; also a spa and gym. Hotel boats for excursions. Fine *enoteca* (wine bar) and an award-winning restaurant, L'Olivo (see p197). **www.capri-palace.com**

Key to Price Guide *see p178* **Key to Symbols** *see back cover flap*

CAPRI Punta Tragara

€€€€€

Via Tragara 57, Capri, 80073 **Tel** *081 837 08 44* **Fax** *081 837 77 90* **Rooms** *47* **Road Map** *C4/5*

In a wonderful quiet position facing the Faraglioni islands, this red-hued hotel combines luxury and design in harmony with nature. Its architect was Le Corbusier and bedrooms are serene, with antiques, art and amazing views. There's a beautiful pool and candle-lit dining is on offer in the renowned restaurant. **www.hoteltragara.com**

CAPRI Villa Brunella

€€€€€

Via Tragara, Capri, 80073 **Tel** *081 837 01 22* **Fax** *081 837 04 30* **Rooms** *18* **Road Map** *C4/5*

This elegant, family-owned hotel stands in lush gardens, with a pool overlooking the Faraglioni islands. Bedrooms and suites are decorated in cool, mellow tones, accentuating the space and light. Suites have sitting rooms and terraces. The terrace restaurant is charming and the sun terrace by the pool has magical views. **www.villabrunella.it**

CAPRI Villa Le Scale

€€€€€

Via Capodimonte 64, Capri, 80071 **Tel** *081 838 2190* **Fax** *081 838 2796* **Rooms** *8* **Road Map** *C4/5*

Perfect for those seeking total hush and relaxation, this award-winning boutique hotel occupies a luxurious and historic private home built by a local baron in the 1800s. The gardens and pool create an enchanted setting outside while a collection of art and antiques adorns the interior. **www.villalescale.com**

CETARA Hotel Cetus

€€€

SS Costiera Amalfitana, Cetara, 84010 **Tel** *089 26 13 88* **Fax** *089 26 13 88* **Rooms** *40* **Road Map** *E4*

A fine hotel on the Amalfi Coast road, Cetus has a spectacular setting jutting out from a cliff top and boasts dazzling views through its glass walls. All bedrooms have sea views, as do the restaurant terrace and bar. There is a private beach, reached by a lift. The hotel is close to the fishing town of Cetara *(see p161)*. **www.hotelcetus.com**

CUMAE (CUMA) Villa Giulia

€€

Via Cuma Licola 178, 80078 **Tel** *081 854 01 63* **Fax** *081 804 43 56* **Rooms** *6* **Road Map** *B3*

Just 1 km (0.5 miles) from the sea and only 20 km (12 miles) from the centre of Naples, this beautiful farmhouse is owned by champion breeders of Siberian huskies. Both self-catering and bed and breakfast are available. Terraces overlook the pool and gardens, with views over Ischia and Cumae. Cookery courses available. **www.villagiulia.info**

FURORE Hostaria di Bacco

€

Via G B Lama 9, 84010 **Tel** *089 83 80 60* **Rooms** *12* **Road Map** *D4*

This 19th-century villa, now a taverna with rooms, borders an olive grove, vineyard and terrace. The individually named bedrooms are simple and whitewashed, with terracotta floors and balconies. Suites have huge glass windows. The excellent restaurant offers its own brand of white wine. **www.baccofurore.it**

FURORE Furore Inn Resort

€€€€€

Via dell'Amore 1, 84010 **Tel** *089 830 47 11* **Fax** *089 830 47 77* **Rooms** *22* **Road Map** *D4*

Set on Italy's only fjord, in the lovely village of Furore on the Amalfi coast. Small, luxurious and modern, all rooms have sea views and whirlpool baths; deluxe rooms and suites are especially grand. Excellent restaurant, three pools and a health spa. Boat excursions and cookery lessons are available as is a regular shuttle bus to Amalfi. **www.furoreinn.it**

ISCHIA Il Vitigno B&B

€

Via Bocca 31, Ischia Porto, 80075 **Tel** *081 99 83 07* **Fax** *081 99 83 07* **Rooms** *13* **Road Map** *B4*

This lovely *agriturismo* includes a large vineyard and an estate where you can walk and enjoy nature. Rooms are within the farmhouse and two outhouses – the decor is rustic and all are en suite. Meals are relaxed communal affairs with guests enjoying the farm produce and the local wine. **www.agriturismoilvitigno.it**

ISCHIA Casa Conchiglia

€€

Via Chiaia delle Rose 1, Sant'Angelo, 80070 **Tel** *081 99 92 70* **Fax** *081 99 92 70* **Rooms** *10* **Road Map** *A4*

In the lovely town of Sant'Angelo, this little hotel has an old-fashioned appeal. Right in the thick of things, with the beach just steps away, this has to be one of Ischia's most beautiful spots – perfect for people-watching and gazing at the sea. The hotel also has a superb fish restaurant. **www.conchigliahotel.it**

ISCHIA Hotel Il Monastero

€€

Via Castello Aragonese 3, Ischia Ponte, 80077 **Tel** *081 99 24 35* **Rooms** *22* **Road Map** *B4*

One of the most distinguished addresses on the island belongs to this hotel as it occupies a former convent within Castello Aragonese. In recent years it has been refurbished by the art collector owners. The rooms (former cells), are cheerfully decorated and some have terraces. The views are breathtaking. **www.albergoilmonastero.it**

ISCHIA La Villarosa

€€

Via G Gigante 5, Ischia Porto, 80077 **Tel** *081 99 13 16* **Fax** *081 99 24 25* **Rooms** *37* **Road Map** *B4*

This family-run hotel stands in a verdant garden with a thermal pool, a short walk from the beach and from Ischia Porto. Public rooms are grand and furnished with antiques; bedrooms are simpler. The terraces are perfect for relaxing. The hotel restaurant is highly recommended; in high season full board is required. **www.lavillarosa.it**

ISCHIA Hotel della Baia

€€€

Via S Montano, Baia di S Montano, Lacco Ameno, 80076 **Tel** *081 98 63 98* **Rooms** *20* **Road Map** *A4*

This comfortable hotel is ideally placed for the beach at San Montano. It also neighbours the breathtaking gardens of Negombo, established by an Italian nobleman. The gardens contain a thermal spa, to which the hotel's guests receive free entry. The hotel has a panoramic terrace, a restaurant and five suites with gardens. **www.negombo.it**

ISCHIA Park Hotel Miramare

📶 🍴 🏊 🏋 🛗 🅿 🗙 €€€€

Via Com Maddalena 29, Sant'Angelo, 80070 **Tel** *081 99 92 19* **Fax** *081 88 83 25* **Rooms** *50*   **Road Map** *A4*

Overlooking Maronti Bay, one of Ischia's most beautiful, is this elegant beach hotel. It has an excellent spa just a short walk from the main building. Rooms have sea views; some have terraces or balconies. Two suites are set in the gardens. Sant'Angelo town is particularly picturesque and favoured by Italians. **www.hotelmiramare.it**

ISCHIA Grand Albergo Mezza Torre

📶 🍴 🏊 🏋 🛗 🅿 🗙 €€€€€

Via Mezzatorre 23, San Montano, Forio d'Ischia, 80076 **Tel** *081 98 61 11* **Rooms** *59*   **Road Map** *A4*

A luxury spa hotel set in a pine forest, on a bluff high above the sea between Forio and Lacco Ameno. All rooms have balconies: comfort rooms have sea views while others overlook the park. Superior rooms and suites are sumptuous; some are within a romantic old Saracen tower. Beautiful pools, beach, restaurant and spa. **www.mezzatorre.it**

ISCHIA Miramare e Castello

📶 🍴 🏊 🏋 🛗 🅿 🗙 €€€€€

Via Pontano 5, Ischia Porto, 80077 **Tel** *081 98 13 55* **Fax** *081 98 45 72* **Rooms** *43*   **Road Map** *B4*

In a beautiful spot between Ischia Porto and Ischia Ponte, with views of Castello Aragonese and the big blue sea beyond, this lovely family-run hotel dates from the 1950s. Bedrooms are elegantly furnished; prices increase with comfort and for views. Breakfast is served on the exquisite roof terrace. **www.miramareecastello.it**

ISCHIA Regina Isabella e Royal Sporting

📶 🍴 🏊 🏋 🛗 🅿 🗙 €€€€€

Piazza S Restuita, Lacco Ameno, 80076 **Tel** *081 99 43 22* **Fax** *081 90 01 90* **Rooms** *132*   **Road Map** *A4*

Built in the 1950s, this is probably Ischia's most luxurious hotel – the choice of Elizabeth Taylor and Richard Burton during filming of Cleopatra. The spa, certainly, is the island's most advanced. Decor is ultra stylish: bedrooms have majolica tiles, antiques and contemporary textiles and most have private terraces or balconies. **www.reginaisabella.it**

MAIORI Casa Raffaele

🛗 🅿 🗙 €€

Via Casa Mannini 10, 84010 **Tel** *089 85 35 47* **Fax** *089 854 18 65* **Rooms** *9*   **Road Map** *D4*

This frescoed house was built and furnished by Raffaele Conforti, a 19th-century lemon merchant. Peaceful and elegant, it is now open as a small hotel in the heart of Maiori. Antique furniture adds to the sense of stepping back in time. The suite has a whirlpool bath under a frescoed ceiling. Private beach. **www.casaraffaeleconforti.it**

MASSA LUBRENSE Piccolo Paradiso

📶 🍴 🏊 🛗 🅿 🗙 €

Piazza Madonna della Lobra 5, 80061 **Tel** *081 878 92 40* **Fax** *081 808 90 56* **Rooms** *54*   **Map** *C4*

Set amid citrus trees near the old parish church, close to the centre of Massa Lubrense, this hotel has a pool and fine views. A quiet, comfortable place, it is a pleasant stroll away from the Marina di Lobra below, where you can watch the fishermen at work and sample their catch. Regular buses run to Sorrento. **www.piccolo-paradiso.com**

MASSA LUBRENSE La Certosa

🍴 🏋 🛗 🅿 🗙 €€

Fraz Marina del Cantone, 80061 **Tel** *081 808 12 09* **Fax** *081 808 12 45* **Rooms** *17*   **Map** *C4*

In a lovely spot, right on the beach in the beautiful Baia di Nerano, where Ulysses was bewitched by the Sirens. The hotel partly occupies a 14th-century convent with medieval vaulting and architectural detail carried through into its modern extension. Rooms are simple, colourful and comfortable. Terrace restaurant serving fish. **www.hotelcertosa.com**

MASSA LUBRENSE Locanda del Capitano

🍴 🛗 🅿 🗙 €€€

Piazza delle Sirene, Fraz Marina del Cantone, 80061 **Tel** *081 808 10 28* **Rooms** *12*   **Road Map** *C4*

Not just a wonderful fish restaurant, but also a small inn overlooking the enchanting bay of Marina del Cantone. The food and wine share the billing here alongside the extraordinary view. The hotel is a pretty white building right on the beach. The stylish bedrooms share the views. Breakfasts are delicious. **www.tavernadelcapitano.it**

PAESTUM Hotel Paistos

🍴 🛗 🅿 🗙 €

Via Laura Mare 39, Capaccio, 84040 **Tel** *0828 85 16 83* **Fax** *0828 85 16 61* **Rooms** *10*   **Road Map** *F5*

This small and comfortable modern hotel with surrounding garden, is not far from the beach at Capaccio and around 3 km (2 miles) from the temples of Paestum. It is a fine place for a short stay. Bedrooms are simple and most have balconies. There is a good restaurant, with summer dining alfresco on the terrace. **www.paestum.com/paistos**

PAESTUM Agriturismo Seliano

🍴 🏊 🏋 🛗 🅿 🗙 €€

Via Seliano, Capaccio Scalo, 84063 **Tel** *0828 72 45 44* **Fax** *0828 72 45 44* **Rooms** *14*   **Road Map** *F5*

Run by the Bellelli family, whose forefathers were famously painted by Edgar Degas, this *agriturismo* is a short drive off the main road between Capaccio Scalo and Paestum. Rooms are in the main house or astate cottages. Pretty gardens, a pool and delicious food. Staying on the buffalo farm is also an option. **www.agriturismoseliano.it**

POMPEII Hotel Amleto

📶 🍴 🏋 🛗 🅿 €

Via B Longo 4, 80045 **Tel** *081 863 10 04* **Fax** *081 863 55 85* **Rooms** *26*   **Road Map** *D3*

Family-run, this is a comfortable modern hotel, with an elegant decor and well-furnished bedrooms. In the heart of new Pompeii, it is convenient for the Circumvesuviana train between Naples and Sorrento and a short walk to the ruins. The roof terrace is very pleasant. Lovely Pompeiian-style frescoes adorn the public areas. **www.hotelamleto.it**

POMPEII Hotel dei Misteri

📶 🍴 🏊 🏋 🛗 🅿 €

Villa dei Misteri 11, 80045 **Tel** *081 861 35 93* **Fax** *081 862 29 83* **Rooms** *40*   **Road Map** *D3*

A fine retreat after a dusty day touring Pompeii's ruins or hiking up Vesuvius, this hotel is located close to the Circumvesuviana train and Pompeii's Villa dei Misteri entrance. Motel-style rooms are available near the cooling pool, or you can choose to stay in the main building. Not all rooms have air conditioning. **www.villadeimisteri.it**

Key to Price Guide *see p178* **Key to Symbols** *see back cover flap*

POSITANO Pensione Maria Luisa €

Via Fornillo 42, 84017 **Tel** *089 875 20 23* **Fax** *089 81 20 49* **Rooms** *10* **Road Map** *D4*

Positano's oldest hotel is a delightfully simple place at Fornillo beach. Unlike luxurious Positano, it has minimal facilities, though some rooms have private terraces. Fridges are provided. Prime views can be savoured from the breakfast terrace. The owner keeps several cats on the premises. **www.pensionemarialuisa.com**

POSITANO Albergo Casa Albertina €€€

Via della Tavolozza 3, 84017 **Tel** *089 87 51 43* **Fax** *089 81 15 40* **Rooms** *21* **Road Map** *D4*

Above the beach, this lovely hotel, once the haven of Italian playwright Luigi Pirandello, has old wooden doors and airy bedrooms with colourful tiled floors and antiques. Some rooms have whirlpool baths. Overhanging flower-filled terraces provide guests with lovely views. The restaurant is excellent. **www.casalbertina.com**

POSITANO Hotel California €€€

Via Cristofero Colombo 14, 84017 **Tel** *089 87 53 82* **Fax** *089 81 21 54* **Rooms** *15* **Road Map** *D4*

A delightful family hotel in the Palazzo Bruno, a noble residence with a modern annexe. The spacious terrace affords wonderful views. Some of the old bedrooms have 18th-century frescoes; the new ones have whirlpool baths. All have balconies and sea views. There is a bus stop nearby. **www.hotelcaliforniapositano.com**

POSITANO Villa La Tartana €€€

Via Vicolo Vito Savino 6/8, 84017 **Tel** *089 81 21 93* **Fax** *089 812 20 12* **Rooms** *8* **Road Map** *D4*

A good value, popular bed and breakfast. Family-run, it is a climb uphill from Piazza Molino, where there is a public car park and a bus stop. The house is on four levels and all rooms have balconies and views. Breakfast is served in a lovely dining room. Porter service. Reasonably close to the beach. **www.villalatartana.it**

POSITANO Poseidon €€€€

Viale Pasitea 148, 84017 **Tel** *089 81 11 11* **Fax** *089 87 58 33* **Rooms** *52* **Road Map** *D4*

A beautiful family-run villa immersed in lush vegetation. All rooms have private terraces, with views over the bay or the garden. Quiet and intimate, the hotel has a renowned spa and an excellent restaurant in a romantic setting. Bedrooms are large and stylish, with tiled floors and antique furniture. **www.hotelposeidonpositano.it**

POSITANO Palazzo Murat €€€€

Via dei Mulini 23, 84017 **Tel** *089 87 51 77* **Fax** *089 81 14 19* **Rooms** *30* **Road Map** *D4*

The genteel Palazzo Murat was once the summer residence of Napoleon's brother-in-law. It is set around an enchanting courtyard with a fine restaurant. Bedrooms in the 18th-century wing come complete with stucco, wooden beams and frescoes. Those in the elegant modern annexe have air conditioning. **www.palazzomurat.it**

POSITANO San Pietro €€€€€

Via Laurito 2, 84017 **Tel** *089 87 54 55* **Fax** *089 81 14 49* **Rooms** *60* **Road Map** *D4*

Far out of town, this luxurious hideaway in an extraordinary setting is the choice of many celebrities and royals. Built in the 1970s, it nevertheless has a magnificent decor, with Vietri majolica, wrought ironwork and antiques. Privacy is key on the sea-facing terraces leading from the bedrooms. Private beach. **www.ilsanpietro.it**

POSITANO Le Sirenuse €€€€€

Via Cristofero Colombo 30, 84017 **Tel** *089 87 50 66* **Fax** *089 81 17 98* **Rooms** *61* **Road Map** *D4*

With its excellent Swiss-trained management team, Le Sirenuse vies with the San Pietro to be Positano's top hotel. Occupying an 18th-century town house, it boasts exquisitely furnished rooms. Guests luxuriate under pergolas, on vine-laden terraces and beside possibly the world's most glamorous pool. Breathtaking views. **www.sirenuse.it**

PRAIANO Hotel Margherita €€

Via Umberto I, 70, 84010 **Tel** *089 87 46 28* **Fax** *089 87 46 28* **Rooms** *28* **Road Map** *D4*

A family home converted into a hotel, with slightly old-fashioned decor but lovely views and a peaceful location. Bedrooms are extremely comfortable; it is worth paying extra for one with French windows leading to a private balcony. There is a restaurant and a small pool offering hydromassage. **www.hotelmargherita.info**

PRAIANO Onda Verde €€€€

Via Terra Mare 3, 84010 **Tel** *089 87 41 43* **Fax** *089 813 10 49* **Rooms** *20* **Road Map** *D4*

In a quiet town midway between Amalfi and Positano, this family-run hotel has a panoramic terrace with a restaurant. Bedrooms are located within five villas clustered on a cliff top; many have balconies. There is a path down to a small sandy beach, beside which is a private lido. Daily boat excursions. Bus connections. **www.ondaverde.it**

PROCIDA Hotel La Corricella €€

Marina Corricella 88, Corricella, 80079 **Tel** *081 896 75 75* **Fax** *081 896 75 75* **Rooms** *10* **Road Map** *B3*

Pastel-coloured houses tumble down to the sea in this picturesque fishing harbour. Part of this scene is the charming pink-and-turquoise Hotel La Corricella, where bedrooms are calm, airy and spacious and the views are picture-postcard perfect. There is a terrace where guests can sit and admire the view. **www.procida.net/lacorricella**

PROCIDA Hotel Crescenzo €€

Via Marina Chiaiolella 33, Chiaiolella, 80079 **Tel** *081 896 72 55* **Fax** *081 810 12 60* **Rooms** *10* **Road Map** *B4*

A charming blue-painted hotel with a view over the harbour at Chiaiolella, Crescenzo is also one of the island's finest fish restaurants, so half board is an additional bonus. Rooms are either rear facing and quiet or overlook the harbour. Some have balconies and all are prettily decorated with a blue-and-white nautical theme. **www.hotelcrescenzo.it**

PROCIDA La Casa sul Mare   📄 🖼   €€€
Via Salita Castello 16, Terra Murata, Corricella, 80079 **Tel** *081 896 87 99* **Rooms** *10*   **Road Map** *B3*

High up beside the Terra Murata, this small hotel boasts views over the harbour of Corricella, where *Il Postino* was filmed. It has elegant public areas and a charming sea-facing garden, where breakfast is served. All bedrooms have their own private terraces. A yacht takes guests to the beach at Chiaia every day in summer. **www.lacasasulmare.it**

RAVELLO Da Salvatore   🍽 📄 🖼   €€
Via della Repubblica 2, 84010 **Tel** *089 85 72 27* **Fax** *089 85 72 27* **Rooms** *6*   **Road Map** *D4*

Six comfortable rooms are available at this inn, which is well-known for its excellent seafood. Recently refurbished, they share the same fabulous view as the restaurant upstairs. Each room has a beautifully finished en suite bathroom, as well as a private balcony perfect for sitting out and enjoying the wonderful view.

RAVELLO Hotel Graal   🏊 🍽 🏫 📄 P 🖼   €€
Via della Repubblica 8, 84010 **Tel** *089 85 72 22* **Fax** *089 85 75 51* **Rooms** *35*   **Road Map** *D4*

Far less grand than the other choices in Ravello, this modern hotel is on the main road entering the upper part of town. Views are wonderful and among its facilities are a pool, a lovely sun terrace and a pleasant restaurant. The tasteful decor includes colourfully tiled floors. Some rooms have whirlpool baths and balconies. **www.hotelgraal.it**

RAVELLO Punta Civita B&B   📄 P 🖼   €€€
Via Civita 4, 84010 **Tel** *089 87 22 36* **Rooms** *3*   **Road Map** *D4*

Idyllic views and helpful owners are pluses at this bed and breakfast set amid an olive grove some 2 km (1 mile) from Ravello, on the winding road leading to Amalfi. Bedrooms are cool and airy, with tiled floors, old-fashioned furniture and white bedspreads. Guests can make use of several terraces. Buses pass outside. **www.puntacivita.it**

RAVELLO Hotel Giordano   🍽 🏫 📄 P 🖼   €€€
Via Boccaccio 4, 84010 **Tel** *089 85 71 70* **Fax** *089 85 70 71* **Rooms** *30*   **Road Map** *D4*

Owned by the local Palumbo family, this pretty hotel has a lovely pool and a central position. Bedrooms are large, airy and whitewashed, with terraces or balconies facing the garden and pool side. A generous breakfast is served out on the terrace. Good parking facilities which is a definite perk in busy Ravello. **www.giordanohotel.it**

RAVELLO Marmorata Best Western   🏊 🍽 🏫 🚶 📄 P 🖼   €€€
Via SS Amalfitana 163, Marina di Ravello, 84010 **Tel** *089 87 77 77* **Fax** *089 85 11 89* **Rooms** *37*   **Road Map** *D4*

Located in Marina di Ravello, a tiny bay below Ravello, this converted 15th-century paper mill is in a prime secluded spot. Perfect sea views, a pool and a private beach are part of the package. Bedrooms are stylish. A shuttle bus takes guests up to Ravello daily and there is also a local bus stop outside the hotel. Good restaurant. **www.marmorata.it**

RAVELLO Caruso Belvedere   🏊 🍽 🏫 🚶 📄 P 🖼   €€€€€
Via S Giovanni del Toro 52, 84010 **Tel** *089 85 88 01* **Fax** *089 85 88 06* **Rooms** *52*   **Road Map** *D4*

This wonderful place was recently re-opened by Orient Express, who spent several years refurbishing it. The result is a stylish hotel offering excellent service. Once popular with the Bloomsbury Group, it has sumptuous bedrooms, gardens now restored to their former glory and an exquisite pool. **www.hotelcaruso.com**

RAVELLO Hotel Palumbo   🏊 🍽 🚶 📄 P 🖼   €€€€€
Via S Giovanni del Toro 16, 84010 **Tel** *089 85 72 44* **Fax** *089 85 81 33* **Rooms** *21*   **Road Map** *D4*

This *palazzo* dating from the 1700s is one of the prettiest hotels in Italy with romantic Moorish architecture in pale pink stonework. Terraces and gardens, alcoves and intimate corners – elegance and relaxation are the bywords here, as well as old-fashioned family hospitality. Every room is individually decorated. **www.hotelpalumbo.it**

RAVELLO Palazzo Sasso   🏊 🍽 🚶 📄 P 🖼   €€€€€
Via S Giovanni del Toro 28, 84010 **Tel** *089 81 81 81* **Fax** *089 85 89 00* **Rooms** *38*   **Road Map** *D4*

This beautiful 12th-century *palazzo*, converted into a hotel in 1880, was a bolt hole for Wagner and countless other artists. Now owned by Virgin, it has become a style powerhouse worthy of its five stars. Most of the rooms have Jacuzzis and the views are amazing. The restaurant is one of the area's best. **www.palazzosasso.com**

RAVELLO Villa Cimbrone   🍽 🏫 🚶 📄 🖼   €€€€€
Via Santa Chiara 26, 84010 **Tel** *089 85 74 59* **Fax** *089 85 77 77* **Rooms** *19*   **Road Map** *D4*

Recently re-opened, this 12th-century villa has world-famous romantic gardens, set in a citrus grove high on a cliff top. Bought by an Englishman in 1904, it became a haunt of the Bloomsbury Group. Bedrooms have spectacular vaulting, frescoes, majolica tiles, fireplaces and antiques. Lovely restaurant and pool. **www.villacimbrone.com**

SALERNO Hotel Plaza   🏊 📄 P   €€
Piazza Vittorio Veneto 42, 84123 **Tel** *089 22 44 77* **Fax** *089 23 73 11* **Rooms** *42*   **Road Map** *E4*

A central hotel, opposite the train station and within easy walking distance of the port, the old quarter and the regular bus service along the Amalfi Coast. Bedrooms are large, modern, clean and comfortable, with a choice of bath or shower. There's a bar and a breakfast room. Secure parking is available nearby. **www.plazasalerno.it**

SORRENTO Hotel Nice   📄   €
Corso Italia 257, 80067 **Tel** *081 878 16 50* **Fax** *081 878 30 86* **Rooms** *12*   **Road Map** *C4*

Perfectly placed for central Sorrento, and for those using the town as a base to explore the area, this small hotel is a step from the train station. It provides simple, clean and comfortable budget accommodation, following a refurbishment in 2003. As it is on a main street, rooms at the back are quieter. Friendly owners. **hotelnice@tiscali.it**

Key to Price Guide *see p178* **Key to Symbols** *see back cover flap*

SORRENTO Agriturismo Marecoccola
Via Malacoccola 10, 80067 **Tel** *081 533 01 51* **Fax** *081 533 09 21* **Rooms** *6*   **Road Map** *C4*

A delightful *agriturismo* outside Sorrento, set in countryside beside a WWF reserve and overlooking Li Galli islands. Delicious food and comfortable rooms, ideal for those wishing to go walking. The suite has a hot tub and opens on to a private terrace. Play area and restaurant. Horse riding available. **www.fattoriamarecoccola.com**

SORRENTO Hotel Mignon Meuble
Via Sersale 9, 80067 **Tel** *081 807 38 24* **Fax** *081 877 43 48* **Rooms** *24*   **Road Map** *C4*

In the historic centre of Sorrento, near the cathedral and the old walls, this charming *pensione* offers spacious rooms with traditional furniture, tiled floors and good bathrooms. Breakfast is served in guests' rooms, some of which have French windows and small balconies. Limited hotel parking. **www.sorrentohotelmignon.com**

SORRENTO La Neffola
Via Capo 21, 80067 **Tel** *081 878 13 44* **Fax** *081 807 34 50* **Rooms** *8*   **Road Map** *C4*

These charming apartments, within a stone farmhouse standing in lush gardens, are high on a cliff top above the main harbour. They have great views towards Vesuvius. Guests may make use of the lovely pool, terrace and restaurant of the neighbouring camp site. Kitchens are well equipped and there is a friendly bar. **www.neffolaresidence.com**

SORRENTO Il Nido
Via Nastro Verde 62, 80067 **Tel** *081 878 27 66* **Fax** *081 807 33 04* **Rooms** *23*   **Road Map** *C4*

A pretty hotel some 5 km (3 miles) outside Sorrento, with fine views over the Bay of Naples to Vesuvius. A shuttle bus runs every hour into town; it is also on a local bus route. Bedrooms, in pleasing pastel shades, are large and airy. The family room has a great view. Wonderful home cooking in the restaurant and helpful owners. **www.ilnido.it**

SORRENTO Loreley et Londres
Via A Califano 2, 80067 **Tel** *081 807 31 87* **Fax** *081 532 90 01* **Rooms** *23*   **Road Map** *C4*

This relaxing *pensione* is set in an imposing building in an enviable position and oozes faded grandeur. The lovely terrace, with restaurant, has stunning views. With no airs and graces, it has few mod cons, disarmingly low prices and charming staff. Closed mid-Nov–mid-Mar. **www.sorrentohotelmignon.com**

SORRENTO La Tonnarella
Via Capo 31, 80067 **Tel** *081 878 11 53* **Fax** *081 878 21 69* **Rooms** *16*   **Road Map** *C4*

Perched on a cliff, 3 km (2 miles) outside Sorrento's centre, this hotel was the summer residence of an aristocratic family. Inside, there are majolica floor tiles, Moorish vaulting and antique furniture. With wonderful views over the bay, a room with a sea view, balcony or terrace costs more. Good, if tiny, restaurant. Private beach. **www.latonnarella.it**

SORRENTO Parco dei Principi
Via Rota 1, 80067 **Tel** *081 878 46 44* **Fax** *081 878 37 86* **Rooms** *177*   **Road Map** *C4*

A 1960s hotel with a difference, designed by style icon Gio Ponti and with a location that it would be hard to better. The gardens, including a pool and a cliff-top terrace, afford incredible views. The interior is filled with quirky nautical motifs and pebble or shell mosaics. Other facilities include a beach, lido, spa and gym. **www.hotelparcoprincipi.com**

SORRENTO Bellevue Syrene
Piazza della Vittoria 5, 80067 **Tel** *081 878 10 24* **Fax** *081 878 39 63* **Rooms** *73*   **Road Map** *C4*

A grand hotel in every sense, high on a bluff in Sorrento. Established in 1820 and a perennial favourite of royalty and romantic writers, the Bellevue Syrene is sumptuously decorated with frescoes, vaulting, antiques and fine paintings. Built on the foundations of a Roman villa, views of the sea and Vesuvius abound. **www.bellevue.it**

SORRENTO Gran Hotel Cocumella
Via Cocumella 7, Sant'Agnello, 80065 **Tel** *081 878 29 33* **Fax** *081 878 37 12* **Rooms** *61*   **Road Map** *C4*

A former Jesuit monastery in landscaped gardens, this beautiful hotel is found in a quiet suburb of Sorrento. Famous former guests include the Duke of Wellington and Sigmund Freud. Suites are stylish, with fabulous views over the Bay of Naples, while there is a romantic restaurant on the terrace. Classical concerts in summer. **www.cocumella.com**

TORRE DEL GRECO Casa Rossa 1888 al Vesuvio
Via Mortelle 87, 80056 **Tel** *081 883 15 49* **Rooms** *24*   **Road Map** *C3*

On the coast road between Naples and Sorrento, near Vesuvius, this is a convenient stopping place if you are driving. Stylish modern spaces are filled with light and art. Bedrooms are large, with balconies and sea views. The food in the restaurant is excellent. Also a private beach of black volcanic sand. Popular at weekends. **www.casarossa1888.it**

VICO EQUENSE Agriturismo La Ginestra
Via Tessa 2, S. Maria del Castello, Moiano di Vico Equense, 80069 **Tel/Fax** *081 802 32 11* **Rooms** *8* **Road Map** *D4*

This beautifully positioned pink farmhouse, high above the coast, has spectacular terraces bedecked with flowers. There are splendid walks all around – and down to Positano. Public transport links are via Vico Equense. A delightful place to relax, with an excellent restaurant. Minimum stay of three nights. **www.laginestra.org**

VICO EQUENSE Hotel Capo La Gala
Via L Serio 8, 80069 **Tel** *081 801 57 58* **Fax** *081 879 87 47* **Rooms** *18*   **Road Map** *D4*

A place for gazing at the sea from sunrise to sunset, this hotel is on the Sorrento road just 1 km (0.5 miles) before Vico Equense. Imposing terraces, a pool and a private beach offer great views, as do all the rooms. Charge for air conditioning. There are thermal baths nearby. **www.capolagala.com**

WHERE TO EAT

Neapolitan pizzeria sign

The region known to the Romans as *Campania felix* (happy country) revels in food, especially the fruit, vegetables and vines that grow in abundance on every available slope. Neapolitan cuisine is well known throughout the world, thanks to the emigrants who took pizza and pasta with them wherever they went. Neapolitans have never given up their passion for good food, and

eating is a social occasion here – all important events are celebrated with huge meals that may last half a day. Key elements in Neapolitan cuisine are pasta, olive oil and tomatoes, but all along the coast and on the islands you'll find the freshest seafood and fish dishes, from simple pasta sauces to generous fish stews. This is also the home of ice cream, and delectable cakes and pastries.

TYPES OF RESTAURANTS AND BARS

Naples and the outlying area offer a wide choice of restaurants, trattorias and bars to suit all budgets. A *ristorante* may be smarter (and more expensive) than a *trattoria*, and a trattoria may be more informal. Every part of Campania has its own specialities and similar recipes may be interpreted in quite different ways in different locations. Family-run trattorias usually offer excellent home-style cooking. Many of the most exclusive restaurants in Naples are located in the seafront area. In Posillipo the famous restaurants are expensive but you will be seated in front of breathtaking views and the mild climate means you can eat outdoors practically all year round.

The city centre is the place to go for less pretentious and cheaper trattorias and pizzerias with typical Neapolitan food. A pizzeria will offer pasta,

A Finestella (see p195) looking out on to the Bay of Naples

meat and fish dishes as well as pizza. In the Spaccanapoli and Decumano Maggiore districts there are trattorias known as *vini e cucina* where you can eat quite cheaply. Besides good wine served by the bottle or from the barrel, these are good places for trying genuine Neapolitan home cooking. They are usually family–run and small, located in the popular areas; the interiors may be quite plain, with plastic tablecloths and paper napkins; and the menu will either be written on a blackboard or recited at your table by the waiter. *Vini e cucina* are popular with locals and students, so you can also experience authentic Neapolitan life. At *tavole calde* (snack bars) first and second courses are economically priced.

The food on sale at the stalls and *friggitorie* (for fried food) is often very good: potato croquettes, fried pizzas *(pizzelle)* and panzerotti (ravioli). Bars usually offer filled rolls *(panini)* and sandwiches *(tramezzini)*, as well as cakes and pastries, and assorted drinks. Many bars also operate as *gelaterie*, with a tempting range of ice creams.

HOW MUCH TO PAY

The average price for a full meal at a trattoria is about €20, and it can be as little as €8 in pizzerias and *vini e cucina*. Restaurants cost from €18–€20 upwards. *Vino sfuso*, or house wine, is often served in jugs and is inexpensive. Fresh fish is usually sold by weight, which can make calculating the cost of your meal difficult. You may find it can be quite expensive.

The Da Carmine trattoria (see p193)

Eating outdoors, one of the many pleasures of Naples

OPENING HOURS

Restaurants are generally open from 12:30 to 3:30pm and from 8pm to midnight, but this may vary somewhat, especially at weekends and in summer, when you can dine until fairly late. Family–run trattorias have more limited business hours and are usually closed on Sundays and in August, especially around Ferragosto (15 Aug), when many shops in the city are closed for holidays. The restaurants in tourist centres on the islands and along the coast usually close in the winter and open around Easter.

A wood–fired pizza oven

MAKING RESERVATIONS AND PAYING

Restaurants and pizzerias tend to be very crowded on Saturday evening, so it's best to book in advance or arrive early. It is also a good idea to book during the holiday season or on local feast days. Service charges are usually included in the menu prices, but it is customary to leave a tip of around five per cent. The larger restaurants accept major credit cards.

READING THE MENU

A typical Neapolitan menu begins with antipasti, which are so varied and interesting they make a meal in them-selves: seafood salad, sautéed clams and mussels, or tomato, pepper and aubergine (eggplant) cooked in various different ways. The first course *(primo)* will depend on the season: spaghetti with seafood, aubergine baked in tomato sauce *(parmigiana di melanzane)* or a simple tomato, mozzarella and basil salad *(insalata caprese)* for lunch at the seaside; pasta and meat sauce or rice cake with meat and mushrooms *(sartù di riso)* for a heartier winter lunch. Among the main courses *(secondi)*, you can choose calamari or squid in tomato sauce, assorted fried fish *(fritto misto)* or grilled fish

QUI 100 ANNI FA NACQUE LA PIZZA MARGHERITA 1889 1989 BRANDI

Centenary of the Margherita pizza

(grigliata mista), or fried baby mozzarella, artichokes and potato or rice croquettes. Try the vegetable pies; the most famous is made with endive and, in the winter, *friarelli*, a type of broccoli found only in Naples. They are sauteed in a pan with *peperoncino* (hot chilli pepper) and are usually served with sausages.

PIZZERIAS

Naples is the original home of authentic pizza, freshly made and baked in wood–fired ovens. True pizza was originally a peasant dish, made very simply from dough spread with olive oil and tomatoes, and dating from the 18th century. Eaten at any hour of the day in the poorer neighbourhoods of Naples, it was ignored by everyone else until Queen Margherita, wife of Umberto I, decided to try this famous dish. The pizza Margherita, with mozzarella and basil added to create the colours of the Italian flag – red, white and green – was invented in her honour. It is now found in every pizzeria, not only in Italy but wherever pizza is sold. Neapolitan pizza chefs are famous for their creative flair, and as well as classic toppings like the Margherita and the Marinara (tomato, anchovies), you may find they offer to create their own chef's special. Expect to wait for a table at many popular pizzerias.

Inside La Bersagliera restaurant *(see p195)*

The Flavours of Naples and the Amalfi Coast

Juicy red tomatoes, creamy white *mozzarella di bufala* and fragrant green basil, topped with a swirl of olive oil – this is *caprese,* a classic Neapolitan *antipasto.* Its mix of intense flavours and vivid colours is characteristic of a cuisine that reflects the region's sunny Mediterranean climate. Dishes here are generally simple and rely for their success on the freshness that a ready supply of superb local ingredients – grains, pulses, vegetables, fruit, fish and olive oil – can deliver. In Naples' bustling streets, the enticing aromas of recently picked lemons, fresh herbs and grilling fish mingle with the ever-present tang of sea salt.

Fresh herbs

Locals at one of the many freshly squeezed juice stalls in Naples

NAPLES

Neapolitan cuisine has always owed much to the brooding mass of Mount Vesuvius. The fertile volcanic soil on its lower slopes yields a bumper harvest of fruit and vegetables all year round. The superb local aubergines (eggplant), artichokes, fennel and courgettes (zucchini) are

served cooked or preserved in oil or vinegar as *antipasti.* Traditionally, meat has been in short supply and meagre rations of lamb or kid were something to save for special occasions. For many, Sunday is still the day for preparing *ragu,* stuffed rolls of meat that are simmered for hours with wine and tomatoes.

The durum wheat used for pasta was first planted in the the region by the ancient Greeks, but the Neapolitans only became avid pasta-eaters after techniques for making it were introduced by the Sicilians several centuries later. The sunny climate proved perfect for making long strands of *maccheroni,* which were left out to dry in the streets. Spanish rule later brought peppers and tomatoes from South America – and local pasta found its ideal partner.

Superb seafood, caught along the coastline of southern Italy

Labels: Lobster, Tuna, Squid, Sardines, Mussels, Clams

LOCAL DISHES AND SPECIALITIES

Rich tomato sauces with herbs, onion and garlic are central to many dishes. Classic examples are *bistecca alla pizzaiola,* beef cooked with tomatoes, garlic and oregano, and *pollo alla cacciatora,* chicken braised in tomatoes, onions, rosemary and red peppers. *Spaghetti alla puttanesca* (literally, prostitute-style spaghetti) probably got its name because the tomato sauce with olives, anchovies and capers would have been quick for a busy, working woman to prepare. *Timballo di maccheroni,* a pie filled with macaroni, wild mushrooms and tomatoes, is a more elaborate local pasta dish. Neapolitans are also noted for being sweet-toothed. One traditional Easter treat – *pastiera napoletana* (candied fruits and ricotta cheese in a pastry case) – is now popular throughout Italy.

Ripe figs

Parmigiana di melanzane
Aubergines (eggplant) are layered with mozzarella, basil, tomato sauce and parmesan.

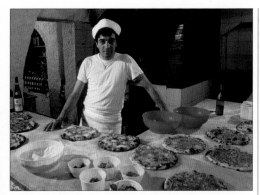

Making pizzas in an Amalfi restaurant

The most highly regarded of all local tomatoes is the strongly flavoured, plum-shaped San Marzano. Naples today is ringed by factories producing pasta and canned tomatoes for export, and the city is known the world over as the home of pasta, pizza and ice cream, or *gelati*.

The famous Neapolitan *gelati*, with three coloured layers, originated in the 19th century. Noted makers, such as Tortoni, used chocolate, cherries and pistachios to colour their creations.

AMALFI COAST AND THE ISLANDS

The people of the Amalfi coast and its many islands have always depended on the daily catch. Buying fish fresh from the habour is still part of local life. Traditional

recipes make the most of the readily available fresh anchovies, mackerel and sardines, as well as larger fish which are becoming increasingly rare in these waters. Fish stews are made from whatever is plentiful

Newly picked olives, ready for crushing to extract their oil

and *frutti di Mare*, such as clams, mussels, octopus, squid and cuttlefish, are served in dozens of ways, including with pasta.

Until the tourism boom of the 1960s, the islands were mainly home to peasant farmers. Dishes relied on whatever was to hand. A typical meal would be *coniglio all'ischitania* (rabbit stew with white wine, garlic, tomatoes and peppers).

All along the coast, bright yellow lemons grow on the steeply stepped terraces. Amalfi lemons are prized for their almost-sweet, tongue-tingling flavour and feature strongly in local desserts.

WHAT TO DRINK

Vesuvio wines The volcano's vines produce fruity reds and crisp white *Lachryma Christi*.

Fiano di Avellino and **Greco di Tufo wines** Both these dry whites are made from ancient Roman grape varieties.

Taurasi wine This powerful red is made from the local Anglianco grapes.

Ischia wines These include good quality reds, whites and sparkling varieties.

Capri wines Dry and white, these are good with seafood.

Limoncello This lemon liqueur is usually served at the end of a meal.

Pizza Napoletana *This thin-crusted pizza is topped simply with tomato, garlic, oregano, basil and anchovies.*

Pesce spada *In Campania, Puglia and Sicily, swordfish steak is pan-fried or grilled with lemon and oregano.*

Sfogliatella *Paper-thin layers of pastry ooze with butter, sugar, cinnamon, orange peel and ricotta.*

Choosing a Restaurant

The restaurants in this chart have been selected for their high quality of food and value for money. They are listed by price category and district (Naples) or region (outside Naples). See the Street Finder on pages 228–43 for map references in Naples; for those in other areas, see the Road Map on the inside back cover.

PRICE CATEGORIES
The following price ranges are for a three-course evening meal for one, including a half-bottle of house wine, tax and service.
€ Under €20
€€ €20–€30
€€€ €30–€40
€€€€ €40–€55
€€€€€ Over €55

NAPLES

TOLEDO AND CASTEL NUOVO Ciro a Medina   📖   €
Via Medina 19, 80133 **Tel** *081 551 53 55*   **Map** *7 B2*

A cheery place with a relaxed feel. At lunch time there is a fixed menu, but a wider choice is available for dinner, including excellent pizzas. Mostly fish-based dishes, with specials such as smoked swordfish with *culatello* (cured pork) sauce and smoked mozzarella, *scialiatelli* (pasta ribbons) with seafood, and *linguine* (pasta) with anchovies and breadcrumbs.

TOLEDO AND CASTEL NUOVO Osteria Il Garum   🍴📖   €
Piazza Monteoliveto 2a, 80134 **Tel** *081 542 32 28*   **Map** *7 A1 (9 B5)*

This friendly *osteria* boasts a fine location in the beautiful square of Piazza Monteoliveto, facing the church of Sant'Ana dei Lombardi. It offers superb value and you can choose between a table outside or one in the cosy dining room. Neapolitan cuisine with innovative touches, often using *garum*, an ancient Roman spice made from fish.

TOLEDO AND CASTEL NUOVO Amici Miei   ♿📖   €€
Via Monte de Dio 78, 80123 **Tel** *081 764 60 63*   **Map** *6 F2*

A welcoming traditional trattoria in Naples' oldest quarter, where the menu is very much meat orientated. Renowned for its excellent pasta and char-grilled pork, lamb, steaks and game. Try the *paccheri* (pasta) with gorgonzola and tomato sauce, followed by steak with a *barolo* wine and radicchio sauce. The wine list is excellent, as are the desserts.

TOLEDO AND CASTEL NUOVO Fratelli La Bufala   📖   €€
Via Medina 18, 80133 **Tel** *081 551 04 70*   **Map** *7 B2*

As popular for its pizzas as its meat – and the meat in question is buffalo. The walls of this stylish restaurant feature colourful modern art and service is efficient and friendly. Excellent *mozzarella di bufala* (buffalo mozzarella) and desserts featuring ricotta made from rich buffalo milk. Buffalo steaks, hamburgers and *polpetti* (meatballs in tomato sauce).

TOLEDO AND CASTEL NUOVO Hostaria Toledo   📖   €€
Vico Giardinetto a Toledo 78a, 80134 **Tel** *081 42 12 57*   **Map** *7 A2*

In the heart of the Quartieri Spagnoli, this *osteria* has been open since 1951 and offers classics from the Neapolitan repertoire. Specials include *ziti al ragu* (pasta with a tomato and beef sauce), *frittura di paranza* (mixed fried fish), *zucchine alla scapece* (courgette gazpacho) and *spaghetti alle vongole* (with clams). The desserts are sublime.

TOLEDO AND CASTEL NUOVO Kukai   📖   €€
Via Carlo de Cesare 55-56, 80132 **Tel** *081 41 19 05*   **Map** *7 A4*

One of Naples' first sushi bars, Kukai features stylish decor. Aquariums, modern lighting and bar stools surround the glass-walled kitchen, in which Japanese chefs prepare the food before your very eyes. Japanese beer and sake are on hand to wash down the excellent sushi, sashimi and *teriaki*. Trendy and popular, it also does takeaways.

SPACCANAPOLI Da Michele   📋   €
Via C Sersale 1/3, 80139 **Tel** *081 553 92 04*   **Map** *4 D5 (10 F3)*

In existence since 1870, this legendary pizzeria produces only two varieties – *margherita* or *marinara* (tomato, garlic, oregano and basil), washed down with beer and soft drinks. Very cheap and extremely good. Try the *frittura* (fried starters). Queues are long – get a number from the cash desk inside and wait your turn. Usually closed Sun.

SPACCANAPOLI Vesi   🍽♿📖   €
Via dei Tribunali 338, 80138 **Tel** *081 45 90 34*   **Map** *3 B5 (9 C3)*

A busy pizzeria with wooden tables. Long queues form in the evenings, when regulars jostle for elbow room and service is brisk. Naturally, the pizzas are excellent – try the Neapolitan classic, the *marinara*, or the *rustica* (ricotta, mozzarella and peppers), along with a cold beer.

SPACCANAPOLI La Cantina del Sole   📖   €€
Via Paladino 3, 80138 **Tel** *081 552 73 12*   **Map** *3 C5*

This intimate and cheerfully decorated restaurant, in the heart of the historic centre, serves up a vast repertoire of dishes made according to traditional Neapolitan recipes dating from the 17th and 18th centuries. The food is fabulous and full of culinary surprises. The menu is complemented by a good wine list.

Key to Symbols *see back cover flap*

SPACCANAPOLI La Fila
Via Nazionale 6c, 80143 **Tel** *081 20 67 17*   **Map** *4 F3*

Cosy and family-run, La Fila offers top-notch food. Ask for the day's specials and you will discover the pleasures of simple Neapolitan cuisine at its best. The welcoming owners help create an ambience that attracts a wide spectrum of people. Pizzas are served in the evening only. Located close to Central Station.

SPACCANAPOLI Lombardi a Santa Chiara
Via B Croce 59, 80134 **Tel** *081 552 07 80*   **Map** *3 B5, 9C4*

This friendly place is found in the heart of old Naples, close to the lovely church of Santa Chiara. Downstairs, customers perching on stools snack on pizzas and calzoni. Upstairs, there is an elegant dining room, where a huge range of antipasti is served, as well as delicious pasta, pizzas and salads. Very popular so book ahead.

SPACCANAPOLI Mimi alla Ferrovia
Via A d'Aragona 21, 80139 **Tel** *081 553 85 25*   **Map** *4 E4*

Extremely popular, this oasis of calm off Piazza Garibaldi provides fine food and wine. The decor is Art-Deco elegance and the service refined. Recipes celebrate the *cucina povera* (literally, "poor cooking") of old Naples and include excellent mozzarella and antipasti and a wide range of pasta, fish and meat dishes, as well as delicious desserts. Closed Sun.

SPACCANAPOLI Il Simposium
Via Benedetto Croce 38, 80134 **Tel** *081 552 05 19*   **Map** *3 B5, 9 C4*

Giovanni Serritelli, an eminent food historian, has re-opened this unique restaurant. Every Friday and Saturday evening, he offers a menu from a specific historical period accompanied by music and entertainment from that era. Guests sit together – groups, couples and individuals are welcome – presided over by their host. Booking essential.

DECUMANO MAGGIORE Da Carmine
Via dei Tribunali 330, 80138 **Tel** *081 29 43 83*   **Map** *3 B5, 9 C3*

This is a charming, old-style family trattoria, bedecked with sepia pictures of old Naples. Classic Neapolitan cuisine is the order of the day, at bargain prices. The atmosphere is cosy and friendly, the fare is hearty and dishes are freshly prepared. Very close to Napoli Sotterranea and convenient for San Gregorio di Armeno.

DECUMANO MAGGIORE Di Matteo
Via dei Tribunali 94, 80138 **Tel** *081 45 52 62*   **Map** *3 B5, 9 C3*

One of the top pizzerias in Naples' historic centre attracts long queues of loyal locals. While you wait for your pizza or a table, nibble on the delicious fried courgettes (zucchini), artichokes and mozzarella. The pizza dough is wonderful and the toppings are made with the freshest ingredients – try sausage and *friarelli* (a type of broccoli).

DECUMANO MAGGIORE Sorbillo
Via dei Tribunali 32, 80138 **Tel** *081 44 66 43*   **Map** *3 B5, 9 C3*

One of Naples' best pizzerias, this tiny place has only a handful of tables and one thing on the menu – pizza. In the family for three generations, its pizza bases are excellent and the finest ingredients are used for the toppings. Service is brisk but friendly. A more upmarket version is further up the same street, but many prefer the original. Worth the queue.

DECUMANO MAGGIORE Europei di Matozzi
Via Marchese Campodisola 4–10, 80133 **Tel** *081 552 13 23*   **Map** *7 B1, 9 C5*

A welcoming restaurant near Piazza Borsa with a rustic feel with copper ware and early 20th-century photos hanging from the walls. Delicious and decidedly seasonal Neapolitan fare: antipasti, hearty soups with chickpeas, beans and peas, and excellent pastas. Try the fresh *gragnano* pasta with *genovese* (mince and onion) sauce. Great wine list.

DECUMANO MAGGIORE La Chitarra
Rampe San Giovanni Maggiore 1/b, 80134 **Tel** *081 552 91 03*   **Map** *7 B1*

Not far from the University of Federico II, this trattoria only has a few tables. The lunch time set menu is a bargain. Try the soups, *parmigiana di melanzane* (baked aubergine (eggplant) with tomato sauce and cheese), pizza with *scarola* (endive), and *tubetti* pasta with mussels, *baccala* (salt cod) and chickpeas. Delicious home-made fruit liqueurs.

DECUMANO MAGGIORE La Taverna dell'Arte
Rampe San Giovanni Maggiore 1/a, 80134 **Tel** *081 552 75 58*   **Map** *7 B1*

With only a few tables inside, and a lovely pergola for alfresco dining in summer, the ambience here is intimate and old-fashioned. Elegantly decorated with antique chandeliers and 17th-century furnishings. The cuisine is traditional Neapolitan, using old recipes, with the menu changing daily according to the owner's whim. Delectable desserts.

DECUMANO MAGGIORE Osteria da Carmela
Via Conte di Ruvo 11/12, 80135 **Tel** *081 49 97 38*   **Map** *3 B4, 9 B2*

Not far from the Archaeological Museum, this friendly *osteria* features traditional Neapolitan home cooking with innovative touches and a welcoming atmosphere – typical Neapolitan paraphernalia hangs from the walls. Try the *pappardelle* pasta with clams and *porcini* (cep mushrooms) or the pasta with white beans and mussels. Excellent wines.

CAPODIMONTE AND I VERGINI Antica Cantina del Gallo
Via Telesino 21, 80136 **Tel** *081 544 15 21*   **Map** *2 F2*

Not far from the Fontanelle in the Sanita quarter, this pizzeria-trattoria has been around for 200 years. Set in a *tuffo* (tufa rock) cave, the decor is basic but the good food ensures its popularity. Choose from pizzas, *pizzicotti* (calzoni stuffed with aubergine (eggplant), mozzarella, sausage and broccoli), bean soups and pastas.

CAPODIMONTE AND I VERGINI Lombardi

Via Foria 12, 80137 **Tel** *081 45 62 20*   **Map** *4 D2*

A stylish trattoria, not far from the *Orto Botanico* (botanic gardens), this is an oasis away from the traffic of Via Foria. While the menu is limited, all dishes are freshly made to order and there are daily specials. Delicious antipasti and good seafood pasta and risotto. There is a little outside terrace, but the street is rather busy.

VOMERO Acunzo

Via Domenico Cimarosa 64, 80127 **Tel** *081 578 53 62*   **Map** *2 D5*

An unpretentious local trattoria and pizzeria offering simple home cooking and a low-key atmosphere. Both the pasta dishes and pizzas are delicious, using well-sourced ingredients. Convenient for the funicular down to Via Roma, it is the perfect pitstop before or after a visit to San Martino or Castel Sant'Elmo. In the evening expect to queue.

VOMERO Toto, Eduardo e Pasta e Fagioli

Corso Vittorio Emanuele 514, 80135 **Tel** *081 564 26 23*

Another classic Neapolitan trattoria, with very honestly priced food and a proud history of *cucina genuina* (traditional cooking). The menu features both meat and fish dishes, as well as fresh *gragnano* pasta. There is also a wealth of local desserts to tempt you. Choose to eat inside or out on the ample terrace. Good house wine.

VOMERO La Cantina de Sica

Via G Lorenzo Bernini 17, 80129 **Tel** *081 556 75 20*   **Map** *2 D5*

Typically Neapolitan cuisine is to be had here, with a romantic menu on Sundays for couples. Courteous, efficient service and a rustic decor, with a beamed ceiling and wooden tables. Excellent soups, pastas, antipasti and desserts. Try the *parmigiano di peperone* (baked peppers) or *tubettoni* pasta with courgettes (zucchini) and prawns.

VOMERO Il Gallo Nero

Via Tasso 466, 80127 **Tel** *081 64 30 12*   **Map** *5 A1, 5 B1*

This restaurant is set in a beautiful Liberty (Art-Nouveu) villa, high on Vomero hill, with wonderful views over the city. The menu is limited, but features classics from the Neapolitan repertoire created using the finest ingredients – freshly caught fish and the best meat from the Campanian hinterland. A stylish choice; eat in the garden in summer. Good wine list.

CASTEL DELL'OVO AND CHIAIA Da Pasqualino

Piazza Sannazzaro 77–9, 80122 **Tel** *081 68 15 24*   **Map** *5 B3*

Ideally located for the ferry port, the nearby railway station and the seafront at Mergellina, this pizzeria opens onto a pretty but busy square. Here you can watch the locals' fascinating driving style from a safe distance and enjoy a bite to eat. Very cheap and cheerful, its pizzas are more than satisfactory, and pasta and fried nibbles are on offer too.

CASTEL DELL'OVO AND CHIAIA Da Pietro

Via Lucilliana 27, Borgo Marinaro, 80121 **Tel** *081 807 10 82*   **Map** *7 A5*

Flanked on either side by expensive restaurants, this tiny trattoria in the Borgo Marinaro has a basic daily menu with only a few tables inside and out. Excellent seafood dishes are its forte, as well as the low prices. Except to queue or arrive early. Opening hours are somewhat erratic.

CASTEL DELL'OVO AND CHIAIA Dal 1920 Antica Trattoria Da Ettore

Via Gennaro Serra 39, 80132 **Tel** *081 764 35 78*   **Map** *7 A3*

A classic restaurant, run by the same family since the 1920s. Attracting famous customers in years gone by – such as the comedian Totò and playwright De Filippo *(see p37)* – the atmosphere is convivial. The cuisine is deceptively simple, featuring pasta, risotto, fish and meat dishes. Especially good for fresh fish. Superb wine list.

CASTEL DELL'OVO AND CHIAIA Brandi

Salita S Anna di Palazzo 1–2, Via Chiaia, 80121 **Tel** *081 41 69 28*   **Map** *6 F2*

Laying claims to the invention of the *pizza margherita*, this historic pizzeria has been in business since 1780. Friendly, bustling and very popular, it also serves good pasta dishes. Its ambience makes it a fun place to spend an evening. Yet, purists might point out that they are not the best pizzas the city has to offer and prices are a little steep.

CASTEL DELL'OVO AND CHIAIA Da Ettore

Via Santa Lucia 56, 80123 **Tel** *081 764 04 98*   **Map** *7 A4*

A trattoria-pizzeria, with a loyal following and old-fashioned charm. In summer you can choose from the wood-panelled dining room or street-side tables. Excellent antipasti, especially the *mozzarella di bufala*, (buffalo mozzarella) and good pizzas and pastas. Handy for Santa Lucia or Piazza Plebescito.

CASTEL DELL'OVO AND CHIAIA Da Tonino

Via Santa Teresa a Chiaia 47, 80121 **Tel** *081 42 15 33*   **Map** *6 E2*

At this *enoteca* and *osteria*, run by the same family for over a hundred years, meals are served in a cosy wood-panelled dining room. Portions are generous; at lunch there is a limited menu, but in the evening a more ample one is on offer. Good wine and typical Neapolitan cuisine: pasta with chickpeas, lentils or meat sauce; fish stews.

CASTEL DELL'OVO AND CHIAIA Dall'Amico Gamberone

Via F Crispi 93–5, 80100 **Tel** *081 66 53 44*   **Map** *5 C2*

This pizzeria-trattoria has a rustic feel and a pretty garden. The menu changes with the season, but is predominantly based on fish and seafood combined with lemons and oranges. Try the fried small fish starter, *scialiatelli* pasta with courgette (zucchini) flowers and shellfish, or *musdea* (octopus tentacles in broth). Good wine list.

Key to Price Guide *see p192* **Key to Symbols** *see back cover flap*

CASTEL DELL'OVO AND CHIAIA La Cantina di Triunfo
Riviera di Chiaia 64, 80122 **Tel** *081 66 81 01*   **Map** *5 C2*

A veritable institution, this is a wine shop by day and a trattoria by night. The long, cool room has an open kitchen, so you can watch your food being prepared. The daily changing menu is limited to two options for each course; the chef uses regional recipes and seasonal ingredients. The house wine is excellent and very good value.

CASTEL DELL'OVO AND CHIAIA Ciro
Borgo Marinaro 29–30, 80121 **Tel** *081 764 60 06*   **Map** *7 A5*

At the foot of Castel dell'Ovo, this trattoria has a narrow terrace overlooking the pretty marina, with fine views of Vesuvius. With pizzas, seafood, pasta and risotto on offer, there is something for everyone, and the delicious desserts will tempt you to linger awhile. Extremely popular, so it is a good idea to arrive early if you want a good table.

CASTEL DELL'OVO AND CHIAIA Don Salvatore
Via Mergellina 4a, 80122 **Tel** *081 68 18 17*   **Map** *5 B4*

An abundance of fresh fish and seafood pasta dishes is on the menu at this top restaurant by the harbour at Mergellina. Eat on the leafy terrace or in the elegant dining rooms with chandeliers. The antipasti are sought after and there is pizza and freshly baked bread too. An excellent wine cellar. Closed Wed.

CASTEL DELL'OVO AND CHIAIA La Bersagliera
Borgo Marinaro 10–11, 80132 **Tel** *081 764 60 16*   **Map** *7 A5*

A historic fish restaurant offering turn-of-the-century decor and mandolin music. The romantic terrace faces the harbour, Castel dell'Ovo and Vesuvius. Try the clam and mussel soup, *taglierini* pasta with baby octopus, black olives and tomato, or risotto with gorgonzola. Other classics include *orata* (seabream) in a salt crust and cuttlefish.

CASTEL DELL'OVO AND CHIAIA La Stanza del Gusto
Vicoletto Sant'Arpino 21, 80121 **Tel** *081 40 15 78*   **Map** *6 F2*

This elegant place is located in a small alley off bustling Via Chiaia. Customers can sample *soffrito* (offal in a tomato sauce), as well as other delicacies less common to the Neapolitan repertoire. The delicious seasonal dishes, prepared with considerable creative flair, include choices such as pasta with sausage and fennel and lamb with ginger.

CASTEL DELL'OVO AND CHIAIA Da Dora
Via F Palasciano 28, 80122 **Tel** *081 68 05 19*   **Map** *5 C2*

A deservedly popular, intimate fish restaurant tucked away in an alley off the Riviera di Chiaia. The charming dining room has white walls, nautical ceramic tiles and a laid-back elegance. Seafood, fresh pasta and fish, prepared simply and well, are matched by fine wines. If you are lucky, the chefs may break into song. Book ahead.

CASTEL DELL'OVO AND CHIAIA Vadinchenia
Via Pontano 21, 80122 **Tel** *081 66 02 05*   **Map** *5 C2*

Not far from Piazza Amedeo, this restaurant offers innovative interpretations of Neapolitan classics. The menu is seasonal and fish is the mainstay. Typical fare is *paccheri* pasta with sardines and *pecorino* (sheep's cheese), finely cooked fish and succulent steaks. The atmosphere is stylish and modern and the food too, is beautifully presented.

CASTEL DELL'OVO AND CHIAIA La Cantinella
Via N Sauro 23 (Lungomare di Santa Lucia), 80132 **Tel** *081 764 86 84*   **Map** *7 A4*

Fine dining and an adjoining club are features of this elite restaurant where Naples' movers and shakers congregate. The decor has an emphasis on bamboo. Service is impeccable and both regional and world cuisine are prepared from the finest ingredients. Excellent fish and steaks, and an extensive wine cellar.

CASTEL DELL'OVO AND CHIAIA La Terrazza, Hotel Excelsior
Via Partenope 48, 80121 **Tel** *081 764 01 11*   **Map** *7 A5*

Probably the best dinner view in town is from this hotel restaurant. Stylishly and luxuriously decorated, it serves inspiring food and wines. International cuisine meets Neapolitan classics and the menu features pasta, meat and fish dishes. Service is discreet and charming.

POSILLIPO A Finestella
Calata del Ponticello a Marechiaro 23, 80123 **Tel** *081 769 00 20*   **Road Map** *C3*

The window of this restaurant and its wonderful view over the Bay of Naples, with Vesuvius looming in the distance, is made famous in a classic Neapolitan song by Salvatore di Giacomo. An old-style place, the setting is unmatched and the kitchen produces classic Neapolitan dishes. Try the *linguine* (pasta) with gurnard and tomatoes.

POSILLIPO Da Cicciotto
Calata del Ponticello a Marechiaro 32, 80123 **Tel** *081 575 11 65*   **Road Map** *C3*

This tiny *osteria* has the remains of a temple as its backdrop, while its dining rooms are dug out of a *tufo* (tufa rock) cave and its terrace faces Marechiaro's splendid view of Vesuvius. It is extremely busy, so book ahead or face a long queue. Follow your waiter's advice: have the delicious antipasti, then fish or lobster washed down by excellent wine.

POSILLIPO La Sacrestia
Via Orazio 116, 80122 **Tel** *081 66 41 86*   **Map** *5 B4*

Fabulous views over the Gulf of Naples are to be had from La Sacrestia's terrace high on Posillipo hill. The staff exude an old-fashioned charm, while the decor is attractive. This is a good place for fine dining on a special occasion. Try the *schiafoni con totanetti* (pasta with tiny cuttlefish, black olives, capers and potatoes) and the carefully prepared fish.

POMPEII & THE AMALFI COAST

AMALFI Cantina San Nicola
⊟   €€

Salita Marino Sebaste 8, 84011   **Tel** *089 830 45 49*   **Road Map** *D4*

Set in a former convent, with labyrinthine rooms, this wine bar-restaurant is off the beaten track but well worth seeking out. *Spuntini* (snacks) are on offer, as well as platters of locally cured meats, cheese and some hot dishes. Try the *caponata* (bread with potatoes and peppers, flavoured with *colatura di alici* – a fish sauce). Fine wines too.

AMALFI Trattoria del Teatro
⊟   €€

Via E Marini 19, 84011   **Tel** *089 87 24 73*   **Road Map** *D4*

A former theatre, this trattoria is reached by a maze of stairs and corridors as it is hidden away in the alleyways within the walls of the old town. Inside, the place is convivial and its kitchen serves up pizzas and excellent pasta as well as fresh fish and meat. Always bustling, it is popular with locals and tourists alike.

AMALFI Eolo
⊞⊟   €€€

Via Comite 3, 84011   **Tel** *089 87 12 41*   **Road Map** *D4*

A charming, elegant restaurant with only a few tables. Three of these are outside and command inspirational views of the sea. The menu features seafood and fish – you can even choose your own lobster from the tank near the entrance. All dishes are prepared simply and with great care. Booking is recommended.

AMALFI La Caravella
⊟   €€€€€

Via M Camera 12, 84011   **Tel** *089 87 10 29*   **Road Map** *D4*

Located near the seafront, within the arches of the entrance to the town, La Caravella is renowned for its fresh fish. Inside, the ambience is formal but friendly and the owner has a fine collection of ceramics from masters of Vietri. Try the wonderful antipasti, seaweed croquettes or the swordfish rolls with almonds wrapped in lemon leaves.

AMALFI (ATRANI) Osteria da Luisiella
♿⊞⊟   €

Piazza Umberto, 84011   **Tel** *089 87 10 87*   **Road Map** *D4*

To flee the bustle of busy Amalfi, stroll to Atrani, where this winebar-restaurant awaits with pleasant tables in the shade under the arches or in the main square. While you admire the pretty views, the friendly owner will tell you about the day's specials, usually pasta, salads and antipasti. A lovely place to linger.

AMALFI (POGEROLA) Trattoria Rispoli
▨⊞   €€

Via Riolo 3, 84011   **Tel** *089 83 00 80*   **Road Map** *D4*

An intimate *osteria* in a lovely village, perched on the rocks above Amalfi. Sit inside the cool dining room or on the small terrace. Time-honoured recipes and locally grown ingredients are key here – both fish and meat are served, though the fish has the edge. Popular, so book ahead.

BAIA Il Casolare
⊞   €€

Via Fabris 12, 80070   **Tel** *081 523 51 93*   **Road Map** *B3*

This *agriturismo* with rooms *(see p181)* and wonderful cooking is set within the green, fertile oasis of a 10,000-year-old extinct volcano. It is renowned for its generous portions of seasonal produce from the surrounding farm belonging to the owner and his family. There is a lovely terrace in summer and a cosy dining room in winter. Book ahead.

CAPRI Da Paolino
♿⊞⊟   €€

Via Palazzo a Mare 11, Capri, 80073   **Tel** *081 837 61 02*   **Road Map** *C5*

An enchanting spot, set in its own lemon grove, Da Paolino serves traditional Caprese recipes. Good antipasti and a choice of dishes from land and sea. Choose from rabbit prepared in balsamic vinegar or fresh fish (seleced by the diner). Delicious pasta includes *ravioli alla caprese* or *tubettoni* with mussels. Good dessert and wine lists.

CAPRI La Pergola
⊞⊟   €€

Traversa Lo Palazzo 2, Capri, 80073   **Tel** *081 837 74 14*   **Road Map** *C5*

Regulars come for both the delicious food and the wonderful views from its large terrace. Lemons feature in all dishes: *ravioli al limone* (stuffed with cheese and lemon and served in a lemon sauce), fresh fish marinated in lemon juice and an excellent lemon tart for dessert. Family-run restaurant with very friendly service.

CAPRI La Savardina da Eduardo
♿⊞⊟   €€

Via Lo Capo 8, Capri, 80073   **Tel** *081 837 63 00*   **Road Map** *C5*

Not far from Villa Jovis, this place is effortlessly charming and Eduardo has a faithful clientele. Dine under a lovely pergola with orange trees and fabulous sea views. Specialities include the *ravioli alla caprese*, the *linguini al'Eduardo* (pasta with anchovies and capers) and the rabbit stew, as well as lamb and seafood.

CAPRI Le Arcate
♿⊞   €€

Via de Tommaso 24, Anacapri, 80071   **Tel** *081 837 33 25*   **Road Map** *C4*

Open all year round – a plus since so many restaurants on Capri have seasonal opening – this place is popular with both locals and tourists. Delicious pizzas and pasta dishes, followed by simply cooked fresh fish or lamb roasted with rosemary. There is the option of eating outside on a pretty terrace.

CAPRI Settani

Via Longano 5, Capri, 80073 **Tel** *081 837 01 05*

Road Map *C5*

There is no terrace here, but if you are lucky you can have a table at the back, with fabulous views over the cliff tops to the sea. Lovely seafood and pasta dishes and friendly family service. Not far from the Piazzetta, the house special is *spaghetti alla chiummenzana* (cherry tomatoes, oregano, basil and wild herbs).

CAPRI Add'O Riccio

Via Grotta Azzurra 11, Anacapri, 80071 **Tel** *081 837 13 80*

Road Map *C4*

A narrow stairway separates this charming restaurant from the famous Blue Grotto. It is a perfect stop-off for those arriving by road. Tables are perched on a wooden platform just above the sea and there is also a lovely lido, which customers can use, meaning that you can make a day of it. Delicious seafood, pasta and fresh fish.

CAPRI Aurora

Via Furlovado 18, Capri, 80071 **Tel** *081 837 65 33*

Road Map *C4*

One of the island's oldest restaurants, Aurora has been in the same family for three generations. It is just a short walk from the bustle of the Piazzetta. The chef creates delicious and beautifully presented food based on Neapolitan and Caprese classics. Pizza is also on the menu. Choose from the outdoor tables or the charming dining rooms. Fine wine list.

CAPRI Gelsolmina la Migliara

Via Migliara 72, Anacapri, 80071 **Tel** *081 837 14 99*

Road Map *C4*

This traditional family-run restaurant is set in a garden with a swimming pool, near a romantic walk to La Migliara, some 20 minutes from Anacapri. The cooking is exemplary: try the delicious pasta with beans or the *ravioli capresi*. Also on offer are "brick-baked" chicken, fresh fish and rabbit. Views over Ischia and beyond. Good wine list.

CAPRI Al Grottino

Via Longano 27, Capri, 80073 **Tel** *081 837 05 84*

Road Map *C4/5*

This stylish choice is a magnet for Capri's rich and famous. The pasta is home made – try the vermicelli with *fiori di zucca* (courgette (zucchini) flowers) and prawns, or the catch of the day prepared *all'acqua pazza* (cooked in water, tomato, wine and herbs). There are also appetizing *involtini alla napoletana* (veal rolls in tomato sauce).

CAPRI La Columbaia

Hotel Quisisana, Via Camerelle 2, Capri, 80073 **Tel** *081 837 07 88*

Road Map *C4/5*

For romantic dining beside the pool at one of the world's legendary hotels, La Columbaia is hard to beat. Impeccable service is to be expected and the menu offers a good choice of pasta, fish and meat dishes. There is a lunch-time buffet and pizzas are cooked in a wood-fired oven. Closed Oct–Apr.

CAPRI La Capannina

Via Le Botteghe 14, Capri, 80073 **Tel** *081 837 07 32*

Road Map *C4/5*

Celebrities and visiting royalty flock here to enjoy the fine cuisine. There is a beautiful veranda and it is just a hop, skip and a jump from the legendary *passeggiata* (evening walk) of the Piazzetta. Romantic candle-lit dining, typical Caprese cuisine and fine house wine. Try to book an outside table.

CAPRI L'Olivo

Capri Palace Hotel, Via Capodimonte 2b, Anacapri, 80071 **Tel** *081 978 01 11*

Road Map *C4/5*

Part of one of Italy's finest hotels (Capri Palace, *see p182*), L'Olivo won a Michelin star in 2004. The decor is eminently stylish and the service impeccable. Dishes are a feast for both the eyes and the tastebuds, while the wines are superb. Typical fare includes seabream with peach and fennel puree, or a timbale of prawns, asparagus, caviar and apple sauce.

CASERTA Gli Scacchi

Via Sant'Annunziata 5, 81100 **Tel** *0823 37 10 86*

Road Map *C2*

In Caserta Vecchia, a beautiful Medieval hill-side town, is this restaurant offering wonderful antipasti and dishes using local and seasonal produce such as chestnuts, mushrooms, rabbit, lamb and pork. Try the *cianfotta* (local summer soup) or the fresh pasta. Home-made desserts and good house wine. Generous portions at modest prices.

CASERTA La Cucinotta

Via Pollio 14 (Piazza Vanvitelli), 81100 **Tel** *0823 44 28 07*

Road Map *C2*

A return to his beloved Caserta for the young chef Bartolo, who spent several years honing his art in France and Switzerland. Exploiting only the finest seasonal ingredients from the surrounding area, he infuses the regional cuisine with his creative flair. The stylish dining room is decorated with modern art. Food and wine tastings on Wednesdays.

CASERTA Le Colonne

Via Nazionale Appia 7, 81100 **Tel** *0823 46 74 94*

Road Map *C2*

This elegant family-run restaurant is set inside a villa with a garden. Produce comes from the fertile soil of the *Terra Felix* (Fortunate Earth), as the Romans called Campania. Naturally, cheese and meat dominate, with much use of the fine local buffalo mozzarella and grilled buffalo steaks, but there is also excellent fish. Good wine list.

CETARA Acqua Pazza

Corso Garibaldi 36, 84010 **Tel** *089 26 16 06*

Road Map *D4*

Renowned for its fish, Cetara has a large fishing fleet and local specialities are celebrated in this delightful restaurant. Try the thinly sliced smoked fish *carpaccio* or the fresh tuna, and the famed *colatura di alici* (fish sauce). Other choices include cuttlefish with cannellini beans, potato and *bottarga* (dried fish roe) puree and sardines cooked in tomatoes.

FURORE Hostaria di Bacco
🖼️📋 €€
Via G B Lama 9, Fraz San Giacomo, 84010 **Tel** *089 83 03 60*   **Road Map** *D4*

Set on Italy's only fjord, with its very own microclimate, this hotel *(see p183)* and restaurant is surrounded by vines. Family owned and popular, its excellent cuisine uses local produce from land and sea. Fresh pasta, fish and rabbit may be washed down with the local Furore white DOC wine. Look out for the fjord's prickly pears in season.

FURORE La Volpe Pescatrice
🖼️📋 €€€€€
Furore Inn Hotel, Via dell'Amore 1, 84010 **Tel** *089 830 47 11*   **Road Map** *D4*

Top-notch cuisine, prepared by a gifted young chef from Amalfi, awaits in this hotel set in a prime position with a spectacular terrace. The restaurant's name means "the fishing fox" and the emphasis is on combining ingredients from land and sea, using local seasonal produce. Try the *fusilli* pasta with seafood and pinenuts.

HERCULANEUM (ERCULANO) Viva lo Re
📋 €€
Corso Resina 261, 80056 **Tel** *081 739 02 07*   **Road Map** *C3*

A bar-restaurant, with a wonderful regional wine cellar. The feel is rustic but stylish and the place is run by young, competent staff. Try the *paccheri* pasta with clams and white fish, the courgette (zucchini) flowers filled with ricotta, or the *sardine parmigiana*. Hearty soups in winter, good local lamb and ricotta with wild strawberries in season.

ISCHIA Zi Carmela
♿🖼️📋 €
Via Schioppa 27, Forio, 80076 **Tel** *081 99 84 23*   **Road Map** *A4*

This friendly, lively place is big on seafood and popular with the locals. It is colourful, with ceramic plates and copper paraphernalia. In addition to fish, there is good pizza baked in a wood-fired oven. Try the fried mixed fish, or the *pezogne*, a white fish baked with potatoes and aromatic herbs. There are also good tasting menus on offer.

ISCHIA Da Coco
♿🖼️📋 €€
Via Aragonese 1, Ischia Ponte, 80077 **Tel** *081 98 18 23*   **Road Map** *B4*

With a remarkable location on the side of the causeway between the mainland and the tiny island of the Castello Aragonese, this seafood restaurant serves ultra-fresh fish from the nearby port. It also serves good pasta with shellfish or baby squid. Very popular with the locals.

ISCHIA La Conchiglia
♿🖼️ €€
Via Chiaia delle Rose 3, Sant'Angelo, 80070 **Tel** *081 99 92 70*   **Road Map** *A4*

Located in a fishing village, this rose-coloured villa also has rooms *(see p183)*. You can eat wonderful seafood in the barrel-vaulted dining room or on a patio perched over the waves – with spectacular views. Locally caught fish of the day will not disappoint, nor will the fried squid or prawns and the many seafood pastas. Good local wine.

ISCHIA Lo Scoglio
🖼️📋 €€
Via Cava Ruffano 58, Sant'Angelo, 80070 **Tel** *081 99 95 29*   **Road Map** *A4*

In a panoramic position perched over the sea beside a pretty cove, seafood is the obvious attraction on the menu at Lo Scoglio. A busy place, popular with locals, it specializes in delicious soups and pastas featuring mussels and other shellfish, as well as just-caught fish. The grilled seabass is especially good.

ISCHIA Trattoria Il Focolare
♿🖼️ €€€
Via Cretajo al Crocefisso 3, Barona d'Ischia, 80070 **Tel** *081 90 20 44*   **Road Map** *A4*

The owners of this place also have a winery, so there are some well-chosen vintages. Ischitana cuisine *di terra* (of the land), served on a straw-canopied terrace. For a break from fish, come here for rabbit, snails, mushrooms, asparagus and fresh pastas flavoured with wild aromatic herbs. The sweet honey bread with lavender and rosemary is a must.

ISCHIA Il Melograno
♿🖼️📋 €€€€
Via G Mazzella 110, Forio, 80076 **Tel** *081 99 84 50*   **Road Map** *A4*

On the road heading to Citara beach, this popular and stylish restaurant is run by a native of nearby Procida. Under the shade of lime trees, you can eat steamed fish with lentils, goose liver, fish soup with croutons and good home-made pasta. Also fresh daily fish or Tuscan steaks. Excellent wines and special menus are available.

ISCHIA Umberto a Mare
🖼️ €€€€
Via Soccorso 2, Forio, 80076 **Tel** *081 99 71 71*   **Road Map** *A4*

Perched over the sea and beside one of the island's loveliest churches, the Chiesa di Soccorso, this restaurant is also a popular hotel. The dining terrace has panoramic views over the deep blue sea. Local ingredients and recipes are given an innovative touch. Try the octopus with *peperoncino* (chilli), dark chocolate and roast pumpkin.

MAIORI Il Faro di Capo L'Orso
🖼️📋 €€€€€
Via D Taiani 48, 84010 **Tel** *089 87 70 22*   **Road Map** *D4*

Just beyond Maiori, immersed in the green of the Capo l'Orso, there are splendid views from this restaurant across to Li Galli islands. Stylish decor includes stone walls, floor-to-ceiling glass walls and fine tiles from Vietri. Fresh *gragnano* pasta, seafood and fish dominate the menu and there is also an excellent wine list.

MASSA LUBRENSE Antica Francischiello da Peppino
♿🖼️📋 €€€
Via Partenope 27, 80068 **Tel** *081 533 97 80*   **Road Map** *C4*

Said to be where the local favourite dessert, *delizia di limone* (a kind of lemon cheesecake) was invented, this well-loved restaurant has been in the same family for four generations. With a wonderful terrace offering sea views, it is filled with antiques, ceramic plates and rustic implements. A vast menu and wine list – all dishes are prepared with care.

Key to Price Guide *see p192* **Key to Symbols** *see back cover flap*

MASSA LUBRENSE I Quattro Passi
⟨icons⟩ €€€€

Via Marina del Cantone, Nerano, 80068 **Tel** *081 808 12 71* **Road Map** *C4*

At this stylish restaurant, the chef has put his own interpretation on traditional local recipes for refined dining. Delicious *pappardelle* pasta comes with *fiori di zucca* (courgette (zucchini) flowers), ravioli is stuffed with broad beans and *scapetti* pasta with oysters. Dishes are often served with edible wild flowers. Superb fruit and chocolate mousses.

MASSA LUBRENSE/NERANO Taverna del Capitano
⟨icons⟩ €€€€

Piazza delle Sirene 10, Loc Marina del Cantone, 80068 **Tel** *081 808 10 28* **Road Map** *C4*

A friendly family restaurant, with rooms also available, this place overlooks the enchanting bay of Marina del Cantone. The young and innovative chef produces superb cuisine from traditional recipes, while the wine list is a joy to behold. Freshness is key here, from the bread to the pasta to the fish, all prepared with the minimum of fuss.

PAESTUM La Pergola
⟨icons⟩ €€€

Via Magna Grecia 1, Capaccio Scalo, 80147 **Tel** *0828 72 33 77* **Road Map** *F5*

Creative regional cuisine from fine produce is on offer at La Pergola. The house speciality is *susciello* (soup of wild asparagus, wild onions, herbs and scrambled egg). Other seasonal dishes include fried white fish with artichokes, oven-baked tuna in buffalo yoghurt and swordfish with sweet red Tropea onions. Also buffalo meat and cheeses.

PAESTUM Nonna Sceppa
⟨icons⟩ €€€

Via Laura 45, Loc Capaccio, 80147 **Tel** *0828 85 10 64* **Road Map** *F5*

A large family-run restaurant producing tempting cuisine that represents the Cilento region. Artichokes are one of the house specials, cooked in a myriad of ways, and the fresh *gragnano* pasta is also delicious. The wine list is good and there are delectable local buffalo cheeses from nearby Battipaglia. Service is good. Closed Fri and Oct.

POMPEII Al Gamberone
⟨icons⟩ €€

Via Piave 36, 80045 **Tel** *081 850 68 14* **Road Map** *D3*

A stone's throw from Pompeii's cathedral, this seafood restaurant also serves excellent fresh pasta dishes. Prawns – as the name of the place implies – have top billing. Try the prawns flambéed in brandy. In summer the exterior seating area, situated within an orange and lemon grove, is lovely.

POMPEII Il Principe
⟨icons⟩ €€€€

Piazza B Longo 8, 80045 **Tel** *081 850 55 66* **Road Map** *D3*

This decidedly elegant restaurant is near the ruins of Pompeii and its decor recreates some of the frescoes from the site. Excellent and beautifully presented food is prepared with flair. Fish dominates the menu, often flavoured with *garum*, an ancient Roman fish spice. Family run, the service is charming and highly attentive.

POSITANO Da Adolfo
⟨icons⟩ €€

Localita Laurita 40, 84017 **Tel** *089 87 50 22* **Road Map** *D4*

Hard to get to and hard to leave, in more ways than one, but well worth it. Boats take you to this little beach, where Da Adolfo serves tasty alfresco food under the shade of a straw canopy. Freshly grilled fish, spaghetti with clams, and squid and potatoes with garlic, as well as good grilled vegetable antipasti. Check the return boat times to avoid a wait.

POSITANO Da Vincenzo
⟨icons⟩ €€

Viale Pasitea 172–8, 84017 **Tel** *089 87 51 28* **Road Map** *D4*

In the upper reaches of Positano delicious home cooking is served in this simple place, run by a friendly family. Dishes change according to what is available in the market, but all are cooked with aplomb. Try the *panzarotti* (pastry squares with mozzarella and prosciutto), or the delicious stuffed peppers and salads. Very reasonable prices.

POSITANO Lo Guarracino
⟨icons⟩ €€

Via Positanesi d'America 12, 84017 **Tel** *089 87 57 94* **Road Map** *D4*

Away from the crowds, high on a pathway on the cliff side, this restaurant has a memorable panoramic terrace with views of a quiet bay. On offer are pizzas baked in a wood-fired oven, delicious seafood pasta and meat dishes. The *linguini ai ricci di mare* (pasta with sea urchin) or the grilled swordfish are worth trying.

POSITANO Il Ritrovo
⟨icons⟩ €€€

Via Montepertuso 77, Montepertuso, 84017 **Tel** *089 81 20 05* **Road Map** *D4*

If you book a table in this sought-after restaurant, a shuttle bus will be sent to collect you. High above Positano, in the village of Montepertuso, great food can be had for a lot less. Enjoy home-made pasta with seafood, *scamorza* cheese in lemon leaves, fresh fish, irresistible *semifreddi* and wild fruit liqueurs. Closed Jan; Wed in winter.

POSITANO La Buca di Bacco
⟨icons⟩ €€€

Via Rampa Teglia 8, 84017 **Tel** *089 97 56 99* **Road Map** *D4*

At this ever-fashionable address you can eat anything from a light meal to a feast, while surveying the *passeggiata* (evening walk) and gazing at the sea and Li Galli islands beyond. The *arancini* (rice croquettes with mozzarella) are renowned, as is the mussel soup and fresh fish, especially the seabass. In season, try the caramelized figs and oranges.

POSITANO Ristorante Max
⟨icons⟩ €€€

Via dei Mulini 22, 84017 **Tel** *089 87 50 56* **Road Map** *D4*

Set within an art gallery, this restaurant is cool and chic, with antique furniture and modern art. Tables are on the first floor, in the basement, or on the terrace upstairs for al fresco dining in summer. There is a vast range of wines to choose from and a good a la carte menu, as well as daily specials of both meat and fish dishes.

POSITANO La Sponda

Via Colombo 30, 84017 **Tel** *089 87 50 66*   **Road Map** *D4*

Hotel dining with a difference. The bougainvillea-covered pergola at Le Sirenuse *(see p185)*, one of Italy's most elegant hotels, is the ultimate in candle-lit romance. The refined menu, dominated by seafood, combines traditional recipes with creative flair. The fish is ultra fresh: try the langoustine gratin with white melon and wild aromatic herbs.

POZZUOLI Fattoria del Campiglione

Via Vicinale Campana 2, 80078 **Tel** *081 526 37 33*   **Road Map** *B3*

A cheerful restaurant, where for a change meat – not fish – reigns. There are little copper pots for tableware and a fine array of game and meats to choose from: rabbit, *salumi* (cured meats), grilled beef and steaks, lamb and baby kid; even kangaroo, venison and bison. The wine list is huge, incorporating a choice of wines from all over the world.

POZZUOLI Il Capitano

Via Cristofero Colombo 10, 80078 **Tel** *081 526 22 83*   **Road Map** *B3*

Il Capitano is a convenient and convivial place for dinner after a visit to Roman Pozzuoli or the Solfatara, or when hopping on or off a boat from Ischia or Procida. This elegant restaurant also has five rooms for those who wish to extend their stay to overnight. Fresh fish and a wide range of seafood pasta dishes. Fine wine list.

PROCIDA Osteria del Gallo

Via Roma 28, Marina Grande, 80079 **Tel** *081 810 19 19*   **Road Map** *B3*

This informal trattoria specializes in seafood pasta and fresh fish. Expect no-nonsense cooking, brisk service and fair prices. There is a choice between the traditional dining room, with air conditioning, or the terrace by the bustling port and main drag. Look out for mussels, clams and fish *all'acqua pazza* (cooked in water, tomato, wine and herbs).

PROCIDA Crescenzo

Via Marina Chiaolella 33, Chiaolella Port, 80079 **Tel** *081 896 72 55*   **Road Map** *B3*

A welcoming hotel *(see p185)* and restaurant by Chiaolella's harbour and beach. Arguably Procida's finest culinary experience, the excellent seafood pasta and fish attracts the hordes at weekends and in high season. Tables are in a cool dining room and out on the terrace. In the evenings there is also pizza, prepared with finesse. Booking advised.

PROCIDA Gorgonia

Marina Corricella 50, Corricella, 80079 **Tel** *081 810 10 60*   **Road Map** *B3*

Named after a locally grown seaweed, the focus here is firmly on seafood and fresh fish. In the heart of colourful Corricella and facing the wide Mediterranean sea, this place offers some of Procida's finest cuisine. Try the delectable spaghetti with sea urchins and the turbot with potatoes. The Campanian wines are highly recommended.

PROCIDA Sent'Co

Via Roma 167, Marina Grande, 80079 **Tel** *081 810 11 20*   **Road Map** *B3*

Old-fashioned and friendly, this trattoria prepares outstanding seafood and fish. Select from the abundance of antipasti, then sample the *orecchiette* with broccoli and shellfish or the spaghetti with *riccio di mare* (sea urchins), the house speciality. The catch of the day is always worthwhile. A small but pleasing wine list.

RAVELLO Cumpa Cosima

Via Roma 42–4, 84010 **Tel** *089 85 71 56*   **Road Map** *D4*

Originally a humble wine shop, this trattoria can get very busy. Not far from the Duomo, it is run by a formidable lady, who knows all about good home cooking. She uses meat from her family's butcher's shop next door and fruits and vegetables from her own garden. The pasta and meat dishes are the best choices. Charming decor.

RAVELLO Da Salvatore

Via delle Repubbliche 2, 84010 **Tel** *089 85 72 27*   **Road Map** *D4*

Right beside the bus stop at the entrance to the top of the town, this popular seafood restaurant has a large airy dining room with panoramic windows and a lovely open terrace overlooking the sea. Staff are gregarious and attentive; there is even a friendly resident mynah bird. Fresh fish and seafood pasta. Closed Nov–Mar.

RAVELLO Ristorante Figli di Papà

Via della Marra 7/9, 84010 **Tel** *089 85 83 02*   **Road Map** *D4*

Set in a lovely building dating from the late 13th century, this restaurant has vaulted dining rooms and walls lined with modern art. The food served up by the young chef also balances the classic with the creative. The daily tourist menu is highly recommended, or you could try one of the taster menus. Good local wines are on offer.

RAVELLO Villa Maria

Via Santa Chiara 2, 84010 **Tel** *089 85 72 55*   **Road Map** *D4*

On the pathway leading to the Villa Cimbrone, this small hotel and restaurant has gorgeous views over the Vallone di Dragone towards Scala. Set in an elegant house, with a charming garden in the shade of lime trees, there is a balmy terrace as well as a dining room. The food is excellent: local game, fresh fish and home-made pasta.

RAVELLO Rossellini's

Palazzo Sasso, Via San Giovanni del Toro 28, 84010 **Tel** *089 81 81 81*   **Road Map** *D4*

For romantic candle-lit meals and fine food, dine at this Ravello restaurant, which has two Michelin stars. The view is mesmerising and the food, created by young chef Pino Lavarla, originally from Puglia, is a memorable if expensive experience. Only the finest of ingredients and an impressive wine list. Dinner only. Closed Nov–Mar.

Key to Price Guide *see p192* **Key to Symbols** *see back cover flap*

S'AGATA SUI DUE GOLFI Don Alfonso
Corso Sant'Agata 11, 80064 **Tel** *081 87 80 26*　　　　　　　　　**Road Map** *C4*

One of Italy's finest chefs, Alfonso Laccarino, and his wife Livia run this elegant and much-lauded restaurant. Many ingredients come from the family's own farm on the hill sides above Sorrento: fish and seafood reign, though. Regional traditions combine with creative finesse to great effect, earning the chef two Michelin stars.

SALERNO Antica Pizzeria del Vicolo della Neve
Vicolo della Neve 24, 84121 **Tel** *089 22 57 05*　　　　　　　　　**Road Map** *E4*

This pizzeria in the heart of old Salerno is only open in the evenings. Excellent pizzas and *calzoni* are baked in a wood-fired oven. Also on the menu is typical Salernitana cuisine – *pasta e fagioli* (beans) combined with a delicious peppery oil, *baccala* (salt cod) and potato casserole, and sausages with broccoli. Very popular with the locals.

SCALA Da Lorenzo
Via Fra Gerardo Sasso, 84010 **Tel** *089 85 82 90*　　　　　　　　　**Road Map** *D4*

This friendly family-run restaurant has a light, airy dining room and a pretty terrace affording spectacular views. The fresh pasta is truly delicious and the menu – mostly fish-based – changes from day to day. If you book ahead, you can order your fish and they will get it especially for you. Good local wine from the vines on the hills around.

SORRENTO Sant'Anna da Emilia
Via Marina Grande 62, 80067 **Tel** *081 807 27 20*　　　　　　　　　**Road Map** *C4*

A favourite with the locals, right down by the port, this family-run trattoria prepares simple grilled fresh fish and seafood pasta dishes. All food is prepared to order and the decor is charmingly unpretentious. A great place for watching the comings and goings of the port, although there are only a few tables outside.

SORRENTO Ristorante della Favorita O'Parrucchiano
Corso Italia 15, 80067 **Tel** *081 878 13 21*　　　　　　　　　**Road Map** *C4*

This delightfully meandering glasshouse restaurant, with an open-air terrace under a pergola of citrus trees, was established by a former priest over a century ago. Popular with locals and tourists, it rustles up excellent Sorrentino cuisine, such as white bean soup, cheese baked in lemon leaves and seafood pasta, as well as a great peppered steak.

SORRENTO Il Buco
Rampa Marina Piccola 5, 80067 **Tel** *081 878 23 54*　　　　　　　　　**Road Map** *C4*

A wine cellar formerly used by monks now hosts an excellent restaurant with the emphasis on good home-made cooking. The menu offers a choice of the finest food from land and sea: try the ravioli with pumpkin, pepper and fish sauce or the white bean soup with baby squid and garlic croutons. Good wines and friendly service.

SORRENTO L'Antica Trattoria
Via Padre Reginaldo Guiliani 33, 80067 **Tel** *081 807 10 82*　　　　　　　　　**Road Map** *C4*

This restaurant has been going strong since 1930. Sit either inside or out: the terrace is made for romantic dining. Meat and fish vie for your attention on the menu; all dishes are prepared with great care and creativity. The *pappardelle* pasta with *porcini* (cep mushrooms) and the strawberries are delicious. Resident mandolin player.

SORRENTO Caruso
Via Sant'Antonino 12, Piazza Tasso, 80067 **Tel** *081 807 31 56*　　　　　　　　　**Road Map** *C4*

Imaginative cooking is served in elegant surroundings in a museum-restaurant dedicated to the great tenor, Enrico Caruso, who died tragically at only 48. The dining rooms are charming and the food uses the freshest of ingredients: try the ravioli with prawns or shellfish and delicious home-made desserts, such as *pastiera* (grain and cheese pie).

TORRE DEL GRECO Casa Rossa 1888
Via Vesuvio 30, 80056 **Tel** *081 777 97 63*　　　　　　　　　**Road Map** *C3*

A popular hotel *(see p187)* and restaurant on the A3 between Naples and Vesuvius, this imposing modern building serves superb food: mostly fish but also some meat, all prepared with flair and partnered by good local wines. There are great views over the Bay of Naples, while the bright dining rooms are filled with modern art. Busy at weekends.

VICO EQUENSE Antica Osteria Nonna Rosa
Via Privata Bonea 4, 80069 **Tel** *081 879 90 55*　　　　　　　　　**Road Map** *D4*

Only a few tables are up for grabs in this intimate *osteria*, where the speciality is fresh egg pasta combined with seasonal ingredients from land and sea. Typical delicacies would be pasta in a *fior di latte* cheese, parma ham and *irpino* (black truffle) sauce or baked rabbit with sweet onions. Friendly and well worth seeking out.

VICO EQUENSE Pizza a Metro
Via Nicotera, 15, 80069 **Tel** *081 801 64 47*　　　　　　　　　**Road Map** *D4*

A favourite with locals and tourists alike, this restaurant has been selling pizza by the metre since the 1930's. Cooked in the immense wood-fired ovens, the thin-based pizzas are made using the freshest ingredients. The outdoor terrace, surrounded by shady plants and trees, is lovely in the summer. Situated close to the Vico Equense station.

VICO EQUENSE La Torre del Saracino
Via Torretta 9, Marina d'Acqua, Loc Sciano, 80069 **Tel** *081 802 85 55*　　　　　　　　　**Road Map** *D4*

Owned by the same family, these two eateries stand side by side, with the choice between a good seafood restaurant, with a pleasant terrace for al fresco dining, and the pizzeria next door. The pizzeria, Aurora, serves over 50 types of pizza and is popular with the locals, while the restaurant sometimes stages gastronomic events.

Light Meals and Snacks in Naples

Naples is full of bars, pastry shops, *rosticcerie*, and all kinds of places with stand-up counters where you can stop for a drink and a snack. It is an Italian habit to stop at a local bar to breakfast on a cappuccino and warm croissant, to pause for an apéritif before lunch or have a coffee in the afternoon. A quick and cheap meal can be bought at the numerous fast food establishments that sell sandwiches, small pizzas and filled rolls, as well as prepared meals like pasta with different sauces, to eat on the spot or take away.

BARS AND CAFES

In Naples, unlike most other European cities, the bars generally only have stand-up counters for customers to have a quick coffee. In bars and cafés where seating space is provided, there is usually an additional charge for service at the table. In the summer, however, all available outdoor space is packed with tables. Some of the cafés stay open until the early hours, and are equally popular with the young and the old. Many bars in Naples are also pastry shops (*pasticceria*), ice cream parlours (*gelateria*), quick self-service restaurants (*tavola calda*), or all these combined.

One historic Neapolitan café frequented by celebrities in the past is **Caffè Gambrinus**, one of the most elegant bars in the centre (*see p52*). Here, a short distance from the Palazzo Reale, you can sit outside and admire the lovely Piazza del Plebiscito, which is closed to traffic. Other elegant cafés are **La Caffettiera** in Piazza dei Martiri in Chiaia, or the **Caffetteria Bernini** on Piazza Fanzago in Vomero. Both of these get very busy in the evenings, especially at weekends. **Gran Caffè Cimmino** in Posillipo offers excellent coffee and pastries as well as fine views of the bay.

If you are walking along the seafront (*lungomare*), stop for an apéritif at the **Bar dell'Ovo**. The small and elegant **Bar Prencipe** in Piazza Municipio, which retains its original Art Deco interior, is a good place to pause for breakfast in the city centre. The **Gran Caffè Verdi** on Via Verdi and **Bar Roma** on Via Toledo, with their spacious refreshment areas, are both popular with office workers during their breaks. To taste an excellent coffee, try the **Caffè Mexico** in Piazza Dante with superb blends, or the **Café do Brasil** in the Vomero area opposite the Teatro Diana. In the old city centre the **Bar Nilo** is distinguished for its courteous and friendly service.

During the summer months, popular spots for night owls are the **Caffè dell' Epoca**, opposite the Academy of Art, and the cafés in Piazza Bellini: the **Caffè Arabo** and the **Intra Moenia** that also sells books and promotes cultural events.

PASTRY SHOPS AND ICE CREAM PARLOURS

Neapolitan pastry shops, known throughout the world and descended from a centuries-old tradition, offer a number of specialities. Among these are the shortcrust or puff pastries called *sfogliatelle*, the *pastiera* eaten at Easter, *babà*, *zeppola di San Giuseppe* and Christmas season pastries such as *rococò* and *struffoli* (pastry rings with honey and candied fruit).

A favourite spot for the locals, particularly on Sundays, is **Scaturchio** in Piazza San Domenico Maggiore, one of the best cafés in the historic centre. Also in Piazza San Domenico Maggiore, **Gran Caffè Aragonese** sells excellent pastries and sweets, as do **Augustus** in Posillipo, **Daniele** and **Bellavia** in the Vomero and **Moccia** in the Chiaia district. The **Gran Bar Riviera**, opened in Chiaia in 1870, also offers many treats; the *tartufo* was invented here, a delectable *semifreddo* ice cream with chestnut cream filling. The best *sfogliatella* can be found at **Pintauro** on Via Toledo or **La Sfogliatella Mary** in the Galleria Umberto I. Good ice cream parlours are **La Scimmia** in Piazza Carità, the **Bilancione** in Posillipo, **Carraturo** near the railway station and **Soave** in Vomero.

The *chalets* on the seafront in the Mergellina area are legendary among Neapolitans. The most famous of these is **Chalet Ciro**, specializing in home-made ice cream (*artigianale*). People also come here for coffee or an apéritif. **Chiquito's**, on the Via Mergellina, was once a water vendor and is now famous for his fruit cups and exotic fruit shakes.

TAKE-AWAY FOOD

Founded in 1887 by Gaetano Cecere, the first Neapolitan fast food establishment is aptly named **Vaco 'e pressa** (I'm in a hurry). True to its founder's tradition, it still has marble furnishings and a quaint atmosphere. Rather than **McDonald's**, the locals usually prefer to drop in at a *tavola calda*, where they can eat a quick plate of pasta, or to buy a sandwich prepared in a delicatessen (*salumeria*), eat a local mozzarella or have hot snacks from a *rosticceria*. Excellent take-aways are **Tavola Calda L.U.I.S.E.** in Via Toledo and **Imperatore** in the Vomero area, where you can also buy tasty roast chicken. **La Piazza**, next to Santa Maria La Nova church, offers a quick snack.

If you like sweet or savoury crêpes, **La Crêperie** in the Vomero area is for you. Then there are the many *pizzetterie* such as **Le Focacce Moccia** and **Friggitoria Pizzeria Giuliano** and the *rosticcerie* include **Elettroforno** in Posillipo, which sells pizza by the slice as well as "crocché" (potato croquettes), *arancini di riso* (rice croquettes) and *saltimbocca* (veal). Many of these *pizzerie*, such as the **Napoli, Napoli** chain, also sell roasted meats.

DIRECTORY

TOLEDO AND CASTEL NUOVO

BARS AND CAFES

Bar Prencipe
Piazza Municipio 20.
Map 7 B2.

Caffè Gambrinus
Piazza Trieste e
Trento 38.
Map 7 A3.

Bar Roma
Via Toledo 325.
Map 7 A2 (9 A5).

Gran Caffè Verdi
Via Verdi 23.
Map 7 A2.

PASTRY SHOPS AND ICE CREAM PARLOURS

Pintauro
Via Toledo 275.
Map 7 A2 (9 A5).

La Scimmia
Piazza Carità 4.
Map 7 A1.

La Sfogliatella Mary
Galleria Umberto I, 66.
Map 7 A2.

TAKE-AWAY FOOD

Cibo
Via Cervantes 70.
Map 7 A2.

Tavola Calda L.U.I.S.E.
Via Toledo 266.
Map 7 A1 (9 A5).

McDonald's
Via Sanfelice 16/20.
Map 7 B1 (9 C5).

SPACCANAPOLI

BARS AND CAFES

Bar Nilo
Via San Biagio dei Librai 129/130.
Map 3 C5.

PASTRY SHOPS AND ICE CREAM PARLOURS

Gran Caffè Aragonese
Piazza San Domenico Maggiore 5.
Map 3 B5 (9 C3).

Scaturchio
Piazza San Domenico Maggiore 19.
Map 3 B5 (9 C3).

TAKE-AWAY FOOD

Le Focacce Moccia
Piazzetta Nilo 16 bis.
Map 3 B5 (10 E3).

Friggitoria Pizzeria Giuliano
Calata Trinità Maggiore.
Map 7 B1 (9 B5).

La Piazza
Piazza Santa Maria La Nova.
Map 7 B1 (9 C5).

Napoli, Napoli
Piazza del Gesù 27.
Map 3 B5 (9 B4).

DECUMANO MAGGIORE

BARS AND CAFES

Caffè Arabo
Piazza Bellini 66.
Map 3 B5.

Caffè dell' Epoca
Via Constantinopoli.
Map 3 B4.

Caffè Mexico
Piazza Dante 86.
Map 3 A5 (9 B3).

Intra Moenia
Piazza Bellini 70.
Map 3 B5.

Scaturchio
Via Portamedina 22
Map 3 A5 (9 A4).

PASTRY SHOPS AND ICE CREAM PARLOURS

Carraturo
Via Casanova 97.
Map 4 E3.

TAKE-AWAY FOOD

Antica Gastronomia Ferrieri
Piazza Garibaldi 82.
Map 4 E4.

McDonald's
Piazza Dante 92.
Map 3 A5.

Vaco 'e Pressa
Piazza Dante 87.
Map 3 A5 (9 B3).

VOMERO

BARS AND CAFES

Café do Brasil
Via Giordano 31.
Map 5 B2.

La Caffettiera
Piazza Vanvitelli 10.
Map 2 D5.

Caffetteria Bernini
Piazza Fanzago.
Map 2 D4.

Caffè Mexico
Via Scarlatti 69.
Map 2 D5.

PASTRY SHOPS AND ICE CREAM PARLOURS

Bellavia
Via Luca Giordano 158.
Map 1 C5.

Daniele
Via Scarlatti 104/106.
Map 2 D5.

Soave
Via Scarlatti 130.
Map 2 D5.

TAKE-AWAY FOOD

La Crêperie
Via Donadio 1/3.
Map 2 D4.

Imperatore
Via Scarlatti 180.
Map 2 D5.

McDonald's
Via Scarlatti 209.
Map 2 D5.

Rossopomodoro
Via Cimarosa 144.
Map 1 C5.

CASTEL DELL'OVO AND CHIAIA

BARS AND CAFES

Bar dell'Ovo
Via Partenope 6.
Map 7 A4.

La Caffettiera
Piazza dei Martiri 30.
Map 6 F2.

PASTRY SHOPS AND ICE CREAM PARLOURS

Chalet Ciro
Via Caracciolo.
Map 5 B4.

Chiquito's
Via Mergellina (opposite the funicular).
Map 5 B3.

Moccia
Via San Pasquale 21.
Map 6 E2.

Gran Bar Riviera
Riviera di Chiaia 183.
Map 5 C2.

Remy
Via Galiani 29a.
Map 5 B3.

POSILLIPO

BARS AND CAFES

Gran Caffè Cimmino
Via Petraca 147.
Map 5 A4.

PASTRY SHOPS AND ICE CREAM PARLOURS

Augustus
Via Petrarca 81 a/b.
Map 5 A4.

Bilancione
Via Posillipo 238/b.
Map 5 A5.

TAKE-AWAY FOOD

Elettroforno
Piazza San Luigi 12/b.

SHOPS AND MARKETS

Shopping in Naples is an excellent way to explore the labyrinth of this fascinating city. Expensive boutiques line the main streets such as Via Toledo and Via Chiaia, where good quality, stylish clothes, shoes and jewellery can be bought. However, don't limit yourself to the fashionable areas, but wander around the alleyways in the old town to discover the small specialist shops and artisan workshops. Here visitors can find authentic and hand-made souvenirs.

Nativity figure

These streets often bear the name of the trade practised there, such as Piazza degli Orefici (Goldsmiths' Square).

Perhaps the most enjoyable way to shop is to follow the example of most Neapolitans and buy from the numerous markets and stalls along the roadside. These *bancarelle* sell everything from clothes to kitchenware, and children's toys to jewellery. Common items are cheap seconds from the manufacturer or imitation designer labels.

SALES

From early july to early September and early January to mid-March, sales are held in Naples. You can find excellent bargains with discounts of up to 50 per cent and sometimes as much as 70 per cent. It is a good idea to check goods before you leave the shop as a refund is unlikely.

FASHION AND ACCESSORIES

The exclusive shops are concentrated in Via dei Mille and Via Calabritto, in the elegant Chiaia district. Here the great fashion designers, such as **Emporio Armani**, **Prada**, **Gianni Versace** and **Mario Valentino**, have their stores. A jewellery shop, **Bulgari**, has also opened here. In Riviera di Chiaia, **Marinella** sells his famous ties, which are worn by many VIPs.

The shop window of the elegant Livio de Simone boutique

At **Eddy Monetti** the emphasis is on elegant and classical fashion. Clothes with an innovative touch are offered by **Barbaro** in Galleria Umberto I, while more avant-garde men's and women's wear is sold by **Maxi Ho.** **Livio De Simone**, who is a native of Naples, offers stylish clothes in bright Mediterranean colours, while **Amina Rubinacci** is known for her woollen and soft cashmere jumpers. Naples also has boutiques for **Max Mara** and **Max & Co**.

Clothing at somewhat more accessible prices is sold at **Camomilla** and **Motivi**. Young people have no lack of choice with clothes from the well-known **Benetton** outlets and the **Mastrolonardo** boutique in Via Nisco, which is famous for its stylish clothes. Fun and original second-hand clothes and accessories and personalized T-shirts are sold at **Mu.Mu Frequencies**, a multimedia cultural group.

The **Prénatal** chain caters for mothers-to-be and small children. Handbags, belts and other accessories, which are mostly made by local craftsmen, are sold in the **Spatarella** and **Tramontano** stores.

In the old centre between San Biagio dei Librai and Via degli Orefici there are many jewellers' and goldsmiths' shops. The age-old tradition of engraving and cameo work is still practised in many of these shops.

OPENING HOURS

Shops are open from 10am to 2pm and from 4pm to 8pm. They are closed on Sundays and Monday morning in winter, Saturday afternoon and Sunday in summer. Food shops and markets are shut on Thursday afternoons. Before holiday periods like Christmas, many places are open on Sundays and extend their weekly opening hours. In summer most shops close for two weeks around 15 August (Ferragosto).

HOW TO PAY

Major credit cards are accepted in most boutiques and department stores. After you have made your purchase, make sure you are given the receipt *(ricevuta fiscale)*. By law the police can make a spot check outside the shop and if you are without a receipt, you may be fined.

Coral jewellery in a shop window

Interior of the Colonnese bookshop in Via San Pietro a Majella

Ascione Coralli, a coral and cameo atelier, is open by appointment. **Caso Agostino** has superb coral jewels, and other jewellery shops such as **Ventrella** and **Knight** stock original and attractive designs.

DEPARTMENT STORES AND SHOPPING CENTRES

Most Neapolitans on the whole prefer the smaller, specialist shops, where the service is more personal. However, some of the department stores in particular **La Rinascente** and **Coin** offer a good variety of products ranging from quality clothes, cosmetics and perfumes to household goods and crockery. If you are looking for those stores that specialize in household and kitchen goods, try the **Croff** chain, which also sells a very wide variety of modern furnishings. The large chain stores, such as **Upim**, are, as you would expect, generally cheaper and feature average-quality cosmetics, lingerie, household articles and clothes.

The shopping centres, **Galleria Vanvitelli** and the elegant **Galleria Scarlatti** can be found in the Vomero district of the city, and the extremely smart 19th-century Galleria Umberto I, off Piazza Trieste e Trento, is an attractive arcade of numerous elegant shops.

Coin
Via Scarlatti 100.
Tel 081 578 01 11.

Croff
Galleria Vanvitelli 16–23.
Tel 081 578 96 98.

Galleria Scarlatti
Via Scarlatti.

Galleria Vanvitelli
Piazza Vanvitelli.

La Rinascente
Via Toledo 343.
Tel 081 41 15 11.

Upim
Via A. Doria 40.
Tel 081 239 63 60.
Via dei Mille 59.
Tel 081 40 00 73.

ART, ANTIQUES AND INTERIOR DESIGN

Naples is renowned for its many fascinating antique and second-hand shops. The best-known antique dealers can be found in Via Domenico Morelli: for instance, **Brandi, D'Amodio** and **Florida** are all specialists in 18th-century furniture and paintings. Shops that stock historic objects, such as **L'Antiquario** and **Affaitati**, are in Via Costantinopoli. Old engravings, prints and lithographs, picture frames and other *objets d'art*, are on sale at **Bowinkel**, which is the oldest shop in Piazza dei Martiri. Items such as rare books, prints and gouaches are sold at the **Casella** and **Regina** antiquarian booksellers, while the **Colonnese** bookshop stocks what can be described as traditional Neapolitan articles. The **Archivio Fotografico Parisio**, which has about 100,000 photographs of Neapolitan

The traditional craft of making and restoring string instruments

life and characters, provides a unique record of the city's history. Examples of Naples art galleries that generally have interesting work on show include the **Galleria Navarra, Lia Rumma, E-M Arts** and **Studio Trisorio**. Leading interior design shops include

Neapolitan second-hand dealer with goods on display in the street

The attractive doll display in the Ospedale delle Bambole *(see p63)*

Agorà in the Posillipo area and **Novelli** in Piazza Amedeo, featuring the latest styles in home furnishings. Simple, clean-cut design solutions which may appeal more to a younger generation are on view at **IdeArredo**.

HANDICRAFTS

The many workshops and second-hand shops in the historic centre offer a varied choice of articles, from the kitsch to the well-designed. In Via San Gregorio Armeno

is the workshop of the famous nativity scene artisan, **Giuseppe Ferrigno**, while in Via San Biagio dei Librai can be found the **Ospedale delle Bambole** (hospital for dolls) where porcelain dolls, shepherds, marionettes and puppets are repaired and restored. At the **Liuteria Calace**, which is in the historic centre, they make and restore violins, violas, mandolins and lutes. **Nel Regno di Pulcinella** is a workshop dedicated entirely to the making of Neapolitan masks.

Book restoration, book-binding and elegant objects all made from hand-made Amalfi paper make **Gli Artigiani del Libro** a fascinating place. If you are particularly interested in ceramics, it is worth having a look at **Il Cantuccio della Ceramica** and the workshop of **Lisa Weber**.

FOOD, WINE AND SPIRITS

Two of Naples' leading delicatessens are **La Botteghina** and **Gastronomia L.U.I.S.E.**, both of which sell a fantastic variety of local specialities. **Gay Odin** has the finest chocolate in Naples, including the delicious *Vesuvio* chocolate which is made with rum. The old-fashioned **Scaturchio** sells excellent cakes and sweets, as well as ice cream. A good selection of wines is to be found at both the **Enoteca Dante** and the **Enoteca Belledonne**.

OPEN-AIR MARKETS

Street stalls and markets set up in the early morning and usually pack up after midday. Food stalls selling seasonal fruit and vegetables generally have fresher and less expensive produce than the shops. Clothes and household items will be cheap and, although they may not be designer quality, they are perfectly good. Bargaining is not usually done when buying food, but for clothes and other items try asking for a discount *(sconto)*.

Market at Sant'Antonio Abate

Mercatino di Antignano
Piazza degli Artisti.
◻ *8am–1pm Mon–Sat.*
Clothing, shoes, household articles, fabrics.

Fiera Antiquaria Napoletana
Villa Comunale. ◻ *8am–3pm last & penultimate Sat & Sun of month.*
Antiques market: silverware, jewellery and ornaments.

Mercato del Casale di Posillipo
Posillipo. ◻ *8am–2pm Thu.*
Clothes, accessories, household articles.

Mercato del Ponte di Casanova
Porta Capuana. ◻ *8am–sunset Mon–Sat.*
New and used clothes.

Mercato dei Fiori
Castel Nuovo. ◻ *daily at dawn.*
Flowers.

Mercatino della Pignasecca
Near Piazza Carità. ◻ *8am–2pm Mon–Sat.*
Mainly food.

Mercato di Sant'Antonio
Via Sant'Antonio Abate.
◻ *9am–8pm daily.*
Food market.

Mercato di Porta Nolana
Via Carmignano. ◻ *8am–6pm Mon–Sat (8am–2pm Sun).*
Fresh fish and seafood.

Mercatino della Torretta
Viale Gramsci. ◻ *8am–1pm Mon–Sat.*
Food market and clothing.

The inviting entrance of the famous Scaturchio *pasticceria*

DIRECTORY

FASHION AND ACCESSORIES

Amina Rubinacci
Via dei Mille 16.
Tel 081 41 30 48.

Ascione Coralli
Piazzetta Matilde Serao
19 (2nd floor).
Tel 081 42 11 11.
Open by appointment.

Barbaro
Galleria Umberto 44.
Tel 081 41 12 84.
One of many branches.

Bulgari
Via Filangieri 41.
Tel 081 40 08 56.

Camomilla
Via Toledo 407.
Tel 081 551 14 45.
One of many branches.

Caso Agostino
Piazza San Domenico
Maggiore 16.
Tel 081 552 01 08.

Eddy Monetti
Via dei Mille 45a/b/c.
Tel 081 40 47 07.

**Emporio
Armani**
Piazza dei Martiri 61–62.
Tel 081 40 63 63.

Gianni Versace
Via Toledo 157.
Tel 081 551 06 47.

Knight
Piazza dei Martiri 52.
Tel 081 764 38 37.

**Livio De
Simone**
Via D Morelli 15.
Tel 081 764 38 27.

**Magazzini
Marinella**
Piazza Vittoria 287.
Tel 081 245 11 82.

Mario Valentino
Via Calabritto 9/10.
Tel 081 764 42 62.

Mastrolonardo
Via Nisco 6.
Tel 081 42 31 11.

Max & Co.
Corso Umberto I 28.
Tel 081 552 62 23.
One of many branches.

Max Mara
Corso Umberto I 134/136.
Tel 081 553 85 01.

Maxi Ho
Via Luca Giordano 23.
Tel 081 578 04 39.

Motivi
Via Toledo 157.
Tel 081 551 06 47.

Mu.Mu Frequencies
Piazza Monteoliveto 10.
Tel 081 936 02 09.

Prada
Via Calabritto 9.
Tel 081 764 13 23.

Prénatal
Via Roma 332.
Tel 081 42 12 22.
One of many branches.

Spatarella
Via Filangieri 23.
Tel 081 40 17 03.

Tramontano
Via Chiaia 143.
Tel 081 41 48 37.

Ventrella
Via C Poerio 11.
Tel 081 764 31 73.

ART, ANTIQUES AND INTERIOR DESIGN

Affaitati
Via Costantinopoli 18.
Tel 081 44 44 27.

Agorà
Via Orazio 136/b.
Tel 081 714 33 33.

L'Antiquario
Via Costantinopoli 34.
Tel 081 564 06 07.

**Archivio
Fotografico Parisio**
Largo Carolina 10.
Tel 081 764 51 22.

Bowinkel
Piazza dei Martiri 24.
Tel 081 764 43 44.
Via S Lucia.
Tel 081 764 07 39.

Brandi
Via D Morelli 9/11.
Tel 081 764 38 82.

Casella
Via C Poerio 92/e.
Tel 081 764 26 27.

Colonnese
Via S Pietro a Maiella 32.
Tel 081 459 858.

D'Amodio
Via D Morelli 6 bis.
Tel 081 764 38 72.

E-M Arts
Via Calabritto 20.
Tel 081 763 37 37.

Florida
Via D Morelli 13.
Tel 081 764 34 40.

**Galleria
Navarra**
Piazza dei Martiri 23.
Tel 081 764 35 95.

IdeArredo
Via R Bracco 41/49.
Tel 081 551 09 92.

Lia Rumma
Via V Gaetani 12.
Tel 081 764 36 19.

Novelli
Piazza Amedeo 21/22.
Tel 081 41 53 50.

Regina
Via Costantinopoli
51/103.
Tel 081 29 09 25.

**Studio
Trisorio**
Riviera di Chiaia 215.
Tel 081 41 43 06.

HANDICRAFTS

**Gli Artigiani
del Libro**
Calata Trinità Maggiore 4.
Tel 081 551 12 80.

**Il Cantuccio
della Ceramica**
Via B Croce 38 (inside).
Tel 081 552 58 57.

Giuseppe Ferrigno
Via S Gregorio Armeno 8.
Tel 081 552 31 48.

Lisa Weber
Via G Paladino 4.

Liuteria Calace
Piazza San Domenico
Maggiore 9.
Tel 081 551 59 83.

**Nel Regno di
Pulcinella**
Via San Domenico
Maggiore 9.
Tel 081 551 41 71.

**Ospedale delle
Bambole**
Via S Biagio dei Librai 81.
Tel 081 20 30 67.

FOOD, WINE AND SPIRITS

La Botteghina
Via Orazio 106.
Tel 081 66 05 16.

**Drogheria
Santachiara**
Via B Croce 50.
Tel 081 551 64 44.

**Enoteca
Belledonne**
Vico Belledonne a
Chiaia 18.
Tel 081 40 31 62.

Enoteca Dante
Piazza Dante 189.
Tel 081 549 96 89.

**Gastronomia
L.U.I.S.E.**
Piazza dei Martiri 68.
Tel 081 41 77 35.

Gay Odin
Via Toledo 214.
Tel 081 40 00 63.
One of many branches.

Scaturchio
Piazza San Domenico
Maggiore 19.
Tel 081 551 69 44.

Shops and Markets along the Coast

Every town and village in the region, from the islands to the coast, offers typical local handicrafts such as ceramics or glassware, as well as foods and wines associated with the history and culture of each place. Wandering through the narrow streets in these lovely seaside spots, you will discover all kinds of customs.

FASHION AND ACCESSORIES

Besides shops with designer wear, there are still several old local fashion houses. You can find the top names in Italian and foreign fashion at places such as **Adario & Fiorentino**, who have a shop at Sant'Agata sui due Golfi, or **Loro Piana** in Ischia. **Capricci**, also in Ischia, sells designer lingerie and swimwear. The shopping street in Capri, Via Camerelle, boasts the elegant **Marcello Rubinacci** boutique, known for top-quality cashmere pullovers. Elegant apparel, mostly made of silk, and typical Capri shoes are among the specialities of **Laura Merola**. Two top jewellers in Capri are **La Campanina** and **Cartier**, both sited in Via Vittorio Emanuele, who stock precious stones in every colour as well as diamonds and coral necklaces of very fine quality.

Fashion styles in Positano are famous for their originality. Among the town's leading houses is **Maria Lampo**, who are well known for making their articles quickly (*lampo* meaning "in a flash"). Top designer wear as well as handmade patchwork clothing and quilts are sold at **Nadir's**, while **La Bottega di Brunella** and **La Tartana** are distinguished for their fine fabrics and original patterns. If you want the bikini of your dreams, go to **Susy** on Capri, where you can order swimwear made to measure. For locally designed linen clothes, head for **Capri Naturale** in Anacapri.

Sorrento, Positano and Capri are famous for their handmade sandals; to have a pair made especially for you, go to **Siniscalchi** in Sorrento, **Costanzo Avitabile** in Positano, the imaginative **Canfora** in Capri or Antonio Viva's shop at Anacapri, aptly called **L'Arte del Sandalo Caprese**. On the mainland, cloth shoes decorated in weird and wonderful ways can be found at **La Gabella** in Amalfi.

ART AND HANDICRAFTS

By exploring the craftsmen's shops in the towns and villages outside Naples you can really get to know the heart of a place, and discover its cultural and artistic traditions. The boats known as *gozzi* are built by the **Aprea Mare** company in Sorrento, and are world-famous. The ancient tradition of marquetry in the Sorrento peninsula is carried on by craftsmen such as **Salvatore Gargiulo**, **Peppe Rocco** and **Giliberto Attardi**.

Vietri sul Mare is famous for its decorated ceramics; the **Solimene** factory employs at least 40 craftsmen who, despite the large output of the place, make fine handmade products. The **Perrotti** brothers make splendid stained glass, and accept commissions. Other high-quality ceramics are produced by **Taki** in Ischia and **Artigiò** in Procida, while **La Bottega dell'Arte** in Capri – thanks to the well-known ceramicist Sergio Rubini – now has over 200 outlets in the United States alone. Again in Capri, **Carmelina** offers classic naive painting.

In Amalfi, visit the **Cartiera Amatruda** and **Cavaliere** mills, where fine quality paper is produced. As a souvenir of Capri there are the **Carthusia** perfumes, sold only on the island (you can also visit their laboratories at No. 2 Via Parco Augusto). On the island of Procida, **Maria Rosaria Intartaglia** makes pretty embroidered lingerie to order. Lastly, the **Emporio Scialò** at Ischia sells raffia dolls and Pulcinella puppets, all made by hand.

FOOD, WINE AND LIQUEURS

Many fine dairy products such as cheese come from the area around Naples. In Sorrento you can visit the **Apreda** dairy and buy fresh plaits of *fiordilatte*, a type of mozzarella made from cow's milk, in the nearby shop. The **Caseificio Isola di Capri** and **Gabriele** in Vico Equense are also excellent dairies. At Capri, **Sfizi di Pane** offers 15 different types of *tarallini* biscuits as well as various kinds of bread. For the sweet-toothed, Ischia's **Caffè Calise** has orange *sfogliatelle* and at Positano the **La Zagara** pastry shop has delicious fruit tarts called *crostate*. While in Amalfi, try the delightful lemon pastries at **Andrea Pansa**.

Some wine shops also sell local products such as jam, honey and spices: **Piemme** at Sorrento, **Ischia Sapori** on Ischia and **Gusti e Delizie** in Ravello. Good ranges of wine are on sale at **La Valle dei Mulini** in Amalfi, **I Sapori di Positano** in Positano and **Enoteca Casa D'Ambra** at Ischia. **Limoncello di Capri** is the most famous source of limoncello, or lemon-flavoured liqueur, and **I Giardini di Ravello** also stocks a good range.

MARKETS

There are numerous markets in the outlying areas. The most important in size and tradition is the second-hand market in Resina at Ercolano (Herculaneum), where you will find used clothes and accessories. It is half an hour from the central railway station in Naples: take the Circumvesuviana line and get off at Ercolano.

DIRECTORY

FASHION AND ACCESSORIES

Adario & Fiorentino
Via Nastro Azzurro 1–3
(Sant'Agata sui Due
Golfi).
*Tel 081 878 00 65. One
of two shops.*

L'Arte del Sandalo Caprese
Via G Orlandi 75
(Anacapri).
Tel 081 837 35 83.

La Bottega di Brunella
Via Pasitea 76
(Positano). *Tel 089 87 52
28.*

La Campanina
Via V Emanuele 18
(Capri).
Tel 081 837 06 43.

Canfora
Via Camerelle 3
(Capri).
Tel 081 837 04 87.

Capricci
Via Roma 37
(Ischia Town).
Tel 081 98 20 63.

Capri Naturale
Via Capodimonte 15
(Anacapri).
Tel 081 837 47 19.

Cartier
Via V Emanuele 47
(Capri).
Tel 081 837 06 18.

Costanzo Avitabile
Piazza A Vespucci 1–5
(Positano).
Tel 081 87 53 66.

La Gabella
Via P Comite 37
(Amalfi).
Tel 330 67 54 03.

Laura Merola
Via Fuorlovado 2
(Capri).
Tel 081 837 04 03.

Loro Piana
Corso V Colonna 180
(Ischia).
*Tel 081 99 12 21.
One of two shops.*

Marcello Rubinacci
Via Camerelle 9 (Capri).
Tel 081 837 72 95.

Maria Lampo
Via Pasitea 12–16
(Positano).
Tel 089 87 50 21.

Nadir's
Via Pasitea 44
(Positano).
Tel 089 87 59 75.

Siniscalchi
Corso Italia 203
(Sorrento).
*Tel 081 878 30 65.
One of two shops.*

Susy
Via Le Botteghe 61
(Capri).

La Tartana
Via della Tartana 5
(Positano).
Tel 089 87 56 45.

ART AND HANDICRAFTS

Aprea Mare
Via Santa Lucia 15
(Sorrento).
Tel 081 807 28 18.

Artigiò
Via V Emanuele 10
(Procida).
Tel 081 896 96 69.

Giliberto Attardi
Via Padre R Giuliani 45–49
(Sorrento).
Tel 081 878 12 91.

La Bottega dell'Arte
Via Catena 2–4
(Capri).
Tel 081 837 18 78.

Carmelina
Via Roma (Capri).

Carthusia
Via Camerelle 10
(Capri).
*Tel 081 837 36 68.
One of two shops.*

Cartiere Amatruda
Via delle Cartiere 94
(Amalfi).
Tel 089 87 13 15.

Cartiera Cavaliere
Via M del Giudice 2.
(Amalfi).

Ceramiche Artistiche Solimene
Via Madonna degli
Angeli 7
(Vietri sul Mare).
Tel 089 21 02 43.

Emporio Scialò
Corso Umberto I, 21
(Forio d'Ischia).
Tel 081 99 75 92.

Maria Rosaria Intartaglia
Via Lubrano di Vavarìa 12
(Procida).
Tel 081 896 86 74.

Peppe Rocco
Via San Nicola 12
(Sorrento).
Tel 081 878 48 74.

Perrotti
Via Nazionale Costiera 32
(Vietri sul Mare).
Tel 089 76 15 76.

Salvatore Gargiulo
Via Fuoro 33 (Sorrento).
Tel 081 878 24 20.

Taki
Via Marina 20
(Forio d'Ischia).
Tel 081 98 91 49.

FOOD, WINE AND LIQUEURS

Andrea Pansa
Piazza Duomo 40
(Amalfi).
Tel 089 87 10 65.

Apreda
Via del Mare 20
(Sorrento).
*Tel 081 878 13 34.
One of two shops.*

Caffè Calise
Via A Sogliuzzo 69
(Ischia Porto).
Tel 081 99 12 70.

Caseificio Isola di Capri
Via Roma 38
(Capri).
Tel 081 837 68 75.

Enoteca Casa D'Ambra
Via Porto 24
(Ischia Porto).
Tel 081 99 10 46.

Gabriele
Corso Umberto I, 5–7
(Vico Equense).
Tel 081 879 87 44.

I Giardinidi Ravello
Via Civiltà 19
(Ravello).
Tel 089 87 22 64.

Gusti e Delizie
Via Roma 28–30
(Ravello).
Tel 089 85 77 16.

Ischia Sapori
Via Gianturco 2
(Ischia Porto).
Tel 081 98 44 82.

Limoncello di Capri
Via Roma 85
(Capri).
Tel 081 837 55 61.

Piemme
Corso Italia 161
(Sorrento).
Tel 081 877 35 96.

I Sapori di Positano
Via Mulini 6
(Positano).
Tel 089 81 11 16.

Sfizi di Pane
Via delle Botteghe 15
(Capri).
Tel 081 837 01 06.

La Valle dei Mulini
Via delle Cartiere 55
(Amalfi).
Tel 089 87 32 11.

La Zagara
Via Mulini 8
(Positano).
Tel 089 87 59 64.

ENTERTAINMENT

Naples knows how to entertain: demanding emperors, kings, residents and travellers have enjoyed its delights for over 2,000 years. Once a major European capital, Naples still revels in shows, games, banquets, and horse races, plus newer diversions like opera and football. Perhaps Italy's most energetic city, Naples buzzes with activity. The nightlife is dynamic, the cafés, nightspots and cultural venues are always open late, and just about every taste is catered for. Music and theatre performances take place

Ballet dancer

throughout the year, bolstered by some important international festivals in summertime, mostly held in the holiday resorts. For film buffs there are two main multiplexes as well as some arthouse cinemas. During the week people usually go to the cinema or out to eat; at weekends the piazzas are bustling with life, as it is customary for Neapolitans to meet up to have a drink before going on to nearby nightspots. Clubbers get going after midnight, perhaps winding down at dawn with coffee and a hot brioche at an all-night bar.

Night-time illuminations in a city that is happy to party until dawn

INFORMATION AND BUYING TICKETS

Naples' daily newspaper *Il Mattino* has the most complete listings for the city, but the national newspapers also carry Naples listings in their local editions.

A monthly guide to events in Naples is published by the tourist office. Visit www.inaples.it to check it out online. Alternatively, pick up a copy of the magazine *Qui Napoli* (*see p218*), which is available free from most tourist information offices and hotels.

Tickets for performances can generally be bought at the door on the day. They may be more difficult to obtain for operas at the San Carlo, popular shows at the Diana and Bellini, premieres and special events. The two main booking offices are **Concerteria** and **Box Office**.

THEATRE, OPERA AND DANCE

Naples is one of Italy's leading cities for theatre. It hosts international and national touring productions, as well as prestigious local companies. The main season is from October to May, though some theatres put on extra programmes and there are special events year-round.

Neapolitans are proud of their dialect, so don't be surprised if it features in some theatrical productions. **Teatro Sannazaro**, a 19th-century theatre staging traditional Neapolitan comedy, is the venue where Eleonora Duse, Eduardo Scarpetta and the De Filippo brothers starred. The **Mercadante**, home of Teatro Stabile di Napoli, sometimes

stages plays by Eduardo De Filippo (*see p37*) in English.

Teatro Cilea, founded in the 1970s, focuses on traditional Neapolitan theatre. Italian classic drama and Neapolitan musicals are on at the **Bellini** and leading Italian companies and Neapolitan musicals at the **Diana**. **Teatro Trianon** bills itself as "the Theatre of Neapolitan Song". The **Augusteo** hosts musicals, concerts and visiting theatre companies, while the **Totò** puts on variety shows.

The **Sancarluccio** is a venue where new small companies stage performances in Italian or English. Fringe and experimental theatre are on offer at **Galleria Toledo** and **Nuovo Teatro Nuovo**.

Teatro San Carlo (*see p37* and *p53*) is one of Italy's top three opera houses. It also serves as the city's leading ballet venue and hosts an important symphony season. A premiere here is a great social occasion. The San Carlo stages performances designed to appeal to young people through its Programma Scuole.

An opera at the Teatro San Carlo

Performance at a city music venue

LIVE MUSIC

Naples is home to the prestigious San Pietro a Maiella Conservatoire, as well as the symphony season at the **Teatro San Carlo**.

The **Associazione Alessandro Scarlatti** boasts a critically acclaimed classical repertoire, while the **Cappella della Pietà de' Turchini** stages concerts of music by Baroque Neapolitan composers. Both **Teatro Diana** and **Teatro Bellini** sometimes have chamber music concerts.

Otto Jazz Club, the city's historic main jazz venue, is joined by **Around Midnight**. **Palapartenope** hosts large-scale shows, musicals, rock and pop concerts. Naples is also known for its spontaneous music, so watch out for street performers in the piazzas too.

NIGHTLIFE

La Movada is the Spanish term Neapolitans use to describe their moveable nightlife – snacks here, drinks there – in places that stay open until the small hours. *La Movada* shifts around, but favoured in the Vomero area Via Giotto, Via Ruoppolo, Via Chiaia and Via Piccinni. Piazza dei Martiri sees plenty of action. Piazza Bellini is lively, with cultural associations that host exhibitions and events. **Intra Moenia** appeals to a lefty intellectual crowd with its recorded fusion and jazz. **Rising South**, located in the musical instrument district behind lively Piazza Dante, features live roots music on Wednesdays, lounge/jazz on Sundays and recorded music

on other nights. **Chez Moi** has been around for years and is still fashionable. A more alternative crowd that is into dance music favours **Keste**.

Via Chiaia, an upmarket shopping area by day, attracts a smart evening set. Mixed use is in vogue. **Culti Spacafe** is chic: by day it is a spa; in the evening, trendies flock here for finger food and wine before the cinema. **Kaligola** is an accessories shop by day and a lounge by night. Piazza Santa Maria la Nova draws a younger crowd to chug beer at its stands and cafés.

Look out also for openings at contemporary art galleries clustered around **MADRE** (Museo D'Arte Contemporanea Donnaregina) and **PAN** (Palazzo delle Arti Napoli).

La Notte Bianca, (the White Night), is an endless night of Naples culture, which is generally held during an October weekend.

For dance music two clubs stand out: **Velvet Underground** and **Notting Hill**, both offering varied interactive programmes with theme evenings.

Phone numbers for venues often change, so don't rely on them. A good hotel concierge should be able to provide

advice – or you can simply follow *La Movada* and see where it takes you.

CINEMA

Most foreign films are dubbed into Italian, but movies are also occasionally shown in the original language; newspaper listings will indicate *versione originale*. **Plaza Multisala** shows original version films on Tuesdays. Some foreign language institutes, such as the **Institut Français de Naples "Le Grenoble"**, also show films in their original language.

For around ten days in June, the Napoli Film Festival highlights international cinema. **Warner Village Metropolitan** and **Filangieri Multisala** screen both mainstream and arthouse movies. **Modernissimo** and **Plaza Multisala** have mulitple screens and show childrens' films. **Teatro Augusteo** hosted the 10th Artecinema, an international festival of films about contemporary art.

Some cinemas show new films for half price on Wednesdays. Summertime brings outdoor screenings in squares and at historic sites. Outside Naples there are some drive-in cinemas *(see p212)*.

napoli film festival

Festival logo

Fireworks, a popular tradition in Naples and the Campania region

Orchestra playing at the Festival Internazionale di Ravello

CHILDREN'S ENTERTAINMENT

Edenlandia is the main amusement park in Naples, with over 200 attractions, including the World of Fables, Walt Disney favourites, models of sets from Disney stories and theme merry-go-rounds. **Bowling Oltremare** has table tennis, football and virtual golf, as well as bowling. For computer-mad kids, Internet terminals are available at **Opus Informatica** and **Multimedia IC**; you could try to get them to look at the Naples website *(see p210)*.

Carousel at the Edenlandia funfair

SPECTATOR SPORTS

Stadio San Paolo *(see p42)* hosts *calcio* (football), the sporting event that most fires the passion of Neapolitans. Usually games are held on Sundays and tickets always sell out quickly. Newer to Naples is *basket*: its basketball team is Carpisa Napoli.

The **Ippodromo di Agnano** race track lies in a splendid natural location. Every April it hosts the famous Gran Premio trotting races.

Canoe polo teams, active since the late 1980s, compete in the Coppa Italia di Canoa Polo; check *Il Mattino* sports section for information. If you are lucky enough to

come across a match, don't miss the chance to enjoy a unique experience.

Swimming, diving and, especially, water polo are extremely popular in Naples. All are practised at the **Piscina Scandone**, the city's public swimming pool.

Trotting races at Agnano

OUTSIDE NAPLES

Festivals of classical music in the Amalfi Coast region are often eagerly anticipated annual events. Because of their popularity, it is best to book tickets in advance. Concerts at the Estate Musicale Sorrentina, which are held in the cloister of the church of San Francesco in Sorrento, are

often in demand. The **Festival Internazionale di Ravello** *(see p41)*, which runs from early July until mid September, includes chamber music, orchestral concerts, film, dance and art exhibitions.

Pompeii di Notte offers guided evening visits to the remains of Pompeii *(see pp146–9)* from May to October. One choice includes a light show, with music by Italian composer Ennio Morricone, and has proved popular with Neapolitans and tourists alike.

Settimana della Cultura, an annual week of cultural events held in April, offers visits to archaeological sites in Campania. Some of these sites are not generally open to the public. Others stage special events or entertainment: from art exhibitions to architectural or archival displays; and from film and theatre to sports.

Benevento, Santa Maria Capua Vetere and Caserta all have theatres staging plays, and Pozzuoli and Caserta have drive-in cinemas.

The Phlegraean Fields area has many nightspots, bars and discos. South toward Licola, and on the Sorrento peninsula, the beach bars convert to beach discos on summer evenings. In Capri, after a stroll around La Piazzetta you could try **Number Two** for a night of energetic dancing. On Ischia, dancers at **Valentino** party until well into the night. It is open year round, though in winter only at weekends.

Outdoor café nightlife, La Piazzetta, Capri

DIRECTORY

INFORMATION AND BUYING TICKETS

Box Office
Galleria Umberto I.
Map 7 A2.
Tel 081 551 91 88.
www.boxofficenapoli.it

Concerteria
Via M Schipa 23.
Map 5 B2.
Tel 081 761 12 21.

THEATRE, OPERA AND DANCE

Galleria Toledo
Teatro Stabile
D'Innovazione,
Via Concezione a
Montecalvario 34.
Tel 081 42 58 24.

Nuovo Teatro Nuovo
Via Montecalvario 16.
Map 7 A1.
Tel 081 425 59 58.

Teatro Augusteo
Via Toledo 262 (Piazzetta
Duca d'Aosta). **Map** 7 A1.
Tel 081 41 42 43.
www.teatroaugusteo.com

Teatro Bellini
Via Conte di Ruvo 14.
Map 3 B4.
Tel 081 549 96 88.
www.teatrobellini.it

Teatro Cilea
Via San Domenico 1.
Map 1 A5.
Tel 081 19 57 96 77.

Teatro Diana
Via Luca Giordano 64–72.
Map 1 C5.
Tel 081 556 75 27.
www.teatrodiana.it

Teatro Mercadante
Piazza Municipio 64.
Map 7 B2.
Tel 081 551 33 96.
www.teatrostabilenapoli.it

Teatro Palapartenope
Via Barbagallo 115
(Fuorigrotta).
Tel 081 57 00 08.

Teatro San Carlo
Via San Carlo 93/f.
Map 7 A2.
Tel 081 41 63 05.

www.teatrosancarlo.it
Programma Scuole
Tel 081 40 40 64.

Teatro Sancarluccio
Via San Pasquale a
Chiaia 39. **Map** 6 E2.
Tel 081 40 50 00.

Teatro Sannazaro
Via Chiaia 157. **Map** 7 A3.
Tel 081 41 17 23.

Teatro Totò
Via F Cavara 12/a.
Map 4 D3.
Tel 081 564 75 25.
www.teatrototo.com

Teatro Trianon
Piazza Calenda 9.
Map 4 D5.
Tel 081 225 82 85.

LIVE MUSIC

Around Midnight
Via Bonito 32/a.
Map 2 D4.

Associazione Alessandro Scarlatti
Piazza dei Martiri 58.
Map 6 F2.
Tel 081 40 60 11.

Cappella della Pietà de' Turchini
Via Santa Caterina
da Siena 38.
Map 6 F1.
Tel 081 40 23 95.
www.turchini.it

Otto Jazz Club
Piazzetta Cariati.
Map 6 F1.
Tel 081 551 74 53.

Palapartenope
Via Barbagallo 15.
Tel 081 762 82 16.

Teatro Bellini
*See listing under Theatre,
Opera and Dance.*

Teatro Diana
*See listing under Theatre,
Opera and Dance.*

Teatro San Carlo
*See listing under Theatre,
Opera and Dance.*

NIGHTLIFE

Chez Moi
Via Parco Margherita 13.
Map 6 D1.
Tel 081 40 75 26.

Culti Spacafe
Via Carlo Poerio 47. **Map**
6 E2. *Tel 081 76 44 619.*

Intra Moenia
Piazza Bellini 70. **Map** 3
B5. *Tel 081 29 07 20.*

Kaligola
Via Capella Vecchia.
Tel 081 65 82 796.

Keste
Largo San Giovanni
Maggiore 26–7. **Map** 7
B1. *Tel 081 551 39 84.*

MADRE (Museo D'Arte Contemporanea Donnaregina)
Via L Settembrini 79. **Map**
3 C3. *Tel 081 56 24 561.*

La Notte Bianca
Tel 081 796 6800.
www.nottebianca
napoli.com

Notting Hill
Piazza Dante 88.
Map 3 A5.

PAN (Palazzo delle Arti Napoli)
Via dei Mille 60. **Map** 6 E2.
Tel 081 795 86 05.

Rising South
Via San Sebastiano 19.
Map 3 B5.
Tel 339 794 6826.

Velvet Underground
Via Cisterna dell'Olio.
Map 3 A5.

CINEMA

Filangieri Multisala
Via Filangieri 43–7. **Map** 6
F2. *Tel 081 251 24 08.*

Institut Français de Naples "Le Grenoble"
Via Crispi 86. **Map** 6 D2.
Tel 081 66 96 65.

Modernissimo
Via Cisterna dell'Olio 59.
Map 3 A5.
Tel 081 551 12 47.

Napoli Film Festival
www.napolifilm
festival.com

Plaza Multisala
Via Kerbaker 85.
Map 2 D4.
Tel 081 556 35 55.

Warner Village Metropolitan
Via Chiaia 149. **Map** 7 A3.
Tel 081 25 01 33.

CHILDREN'S ENTERTAINMENT

Bowling Oltremare
Viale J F Kennedy.
Tel 081 62 44 44.

Edenlandia
Viale J F Kennedy.
Tel 081 239 40 90.

Multimedia IC
Via San Giovanni
Maggiore Pignatelli.
Map 3 B5.
Tel 081 551 47 08.

Opus Informatica
Piazza Cavour 146.
Map 3 B3.
Tel 081 29 88 77.

SPECTATOR SPORTS

Ippodromo di Agnano
Via Ruggero Raffaele.
Tel 081 735 72 33.

Piscina Scandone
Viale Giochi del
Mediterraneo.
Tel 081 570 91 59.

Stadio San Paolo
Via Claudio.
Tel 081 239 56 23.

OUTSIDE NAPLES

Festival Internazionale di Ravello
Information *Tel 089 85 84
22.* Advance credit card
booking *Tel 199 10 99 10.*
www.ravellofestival.com

Number Two
Via Camerelle 1 (Capri).
Tel 081 837 70 78.

Pompeii di Notte
Tel 081 81 64 05.
www.pompeiisites.org

Settimana della Cultura
www.beniculturali.it/
settimanacultura

Valentino
Corso V Colonna (Ischia).
Tel 081 99 26 53.

SPECIALIST HOLIDAYS AND OUTDOOR ACTIVITIES

Naples and the Amalfi Coast offer a variety of cultural and sporting activities as well as beautiful and arresting landscapes. You can learn to cook regional dishes and discover wines made from grapes unique to the area, some descended from those of Ancient Greece. Walks can be through small medieval towns, rolling hills, along dramatic cliff tops or over active volcanic

The grape harvest at a local winery

terrain. Horse rides pass mountains, vineyards and ancient temples. Some of the world's most spectacular coastline beckons with its water sports and caves. Those interested in archaeology can join university projects at ancient sites. Alternatively, you can relax at thermal baths, the best of which are on the island of Ischia. Most guided activities are in Italian, unless noted otherwise.

CULINARY COURSES

Cookery courses are run close to Paestum (see pp162–3) by **Azienda Agrituristica Seliano**. The courses focus on cuisine derived from ancient Greek and Roman traditions and are held at Agriturismo Seliano (see p184), a working farm that can provide room and board. The farm raises buffalo, which produce milk for the best mozzarella. Courses usually last three to five days, but can be flexible.

Il Principe (see p199), a restaurant within walking distance of the ruins of Pompeii (see pp146–9), offers cookery lessons in ancient or modern Neapolitan cuisine. The ancient Roman recipes were devised in collaboration with the Archaeological Service of Pompeii. De Gustibus, a recipe booklet fine tuned by the restaurant's award-winning chef, describes how the Romans prepared their food. Courses last from one to five days, but a short lesson after a meal is also possible.

Pastafest, with tastings and demonstrations, is a five-day fair held in October in Torre Annunziata (see p141).

WINE COURSES AND TASTING

Vitignoitalia is an annual wine trade show and tasting experience that began in 2005. For three days in late spring participants visit wine makers, taste wines and enrol at sessions to learn more about single-varietal wines (those made from only one type of grape), most of which are from southern Italy.

Mastroberardino, a winery founded in 1878, has a joint project with the Archaeological Service of Pompeii to research the grapes and growing systems used in Pompeii at the time of the AD 79 eruption. It holds various wine tasting courses and tours of its cellar.

Feudi di San Gregorio is one of the region's larger wine makers and has a modern *cantina* (cellar) of architectural interest designed in 2002 by Hikaru Mori. It runs wine tasting and has recently added guest accommodation.

WALKING AND HORSE RIDING

Hiking through the glorious countryside has increased in popularity in recent years. Free maps with suggested routes are available at EPT offices (see p219), which also have details of guided tours.

The Pozzuoli/Solfatara metro stop is recommended as a starting point for exploring Pozzuoli (see pp136–7). You can walk to the Temple of Serapis and then on to the Solfatara (seep137), with its volcanic phenomena such as fumaroles and bubbling mud.

Naples WWF runs the Cratere degli Astroni nature reserve on Vesuvius' crater. To get there take the Agnano exit on the *tangenziale* (bypass). Paths through the woods lead to stretches of water inhabited by herons and other birds. **Guide Alpine della Campania** leads guided tours in the park around Vesuvius. **Ente Parco del Vesuvio** has information on various self-guided routes to Mount Vesuvius.

Azienda Agrituristica Seliano in Paestum offers horse riding. It is also worth checking with tourist offices for equestrian centres and other *agriturismi* with horses.

Horse riding, an ideal way to appreciate the region's scenery

Treatment at one of the Amalfi Coast's spa resorts

SPA HOLIDAYS

The Amalfi Coast's thermal waters attracted the likes of the Roman emperor Tiberius. Unlike those in northern Italy, the region's spas attract few crowds and charge reasonable prices. Ischia has the best facilities. **Grand Hotel Punta Molino Terme** has a thermal pool and spa, as does **Hotel Grazia Terme**. Thermal waters are also to be found at Lacco Ameno, Casamicciola Terme, Telesia near Benevento and Villamaina near Avellino. Note that many spas close in winter.

WATER SPORTS AND EXCURSIONS BY BOAT

Many Neapolitans head to Capri or Ischia on the ferry *(see p226)* for the day. **Metro del Mare** connects Naples with coastal towns and the islands.

A glimpse of marine life and the features of the sea bed is an experience you should not miss. Scuba lessons and excursions are available at **Circolo Ilva Bagnoli**, **Teresa Lucibello** and (in English as well as Italian) at **Centro Immersione Massa Lubrense**. For diving at Capri and Ischia make enquiries at the **Capri Diving Club** and **Ischia Diving Center** respectively.

Naples' seafront clubs are reserved for members but your hotel may be able to sponsor you as a guest. Many marinas offer sailing. Weekly yacht rentals (2–5 cabins), with or without a skipper, are available year-round at **Eva Mare** in Salerno. *La canoa polo* (canoe polo) grew in popularity in Italy in the 1980s and **HyppoKampos Resort** in Castel Volturno organizes both lessons and rentals.

ARCHAEOLOGICAL PROJECTS

The **Porta Stabia Research Project** explores the development of southern Pompeii in the area of the city's entertainment and theatre district. Recruitment of paying volunteers for the field school session begins in October.

SPELUNKING

Those who fancy having a go at cave exploring can experience it in the **Grotte dell'Angelo** (Angel Cave), a trek suitable for amateurs.

DIRECTORY

CULINARY COURSES

Azienda Agrituristica Seliano
Via Seliano, Paestum.
Tel *082 872 36 34.*

Pastafest
Tel *081 86 17 011.*

Il Principe
Piazza Bartolo Longo 8, Pompeii.
Tel *081 850 55 66.*

WINE COURSES AND TASTING

Feudi di San Gregorio
Via Cerza Grossa, Sorbo Serpico (Avellino).
Tel *082 598 66 11.*
www.feudi.com

Mastroberardino
Altripalda (Avellino).
Tel *082 561 41 11.*
www.mastroberardino.com

Vitignoitalia
Tel *081 410 70 43.*
www.vitignoitalia.it

WALKING AND HORSE RIDING

Azienda Agrituristica Seliano
See Culinary Courses.

Ente Parco del Vesuvio
Municipio di San Sebastiano al Vesuvio.
Tel *081 771 82 15.*

Guide Alpine della Campania
Piazzale di Quota 1000, Ercolano.
Tel *081 777 57 20.*

Naples WWF
Tel *081 726 65 11.*

SPA HOLIDAYS

Grand Hotel Punta Molino Terme
Lungomare Cristofero Colombo 23, Ischia.
Tel *081 99 15 44.*
www.puntamolino.it

Hotel Grazia Terme
Via Borbonica 2, Lacco Ameno, Ischia.
Tel *081 99 43 33.*
www.hotelgrazia.it

WATER SPORTS AND EXCURSIONS BY BOAT

Capri Diving Club
Località Punta Carena 8, Anacapri.
Tel *081 837 34 87.*

Centro Immersione Massa Lubrense
Marina del Massa Lubrense, Via Fontanelle 18/Via Cristofero Colombo, Massa Lubrense (Sorrento).
Tel *081 808 90 03.*

Circolo Ilva Bagnoli
Vico Pedigrotta 1, Bagnoli.
Tel *081 761 36 03.*

Eva Mare
Via Porto 12, Salerno.
Tel *089 258 30 67.*
www.evamare.it

HyppoKampos Resort
Via Fiumitello II, Castel Volturno. **Tel** *082 376 21 06* or *338 482 64 15.*

Ischia Diving Center
Via Jasolino 8, Ischia.
Tel *081 98 50 08.*

Metro del Mare
Tel *199 44 66 44*
(SMS *340 439 07 62* for timetable).
www.metrodelmare.com

Teresa Lucibello
Spiaggia Marina Grande, Positano.
Tel *089 87 50 32.*

ARCHAEOLOGICAL PROJECTS

Porta Stabia Research Project
Apply through Stanford University Continuing Studies, USA. **Tel** *650 725 26 50.* **www**.stanford.edu/group/pompeii, or The University of Sydney, Australia. Mediterraneo Service. **Tel** *081 866 36 13.*

SPELUNKING

Grotte dell'Angelo
Petina or Polla exit from A3, then SS19 and follow signs to the cave.
www.grottedellangelo.sa.it

SURVIVAL GUIDE

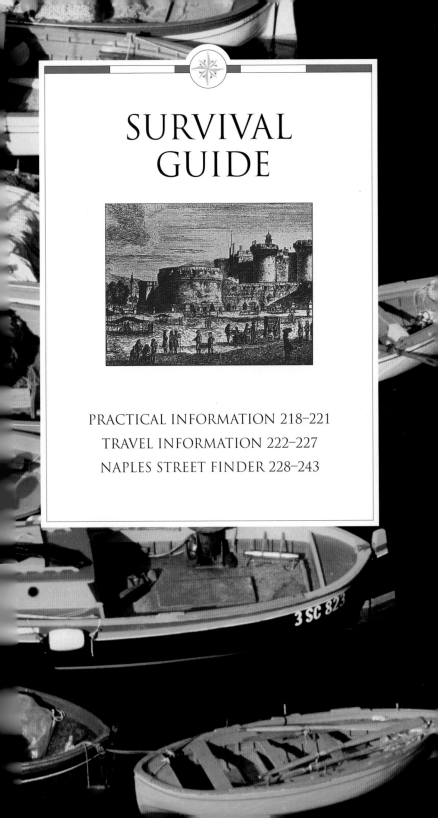

PRACTICAL INFORMATION

Naples is a lively, if somewhat chaotic city which may seem bewildering to visitors. However, over the past few years the city has undergone something of a rebirth. Its rich historic and artistic wealth has been reassessed, with more monuments open at regular hours and reorganization of the major museums to make the most of their world-class collections. Improved facilities and new pedestrian areas have

ENTE NAZIONALE ITALIANO PER IL TURISMO
The ENIT logo

revived public spaces, and cultural and social activities, advertised in the tourist offices, abound.

Visitors will still find the city has its frustrating aspects, with crippling bureaucracy at banks and public offices, and it is wise to be on the lookout for petty crime, keeping money and valuables well out of view. However, only simple guidelines and some forward planning are needed to make the most of this fascinating city and its past.

Looking over Piazza Mercato, one of Naples's liveliest squares

TOURIST INFORMATION

You can begin to organize your own itineraries before you leave for Italy by making enquiries at the **ENIT** office (the Italian national tourist board) in your home country. Once you are in Italy, the network of local tourist offices, known as **EPT** (Ente Provinciale per il Turismo), can provide useful information concerning accommodation, guided tours and excursions in the surrounding area. These information offices can be found at key arrival points such as the airport and the main railway station in Naples, as well as in the city centre.

Outside Naples, the **Azienda Autonoma di Soggiorno, Cura e Turismo**, which is organized by the regional

administration, has offices in Naples and the main tourist resorts. They are reliable sources of information and will provide free maps and guide books. Smaller towns will also have an information office, called a *Pro Loco*, often based in the town hall.

INFORMATION FOR STUDENT TRAVELLERS

Students and young people under 26 can obtain air, rail and ferry discount tickets at the local Centro Turistico Studentesco (**CTS**). The membership card costs €22 and includes the ISIC international student identity card and the Italian *Carta Giovani*. This card offers discounts at theatres, bookshops and other businesses in Naples. CTS will also help with cheap car hire and courses for its members. Students from abroad can purchase the ISIC card or the *Carta Giovani* separately for €8 each. The ISIC card offers a 24-hour telephone helpline providing general advice and information.

The **Associazione Italiana Alberghi per la Gioventù** (Youth hostelling association) operates hostels for members of the YHA (Youth Hostel Association). If you are not already a member, the card can be purchased directly from the hostel for €13. There is one youth hostel in Naples, the Ostello Mergellina,

which is conveniently located and open all year round. For information on hostels outside Naples, inquire at the youth hostel association office.

ENTERTAINMENT

The monthly magazine called *Qui Napoli*, published by the **Azienda Autonoma di Soggiorno, Cura e Turismo** and available from most hotels and information offices, is a free guide to events in and around Naples. It lists opening hours for monuments and museums and each issue has an updated *Agenda* in both Italian and English with information on exhibitions, theatre, concerts and conferences. More detailed information on lectures, seminars, sports and entertainment can be found in the national magazines or in the relevant supplements of the daily newspapers.

Qui Napoli, a free tourist monthly for Naples and Campania

◁ **Fishing boats at Marina Grande, Sorrento**

Modern Neapolitan skyscrapers, a striking contrast with the old city

MUSEUMS AND MONUMENTS

Some streets and squares in the old centre have maps showing the position of major sights. There are also information panels corresponding to audio guides that are available in five languages. Museums are usually open in the morning and closed on Mondays. Entrance is free for under 18s or those over 60. Churches are generally free, though there may be a charge for areas like cloisters.

Visits to underground Naples are organized by **L.A.E.S.** and **Napoli Sotterranea** on Thursdays at 9pm, Saturdays at 10am and noon, and Sundays from 10am to noon. Archaeological sites are usually open every day until one hour before sunset.

Display panel with local map and tourist information

Old-style street clock

IMMIGRATION AND CUSTOMS

European Union (EU) residents and visitors from the United States, Canada, Australia, New Zealand and Japan do not need a visa for stays of up to three months but must have one for a longer stay. Non-European Union citizens must carry a valid passport with them at all times, while for EU citizens an ID card will suffice.

Non-EU citizens can bring in either 400 cigarettes or 100 cigars or 500 grams of tobacco, 1 litre of spirits, 2 litres of wine and 50 grams of perfume. Non- EU citizens can claim back sales tax (IVA) on purchases over €155. For help, call your embassy or consulate.

ITALIAN TIME

Italy is one hour ahead of Greenwich Mean Time in winter and two hours ahead in the summer. The clocks go forward in March and back in September. That means that London is one hour behind Italian time and New York six hours behind; while Tokyo is eight hours ahead of Naples and Sydney is ten hours ahead.

ELECTRIC ADAPTORS

Electric current is 220 volts, with two-pin or three-pin round-pronged plugs.

DIRECTORY

TOURIST INFORMATION

Aziende Autonome di Soggiorno, Cura e Turismo

Naples
Palazzo Reale, Piazza Plebiscito.
Tel 081 252 57 11.
Piazza del Gesù.
Tel 081 557 20 71.
Via Marino Turchi 16.
Tel 081 240 09 11.
www.inaples.it

Sorrento
Via De Maio 35.
Tel 081 807 40 33.
www.sorrentotourism.com

ENIT

United Kingdom
1 Princes Street, London
WlR 8AY. *Tel 020 7408 1254.*
www.italiantouristboard.co.uk

United States
630 Fifth Avenue, New York,
NY 10111. *Tel 212 245 4822.*
www.italiantourism.com

EPT

Central Railway Station.
Tel 081 26 87 79.
Mergellina Station.
Tel 081 761 21 02.
Piazza Martiri 58.
Tel 081 410 72 11.

L.A.E.S.
Tel 081 40 02 56.

Napoli Sotterranea
Piazza San Gaetano 68.
Tel 081 29 69 44.

INFORMATION FOR STUDENT TRAVELLERS

Associazione Italiana Alberghi per la Gioventù
Salita della Grotta 23.
Tel 081 761 23 46.

Centro Turistico Studentesco (CTS)
Via Mezzocannone 25.
Tel 081 552 79 60.

CONSULATES

South Africa
Corso Umberto I.
Tel 081 551 75 19.

United Kingdom
Via dei Mille 40.
Tel 081 423 89 11.

United States
Piazza della Repubblica 2.
Tel 081 583 81 11.

Security and Public Services

While the countryside around Naples does not pose particular problems, petty crime is quite widespread in Naples itself. By taking a few simple precautions you will be able to protect yourself from pickpockets and purse snatchers: don't wear valuable jewellery or watches; handbags are easy targets, so hold onto them tightly and carry your money in your pockets. If possible, keep cameras and video cameras hidden from sight. It's best to be wary in Naples, but don't let apprehension ruin your trip.

Logo of the bank of Naples

LOOKING AFTER YOUR PROPERTY

It's best not to carry large sums of money on you while walking around town – leave it in your hotel safe. Always make photocopies of your vital documents like passports, or at least make a note of the number. Report any loss or theft to the police, while lost or stolen traveller's cheques and credit cards should also be immediately reported to the issuing bank. If you are travelling by car, always park in supervised car parks and do not leave items visible inside the vehicle. In crowded public areas or on public transport, be on your guard against pickpockets, as they are very agile, while purse snatchers on mopeds prefer to take jewels and handbags from strolling pedestrians. The station is best avoided at night, and it is not advisable for single women to go around alone after dark.

A team of policemen

but many Italians usually prefer to drink bottled mineral water. As Neapolitan cuisine includes many seafood dishes, be careful not to eat closed

shellfish and it is advisable to avoid raw seafood.

If you should need urgent medical assistance, call the **Pronto Soccorso** (casualty department) or the **Guardia Medica** at night and at week-ends. All pharmacies will have a list of branches open at night and on public holidays *(farmacia di turno)* posted on their door. The **Farmacia Alma Salus** in Piazza Dante, in the centre of Naples, is open 24 hours a day.

CREDIT CARDS

Major credit cards such as VISA, Access/Mastercard, American Express and Diners Card are accepted by the majority of the larger businesses and restaurants. Smaller trattorias may only accept cash, so it is advisable to carry some cash with you.

Italian pharmacy sign

HEALTH

In the summer, if you go to the seaside, watch out for the no bathing signs *(divieto di balneazione)* on the beaches, as this means that the water is polluted. Tap water is drinkable in Naples,

CURRENCY

Twelve countries have replaced their traditional currencies, such as the lira, with the euro. Austria, Belgium, Finland, France, Germany, Greece, Ireland, Italy, Luxembourg, Netherlands, Portugal and Spain chose to join the new currency; the UK, Denmark and Sweden stayed out, with an option to review their situation. The euro was introduced on 1 January 1999, but only for banking purposes. Notes and coins came into circulation on 1 January 2002. All euro notes and coins can be used anywhere inside the participating member states.

You can exchange currency at an automatic cash dispenser at certain bank branches in Naples, but it's best to have some euros in cash with you when you arrive. Euro bank notes have seven denominations. The €5 note (grey in colour) is the smallest, followed by the €10 note (pink), €20 note (blue), €50 note (orange), €100 note (green), €200 note (yellow) and €500 note (purple). The euro has eight coin denominations: €1 and €2; 50 cents, 20 cents, 10 cents, 5 cents, 2 cents and 1 cent. The €2 and €1 coins are both silver and gold in colour. The 50-, 20- and 10-cent coins are gold. The 5-, 2- and 1-cent coins are bronze.

Euro notes

BANKING HOURS

Banks are open from Monday to Friday. Opening hours vary but generally run from 8:30am to 1:20pm and 2:45pm to 3:45pm. Queues may be very long, especially in the morning, when it is advisable to arrive early. Identification, such as a passport, is required for any transaction. Cash dispensers (Bancomat) display logos of the cards they accept.

Banca di Napoli
Via Toledo 177–178.
Tel 081 791 11 11.

Banca di Roma
Via Verdi 31.
Tel 081 493 21 11.

Banca Intesa
Via Nuova Marina 20.
Tel 081 550 71 11.

An Italian post box

POSTAL SERVICES

Post offices in Naples are open Monday to Saturday from 8:30am to 1:20pm (noon on the last day of the month). The central Post Office in Piazza Matteotti is open from 8:15am to 7:20pm (8:15am–2pm on Sundays). Branch Post Offices are situated all over the city, in the railway stations and at Capodichino airport. The Italian postal service is by no means a model of efficiency, so for urgent communications, whether you are sending letters or parcels, it is advisable to use the *Postacelere* express service. This is a fast and reliable service for a fee. Throughout Italy, stamps can be bought at the tobacconist *(tabaccaio)* as well as in the post office itself. The postcode for Naples is 80100.

Posta Centrale
Piazza Matteotti.
Helpline **Tel** *80 31 60.*
Information **Tel** *081 428 95 85.*

Automatic cash dispenser

PUBLIC TELEPHONES

Public telephone boxes in streets and in bars generally accept coins, telephone cards (which can be bought from a *tabaccaio* or a bar) and, sometimes, credit cards. A number of bars use *telefono a scatti* which monitor the number of units used during the phone call and ask you to pay at the end. Offices run by Telecom Italia (the state telephone company) also operate with this system. You can also place reverse charge calls and pay by credit card with these phones.

For international directory enquiries, dial 176. For international operator assistance, dial 170. General information is given on 1400. With Country-direct service you can call an operator in another country, who will connect you to the number you want: dial 172, followed by the country code. With credit card phones you can have your calls charged to your home phone bill; dial 187 to arrange this service. The area code for Naples is 081. Note that hotel phone calls can be very expensive.

There are limited Internet cafés, but there are a few places on the side streets west of Via Toledo where you can make phone calls or use the Internet.

Telecom Italia Office
Via Depretis 4. ⏲ *9:30am–1pm, 2–5:30pm daily.*
Tel 081 551 09 21.

TRAVEL INFORMATION

In the wake of a campaign to improve transport services in Naples, plans are being made to restructure and develop existing flight, rail and ferry links. The airport, Capodichino, is close to the city and is used for domestic, European and charter flights, with the nearest intercontinental airport in Rome to the north. The fastest means of reaching Naples by land is to travel

An Alitalia airplane

by train, since there are no direct long-distance coach connections with European cities, and cars are far from ideal because of parking and traffic problems in town. Naples also has a large maritime passenger terminal with ferry connections to the islands in the Bay of Naples. Buses, funiculars and two underground lines link all the main sites in the city of Naples itself.

The elegant Campi Flegrei railway station

ARRIVING BY AIR

Daily flights to Naples from London, Paris, Frankfurt and Munich are operated by **Alitalia**, the Italian state airline, as well as non-Italian carriers such as **Air France, British Airways** and **Lufthansa.** Numerous budget and charter airlines also offer flights to Naples. The airport authority's website (www.gesac.it) has a search facility that is useful for finding flights into Naples from foreign cities.

Capodichino airport is fairly small, even though it is the only international one in the region. Travellers from outside Europe will probably

Capodichino airport coach service

transfer to a connecting flight to Naples in Rome, although **Eurofly** operates direct flights from New York in summer.

CLP offers direct coach connections from the airport to the centre of town (Piazza Municipio, on the corner of Via Medina); departures are hourly from 6:30am to 11:30pm (from the airport) and from 7am to midnight (from Piazza Municipio); tickets cost €2 and can be bought on board. The **Alibus** provides a similar service at a cost of €3.

If you go by taxi, make sure you go to the official rank and that the meter is on. There are now set tariffs for journeys such as the airport to the centre: these should be displayed. The trip lasts about 20 minutes and the fare will be around €25.

If you have organized a fly-drive deal, you will need to report to the car hire company desk in the airport on arrival. It is usually cheaper to book car hire in advance.

ARRIVING BY TRAIN

There are three main railway stations in Naples – **Napoli Centrale** (Piazza Garibaldi), **Mergellina** (on the seafront) and **Campi Flegrei** (at Fuorigrotta).

The main station in Piazza Garibaldi is also the main interchange for the city's transport systems. Access to the underground (*metropolitana*) and the Circumvesuviana railway (for trains to Pompei-Villa dei Misteri and the coast) is from inside the station. In the square in front you will find the main terminal for the city and suburban buses as well as buses for destinations in Southern Italy.

A programme for the development of high-speed trains called **TAV** (*Treni ad Alta Velocità*) is now under way; it will connect all the major stations. In the meantime, the fastest and most convenient way of travelling by train is the Eurostar (ES), for which you pay a supplement. There is a train every hour on the Naples-Rome line. For

The Mergellina railway station

Passenger ferry at the Naples seaport

journeys of less than 200 km (120 miles) you can purchase a discount ticket *(biglietto a fasce chilometriche)* at newsagents in all stations.

Toll booths on the motorway

ARRIVING BY CAR

Should you decide to travel into Naples by car, be prepared for highly stressful driving, heavy traffic and parking problems. A car may be convenient for visiting other sites in the region, but in Naples itself it is advisable to use the public transport system or walk.

The **Automobile Club d'Italia** (ACI) provides maps and a towing and repair service to its members as well as to members of affiliated foreign associations. Tolls are charged on the *autostrada* (motorway) and can be paid in cash or with a Viacard magnetic card, available at a

tabaccaio (tobacconist's) or an ACI agency. Emergency telephones are located at intervals along the motorway.

Autostrada A2 exits into the Naples bypass road *(tangenziale)*, which takes you quickly to the centre or the outskirts. For the coastal resorts, follow signs for Autostrada A3, signposted Salerno. The state road 163 runs the length of the beautiful Amalfi coastline.

ARRIVING BY BOAT

The main maritime passenger terminal (Stazione Marittima), used by large and medium-sized ships, is the **Molo Angioino**, located opposite Piazza Municipio.

Ferries and hydrofoils for connections to the islands in the bay and the Sorrento peninsula depart from the nearby **Molo Beverello** and **Mergellina** *(see p119)* passenger terminals.

The **Tirrenia** ship line offers direct connections between Naples and Sardinia and Sicily. **Medmar** has services to Tunisia and **Siremar** operates the route from Naples to the Aeolian Islands off the coast of Sicily. **SNAV** and **AliLauro** run high-speed hydrofoil services for the Aeolian islands, Ponza and Ventotene. Some of these routes are only operated in the summer.

DIRECTORY

AIRLINE INFORMATION

Alitalia
Tel 06 22 22.
Tel 081 751 14 94.

British Airways
Tel 199 71 22 66.

Eurofly
Tel 199 50 99 60.

Lufthansa
Tel 199 40 00 44.

Gesac (airport services)
Tel 081 789 62 59.
Tel 848 88 87 77.
www.gesac.it

CLP
Tel 081 251 41 57.

TRAIN INFORMATION

Ferrovie dello Stato
Centrale Railway Station.
Information *Tel* 89 20 21.
www.trenitalia.com

Stazione di Mergellina
Tel 081 68 06 35.

Stazione di Campi Flegrei
Tel 081 239 54 02.

FOR MOTORISTS

Automobile Club d'Italia
Piazzale Tecchio, 49/d.
Tel 081 62 28 16.
Emergencies *Tel* 116.

PASSENGER SHIP LINES

AliLauro
Tel 081 66 02 30.

Medmar
Tel 081 551 33 52.

Siremar
Tel 081 580 03 40.

SNAV
Tel 081 428 55 55.

Tirrenia
Tel 199 123 199.

Consorzio Autonomo Porto di Napoli
Stazione Marittima,
Molo Angioino.
Tel 081 552 39 68.

A SNAV express hydrofoil to the Aeolian Islands and Ponza

Getting Around Naples

The city transport system is being improved and expanded in stages, but it is still fairly unreliable and often rather slow. In fact, it will usually take you less time to travel around the central districts on foot rather than on a bus or tram. With the exception of the underground system *(metropolitana)*, public transport is only really recommended for longer distances. In the main squares in the centre there are display panels with a map of Naples which indicate the main bus, tram and metro stops.

The funicular railway

UNDERGROUND RAILWAY

Naples has two underground lines *(metropolitana)*: one is part of the Ferrovie dello Stato (FS, or state railway), and the other is the hill metro *(collinare)*. The former uses normal train routes and is often subject to delays. It runs from 5:30am to 11pm, with departures every 10–20 minutes. It goes through the main areas in Naples. The hill metro links Vomero with the hospital and the Chiaiano and Secondigliano quarters. It runs from 6am to 11pm, with departures every 6–15 minutes.

FUNICULAR RAILWAYS

There are four funicular routes, three of them run by the Azienda Napoletana Mobilità (ANM) Naples city transport system. Funicolare Centrale, Funicolare di Montesanto and Funicolare di Chiaia connect the centre of the city with the Vomero district. The Mergellina funicular connects the sea-front area (Via Mergellina) with Via Manzoni. The funiculars are reliable and fast and run from 7am to 10pm, though Piazza Fuga operates until 12:30am at weekends. Departures are every 10 minutes.

BUSES AND TRAMS

Bus and tram networks are run by the ANM. You need patience to travel by bus in Naples; even short journeys take time because of the heavy and famously chaotic traffic. Buses and trams are often crowded and have their share of pickpockets, so be alert, and keep valuables carefully tucked away. Four new bus lines (red lines R1, R2, R3, R4) improve the general standard of service; they depart every 5 to 10 minutes between 6am and midnight, while electric buses (E1, E2, E3) serve the old town and the Quartieri Spagnoli.

Citysightseeing Napoli runs a hop-on, hop-off service with three routes: two covering the main city sights and areas, and one along the Bay to Posillipo. The well-marked main stop is outside Castel Nuovo.
Citysightseeing Napoli
Tel 081 551 72 79.
www.napoli.city-sightseeing.it

TICKETS AND PASSES

The "Uniconapoli" system of tickets operates in Naples for all local buses, trams, funiculars, the hill metro and the FS metro. A Uniconapoli ticket costs €1 and is valid for 90 minutes. A ticket costing €3 can be used all day. Uniconapoli tickets are sold in the stations, at newsstands and tobacconists. You must validate each ticket before departure by stamping it in

THE STATE (FS) AND HILL METRO (COLLINARE) UNDERGROUND RAILWAYS (METROPOLITANA)

Chiaiano

Piscinola

Frullone

Colli Aminei

Policlinico

Rione Alto

Piazza Medaglie D'Oro

Piazza Garibaldi/ Stazione Centrale

Monte Donzelli

Materdei

Salvator Rosa

Cavour/ Museo

Montesanto

Cilea Quattro Giornate

Piazza Vanvitelli

Via Toledo

FS

Dante

Gianturco

Piazza Amedeo

Mergellina **FS**

Bagnoli

Campi Flegrei

Piazza Leopardi

C

Pozzuoli

C

Cavalleggeri Aosta

KEY

FS State Railway line

Line 1 (FS)

Line 2 (Collinare)

Funicular line

C Cumana Line

A taxi rank

a machine. When changing to another form of transport within your 90-minute journey, you must revalidate your ticket.

The Artecard and the Unico 3T are special three-day passes designed for tourists. If you are in Naples for a few weeks it is worth buying the monthly Uniconapoli pass.

TAXIS

If you take a taxi, make sure it is from an official rank. The meter should read €4 at the start of the ride, which is the local tax. The minimum fare is €3, double for out-of-town trips and rides from the airport to the centre cost an extra €2–3. There is an extra charge of €2 at weekends and public holidays; and €2 from 10pm to 7am; and 50 cents for each item of luggage.

The Neapolitan taxi logo

Taxis now have set rates for key journeys – these should be displayed inside the cab. You can easily find taxis in the official ranks outside the train and metro stations, and in the main squares, or you can phone for one.

Cotana
Tel 081 570 70 70.

Napoli
Tel 081 556 44 44.

Partenope
Tel 081 556 02 02.

WALKING

The pedestrian zones are a recent, much-needed development in a city with immense traffic problems. You can now walk along streets in the historic centre and admire the monuments in relative peace and quiet. To shop away from traffic, go to the pedestrian-only Via Chiaia, Via Toledo or Via Scarlatti (in Vomero). Every Sunday part of Via Partenope is closed to traffic, enabling you to admire Vesuvius and Castel dell'Ovo. However, be careful crossing the road elsewhere: drivers often ignore traffic lights and people waiting at zebra crossings, and fast-moving scooters appear from nowhere. Fortunately, Neapolitans have quick reflexes and usually manage to avoid accidents. **Traffic policeman**

DIRECTORY

PARKING

Parcheggio di Interscambio
Via Benedetto Brin.
Tel 081 553 99 92.

Grilli
Via G Ferraris 40.
Tel 081 26 43 44.

Mergellina
Via Mergellina 112.
Tel 081 761 34 70.

Santa Chiara
Pallonetto Santa Chiara 30.
Tel 081 580 25 28.

Supergarage
Via Shelley 11.
Tel 081 551 31 04.

Turistico
Via A De Gasperi 14.
Tel 081 552 54 42.

PARKING

In 1998 designated parking areas were introduced to relieve congestion in Naples. They are marked with blue lines and cost a €1–2 per hour to use. Cheaper parking can be found at Brin and Lungomare. Brin's **Parcheggio di Interscambio** also offers electric cars for rent, enabling you to drive in areas normally closed to traffic and enjoy free parking in the city centre car parks.

SCOOTER AND MOPED HIRE

The brave may find that mopeds and scooters are the best method of negotiating the heavy Naples traffic. At least you can easily find parking space. They can be hired at some car-hire agencies:

Italrent
Via del Riposo 12.
Tel 081 751 31 67.

Motorbike hire:
Bernini
Via Torrione San Martino 29.
Tel 081 556 71 12.

A scooter, the most practical way of getting around Naples

Travelling Outside Naples

SEPSA coaches logo

Even if you are based in Naples it is not difficult to visit ancient sites such as the Phlegraean Fields, the archaeological sites at Pompeii and Herculaneum, the towns on the Amalfi coast (Amalfi, Positano and Ravello) and the enchanting islands of Capri, Ischia and Procida. Most places are accessible by local train or bus, and excursions are available from bigger hotels and local travel agents.

Interior of the Centrale station

A Circumvesuviana train

LOCAL TRAINS

The Circumvesuviana train service connects Naples with the towns around Mount Vesuvius (including ancient Pompeii) and those on the Sorrento peninsula. The main terminus is in Corso Garibaldi, with the next stop in Piazza Garibaldi (at underground level), where moving walkways connect the metro station to the **Circumvesuviana**. There are four routes: Naples-Sorrento, Naples-Pompei-Poggiomarino, Naples-Ottaviano-Sarno and Naples-Nola-Baiano. In addition there are three types of train: the *accelerato* (ACC), which stops at all stations, the *diretto* (DIR), stopping only at the main

ones, and the *direttissimo* (DD), stopping at even fewer. Services run from 5am to 10pm (midnight in summer), with trains departing roughly every 20 minutes. You may want to avoid travelling late at night, though, because trains are infrequent and there are fewer people around. From 1 March to 1 November there is a seasonal service run by the Funivia di Monte Faito cableway, starting from Castellammare di Stabia station.
To reach the towns on the Phlegraean Fields and the coast you can take the **Ferrovia Cumana**, while the **Ferrovia Circumflegrea** serves the towns in the interior. The main station is in Piazza Montesanto and the service is fast and efficient. The Cumana service has departures every 10 minutes for Bagnoli and every 20 for Pozzuoli and runs from 5:21am to 9:21pm. The main stops on the Circumflegrea

line are Montesanto, Soccavo, Quarto, Licola and Torregaveta; departures are every 20 minutes until 9:43pm. Six trains per day stop at Cuma, Lido Fusaro and Torregaveta.

HYDROFOILS AND FERRIES

Various shipping lines offer frequent crossings from Naples to the islands in the bay. The Sorrento peninsula and some Amalfi coast towns can also be reached by boat. Ferries and hydrofoils depart from the Molo Beverello in Piazza Municipio, near the Stazione Marittima, and from Mergellina (hydrofoils only). From the port of Pozzuoli the crossing to Procida and Ischia is shorter and cheaper; you can also take your car on board, but check on available space beforehand. The **Caremar** line operates a ferry to Procida, Ischia and Capri which departs from the Molo Beverello and from Pozzuoli. **Metro del Mare** is a summer-only boat service operating from Naples along the coast and to the islands, with departures leaving from Beverello and Mergellina.
Mergellina is also the

SNAV logo

A hydrofoil in the Bay of Naples

Coach for the Amalfi coast

departure point for the **SNAV** line's hydrofoils for Procida, Ischia (Casamicciola) and Capri. **AliLauro** offers a hydrofoil service to Ischia, Sorrento and Capri from the Molo Beverello and to Ischia, Capri and the Amalfi coast (Amalfi, Positano and Salerno) from Mergellina. Hydrofoils run by **Navigazione Libera del Golfo** go to all the islands from Mergellina and to Capri, Amalfi and Positano from the Molo Beverello. For daily departures check local newspaper *Il Mattino*.

TRAVELLING BY COACH

You can also reach towns and resorts in the region by coach. Local companies depart from the terminus in Piazza Garibaldi or from the airport at Capodichino. The bus company **CTP** serves the towns in the Vesuvius area and Caserta, with departures every 20 minutes on weekdays and every 40 minutes on Sundays and public holidays. The **SEPSA** company covers the towns

in the Phlegraean Fields area (Baia and Bacoli), while the blue SITA coaches go to various towns and resorts on the Sorrento peninsula, the tourist sights on the Amalfi coast (Amalfi, Maiori, Minori, Positano, Ravello, and so on) and Salerno. The **SITA** terminus is at Nos. 3–7 Via Pisanelli (near Piazza Municipio). It operates its services from its city centre terminus and from Molo Immacolatella, with departures twice daily.

Three of the main car hire firms

CAR HIRE

In Italy car hire is quite expensive, and driving in Naples is highly stressful. If you are determined to drive, it is best to pre-book through an international agency or organize a fly-drive deal and use the vehicle only for visiting the tourist attractions outside the city. To rent a car you must be over 21 and have held a valid driver's licence for at least a year. Agencies are listed in the Yellow Pages *(Pagine Gialle)* under Autonoleggio.

DIRECTORY

LOCAL TRAINS

Circumvesuviana
Corso Garibaldi 387.
Tel 081 772 21 11.
www.vesuviana.it

Ferrovia Cumana/Circumflegrea
Piazza Montesanto.
Tel 800 00 16 16. www.sepsa.it

HYDROFOILS AND FERRIES

AliLauro
Molo Beverello.
Tel 081 66 02 30.
www.alilauro.it

Caremar
Molo Beverello. *Tel 081 551 38 82.*
Pozzuoli. *Tel 081 526 27 11.*
www.caremar.it

Metro del Mare
Tel 199 44 66 44.
www.metrodelmare.com

Navigazione Libera Del Golfo
Tel 081 552 72 09.
www.navlib.it

SNAV
Tel 081 428 55 55.

COACH COMPANIES

CTP
Via Sannio 19.
Tel 081 700 11 11. www.ctpn.it

SEPSA
Via P Montesanto.
Tel 800 00 16 16. www.sepsa.it

SITA
Via Pisanelli 3–7.
Tel 199 93 07 49. www.sitabus.it

CAR HIRE

AVIS
Piazza Garibaldi 1
(Centrale Railway Station).
Tel 081 28 40 41.
Via Partenope 32.
Tel 081 248 13 36.
Capodichino Airport.
Tel 081 780 57 90.

Hertz
Piazza Garibaldi 93
(Centrale Railway Station).
Tel 081 20 62 28.
Capodichino Airport.
Tel 081 780 29 71.

CIRCUMVESUVIANA

Napoli — Torre Annunziata — Castellammare — Sorrento

Torre del Greco — Pompei — Meta

The main stations on the Circumvesuviana line

NAPLES STREET FINDER

The page grid superimposed on the *Area by Area* map below shows which parts of Naples are covered by this Street Finder. The map references given for the restaurants, hotels and sights in Naples refer to the maps in this section. Central Naples has been enlarged on map pages 9 and 10 to make it easier to read. Sights in this area will give both map references. A complete index of the street names and major sights in the city follows on pages 230–33. The key on the opposite page shows the scales of the maps and explains the symbols. All the main sights in the city are clearly indicated in pink so they are easy to find.

0 metres 500

0 yards 500

1

2

3
Capodimonte and I Vergini

9
Decumano Maggiore

Spaccanapoli

Vomero

5

6

7
Toledo and Castel Nuovo

Castel dell'Ovo and Chiaia

HOW TO USE THE MAPS

The first number corresponds to the Street Finder map.

Gesù Nuovo ❸

Piazza del Gesù Nuovo. **Map** 3 B5 (9 B4).
Tel 081 44 05 11. ⬜ 6:30am–12:45pm
(1:30pm Sun), 4:15–7:30pm daily.

The letters and numbers form the map coordinates. Letters are along the top, numbers are along the sides.

The map continues on page 7 of the Street Finder.

View of the centre of Naples

KEY TO STREET FINDER

⬜	Major sight
⬜	Place of interest
⬜	Railway station
Ⓜ	Metro station
🚍	Bus stop
⛴	Ferry boarding point
🚡	Funicular station
🅿	Parking
ℹ	Tourist information
➕	Hospital with casualty unit
🚓	Police station
⛪	Church
✡	Synagogue
⊠	Post office
▬	Railway line
▬	Funicular line

SCALE OF MAPS 1–8

0 metres	200	
0 yards	200	1:11,100

SCALE OF MAPS 9–10

0 metres	125	
0 yards	125	1:7,300

Street Finder Index

SEE PAGES 9-10 FOR ENLARGEMENT OF THIS AREA

SEE PAGES 9–10 FOR ENLARGEMENT OF THIS AREA

V. DUOMO

D VIA CONCERIA

P PIAZZA MASANIELLO

MARSELLI VC. ZABATTERIA

NUOVA MARINA

CALATA VILLA DEL POPOLO

MOLO C. PISACANE

SEE PAGES 9–10 FOR ENLARGEMENT OF THIS AREA

10

E

VIA AMERIGO VESPUCCI F

VIA DELLA MARINELLA

P.ZA DUCA DEGLI ABRUZZI

MOLO DEL CARMINE

MOLO CESARIO CONSOLE

CALATA DELLA MARINELLA

1

Bacino del Piliero

PONTILE VITTORIO EMANUELE II

2

Bacino Vittorio Emanuele III

3

4

Napoli

5

D E F

General Index

Acknowledgments

Dorling Kindersley would like to thank the following people whose contributions and assistance have made the preparation of this book possible: Guido Bevilacqua, Luigi Consiglio, Diana Georgiacodis, Costantino Pantano, Adriana Sandrini Maione. Dorling Kindersley would also like to thank all the museums and tourist information offices, too numerous to mention individually, for their assistance and kind permission to photograph at their establishments.

Editorial and Design Assistance
Gillian Allen, Riccardo Baldini, Julie Bond, Cooling Brown, Michelle Crane, Felicity Crowe, Vivien Crump, Annette Jacobs, Felicity Laughton, Georgina Matthews, Ferdie McDonald, Jane Oliver-Jedrzejak, Giorgio Padovani, Sargasso, Ingrid Vienings.

Additional Contributors
Sima Belmar, Judy Edelhoff, Julius Honnor, Leonie Loudon.

Additional Photography
Demetrio Carrasco, Ian O'Leary

Picture Credits
Key: t = top; tl = top left; tlc = top left centre; tc = top centre; trc = top right centre; tr = top right; cla = centre left above; ca = centre above; cra = centre right above; cl = centre left; c = centre; cr = centre right; clb = centre left below; crb = centre right below; cb = centre below; bl = bottom left; br = bottom right; b = bottom; bc = bottom centre; bcl = bottom centre left; bcr = bottom centre right.

Every effort has been made to trace the copyright holders. The publisher apologizes for any unintentional omissions and would be pleased, in such cases, to add an acknowledgment in future editions. All the photographs reproduced in this book are from the Overseas S.r.l. Milano picture library except for the following:

4CORNERS IMAGES: Giovanni Simeone 130–131. ADNKRONOS COMUNICAZIONE: 212tl; ALAMY IMAGES: AA World Travel Library 190cl; CuboImages srl 210br; culliganphoto 85t, 123tl; Danita Delimont 154tl; Adam Eastland 154bl; Peter Horree 2–3. 216–217; Ilianski 210tc; Pangea Images 155tl; Sergio Pitamitz 174–175; Rolf Richardson 153tr; Vittorio Sciosia 211br; ASSOCIAZIONE CULTURALE ARCHIVIO PARISIO, NAPLES: 24br, 26c, 26bl, 27tl, 28bc, 42tr, 55cl, 85cl, 129c, 131c, 135cra, 143cr. CORBIS: Jonathan Blair 27bl, 191tl; Owen Franken 191c; Mimmo Jodice 46. IL DAGHERROTIPO: Roberto Della Noce 10cl, 28–29, 120clb, 122bl, 123br, 123c, 124, 153bl, 154cr. GIUSEPPE AVALLONE, NAPLES: 1, 21cr, 23cr, 29cr, 31bl, 33tl, 35tl, 38cl, 38br, 41tl, 41br, 55cr, 60, 63tl, 65tc, 76tr, 77bc, 89bl, 92br, 102, 124, 128, 134bc, 134cl, 135br, 140cl, 144cl, 157tr, 157b, 158tl, 160tr, 161tr, 161bl, 169tl, 171b, 172b, 205cl, 206c, 210cl; GRAND HOTEL PARKER'S: 177tl; GRAND HOTEL PUNTA MOLINO: 215tl; GRAZIA NERI: Stefano Cellai 11bc; Toty Ruggeri 211tl; M. Sestini fotogiornalismo/M. Tramonte 29crb; Francesco Vignali 153cr. FORNASS S.A.S., PORTICI (NAPOLI): 83cr, 206tl. HOTEL IL NIDO: 177c, 222bl. IMAGE BANK, MILAN: 2–3, 12–13, 30–31, 32tr, 32cl, 38tr, 38tl, 39cl, 40cr, 42br, 44–45, 105cl, 107tl, 112, 115c, 117b, 130–131, 135tl, 136bc, 136cl, 137ca, 143bl, 146tr, 149tl, 156tl, 156br, 158tr, 159tr, 159cl, 162cl, 165cl, 165tr, 166tl, 168tl, 169bl, 169br, 170cl, 170bl, 171tl, 171cr; MIMMO JODICE, NAPLES: 40tc, 68bc, 80tr, 96bc. MARKA, MILAN: R. Benzi 220bl; Danilo Donadoni 122tr; D. Donati 62bc; Nunzio Mari 11tr; L. Sechi 223t.; Metronapoli S.p.A: 29br. NAPOLI FILM FESTIVAL: 211cr; NEWIMAGE s.r.l: Sandro Battaglia 214ca; Ronaldo Fabrini 214br. LUCIANO PEDICINI, NAPLES: 21tc, 68c, 69tl, 71c, 81c, 84c, 84bl, 97bl, 151br, 162tr, 163cl, 163tr, 163tc, 166bl, 167cr, 219tr. SCALA GROUP S.P.A: 72tl, 86bc.

Jacket
Front – ALAMY IMAGES: SHOTFILE main; DK IMAGES: Ian O'Leary clb. Back – ALAMY IMAGES: Pat Behnke clb; Mark Dyball tl; Stephen Saks Photography bl; DK IMAGES: Demetrio Carrasco cla. Spine - ALAMY IMAGES: SHOTFILE t; IL DAGHERROPTIO: Giovanni Rinaldi b. Front Endpapers – CORBIS: Mimmo Jodice.

Phrase Book

In Emergency

Help!	Aiuto!	*eye-yoo-toh*
Stop!	Fermate!	*fair-mah-teh*
Call a doctor.	Chiama un medico.	*kee-ah-mah oon meh-dee-koh*
Call an ambulance.	Chiama un' ambulanza.	*kee-ah-mah oon am-boo-lan-tsa*
Call the police.	Chiama la polizia.	*kee-ah-mah lah pol-ee-tsee-ah*
Call the fire brigade.	Chiama i pompieri.	*kee-ah-mah ee pom-pee-air-ee*
Where is the telephone?	Dov'è il telefono?	*dov-eb eel teh-leh-foh-noh?*
The nearest hospital?	L'ospedale più vicino?	*loss-peh-dah-leh pee-oo vee-chee-noh?*

Communication Essentials

Yes/No	Sì/No	*see/noh*
Please	Per favore	*pair fah-vor-eb*
Thank you	Grazie	*grah-tsee-eb*
Excuse me	Mi scusi	*mee skoo-zee*
Hello	Buon giorno	*bwon jor-noh*
Goodbye	Arrivederci	*ah-ree-veh-dair-chee*
Good evening	Buona sera	*bwon-ah sair-ah*
morning	la mattina	*lah mah-tee-nah*
afternoon	il pomeriggio	*eel poh-meh-ree-joh*
evening	la sera	*lah sair-ah*
yesterday	ieri	*ee-air-ee*
today	oggi	*oh-jee*
tomorrow	domani	*doh-mah-nee*
here	qui	*kwee*
there	la	*lah*
What?	Quale?	*kwab-leh?*
When?	Quando?	*kwan-doh?*
Why?	Perchè?	*pair-keh?*
Where?	Dove?	*doh-veh?*

Useful Phrases

How are you?	Come sta?	*kob-meh stah?*
Very well, thank you.	Molto bene, grazie.	*moll-toh beb-neh grah-tsee-eb*
Pleased to meet you.	Piacere di conoscerla.	*pee-ah-chair-eh dee coh-nob-shair-lah*
See you later.	A più tardi.	*ah pee-oo tar-dee*
That's fine.	Va bene.	*va beb-neh*
Where is/are ...?	Dov'è/Dove sono...?	*dov-eb/doveb sob-noh?*
How long does it take to get to ...?	Quanto tempo ci vuole per andare a ...?	*kwan-toh tem-poh chee voo-oh-leh pair an-dar-eb ah ...?*
How do I get to ...?	Come faccio per arrivare a ...?	*koh-meh fab-chob pair arri-var-eb ah...?*
Do you speak English?	Parla inglese?	*par-lah een-gleb-zeh?*
I don't understand.	Non capisco.	*non ka-pee-skoh*
Could you speak more slowly, please?	Può parlare più lentamente, per favore?	*pwob par-lah-reh pee-oo len-ta-men-teh pair fah-vor-eb?*
I'm sorry.	Mi dispiace.	*mee dee-spee-ab-cheb*

Useful Words

big	grande	*gran-deb*
small	piccolo	*pee-koh-lob*
hot	caldo	*kal-doh*
cold	freddo	*fred-doh*
good	buono	*bwob-noh*
bad	cattivo	*kat-tee-voh*
enough	basta	*bas-tah*
well	bene	*beb-neh*
open	aperto	*ah-pair-toh*
closed	chiuso	*kee-oo-zob*
left	a sinistra	*ah see-nee-strah*
right	a destra	*ah dess-trah*
straight on	sempre dritto	*sem-preb dree-toh*
near	vicino	*vee-chee-noh*
far	lontano	*lon-tab-noh*
up	su	*soo*
down	giù	*joo*
early	presto	*press-tob*
late	tardi	*tar-dee*
entrance	entrata	*en-trab-tah*
exit	uscita	*oo-sbee-ta*
toilet	il gabinetto	*eel gab-bee-net-toh*
free, unoccupied	libero	*lee-bair-oh*
free, no charge	gratuito	*grab-too-ee-toh*

Making a Telephone Call

I'd like to place a long-distance call.	Vorrei fare una interurbana.	*vor-ray far-eb oona in-tair-oor-bab-nab*
I'd like to make a reverse-charge call.	Vorrei fare una telefonata a carico del destinatario.	*vor-ray far-eb oona teh-leh-fon-ab-tah ab kar-ee-koh dell dess-tee-nah-tar-ree-ob*
Could I speak to... I'll try again later.	Potrei parlare con... Ritelefono più tardi.	*po-tray par-lab-reb con ree-teh-leb-foh-nob pee-oo tar-dee*
Can I leave a message?	Posso lasciare un messaggio?	*poss-ob lash-ab-reh oon mess-sab-job?*
Hold on.	Un attimo, per favore.	*oon ab-tee-mob, pair fab-vor-eh*
Could you speak up a little please?	Può parlare più forte?	*pwob par-lab-reb pee-oo for-teb?*
local call	telefonata locale	*te-leb-fon-ab-tah lob-cab-leb*

Shopping

How much does this cost?	Quant'è, per favore?	*kwan-teb pair fab-vor-eb?*
I would like ...	Vorrei ...	*vor-ray...*
Do you have ...?	Avete ...?	*ab-veh-teb... ?*
I'm just looking.	Sto soltanto guardando.	*stob sol-tan-tob gwar-dan-dob*
Do you take credit cards?	Accettate carte di credito?	*ab-cbet-tab-teh kar-teb dee creb-dee-toh?*
What time do you open/close?	A che ora apre/ chiude?	*ah keb or-ab ab-preb/kee-oo-deb?*
this one	questo	*kweb-stob*
that one	quello	*kwell-ob*
expensive	caro	*kar-ob*
cheap	a buon prezzo	*ah bwon pret-sob*
size, clothes	la taglia	*lah tab-lee-ab*
size, shoes	il numero	*eel noo-mair-ob*
white	bianco	*bee-ang-kob*
black	nero	*neb-rob*
red	rosso	*ross-ob*
yellow	giallo	*jal-lob*
green	verde	*vair-deb*
blue	blu	*bloo*

Types of Shop

antique dealer	l'antiquario	*lan-tee-kwab-ree-ob*
bakery	il forno/ il panificio	*eel forn-ob/ eel pan-ee-fee-cbob*
bank	la banca	*lah bang-kab*
bookshop	la libreria	*lah lee-breb-ree-ab*
butcher	la macelleria	*lah mab-cbell-eb-ree-ab*
cake shop	la pasticceria	*lah pas-tee-chair-ee-ab*
chemist	la farmacia	*lah far-mah-chee-ab*
delicatessen	la salumeria	*lah sab-loo-meb-ree-ab*
department store	il grande magazzino	*eel gran-deb mag-gad-zee-noh*
fishmonger	il pescivendolo	*eel pesh-ee-ven-dob-loh*
florist	il fioraio	*eel fee-or-eye-ob*
greengrocer	il fruttivendolo	*eel froo-tee-ven-dob-loh*
grocery	alimentari	*ab-lee-men-tab-ree*
hairdresser	il parrucchiere	*eel par-oo-kee-air-eb*
ice cream parlour	la gelateria	*lah jel-lab-tair-ree-ab*
market	il mercato	*eel mair-kab-toh*
newsstand	l'edicola	*leb-dee-koh-lab*
post office	l'ufficio postale	*loo-fee-cbob pos-tab-leb*
shoe shop	il negozio di scarpe	*eel neb-gob-tsiob dee skar-peb*
supermarket	il supermercato	*eel su-pair-mair-kab-toh*
tobacconist	il tabaccaio	*eel tab-bak-eye-ob*
travel agency	l'agenzia di viaggi	*lah-jen-tsee-ab dee vee-ad-jee*

Sightseeing

art gallery	la pinacoteca	*lah peena-koh-teb-kab*
bus stop	la fermata dell'autobus	*lah fair-mab-tah dell ow-tob-booss*
church	la chiesa/ la basilica	*lah kee-eb-zah/ lah bah-seel-i-kab*
closed for holidays	chiuso per le ferie	*kee-oo-zob pair leb fair-ee-eb*
garden	il giardino	*eel jar-dee-no*
library	la biblioteca	*lah beeb-lee-ob-teb-kab*
museum	il museo	*eel moo-zeb-ob*
railway station	la stazione	*lah stab-tsee-ob-neb*
tourist information	l'ufficio di turismo	*loo-fee-cbob dee too-ree-smob*

Staying in a Hotel

Do you have any vacant rooms?	Avete camere libere?	ah-veh-teh kah-mair-eh lee-bair-eh?
double room	una camera doppia	oona kah-mair-ah dob-pee-ah
with double bed	con letto matrimoniale	kon let-toh mah-tree-moh-nee-ah-leh
twin room	una camera con due letti	oona kah-mair-ah kon doo-eh let-tee
single room	una camera singola	oona kah-mair-ah sing-goh-lah
room with a bath, shower	una camera con bagno, con doccia	oona kah-mair-ah kon ban-yob, kon dot-chah
porter	il facchino	eel fah-kee-nob
key	la chiave	lab kee-ah-veh
I have a reservation.	Ho fatto una prenotazione.	ob fat-tob oona preb-nob-tah-tsee-ob-neb

Eating Out

Have you got a table for …?	Avete una tavola per … ?	ah-veh-teh oona tab-vob-lah pair …?
I'd like to reserve a table.	Vorrei riservare una tavola.	vor-ray ree-sair-vah-reh oona tab-vob-lah
breakfast	colazione	kob-lab-tsee-ob-neh
lunch	pranzo	pran-tsob
dinner	cena	cheb-nah
The bill, please.	Il conto, per favore.	eel kon-tob pair fab-vor-eb
I am a vegetarian.	Sono vegetariano/a.	sob-nob veb-jeb-tar-ee-ah-nob/nah
waitress	cameriera	kah-mair-ee-air-ah
waiter	cameriere	kah-mair-ee-air-eh
fixed price menu	il menù a prezzo fisso	eel meb-noo ah pret-sob fee-sob
dish of the day	piatto del giorno	pee-ah-tob dell jor-no
starter	antipasto	an-tee-pass-tob
first course	il primo	eel pree-moh
main course	il secondo	eel seb-kon-doh
vegetables	il contorno	eel kon-tor-nob
dessert	il dolce	eel doll-cheb
cover charge	il coperto	eel koh-pair-tob
wine list	la lista dei vini	lab lee-stah day vee-nee
rare	al sangue	al sang-gweb
medium	al puntino	al poon-tee-nob
well done	ben cotto	ben kot-tob
glass	il bicchiere	eel bee-kee-air-eb
bottle	la bottiglia	lab bot-teel-yab
knife	il coltello	eel kol-tell-ob
fork	la forchetta	lab for-ket-tab
spoon	il cucchiaio	eel koo-kee-eye-ob

Menu Decoder

l'acqua minerale gassata/naturale	lah-kwah mee-nair-nah-too-rah-leh ab-leh gab-zab-tab/	mineral water fizzy/still
aceto	ab-cheb-tob	vinegar
aglio	al-ee-ob	garlic
l'agnello	lab-niell-ob	lamb
al forno	al for-nob	baked/roasted
alla griglia	ab-lah greel-yab	grilled
l'aragosta	lab-rah-goss-tab	lobster
arrosto	ar-ross-tob	roast
basilico	bab-zee-lee-koh	basil
la birra	lab beer-rah	beer
la bistecca	lab bee-stek-kab	steak
il brodo	eel brob-doh	broth
il burro	eel boor-ob	butter
il caffè	eel kah-feb	coffee
i calamari	ee kab-lah-mab-ree	squid
i carciofi	ee kar-choff-ee	artichokes
la carne	la kar-neb	meat
la cipolla	la chip-ob-lab	onion
i contorni	ee kon-tor-nee	vegetables
le cozze	leb cob-tzeb	mussels
i fagioli	ee fab-job-lee	beans
il fegato	eel fay-gab-tob	liver
il finocchio	eel fee-nok-ee-ob	fennel
il formaggio	eel for-mad-job	cheese
le fragole	leb frab-gob-leb	strawberries
il fritto misto	eel free-tob mees-tob	mixed fried dish
la frutta	la froot-tab	fruit
frutti di mare	froo-tee dee mab-reb	seafood
i funghi	ee foon-gbee	mushrooms
i gamberi	ee gam-bair-ee	prawns
il gelato	eel jeb-lab-tob	ice cream
l'insalata	leen-sab-lab-tab	salad

il latte	eel labt-teb	milk
lesso	less-ob	boiled
la melanzana	lab meb-lan-tsab-nab	aubergine
la minestra	lab mee-ness-trab	soup
l'olio	lob-lee-ob	oil
il pane	eel pab-neb	bread
le patate	leb pab-tab-teb	potatoes
le patatine fritte	leb pab-tab-teen-eb free-teb	chips
il pepe	eel peb-peh	pepper
la pesca	lab pess-kab	peach
il pesce	eel pesb-eb	fish
il polipo	eel pob-lee-pob	octopus
il pollo	eel poll-ob	chicken
il pomodoro	eel pob-mob-dor-ob	tomato
il prosciutto cotto/crudo	eel pro-shoo-tob kot-tob/kroo-dob	ham cooked/cured
il riso	eel ree-zob	rice
il sale	eel sab-leb	salt
la salsiccia	lab sal-see-chab	sausage
le seppie	leb sep-pee-eb	cuttlefish
secco	sek-kob	dry
la sogliola	lab soll-yob-lab	sole
i spinaci	ee spee-nab-chee	spinach
succo d'arancia/ di limone	soo-kob dab-ran-chab/ dee lee-moh-neb	orange/lemon juice
il tè	eel teb	tea
la tisana	lab tee-zab-nab	herbal tea
il tonno	eel ton-nob	tuna
la torta	lab tor-tab	cake/tart
l'uovo	loo-ob-vob	egg
vino bianco	vee-nob bee-ang-kob	white wine
vino rosso	vee-nob ross-ob	red wine
il vitello	eel vee-tell-ob	veal
le vongole	leb von-gob-leb	clams
lo zucchero	lob zoo-kair-ob	sugar
gli zucchini	lyee dzu-kee-nee	courgettes
la zuppa	lab tsoo-pab	soup

Numbers

1	uno	oo-nob
2	due	doo-eb
3	tre	treb
4	quattro	kwat-rob
5	cinque	ching-kweb
6	sei	say-ee
7	sette	set-teb
8	otto	ot-tob
9	nove	nob-veb
10	dieci	dee-eb-chee
11	undici	oon-dee-chee
12	dodici	dob-dee-chee
13	tredici	tray-dee-chee
14	quattordici	kwat-tor-dee-chee
15	quindici	kwin-dee-chee
16	sedici	say-dee-chee
17	diciassette	dee-cbab-set-teb
18	diciotto	dee-cbot-tob
19	diciannove	dee-cbab-nob-veb
20	venti	ven-tee
30	trenta	tren-tab
40	quaranta	kwab-ran-tab
50	cinquanta	ching-kwan-tab
60	sessanta	sess-an-tab
70	settanta	set-tan-tab
80	ottanta	ot-tan-tab
90	novanta	nob-van-tab
100	cento	cben-tob
1,000	mille	mee-leb
2,000	duemila	doo-eb mee-lab
5,000	cinquemila	ching-kweb mee-lab
1,000,000	un milione	oon meel-yob-neb

Time

one minute	un minuto	oon mee-noo-tob
one hour	un'ora	oon or-ab
half an hour	mezz'ora	medz-or-ab
a day	un giorno	oon jor-nob
a week	una settimana	oona set-tee-mab-nab
Monday	lunedì	loo-neb-dee
Tuesday	martedì	mar-teb-dee
Wednesday	mercoledì	mair-kob-leb-dee
Thursday	giovedì	job-veb-dee
Friday	venerdì	ven-air-dee
Saturday	sabato	sab-bab-tob
Sunday	domenica	dob-meb-nee-kab